Readings in Historical Phonology

Readings in
Historical Phonology:

*Chapters in the
Theory of Sound Change*

edited by
Philip Baldi
Ronald N. Werth

The Pennsylvania State University Press
University Park and London

Library of Congress Cataloging in Publication Data
Main entry under title:

Readings in historical phonology.

   Includes bibliography.
   1. Grammar, Comparative and general--Phonology--
Addresses, essays, lectures. I. Baldi, Philip.
II. Werth, Ronald N.
P217.R35   415   77-13895
ISBN 0-271-00525-4 cloth
ISBN 0-271-00539-4 paper

Printed in the United States of America

Preface

Surely the primary consideration one must take into account when
deciding whether or not to publish a book today is that of <u>need</u>.
It appears that anthologies, especially, must be more than complete
--they must be timely and must fill an existing gap in the current
literature. In recent years there has been a remarkable surge in
interest in the field of historical-comparative linguistics, most
notably in the area of phonology. Coupled with this is a renewed
interest in the history of linquistics and the opinions of past
generations of language scholars, much of whose work has gained the
spotlight in current debates.

By editing such an anthology as this, we feel that we are answer-
ing a need which we have found from our own classroom experience
and from discussions with other linguists. The need manifests itself in at least two ways: first, the use of any text in historical-
comparative linguistics requires access to an extensive reading list,
and the elements of such a list are often hard to find or completely
unavailable. *Readings in Historical Phonology* selectively provides
the essential items of this list.

Secondly, there exists in the current literature a serious gap
which this anthology will help to fill. That is, there is nowhere
to be found a book which deals exclusively with diachronic phonology,
though the need clearly exists, both for the student and the skilled
practitioner. With these ideas in mind, the time seems right for a
synthesis of the major traditions in linguistics on the question of
sound change.

We wish to express our gratitude to the Linguistics Program of
the Pennsylvania State University and the Organized Research Program
of the University of Texas at Arlington for their financial support.
We would also like to thank Caroline van Antwerp and Dennis Dompert
of Penn State University for their invaluable editorial assistance,

and our wives, Jill Baldi and Liz Werth, for their limitless
patience.

August 1978   Philip Baldi
                                 The Pennsylvania State University

                                 Ronald N. Werth
                                 University of Texas at Arlington

Editors' Note: The following editorial conventions are used
                 throughout this volume: a single underscore
                 indicates emphasis (small caps); a double under-
                 score indicates boldface type.

Contents

General Introduction   ix

SECTION I.   NINETEENTH CENTURY   1

Introduction   1

1. On Sound Change / Hermann Paul (trans. by H. A. Strong)   3
2. Sound Change / Georg von der Gabelentz (trans. by
      Ronald N. Werth)   23
3. An Exception to Grimm's Law / Karl Verner (trans. by
      Richard Stanley)   32
4. On Sound Alternation / Nikolai Kruszewski (trans. by
      Robert Austerlitz)   64

SECTION II.   TWENTIETH CENTURY: STRUCTURALISM   92

Introduction   92

5. Phonetic Changes / Ferdinand de Saussure (trans. by
      Wade Baskin)   94
6. Principles of Historical Phonology / Roman Jakobson
      (trans. by Alan Keiler)   103
7. Function, Structure, and Sound Change / André Martinet   121
8. Graduality, Sporadicity, and the Minor Sound Change
      Processes / Henry M. Hoenigswald   160
9. Synchronic and Diachronic Universals in Phonology /
      Joseph H. Greenberg   172

SECTION III.   TWENTIETH CENTURY: GENERATIVE THEORY,
                SOCIOLINGUISTICS, AND OTHER RECENT
                CONTRIBUTIONS   185

Introduction   185

10. Functional Load and Sound Change / Robert D. King   190
11. Rule Reordering / Paul Kiparsky   218
12. Competing Changes as a Cause of Residue / William S-Y
      Wang   236
13. Phonetic Analogy and Conceptual Analogy / Theo
      Vennemann   258
14. On the Use of the Present to Explain the Past /
      William Labov   275
15. Abductive and Deductive Change / Henning Andersen   313
16. Formalization as Degeneration in Historical
      Linguistics / Raimo Anttila   348

General Introduction

The intention of *Readings in Historical Phonology* is to trace the
evolution of the concept of sound change as it is viewed in various
theories of language from roughly the Neogrammarian era to the
present. This is accomplished by means of excerpts from the writings of prominent spokesmen for these theories. If there seems to
be a bit more emphasis on the present than on the past, this
emphasis is, we believe, justifiable, because never before in the
history of linguistics have there been so many and varied attempts
at explaining (in addition to describing) the phenomenon of sound
change as there are at present. At the same time, this emphasis is
meant to reflect only the relative richness of current research,
rather than indicating an endorsement by the editors of any one
theoretical framework over another.

This anthology is divided, somewhat arbitrarily, into three
sections. Section I represents pre-structural nineteenth-century
linguistics; Section II the various 'schools' of structuralism,
i.e. Bloomfieldian, Prague, Geneva; and Section III the developments of roughly the past ten years, including generative grammar
and sociolinguistics. In the assigning of papers to their sections,
chronological considerations outweighed theoretical ones. For
example, Kruszewski's paper (1881) is in many ways more 'structural
(ist)' than the excerpt from de Saussure (first edition 1915), but
is placed in Section I by virtue of its earlier date. Each section
carries its own introduction, in which the selections in that
section are discussed individually, in respect to one another, and
within the framework of historical phonology in general. One of
the main criteria in choosing the selections was the interrelation-
ship of theoretical issues over the past 100 years, so that the
same basic theme may appear in three different theoretical formulations and be spread over the three sections. Thus, the essential
concept that synchronic variation reflects diachronic process lies
at the heart of the selections by Verner and Kruszewski (Section I),
Greenberg (Section II), and Labov (Section III), though the treatment is, in each case, as different as each author's theoretical
framework.

As much could be said about selections left out of this anthology as about those that were included. In some cases, easy availability (e.g. excerpts from Bloomfield's *Language*) was the deciding factor against inclusion; this was especially true of selections already reprinted in several other anthologies (e.g. Morris Halle, "Phonology in a Generative Grammar"). In other cases, we decided against excellent papers in which we felt, however, that the theoretical issues played second fiddle to a specific language problem (e.g., Wallace Chafe, "Internal Reconstruction in Seneca"). Regrettably, there was also the one that got away, namely Hockett's "Sound Change", surely the synthesis of the (neo-)Bloomfieldian view of sound change. The author was adamant in his refusal to have this paper reprinted in its original wording, and reluctant to revise it, so that, even though there are many references to it, both in our introductions and in some of the selections, the reader must be referred to the sole appearance of this paper in *Language* 41 (1965), 185-204.

Finally, attention is drawn to the fact that all selections appear in English, three of them (Verner, von der Gabelentz, Kruszewski) in translations published here for the first time. The fine translation of Kruszewski's paper by Robert Austerlitz is particularly noteworthy, not only because it is the first English translation, but also because it will have the effect of rescuing Kruszewski's significant contribution (the German original was published in Kazan!) from the virtual oblivion of unavailability.

Section One
Nineteenth Century

Introduction

Section I contains two theoretical statements regarding sound change
fairly typical of the Neogrammarian school (Paul, von der Gabelentz),
the single most famous nineteenth-century contribution toward the
true meaning of 'sound law' (Verner), and a relatively neglected,
but very important, archetypically Praguian monograph on the relevance of morphophonemic alternation for the interpretation of sound
change (Kruszewski).

The excerpt from Hermann Paul's *Prinzipien* (2nd edition 1886, on
which Strong's translation is based) features many of the concepts
echoed by the structuralists, especially Hockett (1965): imperceptibility and graduality of sound change, mechanistic view of change,
'minor' processes such as metathesis and haplology the result of repeated mispronunciations. Regular sound change is viewed as displacement of the motor sensation (*'Bewegungsgefühl'*): the motor
sensation is modified with each new sound perception, thus causing
deviations (Hockett's 'local frequency maxima') from the central
point of articulation. The accumulation of deviations results in
an ever greater divergence from the center; the sound change is complete when the sound-picture (*'Lautbild'*, roughly = 'phoneme') no
longer matches the original motor sensation.

There is basic agreement between Paul and von der Gabelentz (2nd
edition 1901). The process of sound change is viewed as follows.
Each sound has a certain articulatory and auditory range, described
by a circle with a center of gravity (the basic sound, roughly =
'phoneme'). When the (permissible) range is over-extended, native
intuition (*'Sprachgefühl'*) objects; when the center itself shifts,
a sound shift occurs. Sound change is geographically and lexically
gradual. Sound shifts, such as the one labelled Grimm's Law, are
marked by uniform tendencies, whereby natural classes of sounds
change uniformly. Von der Gabelentz also aims a broadside against
the strict regularity hypothesis (*'Ausnahmslosigkeit'*) of the Neo-

grammarians, mainly because it neglects articulatory considerations in assuming uniform pronunciation.

In his article (written 1875), Karl Verner accounts for *en masse* 'irregularities' left unexplained up to that date in the traditional statements of the First (Germanic) Sound Shift, often referred to as Grimm's Law. Verner adduces evidence from the morphophonemic alternation of voiceless fricatives and voiced stops in Germanic verb paradigms to show that originally voiceless fricatives were voiced in Proto-Germanic in medial voiced environments under certain intonational conditions. Verner's paper was pioneering for several reasons: (1) he was among the first to allow morphological and suprasegmental criteria in the statement of a phonological change; (2) he used synchronic evidence for the explanation of a diachronic change; (3) he strengthened the regularity hypothesis in the sense that he showed surface irregularities as reflecting an underlying regularity in the evolution of the languages in question.

Kruszewski's monograph (1881) is important for the same reasons as Verner's article. In addition, Kruszewski sets up three categories of morphophonemic alternation, two of which require diachronic information to account for the causes and conditions of the alternation. Sound change comes about as the result of two interlocking processes: (1) the combinatory process, a purely physiological process in which the sound is 'accommodated' to its conditions; Kruszewski calls this the quantitative stage; (2) the spontaneous process, called the qualitative stage, in which a sound infringes on the domain of another sound, though psychic factors, such as analogy, can impede this process. Thus, the change of [s] to [z] in Germanic under conditions of Verner's Law is seen as combinatory, the change of [z] to [r] as spontaneous. It is interesting to note that de Saussure [5][1] advances exactly the same explanation for Latin [s] > [z] > [r].

Note

[1] Bracketed numbers refer to selections so numbered in this anthology.

2

1 On Sound Change

HERMANN PAUL

In order to understand the phenomenon which we usually designate as
sound-change, we just get a clear idea of the physical and psychical
processes which operate in the production of groups of sound. If we
disregard--as in this case we ought, and indeed must do--the function
which these subserve, the following points challenge our consideration: In the first place, the movements of the organs of language,
as originated by the excitement of the motor nerves, and the muscular
activity thereby awakened; secondly, the series of sensations by
which these movements are necessarily accompanied--the 'motory sensation' (*Bewegungsgefühl*, as Lotze and, following him, Steinthal have
named it);[1] thirdly, the sensations of tone produced in the hearers,
among whom, under normal circumstances, the speaker himself must be
reckoned. These sensations are, of course, not merely physiological
processes, but psychological as well. Even after the physical excitement has passed away, these sensations leave a lasting psychical
effect, viz., in the shape of memory-pictures, which are of the
greatest importance for sound-change. For these are the only means
of connecting the single physiological processes, and these set up a
connexion of cause and effect between the earlier and later production of the same combination of sounds. The memory-picture left
behind by the sensation of the movements carried out before is that
which renders possible the reproduction of similar movements. Motory
and sound sensations need necessarily stand in no intimate connexion
with each other. But both enter into an external association, since
the speaker hears himself speaking at the same time. The mere act
of listening to others gives no motory sensation, and thus gives no
capacity of reproducing the combination of sounds once heard. For
this reason, an effort and a certain amount of practice is necessary,
in order to enable us to reproduce in speaking any sound which we
have not been hitherto accustomed to utter.

From *Principles of the History of Language* (London, 1891), 36-64.
Translated by H.A. Strong from the 2nd edition (1886) of the German
original, *Prinzipien der Sprachgeschichte*.

The question naturally presents itself--What is the analysis of the motory and sound sensations respectively, and to what grade are the special factors in their analysis consciously perceived? Probably nothing has hindered a correct appreciation of the nature of sound-change so much as the fact that the extent and the distinctness of consciousness in this subject has been overrated. It is a great mistake to suppose that for the apprehension of the right sound of any word in its peculiarity--in fact, for the possibility of an excitement of the ideas bound up with it--the single sounds composing the word need come into consciousness at all. Indeed, it is not always indispensable to the apprehension of an entire sentence that even the single words composing it should come into consciousness according to their sound and their signification. The self-deception under which grammarians labour depends on their having regarded the word not as a portion of the living language--audible for a moment, and then passing away--but as something independent to be analysed at leisure, with a view to its leisurely dismemberment. A further source of deception lies in the habit of starting not from the spoken, but from the written word. In writing, no doubt, the word seems separated into its elements, and it may appear requisite that every one who writes should presuppose this dismemberment. But in real truth the matter is somewhat different. No doubt when writing was discovered, and each time that it was applied afresh to a language not hitherto expressed by its aid, such dismemberment must necessarily have been presupposed. Further, it must continuously happen that each time that handwriting is learned anew, an exercise in the spelling of spoken words must go hand in hand with it. But after a certain facility has been attained, the process in writing is not exactly in the first place the dismemberment of each word into its single component sounds, and then for each single sound the setting down of its proper letter. The speed with which the process is carried out excludes the possibility of the single factors coming clearly into consciousness, and demonstrates at the same time that it is unnecessary that they should do so for a regular and normal course. But a really abbreviated process comes in, whereby writing is to some extent emancipated from language--a process which we shall on a later occasion have to consider rather more closely. And if we observe a little more accurately the facts connected with this dismembering faculty of the man who can write, it will clearly force itself on our notice how little consciousness intrudes into the elements of word-sound. We can daily make experience of the fact that the manifold discrepancies between writing and pronunciation pass to a great extent unheeded by the members of any given linguistic community, and strike the

foreigner first, though he can give himself no satisfactory explanation of what these discrepancies repose on. Thus every German who
has not enjoyed a training in the physiology of sound is convinced
that he writes as he speaks. Suppose, however, that he really is
justified in entertaining this conviction as against the Englishman
and the Frenchman, still, to omit niceties, there are plenty of
striking instances in which the pronunciation differs greatly from
the writing. It occurs to few that the final consonant in *Tag*, *Feld*,
and *lieb* is a different sound from that caught in *Tages*, *Feldes*,
liebes, or that the *n* in the German word *Anger* represents a sound
essentially different from that of the *n* heard in *Land*. In the
common pronunciation of *Ungnade* we have a guttural nasal, in that of
unbillig a labial nasal; but no one thinks of this. It excites
actual surprise to assert that in the German word *lange*, *g* is not
heard; that in the second syllable of *legen*, *reden*, *Ritter*, *schüt-
teln*, *e* is not heard; that the final consonant of *leben* in the
ordinary pronunciation contains no *n*, but is an *m* with no *e* preceding it. Indeed, it is safe to assert that most people will dispute
these facts, even after their attention has been drawn to them.
This holds true in many cases even of good scholars. We see from
this how entirely the analysis of the word is learnt with the writing, and how small is the consciousness of the actual elements of
the spoken word.

A real analysis of the word into its proper elements is not merely
extremely difficult, but is actually impossible. A word is not a
united compound of a definite number of independent sounds, of which
each can be expressed by an alphabetical sign; but it is essentially
a continuous series of infinitely numerous sounds, and alphabetical
symbols do no more than bring out certain characteristic points of
this series in an imperfect way. The remainder, which remains un-
denoted, no doubt necessarily reveals itself from the definition of
these points, but reveals itself only up to a certain point. The
continuity of sound is seen with the greatest clearness in the case
of the so-called diphthongs, which exhibit such a series of very
numerous elements (cf. Sievers' *Phonetik*, § 19, i.a.). Sievers was
the first to expressly bring out the significance of the transitional sounds. But it follows from this continuity of the word that an
idea of the individual parts cannot be a self-yielded result, but
must be the fruit of scientific reflection, however primitive this
may be, and it is the practical need of writing to express sounds
which has conduced to this.

What is true of the sound-picture is also naturally true of the
motory sensation. Indeed, we must go further in this point. No
one can maintain that the individual ever has any idea of the

different movements made by his organs in the act of speaking. It is
plain that these can only be ascertained after the most careful scientific observation, and that scientific men are not agreed upon
many points in connexion with this question. Even the most superficial and roughest views as to these movements are not possible without a voluntary habit of careful and protracted observation. They
are superfluous, and not needed to produce sounds and sound-groups
which we are trained to produce. The process seems to be the following. Each movement excites in a definite manner certain sensitive
nerves, and thus evokes a feeling which associates itself with the
direction of the movement of their centre by means of the motor
nerves. If this association is sufficiently established, and if the
memory-picture left by the feeling is sufficiently strong--a condition which, as a rule, is not reached without practice (i.e. without
frequent repetition of the same movement, varied, it may be, with
many vain attempts)--then the memory-picture of the sensation may
have power to reproduce the movement associated therewith as its
reflection; and if the sensation called up thereby corresponds with
the memory-picture, then we may also rest assured that we have
carried out the same movement as formerly.

But we might concede that the degree of consciousness which the
single factors of the sound-picture and of the motory sensation
attain by dint of mastery of writing, and, further, by reflection,
was even greater than it is; we might concede that an absolutely
clear consciousness of these elements was absolutely necessary for
a mastery of the mother-tongue as of any foreign language (and
certainly a higher degree of clear consciousness is necessary than
in the application of what has been learnt by practice); still from
this it would not follow that the same degree of clearness must be
attained in common daily discourse. It rather lies in the nature
of the psychical organisation that all ideas which originally operated merely by consciousness receive by practice the capacity of
operating automatically; and that this automatic operation is the
first and indispensable condition of the speedy course of ideas
demanded in every position of daily life and in languages as well.
Even the professed student of the physiology of sounds will speak
much and hear much without a single sound revealing itself distinctly to his consciousness.

For the proper judgment, then, of the natural life of language,
regulated by no species of pedantry, we must cling to the fundamental maxim that sounds are produced and taken cognisance of without any clear consciousness. This statement contradicts all such
explanatory theories as presuppose in the minds of individuals an
idea of the sound-system of language; under which head come several
hypotheses as to the German sound-shifting process.

On the other hand, however, the unconsciousness of the elements does not exclude an exact control over them. We may utter or hear a group of sounds to which we are accustomed without ever thinking that it is in fact precisely this group, made up in such and such a way; but as soon as in a single element a departure from the usual is observed--which departure needs to be but very slight--it is noticed, unless indeed any extraordinary obstacles supervene to prevent it; and each departure from the accustomed unconscious course of ideas naturally forces itself upon our consciousness. Of course it does not follow that, with the consciousness of the departure, the consciousness of its nature and cause is also given.

The possibility of control extends as far as the power of perceiving differences. This, however, is not limitless, while the possibility of gradual transitions in the movements of the organs of speech, and of course also in the sounds produced thereby, is certainly limitless. Thus, between a and i, as well as between a and u, there lies an unbounded number of possible transitions of vocal sound. In the same way the places of the articulation of all the lingual-palatal sounds lend themselves to representation by the picture of a continuous line in which each point may be the one preferred. Between them and the labial sounds certainly such an imperceptible transition is impossible; still the denti-labials stand in close relationship to the denti-linguals (th, f). In the same way the transition from check [stop] to fricative, and *vice versa*, may be gradually brought about; for complete closure and the greatest possible narrowing process approach each other nearly. All differences of quantity, of pitch, of energy in articulation, as in expiration, are conceivable in all possible transitions. And so with much besides. It is this circumstance specially which renders sound-change intelligible.

Now, if we reflect that it does not depend merely upon the differences in those sounds into which we commonly, though inaccurately, divide the word, but also upon the differences in the transition sounds, in the accent, the time, etc.; and further, if we reflect that unequal portions may always be brought into combination with a series of equal portions, it must then be clear that a manifold variety is possible in the groups of sound, and this even in the case where the actual difference is comparatively small. For this reason it is possible that strikingly different groups may be still conceived of as essentially identical, owing to their, on the whole, superior resemblances; and this is what renders an understanding possible between speakers of different dialects, so long as the differences do not pass beyond a certain limit. But for this very reason a number of variations may set in whose difference it is hard to note, or indeed impossible, until attention has been specially drawn to them.

Early childhood is for every one an experimental stage, in which the individual gradually learns by manifold efforts to imitate what has been spoken before him by those who surround him. When the greatest amount of success has crowned his efforts a period of comparative rest ensues. The former important vacillations cease, and there exists from this time forward a great uniformity in the pronunciation and freedom from disturbing causes, unless indeed the evident influences of foreign dialects, or of a written language, come between. This uniformity, however, can never become absolute. Less important vacillations in the pronunciation of the same word in the same place in the sentence are inevitable. For, speaking generally, in the case of every movement of the body, however much such movement may be the result of training, however fully the motory sensation may have been developed, there still remains a certain amount of uncertainty; it still remains left to chance (in a certain extent, however limited), whether the pronunciation be uttered with absolute exactness, or whether a slight deviation from the correct path towards one side or the other manifests itself. Even the most practised marksman misses his mark sometimes, and would miss it in most cases if it were a mere point with no extension, and if his weapon had only a single point which could touch the goal. Any one's handwriting may be as defined and characteristic as you please, and his general peculiarities may be at once recognisable, still he will not reproduce, each time he writes, the same letters and the same combinations of letters in absolutely the same way. It must be the same with the movements whereby sounds are produced. This variability of pronunciation, which remains unnoticed because of the narrow limits in which it moves, gives the key to our comprehension of the otherwise incomprehensible fact that a change of usage in the sounds of a language sets in and comes to its fulfilment without the least suspicion on the part of those in whom this change is being carried out.

If the motory sensation were always to remain unchanged as a memory-picture, the insignificant deviations would always centre round the same point with the same maximum of distance. In fact, however, this sensation is the product of all the earlier impressions received in the course of carrying out the movement in question, and, according to a common law, the impressions, not merely those which are absolutely identical, but also those that are imperceptibly different from each other, are fused into one. Correspondingly to their difference, the motory sensation must be somewhat modified with each new impression, to however insignificant

an extent. It is, in this process, of importance that the later
impressions always have a stronger after-influence than the earlier.
It is thus impossible to co-ordinate the sensation with the average
of all the impressions received during the whole course of life;
rather, the numerically-speaking inferior may, by the fact of their
freshness, outbalance the weight of the more frequent. It must,
however, be observed that supposing the distance of the possible
divergence to remain the same, a displacement of the limits of this
divergence is brought about with each alteration of the sensation.

Let us now take a line in which every point is exactly fixed as
the proper normal path of movement to which the motory sensation
leads; then, of course, the distance from that point which is
possible as maximum when the movement is really carried out without
conflicting with the sensation, is commonly as great upon one side
as upon the opposite. But it does not follow from this that the
deviations which really set in must be uniformly divided on either
side according to number and extent.

These deviations, which are not defined by the motory sensation,
have, as is natural, their independent causes--causes, moreover,
wholly unconnected with the motory sensation. If such causes act
at the same moment, with exactly the same force, in opposite
directions, then their operations cancel each other, and the movement is carried out with absolute exactness. This case will occur
very seldom indeed. In by far the most numerous cases the balance
will incline to one side or the other. It is, however, possible
for the relation of the forces to undergo manifold changes according to circumstances. If this change is as favourable for one
side as for the other; if a deviation towards one side always
alternates with a corresponding deviation towards the other side,
in this case the very smallest displacements of the motory sensation will be immediately arrested. Matters are, however, very
different when the causes which impel to one side have the prepond-
erance over those which have an immediately opposite tendency,
whether this be in each particular case or only in the generality.
The original deviation may have been ever so insignificant, the
motory sensation having suffered thereby the slightest possible
displacement, still for the next time a somewhat greater displacement from the original is rendered possible, and with this coinci-
dently a displacement of the sensation. There thus gradually arises,
by adding together all the displacements (which we can hardly
imagine small enough), a notable difference--whether it be that the
movement progresses steadily in a special direction, or that the
advance is regularly interrupted by relapses, if only the latter
are less frequent and smaller than the first.

The reason why the inclination to deviation is greater on one side than on the other must be probably sought in the fact that the deviation towards the side to which it tends is in some respect more convenient. The examination of the nature of this greater or less degree of convenience is a purely physiological task. It must not, however, be supposed that it is not at the same time conditioned by psychology. Accent and time, which are of such decisive significance in the process, and also the energy displayed in muscular activity, are essentially dependent on psychical conditions, but their operation upon sound relations is nevertheless physiological. In the process of progressive assimilation it can be nothing but the idea of the sound yet to be uttered which operates upon the preceding one; but this is psychical relation of a very simple kind manifesting itself uniformly throughout, while all special definition of the process of assimilation must be based upon an examination of the physical generation of the sounds in question.

For the task which we have set ourselves, it is sufficient to point to certain general points of view. There are a great number of cases in which we may say quite simply, this sound-group is more convenient than that. Thus the Italian words *otto* and *cattivo* are without any doubt easier to pronounce than the Latin *octo*, and the NHG *empfangen* than a form *entfangen*, unaffected by assimilation, would be. Assimilation, either partial or entire, is a phenomenon occurring in all languages. When, on the other hand, the single sounds come into question, hardly any general principles can be laid down as to the greater or less facility of pronouncing one rather than another, and all theories on this point based on abstractions from narrow grounds show themselves worthless when confronted with a fuller experience. And, further, no perfectly general definitions can be given for the combination of several sounds. Facility depends to a great extent upon conditions of quantity and upon the accentuation, expiratory as well as musical. One sound-group is convenient in the long syllable, another in the short; one in the syllable which bears the stress, another in that which has no stress; while the circumflex makes other demands than the grave or the acute. But, further, the measure of convenience adapts itself to a quantity of circumstances which may be different for each individual, but which may attach themselves to larger groups as well in the same or in a similar way without being shared by the others. One point requires specially emphasising in this case. A certain harmony of the sound-system is found existing in all languages. We see from this that the direction in which a sound deviates must be partially conditioned by the direction taken by the other sounds. Much depends, as Sievers has shown, in this

ease on the so-called neutral position of the organs. Each variation in this entails, of course, also a variation in relation to
the convenience of single sounds. A gradual displacement of this
neutral position will have to be judged precisely after the analogy
of what we have said above about the similar displacement of the
motory sensation.

It is of great importance never to lose sight of the fact that
the consideration of convenience in each production of sound affords
in every case only a very subordinate and secondary cause; the
motory sensation always remains the really decisive motive power.
One of the commonest errors is the supposition that a change which
has arisen in a long period by numerous small displacements is to
be referred to a single act resulting from a desire for convenience.
This error partly results from the method in which rules for sound
are apprehended in practical grammars and even in grammars which
claim to teach on scientific principles. For instance, it is
commonly said that if a sonant [voiced] consonant appears as a
check, it takes the form in this language of the corresponding
surd [voiceless] (cf. MHG $m\hat{i}de$--$meit$, $r\hat{i}be$--$reip$), just as if we
had to do with a change occurring each time occasioned by the fact
of the surd being better adapted to the close of the word. The
truth is that it is in this case the motory sensation developed by
tradition which produces the surd, while the gradual reduction of
the voice-tone to absolute annihilation, and strengthening of the
pressure of expiration connected therewith, belong to a period
perhaps long past and gone. It is equally mistaken to refer the
appearance of a sound-change in each case to some particular manifestation of laziness, weariness, or neglect, and to ascribe its
non-appearance in other cases to some special care and observation.
It may well be that the motory sensation is not in every case
developed to the same degree of certainty. But there is no such
thing as a conscious effort made to prevent a sound-change. For
those who are affected by the change have no suspicion that there
is anything to guard against, and they habitually pass their lives
in the belief that they speak today as they spoke years ago, and
that they will continue to the end to speak in the same way. Were
any one able to compare the movements which his organs made in the
utterance of a word many years before with those which they make
at present, he would most likely find a striking difference. But
to make any such real comparison would be an impossibility. The
only possible test is in each case the motory sensation; and this
is correspondingly modified--in fact, exists no longer in his mind
as it existed on the previous occasion.

There is, however, a controlling source which opposes a powerful

barrier to the development of the single individual just described--
that is, the sound-picture. Motory sensation is formed from the
movements of the speaker only; the sound-picture, on the other hand,
takes shape not merely from our own utterances, but also from all
that we hear from those with whom we enter into communication. Now,
if it were the case that a notable displacement of the motory sensation were to occur, accompanied by no corresponding displacement
of the sound-picture, a discrepancy would be felt between the sound
produced by the first and the sound-picture obtained by the previous
sensations. Such a discrepancy is avoided by the motory sensation
correcting itself after the sound-picture. This happens in the same
way as the motory sensation directs itself at first in childhood
according to the sound-picture. It belongs to the very essence of
language as a means of communication, that the single individual
should always find himself in agreement with the companions with
whom he communicates. Of course no such thing as a conscious effort
at this result exists, but the demand for such agreement remains,
as something self-intelligible, unconscious. This demand cannot
either be complied with with absolute exactness. If the motory
sensation of the individual cannot fully master his movements, and
is actually exposed to slight deviations, the free room for the
movement which finds play within a group of individuals must of
course be still greater, for it will certainly never be in the
power of the motory sensation of each individual to satisfy completely the sound-picture which floats before him. And there is
this further consideration, that this sound-picture as well must
take a somewhat different shape in the case of each individual,
thanks to the differences which exist in sound-sensations, and is
likewise subject to perpetual vacillations. But these vacillations,
within a group connected by active communication, cannot pass beyond
rather narrow limits. They are in this case unnoticed, or, even
should they be noticed on nearer observation, they still hardly admit of definition, or indeed of expression, even by the aid of the
most perfect alphabet. This is not merely a matter of *a priori*
suspicion, but lends itself to objective observation in the case of
living dialects--of course not in the case of those which show a
graduated influence of the written language. If deviations more or
less violent in the case of an individual are found--for instance,
as the result of an organic fault--this makes little difference in
the result of the whole.
  As long, then, as the single individual with his tendency to
deviation stands alone opposed to his companions in intercourse,
he can only yield to this tendency in a very limited measure, seeing that its operations are always counteracted by counter-opera-

tions, which regulate the result. A displacement of greater extent can only appear if it prevails throughout the entirety of the individuals in a group which is to some extent secluded from all external influences, at least in comparison to the activity of the communication prevailing within its circuit. The possibility of such a process needs no demonstration in cases where the deviation suits the convenience of all, or almost all, the organs of speech better than the strict conservancy of the direction of the motory sensation. It must be specially noticed in this connexion that the already existing correspondence in accent, time, etc., gives an impulse towards the same path. The same holds good of correspondence in the neutral position. But this is not nearly sufficient to explain the whole proceeding. We see, of course, that manifold developments proceed from the same starting-point, and this without necessarily in every case being conditioned by changes in accent or other circumstances of any kind which claim as their exciting cause psychology; and we must ever put the question anew: how comes it that precisely the individuals composing this group undergo in common the influence of such and such change? Similarity of climate, of soil, of life has been cited to explain the difficulty. We have, however, to state with reference to this that up to the present date not even the first steps have been taken for methodically collecting materials relating to these which might tend to prove dependence of the development of language on such influences. What is advanced in favour of this theory in individual cases may be easily reduced to a *reductio ad absurdum*. It hardly admits of doubt that peculiarities in the organs of speech are transmitted by inheritance, and hence a degree of relationship, closer or more remote, is to be reckoned among the other factors which condition a greater or less correspondence in the construction of the organs. But this is not the only cause on which the latter depends. And just as little does the development of language depend solely on the construction of the organs. In addition, however, dialectic separation and dialectic reconciliation seem in very many instances to belie the actual physical relationship. It will then be labour in vain to endeavor to explain the fact of the agreement of all the individuals in a single group as a spontaneous result, and therein to overlook the other factor, which is operative side by side with this spontaneity, viz., the force of community of intercourse.

If we start from the assumption that each individual has his special bent and his special development, the possibility of very numerous variations is certainly admitted. But if we take each factor which comes under our consideration as isolated, then the number of the possible variations is indeed very limited. If we

observe the changes of each single sound taken singly, and if we
again differentiate in this process the displacement of the local-
ity of articulation, transition of closure to narrowing, and *vice
versa*, strengthening or weakening of the pressure of expiration,
etc., we shall often be in the position of obtaining two possible
cases, and only two, of deviation. Thus, for instance, the *a*
sound may gradually change into that of all possible vowels; but
the direction in which it moves can still in the first instance be
only that towards *i*, or that towards *u*. Now it can certainly
easily occur that the two or three possible directions may, in a
large linguistic area, all things considered, be fairly balanced.
But it is very unlikely that this should occur in all the different
points at every time. The case that, in an area held together by
an extremely active intercourse, one tendency should gain the upper
hand may easily occur, solely by the caprice of chance--i.e. even
if the agreement of the majority is not conditioned by a more close
inner connexion as against the individuals who stand outside the
group, and if the causes which impel to this definite direction are
different, as they may be, in the case of different individuals.
The fact of the prevalence of a tendency in such a narrow circle
suffices to prevail against the opposing barriers. The active
cause is, that the displacement of the motory sensation to which
the majority leans entails a simultaneous displacement of the sound-
picture in the corresponding direction. The individual is, in fact,
not dependent on the entirety of the members of the whole linguistic
community with respect to the arrangement of his ideas of sound,
but only, as an invariable rule, on those with whom he enters into
intercourse. Nor is his dependence even on these uniform, but
differs widely, according to the frequency of the communication,
and according as each individual brings his activity to bear in the
process. It does not matter from how many persons he hears such
and such peculiarity of language; the whole consideration is how
often he hears them. We must, while on this topic, observe that
the speakers who deviate from the commonly adopted standard may
again differ among themselves, and that their several influences
may thus reciprocally neutralise each other. If, however, a definite displacement of the motory sensation has set in owing to the
removal of the retarding influence of communication, we then find
that in the course of this tendency a further slight deviation is
rendered possible. Meantime, however, the minority as well is
swept into the current by the movement. Precisely the same causes
which prevent the minority from departing too far from the common
usage in their progressive movement, forbid also that it should
lag much behind the advance of the majority. For the superior

14

frequency of any pronunciation is the only measure for its correctness and fitness to serve as a standard. Thus the movement progresses in this way--there is always a part somewhat in front of the average and another part somewhat behind it; but the whole advances with so little difference between its parts that a striking contrast never occurs between individuals who stand in equally close communication with each other.

In this way it will always be found that the displacements which occur within the same generation are slight and scanty. More notable displacements do not occur until an older generation has been thrust aside by a new one springing up. In the first place, if a displacement has already penetrated to the majority, while a minority still opposes it, it will be found that the coming generation will naturally adapt itself to the majority, especially when the majority has the more convenient pronunciation. Even if the minority in these cases should cling to the old custom, it must yet die out. It may, however, be the case that the impulse of the younger generation may set in a special direction differing from the elder one. The same motives which in the case of the elder generation impel to a particular kind of deviation, from the impulse already formed, must in the case of the younger generation operate at the very outset upon the shape to be taken by their language. It may therefore be properly said that the main occasion of sound change consists in the transmission of sounds to new individuals. For this process, then, the expression 'change', if we would remain true to facts, is quite inapplicable; we have rather to deal with a new creation deviating from the old form.

In the process of mastering language the sounds alone are transmitted, and not the motory sensations as well. The agreement of the sounds which are self-generated with those heard from others gives the individual the assurance requisite that he is speaking correctly. That the motory sensation has taken an approximately identical form can only be assumed on the supposition that approximately similar sounds can only be produced by approximately identical movements of the organs of language. If it is possible to produce an approximately identical sound by means of different movements, it must also be possible that the motory sensation of any learner of language may take a different shape from that of the persons from whom he learns it. For a few particular cases such deviation of the form taken by motory sensation must be conceded as possible. Thus, for instance, the dorsal t and s sounds are not very different from the alveolar in sound, although their articulation is essentially different. Lingual and uvular r are still fairly easy to distinguish, and it seems that in different German

dialects the one or the other prevails all through; but the transition of the one into the other can hardly be explained in any other
way than by the fact that deviating utterances were not corrected
because the sound-deviations were not sufficiently marked.

There are other sound changes which do not depend up the displacement or deviating form taken by the motory sensation, which, therefore, have to be separated from sound change in the narrower sense
hitherto described. These changes, however, have this much in
common with that, that they proceed to their fulfilment without any
regard to the function of the word. The effect of these processes
is not the change of the elements of which the sentence is composed,
by substitution, but merely an interchange of these elements in
certain definite cases.[2]

The first of the changes which fall under this head is that of
metathesis. Of this there are two main divisions. The first of
these is when two sounds immediately following are transposed, as
in the case of AS *fix* = OHG *fisc*; *first* = *frist*; *irnan* = *rinnan*.
The second is when two sounds not immediately following change their
places; cf. the case of OHG *erila* by the side of *elira* = NHG *erle*
and *eller*; AS *weleras*, the lips, as against the Gothic *wairilos*;
OHG *ezzih*, which must have had the sound of **etik* before the sound-
shifting process set in = Lat. *acetum*; Ital. dialectically *grolioso*
= *glorioso*; *crompare* = *comprare*; MHG *kokodrille* = Lat. *crocodilus*
[*cokodrilles (Maundevile)*].

Under this head, too, must be ranged assimilations between two
sounds not related, as Lat. *quinque* from **pinque*; PGmc. **finfi* (five)
= **finhwi*, etc.

We more commonly find dissimilations between two similar sounds
not in contact; cf. OHG *turtiltûba*, from the Lat. *turtur*; *marmul*,
from Lat. *marmor*; MHG *martel* with *marter*, from *martyrium*; *prîol* with
prîor: and conversely, MHG *pheller* with *phellel*, from Lat. *palliolum*;
OHG *fluobra* 'consolation,' as against OS *frôfra* and AS *frôfor*; MHG
kaladrius with *karadrius*; Middle Lat. *pelegrinus* from *peregrinus*.

Further, the falling out of a single sound may be regarded as
assimilation, if this be caused by the fact of the same sound occurring in its neighborhood: cf. Greek *drúphaktos* 'wooden barrier',
derived from *phrássō*, and *ékpaglos* from *plḗssō*. It is just so with
the disappearance of an entire syllable occurring near a similar
one closing with the same consonant: cf. *hēmédimnon*, a double of
hēmimédimnon, *amphoreús* of **amphiphoreús*, *kelainephḗs* instead of
kelainonephḗs; Lat. *semestris* for **semimestris*.

These processes seem to admit of no other explanation than that
they are based upon repeated mispronunciations affecting spontaneously a considerable part of the linguistic community. It is a

well-known circumstance that in the act of speaking the order of
the words, syllables, or single sounds becomes displaced, owing to
one element forcing itself prematurely into consciousness. It is
equally well known that of two similar elements one is easily dropped. It is further notoriously difficult to pronounce with accuracy
a succession of similar and yet different sounds uttered quickly.
It is on this that the joke depends about *If Peter Piper picked a
peck of pickled pepper*, etc.; *Round about the rugged rock the
ragged rascals ran*, etc. It will also be impossible to deny that
conditions favourable to certain mispronunciations exist, and that
hence these mispronunciations occur in the mouths of quite different
persons, and this repeatedly. The mispronunciations may then pass
by inheritance as a normal form to the younger generation. These
processes are most easily understood when they affect foreign words
which contain series of sounds repugnant to the genius of the language which adopts them. In these cases inexact perception and
defective recollection will likewise occur. It suggests itself
also often for our consideration if popular etymology is not also
at work in producing them. Everything is not yet clear in these
processes.

   We have now to answer the important question, which has been in
recent times the subject of so much dispute: Can we assert uniformity in sound-laws? In the first place, we must full understand
what we mean, generally speaking, by a sound-law. The word 'law'
is itself used in very different senses, and this very fact induces
errors in its application.[3] The idea of sound-law is not to be
understood in the sense in which we speak of 'laws' in Physics or
Chemistry, nor in the sense of which we were thinking when we contrasted exact sciences with historical sciences. Sound-law does
not pretend to state what must always under certain general conditions regularly recur, but merely expresses the reign of uniformity
within a group of definite historical phenomena.

   In the statement of sound-laws the rule has been to start with a
comparison. The circumstances of one dialect have been compared
with those of another; those of an older stage of development with
those of a more recent. Abstractions have been made by comparing
the relations of one dialect with those of another, those of an
older stage of development with those of a later one. Sound-laws
have also been formed by abstraction by comparing the different
relations within the same dialect existing at the same time. The
rules commonly adopted even into practical grammars are of the
latter kind. Thus, to cite a sentence taken word for word from
Krüger's Greek Grammar: A *t* sound, followed by another, passes regularly into *s*. Examples: *anusthênai* from *anúto*, *ereisthênai* from

ereídō, peisthênai from *peíthō*. It has been before remarked that
we must not allow ourselves to be led away by such rules to adopt
the view that the sound transitions in question are each time
effected anew by the creation of the one form out of the other.
The forms in question which stand in such a relation to each other
are either both taken up by the memory, or one is formed from the
other by analogy. This relation will be designated not as a sound-
change (*Lautwandel*), but as sound-substitution (*Lautwechsel*).
Sound-substitution is not identical with sound change, but is merely
an after-effect of it. Accordingly we ought never to apply the term
'sound-law' to sound-substitution, but only to sound change. A
sound-law may no doubt reflect itself in the effects left in the
conditions of any given language as they exist side by side; but as
a sound-law it never applies to such language, but invariably to a
historical development carried out in a definite period.

If we, therefore, speak of the uniform operation of sound-laws,
this can only mean that in the case of sound-change occurring within the same dialect, all the separate cases, in which the same
sound-conditions occur, are treated uniformly. It must either
happen, therefore, that where the same sound existed previously,
the same sound always remains in the later stages of development as
well; or, where a separation into different sounds has occurred,
there must be a special reason to be assigned; and, further, a
reason of a kind affecting sound alone--such as the effect of neighboring sounds, accent, place of syllable, etc.--for the fact that
in one case one sound has arisen and in another a different one.
No doubt we must take into account in this all the different factors
in the production of sound. Especially we must regard the word not
as isolated, but in the light of its place within the sentence taken
as a whole. Not till then is it possible to recognize the real
uniformity of sound changes.

It is not difficult, after the enunciation of these principles,
to show the necessity of this uniformity as far as it turns on
actual sound-change depending on a gradual displacement of the
motory sensation; to speak more accurately, we should no doubt
rather say, not 'uniformity', but the occurrence of all deviations
from it within limits too fine for our detection.

It must be plain to every one who acknowledges in all phenomena
the operation of general laws, that the process of development works
uniformly to its fulfilment. A motory sensation does not form itself specially for every word, but in every case where the same
elements recur in language their production is guided by the same
sensation. Should, then, the motory sensation suffer displacement
by reason of the pronunciation of an element in any word, then this

displacement is also a precedent for the same element in another word. Thus the pronunciation of this element in the different words vacillates just as much as does that of the same word within the same narrow limits. Vacillations in pronunciation caused by quicker or slower, louder or gentler, more careful or more negligent utterance, will always affect the same element in the same manner, in whatever word it may occur, and these must always move in corresponding distances from the normal or standard manner.

The development of sound change in the case of a single individual is always urged as an objection against the uniform working of sound-laws. It is maintained that our etymological consciousness-- our regard for related forms, stands in the way of the operation of a sound-law. Whoever maintains this, must, in the first place, clearly understand that it involves no denial of the continuous activity of the factor which impels to sound change--only the supposition of a factor of an entirely different nature which operates against this. It is decidedly not a matter of indifference whether we assume that a factor is at one time operative, and at another time inoperative; or whether we maintain that it is under all circumstances operative, and that its operating power is counteracted by that of another factor. But how are we to conceive of the chronological condition in the operation of these factors? Do they both operate simultaneously, so that no change occurs, or does the one operate after the other, so that the operation of the latter is always cancelled? The first alternative could only be conceivable on the assumption that the speaker knew something of the threatened change, and sought to guard himself against it beforehand. I think that I have made it sufficiently clear that there can be no question of this at all. If we, however, allow that the effect of the factor of sound makes its influence first felt, but is then counteracted by the other factor, which we shall have in a following chapter to characterise more closely, the uniformity of the sound-laws is hereby admitted. We can advantageously discuss this point at most: Whether it is a rule that analogy asserts itself immediately after the appearance of a very slight difference between the etymologically connected forms, or that it does not show itself operative until the contrast declares itself more unmistakeably. In principle, there is no difference. That the latter case is however very frequent, we can see by experience, and we shall discuss it at greater length later. But it is in the nature of the case that differences which are not yet felt as such cannot circumscribe the feeling for etymology, and are not circumscribed by this feeling.

Equally inadmissible is the supposition that considerations as to the clearness and intelligibility of a form stand in the way of a transition of sound. We come sometimes upon conditions which seem to prove the affirmative. Thus, for instance, in NGH the medial *e* of the weak preterites and participles after *t* and *d* is maintained as in *redete*, *rettete*, while it is in other cases rejected. But if we revert to the sixteenth century we find that double forms are the rule in every verb; on one hand we find *zeigete* by the side of *zeigte*; on the other, *redte* by that of *redete*. Sound change has thus made its appearance with no consideration of utility; and the greater utility of one set of forms has served to guarantee merely their continued existence.

Thus the question can only remain whether the communication of the different individuals among each other can occasion breaches of uniformity. This would only be conceivable under the supposition that the single individual were to be exposed simultaneously to the influence of several groups of persons who had plainly parted asunder owing to a different system of sound-development, and that he learnt some words from one, and others from the other group. This, however, presupposes a wholly exceptional state of things. Normally speaking, there exist no such differences within the linguistic community within which the individual grows up, and with which he stands in far more intimate connexion than with more distant associates. Where it does not happen that, in consequence of special historical causes, larger groups are detached from their original dwelling-place, and thrown together with others where the population is, at most, modified by slight accessions or departures, but remains constant as far as its main body is concerned, no differences can be developed, which are apprehended as such. Even if A pronounces a somewhat different sound from B in the corresponding place, still the apprehension of the one sound as well as that of the other fades into the sound-picture which the hearer already carries in his mind; and thus it follows again that only the same motory sensation can correspond with them. It is absolutely impossible that, owing to two differences so slight, two different motory sensations should form in the same individual. As a general rule it would be impossible, even supposing that the extremes which occur within a small linguistic domain were the only existing ones. But even if the hearer were in a position to apprehend the difference between these two, still the series of fine transition-steps, which he always hears without any break, would render it impossible to keep a frontier line unbroken. And so, even assuming that he hears one word more frequently and earlier from people who tend to this extreme, and the other more frequently and earlier from people who tend to the other extreme, still this can never produce the result that, in his efforts to repeat the word, the production of a sound in one word should be guided by a different motory sensation from the production of a sound in the other word, if the same individual would set an identical sound in both places.

Thus within the same dialect no irregularity develops, excepting either as the result of a mixture of dialects, or, as we shall have to detail with more accuracy, as the result of the borrowing of a word from a foreign dialect. We shall have later to examine to what extent and under what conditions such borrowing appears. Of course in our statement of sound-laws we do not have to reckon with any such apparent irregularities.

The attempts which have been made to explain sound change as dependent on individual caprice or on an inaccurate ear are hardly worth mentioning. A single inaccuracy of ear cannot possibly have any lasting results for the history of language. If I do not accurately catch a word from any one who speaks the same dialect as myself, or another with which I am well acquainted, but if I guess his meaning from the context of his discourse, then I supply the word in question according to the memory-picture which I have in my mind. If the connexion is not sufficient to explain clearly the meaning, it may be that I shall supply a wrong meaning, or I may supply nothing at all, and satisfy myself with understanding nothing, or I may ask again. But how I should come to think that I have heard a word of different sound, and still to set this word in the place of the one I understand, is to me incomprehensible. Certainly it may more easily happen to a child who has never yet heard a particular word to apprehend that word imperfectly, and to reproduce it again imperfectly. But the child will also frequently reproduce imperfectly that which it has apprehended more correctly because, in its case, impulse is not yet adequately formed. Its apprehension, as its reproduction, will correct itself, if it always hears the word anew; if this be not so, it will forget it. Wrong apprehension of sound is only regularly seen when people who belong to different dialectic areas or different languages converse with each other, and the shape in which foreign words are adopted is no doubt much influenced by this circumstance, but certainly more by the want of motory sensations for the sounds which are wanting to their own dialect.

There remain now certainly some kinds of sound changes in which uniformity of action cannot theoretically be proved necessary. These, however, make up a relatively small part of the entire sound changes, and they admit of sharp delimitation. Thus, on the

one hand, we have to reckon under this head the cases in which a
sound is imitated by means of a deviating articulation. On the
other side we must include the metatheses, assimilations, and dissimilations referred to above. For the rest, even in this case,
we find as a matter of fact, to some extent, that regularity is the
rule, especially in the case of the metathesis of sounds immediately
following each other, and further, e.g. in the case of the dissimilation of the aspirates in Greek, as in *kékhuka*, *pépheuga*, and
elsewhere.

The question, as to how far sound-laws are to be regarded as ad-
mitting of no exceptions, cannot be absolutely decided by the materials of language before us, because there are changes in language
which, although in their nature absolutely different from sound
change, still produce corresponding results with this. Thus our
question is intimately connected with the second question: How far
does the operation of these other changes extend, and how are they
to be divided from sound change?

Notes

[1]See his *Medizinische Psychologie* (1852) § 26, p. 304; also his
Metaphysik, ii, p. 586, sqq. For motory sensation, see G.E. Müller
Zur Grundlegung der Psychophysik, §110-111, and A. Strümpell in
Archiv für klinische Medizin, xxii, p. 321, sqq. Wundt employs
the expression 'innervation'.

[2]Cf. Brugmann, *Zum heutigen Stand der Sprachwissenschaft*, p. 50.

[3]Cf. L. Tobler, "Über die Anwendung des Begriffs von Gesetzen
auf die Sprache," *Vierteljahrschrift f. wiss Phil.*, iii., p. 32
sqq.

2 Sound Change

GEORG VON DER GABELENTZ

The science of historical linguistics correctly assigns virtually
fundamental significance to the phenomena of organically regular
sound change. Its method demands that these phenomena be determined first, that is, that only those be compared whose differences
are due exclusively to the disparate phonological development of
the same proto-form. It might seem as though this method were moving in a circle, as if it were guilty of a *petitio principii*.
Certain rules must be discovered. Let us grant that these rules
do not explain all phenomena of historical linguistic change, and
that therefore not all phenomena are equally useful for induction.
How then can the useful be distinguished from the not useful, before the rule is known? Here, as always, the history of Indo-
European scholarship is instructive, even when it has pursued a
wrong or roundabout path.

At first, taking Sanskrit as the basis, everything with a similarity in meaning and sound was compared: *pitṛ, patér, pater* 'father';
mâtṛ, mētér, mater 'mother'; *pra, prò, pro* 'for'; *asti, esti, est*
'is'--but also *hṛd, kardía, cor(d)* 'heart'; *yakṛt, hépar, jecur*
'liver'; *jihvã, lingua* 'tongue', etc. Later, when the [individual]
sounds were examined more closely, the association of items in the
second group became suspect.

One reasoned inductively: in such cases, sounds standing in the
same position developed from the self-same proto-sounds. Thus
Schleicher was led to rediscover the *k* of the proto-language in
the Sanskrit sounds *k, c, ś*, more rarely *p*, even more rarely *h*.
These are rules with exceptions, in which, to be sure, new rules
are sometimes detected, though they are not absolutely required.

This state of affairs seemed intolerable in the long run. What
develops mechanically must develop regularly, i.e. uniformly.
Where something has developed disparately, the differences also

From *Die Sprachwissenschaft*, 2nd ed. (Leipzig, 1901), 185-192.
Translated by R. N. Werth.

demand explanation. Several possible explanations presented themselves.

(a) The resemblance was deceptive, in that the underlying
words themselves were different in the proto-language. For example,
the original of Greek *theós* is different from that of Sanskrit *deva*;
Sanskrit *hṛd* by origin has nothing to do with [Gk.] *kardia*, [Lat.]
cor 'heart'.

(b) What is responsible for the difference in sounds is
that these sounds were already distinct in the proto-language.
Thus, in Indo-European, in addition to short *a*, short *e* and *o*, preserved in the European languages, were discovered; further, syllabic
ṛ, ḷ, m̥, n̥ or, according to others, a reduced vowel preceding these
liquids: *ər, əl, əm, ən*, and a double series of gutturals, by
which apparent irregularities were explained.

(c) The same sound of the proto-language must have developed
disparately under various conditions, which had to be specified.
Thus Verner's well-known Law all at once brought light and order to
an apparent wilderness.

(d) The words or word-forms were pulled from their original
relationship into another by means of a very natural mental process.
This is the case of the so-called false analogies, of which there
are various subtypes. Latin *lingua* owes its initial sound to the
semantically related *lingere* 'lick'. The German form *frug* instead
of *fragte* is based on the analogy of *trug, schlug*. In Sanskrit and in
some of the Slavic languages, the conjugation with *-mi* has taken
over completely in a few of the most common verbs.

(e) Loans from language to language may also have taken
place; this leads one to ask: At which stage of phonological development in the borrowing language? How much time was there for
the foreign form to assimilate to the native sound system? Consider those words where a German *k* corresponds to Latin *c*: *carcer*
- *Kerker* ['dungeon'], *cicer* - *Kichererbse* ['chick-pea'], *cerasus*
- *Kirsche* ['cherry']. There are also words where Latin *p* is retained as *p*, and those where it is changed into *pf*: *palatium* -
Palast ['palace'] - *Pfalz* ['Palatinate'].

In light of all these possibilities, the following principle has
been set up: sound laws are inviolable; where they seem to be
violated, the violation is only apparent (a), or it is due to
sound laws not yet recognized (b,c), or else it is caused by unrelated, non-articulatory ['nicht lautmechanisch'] factors.

If this principle were correct as stated in this crude form,
then there would be no deviations of articulation, and the factors
which enabled the sounds to shift would be incomprehensible. Given
that all speakers in the same dialect community have exactly the

same pronunciation, how then can it change? For one individual must
initiate the change before it can spread and become dominant. Questionable from the outset is the tenet that an individual would always
pronounce the same thing in the same way under the same circumstances.
Let us look at this matter closely, even if it appears that we are
splitting hairs.

Am I the same person today that I was forty years ago, twenty
years ago, two years ago, three weeks ago, yesterday? Probably the
same person ['derselbe'], but no longer the same being ['dasselbe'].
And whether my pronunciation is still the same remains doubtful. I
need not even consider the possibility that I had contact for a few
days with speakers of another dialect, and that I (like others in
the same circumstances) unconsciously adopted something of their pronunciation. Any pathological change in my speech organs, a cold, a
chipped tooth, even general physical fatigue or emotional agitation,
changes something in the way I produce sounds. Furthermore, what is
meant by the 'same circumstances'? The circumstances are different
when I say the same thing to different persons, or to the same person
but at various distances, or as an answer to a question, or as a
counter-statement in a discussion. Finally, what is meant by the
'same pronunciation'? Is only articulation involved, or also intonation and pace? Does articulation involve only the acoustic effect,
or also the manner in which this effect is produced by movements of
the speech and respiratory organs? No doubt all of these are involved. In the case of languages with lateral sounds, no auditory
differentiation can be made to determine whether the tongue has
moved to the left or to the right. If we want to spur a horse to
gallop, we click laterally, and this sounds exactly like the lateral
click of the Hottentots and Bushmen. The latter, however, articulate
the sound against the right molars, whereas with us it is usually the
left. If we wanted to do that in those languages, the natives would
criticize us. When a learned Arab was asked whether it was permissible to produce the lateral s in the left side of the sound, he re-
plied wittily: "Il n'y a pas d'exemple d'une telle gaucherie!"
Hence not only the ears but also the eyes judge the correctness of
articulation. All things considered, one is entitled to ask: when
are the prerequisites of the principle of uniform pronunciation
applicable? Is the principle viable at all? Language, after all,
is shaped not by the individual, but by the community; even my
brother or village neighbor does not speak exactly as I do.

All these misgivings had to be considered in order that they might
be overcome. I have already pointed out that the *Sprachgefühl* of
native speakers has a broader conception of sounds than does sound
physiology; it permits a certain latitude, large or small, in sound

production and auditory perception. Only when this range is over-
extended does the *Sprachgefühl* object. Each individual by nature
acts in much the same way as he hears and sees it done by those
closest to him, but there are limits to his whims and carelessness:
the bird flutters on the string [i.e. its movement is constrained by
attachment to a fixed point]. Now it may very well happen that within these limits certain directions are gradually preferred. Let us
take, for example, the sound *a*. It may move slightly in the direction of *ä* or just as much in the direction of *a* or *ö*; the ideal *a*
forms the center of a circle which describes its permitted articulatory range. Let us say that within this circle, usage decides in
favor of the direction toward *å*. To begin with, the center of gravity shifts, for the other directions are less frequently made use of.
Later, however, as the center itself shifts, the circle will increase
in the direction toward *å* and decrease in the direction toward *ä* and
ö. Whether it becomes wider or more narrow in the process is another
matter. The essential point, namely the sound shift, is rather
simply explained in this way, and one must admit that no more appropriate term could have been chosen.

What then determines the narrowness or width of those circles?
First of all, it depends, of course, on the greater or lesser sensi-
tivity of sound perception: something may still seem acceptable to
one person, while to another it already sounds unacceptable. It may
be that entire nations are variously endowed or differently conditioned by fate. We often read of languages in which voiced and
voiceless stops are not distinguished, and where in the same instance
either *k* or *g*, *t* or *d* may be produced, and we certainly cannot doubt
the sound perception of the writers. Where there is active contact
between people of different dialects, one certainly is able to distinguish the dialects from each other, but one also tolerates foreign
elements, since they are hardly perceived as foreign anymore; one
might even unconsciously use some of them. If I have observed correctly, the bilabial and labiodental pronunciation of *f* and *w* in
Germany is regionally determined, with the labiodental probably
throughout the north, and the bilabial primarily in the old Upper
German area. Only a small number of Germans are struck by the difference; however, a labiodental pronunciation of *w* in Dutch and
Swedish is deemed unacceptable. On the other hand, no doubt, certain
other deviations are permitted in those languages.

It is always hazardous to make statistical assertations, to talk
of 'always' or 'never', 'mostly' or 'rarely', as long as one cannot
adduce the statistical proof. In our case, the situation is such
that one may have doubts about which of the two principles is the
more accurate, (1) that the same individual under identical circum-

stances always pronounces the same thing in exactly the same way, or (2) that only rarely and accidentally is the same thing articulated in exactly the same way several times, since the individuals, the circumstances, and the pronunciation are subject to countless minute fluctuations. Let us suppose that the latter principle applies: it still would not be tantamount to saying that the evolution of sounds can proceed completely irregularly. And vice-versa: suppose that one could adduce everywhere such sharply delineated and inviolable sound laws as have been discovered in the Indo-European family, and are still being sought: this still would not refute the assertion that articulation everywhere permits a certain amount of latitude, even if it is highly constrained.

However, as long as this kind of progress has not been made in regard to the historical phonology of other language families (as in part must still be made for Indo-European), I will not accept the principle of invariability ['*Ausnahmslosigkeit*'] as dogma, much less as a proven theorem. I would rather see it as a methodological principle which states: "Proceed as if this were the case; adapt your investigations accordingly; do not cease until you have discovered the sound law or the reason why, in a particular instance, it has been violated. In this way you will be as secure as possible under the circumstances." For a start, this is a useful pretense; under the best conditions, it is a plausible postulate. If one wants to pursue it in earnest, put it to the test, one should begin where the sources of linguistic history are the richest and relatively purest, perhaps with the Romance languages. For the present, one is better off speaking of a frequently verified precept rather than of an incontrovertible, proven, or provable theorem. Even if it were proven for the Indo-European languages, it does not follow that it would be proven for the others.

In this sense, which seems also to be approved by many of our most progressive Indo-Europeanists, the principle of recent Indo-European studies may well be valid elsewhere, too. It will prove to be a restraint on precipitate judgments, guarding against accidents on precipitous slopes; on level ground, however, it will hamper progress; on ascending ground, it will thwart progress. Even before the discovery of Verner's Law, one could not reasonably deny that the German words *Vater, Mutter, Bruder* are cognate with Latin *pater, mater, frater*, even if one was at a loss when confronted by the apparent irregularity of the sound correspondences. But to those who forget to look for the probable out of the single-minded desire for absolute certainty, the following quote from *Faust* applies: "By this do I recognize the learned man . . . " ['Daran erkenn' ich den gelehrten Herrn . . .']. Such people deprive themselves of that feeling for the variety of life which no historian must forsake. There will always be enough of the inexplicable; there will always be a time when sound laws will desert us, and we will be unable to explain where they have been violated. Italian and Spanish *gato* 'cat' obviously should not be dissociated from Latin *catus*. However, there is no sound law which accounts for the change of *k* to *g*, and it will be difficult to show why it should have occurred just there.[1] In Germanic, ð *(þ)* replaced Indo-European *t*; in High and Low German this became *d*; in English the fricative split into a voiceless and a voiced sound; and in Danish and Swedish *t* corresponds to the former, *d* to the latter: *du denkst, thou thinkest, du tänker*. What accounts for this?

Sound shifts spread gradually, both in a geographical and lexical sense. The example of the High German dialects is instructive in this respect. The inhabitants of the Lower Rhine area and their kinsmen in Transylvania still say *et, dat, wat* for *es, das, was*; in other items, however, they have adopted the High German *s (ß)* for the word-final *t*. The word *bloss* is still found in Alemannic in its older and Low German form *blutt* (Cf. Kluge, *Etym. Wb. der d. Spr.*, under *bloss*). Only in New High German did *zwerch* 'athwart, across' and *zwehle* 'towel' develop from Middle High German *twerch, dwerch, twehele, dwehele*. The change of *t* to *z* (the Old High German Sound Shift), therefore, occurred here for the second time after several centuries. In Japanese, the tendency to replace unstressed syllables in initial *m* or *n* with *u* - operative for a millenium - is constantly claiming new victims. H. Oldenberg's warning to exercise caution with such assumptions (*Zeitschr. f. deutsche Philol.* XXV, 116) is, however, worth heeding. The afore-mentioned double fate of Germanic *th* and also Lower Rhenish *et, dat, wat* seem indeed to have found a more or less satisfactory explanation in terms of sound laws. I cannot rule out that the other exceptional phenomena I mentioned might not also be due to phonological mechanisms, even though I find this difficult to imagine. But that is less significant here than the fundamental question of what is possible, necessary, or impossible in language. In no instance can the possibility be flatly negated that sound shifts have stalled in certain places, have penetrated farther in others, and that they may be able to burst forth anew after long intervals like atavistic traits. Basque offers copious examples for the fact that sound laws are capable of affecting only certain segments of the language, while passing over others completely. That sound laws do not always take effect suddenly, but also gradually, is shown e.g. by Latin *quintus* for *quinctus*, whereas *junctus, punctum* etc. did not lose the *c* until Italian: *giunto, punto*. In certain cases in Italian, word-final *s*

has changed to *i: noi, voi, poi, sei = nos, vos, post, sex*. If we
suppose that a similar tendency was already present in early Indo-
European times, then we would have an explanation for Sanskrit *tē*,
the nominative plural masculine of the demonstrative pronoun *sa, sā,
tad*, for the Latin and Greek forms *equi, híppoi* as opposed to
Sanskrit *aśvas*, also perhaps - with the aid of the reflexive pronoun - for the endings of the middle in Sanskrit and Greek as well
as the Sanskrit imperative *ǝdhi = sei*. But this will presumably
remain a hypothesis at best; it is already enough if it does not
appear too daring.

No sound is equipped with the tendency to shift in a specific
direction; each sound can avail itself of all imaginable directions
possible within the range of the speech organs. Let us recall what
has been said before. Each alteration, even the most minute, in
the position or movement of any part of the speech organs produces
a new phonetic element, and there are innumerable intermediate
stages between any two different sounds. Therefore one can boldly
assert: in due time and by a longer or shorter route, any sound
can turn into any other sound. It is not necessary, perhaps not
even possible, to demonstrate this in every detail. There is room
here for only some rather general observations.

The weaker the stress on a syllable or word, the more its sounds
are subject to reduction and loss. This can be seen in, e.g. the
suffixes and prefixes of our languages. On the other hand, strong
stress can lead to emphatic phonological development: vowels are
lengthened or diphthongized, consonants are doubled, devoiced,
aspirated, etc. Here we are but one step removed from what is
called euphonics, and if we are to ask what causes stronger or
weaker stress we are directed into the area of psychology.

One can assume as a rule, though hardly a rule without exceptions,
that there is a certain consistency in the sound shifts of a language, that related sounds share related fates. If we were talking
about handwriting, I would put it this way. Not just the individual
letters change, but also the script [ductus] as a whole; it becomes
more pointed or more rounded, more vigorous or more subdued, etc.
Analogous to script [ductus] in the spoken language are all those
habits which govern articulation: condition and movement of the
speech organs, position of the lips, the tongue, the velum, the
larynx, greater or lesser activity of the respiratory organs, etc.
Such habits can change imperceptibly from one generation to the
next, and these changes are decisive for the direction of a sound
shift. We and particularly the naive [uneducated] speakers, who
are very sensitive in such matters, have a wealth of expressions
pertaining to this. It is said that the language sounds harsh or

soft, slow or hurried, drawled or blustery, rasping, snorting,
gurgling, squeaky, nasal, lisping, hissing, garbled; each of these
words contain a highly suggestive descriptive element, a total
picture with a given number of individual traits. It may not always
be easy to reduce the data of a sound shift to such a common denomi-
nator; at any rate, the attempt should be made. The change in Germanic from voiceless stops to aspirates, then to fricatives, from
non-aspirated voiced stops to voiceless ones, from aspirated voiced
stops to non-aspirated ones: all of this must have been governed
by a uniform tendency.

Of course, things have not always worked out this consistently.
In many German dialects, the *g* has been fronted and palatalized to
j, whereas *k* has remained in its original position. Of the Latin
voiceless stops, only *k* has undergone frication (to *x*) in Old French
and the dialect of Florence, whereas *t* and *p* remained unchanged.
In Malagasy, initial *k* changed to *h*, *p* to *f*, but *t* (with some exceptions) remained. This should also be explained.

Infrequent sounds and combinations of sounds tend to disappear
and be replaced by more common ones, for the uncommon becomes un-
comfortable. Thus, Johannes Schmidt (*Pluralbildungen der indogerm.
Neutra*, pp. 198-99), in order to reconcile German *Leber*, Armenian
leard, Old Prussian *lagno* with Sanskrit *yakṛt*, Latin *jecur*, Greek
hêpar, Lithuanian *jeknos*, posits an original *ljêk_ert*, and also
assumes the same rare initial sound *lj* for Greek *eíbō* and *leíbō*.

But our science should strive to delve even more deeply. Why, in
this one out of many related dialects or languages, did a sound
change proceed in this particular way, why in a different direction
somewhere else, and why in yet a third direction in another language? We need think only of the Indo-European languages and the
developments of their vowels, their velars, palatals, aspirates,
and *s*-sounds: what accounts for the various tendencies among the
Aryans, Greeks, Slavs, and the Italic peoples? Climate, life
style, contact with neighboring tribes, perhaps temperament and
occasionally a certain esthetic feeling (fashion) - all of these
may have played a role, but to what degree and in which direction?
It would seem that only with an enormous amount of inductive
scholarship will the objective be reached, proceeding microscopi-
cally at one time, investigating the nearest, smallest dialects,
then again looking far afield at all the language families in all
parts of the world. For a science, which aims to probe the laws
of events, those common denominators, no matter how neatly they
have been worked out, are still merely first steps; they are
simplified descriptions, but not explanations.

Note

[1]Cf. Meyer-Lübke, *Gramm. der roman. Spr.* I, 353.

3   An Exception to Grimm's Law

KARL VERNER

In the XIth volume of this Journal (pp. 161-205) the late scholar
Lottner carefully examined the exceptions to Grimm's Law. He investigated all developments of Indo-European (IE) plosives (voiceless, voiced, and aspirated stops) which seemed to violate the
schema

$$\begin{array}{llllllll}
\text{IE} & k & = \text{Gmc.} & h & \text{IE} & g & = \text{Gmc.} & k \\
 & t & = & \theta & & d & = & t \\
 & p & = & f & & b & = & p
\end{array}$$

$$\begin{array}{lll}
\text{IE} & gh = & \text{Gmc.} \quad g \\
 & dh = & d \\
 & bh = & b
\end{array}$$

and came up with two categories of exceptions (not including the
cases where the lack of shift is conditioned by certain consonant
combinations:

$$\begin{array}{lll}
\text{IE} & sk, \ st, \ sp & = \text{Gmc.} \ sk, \ st, \ sp \\
\text{IE} & kt, \ pt & = \text{Gmc.} \ ht, \ ft \qquad).
\end{array}$$

On the one hand Lottner found that g, d, b occasionally appear unchanged in Germanic, as, for example, Goth. *gredu-s* 'hunger' -
Sk. *gṛdh-yati* 'he is greedy for'; Goth. *dauhtar* 'daughter' - Sk.
duhitar 'id.'; Goth. *bindan* 'to bind' - Sk. root *bandh* 'id.'; etc.
On the other hand he found that in many cases these same Germanic
voiced stops (g, d, b) do not appear as the reflexes of IE aspirates,
as would be expected, but rather as the reflexes of IE voiceless
stops (k, t, p); for example Gmc. *tegu* 'decade' is related to IE
dakan 'ten'; Gmc. *modar* = IE *mātar*; OHG *ebar* = Lat. *aper*; Goth.
bairand 'they carry' = Sk. *bharanti*; etc.

The first class of exceptions was soon eliminated by Grassman. In
his well-known article in the XIIth volume of this Journal, "On the
original existence of roots whose initial and final sound is an

Original title: "Eine Ausnahme der ersten Lautverschiebung",
Zeitschrift für vergleichende Sprachforschung 23 (1877), 97-130.
Translated by Richard Stanley.

aspirate" (p. 98), he demonstrated that the anomalies given by Lottner were only apparent since in Sanskrit *gṛdhyati, duhitar, bandh*,
etc., we do not have the original IE initial sound - this sound
really was an aspirate as a comparison with other IE languages shows.
Thus the appearance of the voiced stops in the Germanic forms becomes
completely justified.

Lottner's second class of exceptions (which, compared with the
first class, is quite extensive) cannot be eliminated in this fashion. Here there is really a violation of the sound laws, and evidently it is exclusively Germanic which is at fault. The irregular
sound change appears only in medial position, and then only in a
voiced environment. I give here a few examples of this irregular
sound change in various medial environments.

$$Gmc. \quad g = IE \ k$$

Gmc. *saga* f. 'saw' (ON *sǫg*, OHG *saga*); compare Lat. *sec-o*, OSl.
sěkǫ 'I cut, hew', Lit. *sýki-s* 'blow, stroke'.

Gmc. *sagjan* 'to say, to tell' (ON *segja*, OSax. *seggian*, OE *secgan*,
OHG *sagian*) = Lit. *sak-ýti, -aú* 'id.'; compare Gk. *én-nep-e* for
én-sep-e and OLat. *in-sec-e* 'I show, tell, relate'.

Goth. *hals-aggan* -m. 'curvature of the neck', OE *angan-* m.'point,
arrow-head'; compare Sk. *aṅka-* m.'hook, clamp; bow, side, lap'
= Gk. *ógkho-s* = Lat. *uncu-s* 'hook'.

Gmc. Θ*egna-* m.'boy, man, servant' (ON Θ*egn*'freeman, soldier', OSax.
thegan 'boy, man, soldier', OE Θ*egn* 'knight', OHG *degan* 'boy,
servant, soldier') = Gk. *tékhno-n* 'child'.

Compare each of these with the following series of regular shifts
in similar medial environments.

Goth. *haiha-* 'one-eyed' = Lat. *caecu-s* 'blind'.

Gmc. *hlahjan* 'to laugh' (Goth. *hlahjan*, ON *hlæja*, OE *hlehhan*,
hlyhhan, OHG *hlahhan*); compare Sk. *kark* 'to laugh', Gk. *khlóssō*
for *khlōkh-jō* 'I cluck, make a clicking sound'.

Gmc. *fanhan* 'to catch' (Goth. *fāhan*, ON *fâ*, OSax. *fāhan*, OE *fōn*,
OFris. *fā*, OHG *fāhan*); compare Sk. *pāś-aya-ti* 'he binds', Lat.
pac-iscī, pax, pāc-is.

Gmc. *laihna* - n. 'fief, fee' (ON *lān*, OE *læn*, OHG *lēhan*) derived
from *līhvan* 'loan' (Goth. *leihvan*, ON *ljâ*, OSax. *far-līhan*, OE
līhan, OHG *līhan*); compare Sk. *ric*, pres. *riṇak-ti* and *recati*
'leave' = Gr. *leípō, é-lip-on* = Lat. *linquo, līqui* = Lit. *lëk-u,*
lìk-ti.

Goth. *fadi-* m. 'man, lord', only in compounds such as *brū̄θ-fadi-*
'bridegroom' = Sk. *pati-* m. 'lord, husband' = Gk *pósi-s* = Lit.
pàt-s 'husband'.

Gmc. Θ*euda-* f. 'people' (Goth. Θ*iuda*, OSax. *thioda*, OHG *diota*) =
(low) Lit. *tautà*, Latvian *tauta*, Umbrian *tūtu*.

Gmc. Θ*ridjan* 'the third' (Goth. Θ*ridjan-* ON Θ*ridi*, OSax. *thriddio*,
OE Θ*ridda*, OHG *dritjo*, *dritto*) = Sk. *tr̥tīya-*, Lat. *tertiu-s*, Lit.
trécza-s, OSl. *tretii*.

Gmc. *fedvōr* 'four' (Goth. *fidvor*, ON *fjórir*, OSax. *fiuuar*, OE *feóver*,
OHG *fior*) = Sk. *catvāras*, Gk. *téssares*, Lat. *quatuor*, Lit. *keturì*,
OSl. *četyrije*.

Gmc. *and-*'against' (Goth. *anda-*, *and-*, ON, OE *and-*, OHG *ant-*); compare Sk. *anti* 'opposite', Gk. *antí*, *ánta*, 'against, Lat. *ante*.

Gmc. *andja-* m. 'end' (Goth. *andja-*, ON *endi-r*, OSax. *endi*, OE *ende*,
OHG *enti* m. n.); compare Sk *anta-* m. 'id.', *antya-* adj. 'the one
at the end, the last one'.

Gmc. *skordi-* f. 'shear, cut' (ON *skurð-r* m. *i*-stem 'the cutting,
the mowing', OHG *scurt* f. 'tonsura'), formed from the root *skar*
'cut' through the suffix *-di* = Sk. *-ti*.

Gmc. *skoldi-* f. 'fault' (ON *skuld*, *skyld*, OSax. *sculd*, OE *scyld*,
OHG *sculd*) formed by means of the same suffix from the root *skal*
'shall, should'.

Compare with these the following cases of regular shift.

Gmc. *hvaθara-* 'uter' (Goth. *hvaθar*, ON *hvár-r*, OSax. *hueðar*, OE
hväðer, OHG *hwedar*, *wedar*) = Sk. *katara-* = Gk. *pótero-s*, Ion.
kótero-s = Lit. *katrà-s*

Gmc. *hleuθa-* n. 'the hearing, listening, silence' (Goth. *hliuθa-*,
ON *hljóð*) = Avestan *śroata* - n. 'the hearing'.

Gmc. *niθja-* m.' relation, cousin' (Goth. *niθja-*, ON *nið-r* OE
niddas pl. m. 'homines'); compare OSl. *netii* m. 'nephew', Gk.
a-ne-psió-s 'cousin, relation', from a base form **napatja-* ; compare Sk. *napāt-*, *naptar-* 'grandson, nephew, descendant', Lat.
nepōt-.

Goth. *saliθva* f. only in the plural *saliθvos* 'lodge, inn', formed
through the suffix *-θva* = Sk. *-tva* from the verb stem *salja-*
'stop at'.

Gmc. *tanθu-*, *tanθ-* m. 'tooth' (Goth. *tunθu-*, ON *tönn* f., OSax.
tand m., OE *tōð*, OHG *zand*) = Sk. *dant-*, *danta-* m., Gk. *o-doús*,
o-dónt-os m., Lit. *dantì-s* m.f.

Gmc. *an-θja-* n. 'forehead' (ON *enni*, OHG *andi*); compare Gk. *antío-s*
'the one opposite or opposed', Lat. *antiae* 'hair in the forehead'.
Gmc. *morθa-* n. 'murder' (ON *morð*, OE *morð*, OSax. *morð*, OHG *mord*),
formed from the root *mar-* 'die' through the suffix -θ*a* = IE -*ta*.
Goth. *vulθu-* m. 'glory' = Lat. *vultu-s*, formed from the root *val* 'to
want' through the suffix -θ*u* = IE -*tu*.

Gmc. *b* = IE *p*:

Gmc. *seban* 'seven' (Goth. *sibun*, ON *sjau*, OSax., OHG *sibun* , *siban*,
OE *seofon*) = Sk. *saptan*, Gk. *heptá*, Lat. *septem*.

On the other hand with regular shift we have

Gmc. *nefan-* m. (the Germanic base form is to be posited with *f* after
the OHG *nevo* 'nephew, sister's son, uncle, relation'; ON *nefi*, OE
nefa); compare Sk. *napāt-* m. 'descendant, grandson', Lat. *nepōt-*.

This split in the development of the original voiceless stops does
not occur only in forms which come from different roots, as in the
above examples - even among word forms which have the same root it
is very common. Thus one derivational form of a Germanic root may
have a voiceless fricative whereas another derivational form of the
same root may have a voiceless stop. For example, along with Gmc.
tehan 'ten' (Goth. *taihun*, ON *tíu*, OSax. *tehan*, OE *tȳn*, OHG *zehan* =
Sk. *dašan*, Gk. *déka*, Lat. *decem*) there is a substantive *tegu-* m.
'decade' (Goth. *tigu-*, ON *tig-r, tug-r*, OHG -*zig*, -*zog*); along with
Gmc. *hauha-* 'high' (Goth. *hauha-*, ON *há-r*, OSax. *hōh*, OE *heáh*, OHG
hōh) there is *hauga-* m. 'hill' (ON *haug-r*, MHG *houc*, gen. *houges*);
along with *teuhan* 'to pull' (Goth. *tiuhan*, OSax. *tiohan*, OHG *ziohan*
= Lat. *dūco*) there is Gmc. *tuga-* '(a) pulling' (ON *tog* n., OHG *zug*
m.), Gmc. *taugi-* f. 'rope' (ON *taug* f., OE *teág*), and Gmc. *haritu-
gan-* m. 'general' (ON *hertogi*, OSax. *heritogo*, OE *heretoga*, OHG
herizogo); along with Gmc. *fanhan* 'to catch' there is the substantive *fanga-* 'a catch' (ON *fang* n., OHG *fang* m.); along with Gmc
slahan 'to strike' (Goth., OSax., OHG *slahan*, ON *slá*, OE *sleán*) there
is Gmc. *slaga-* '(a) blow' (ON *slag* n., OE *slagu* f. OHG *slaga* f.);
along with OHG *swehur* m. and OE *sveor* m. 'father-in-law (= Sk.
śvaśura-, Gk. *hekhuró-s*, Lat. *socer*, OSl. *svekrŭ*, Lit. *szeszura-s*)
there is OHG *swigar* f., OE *sveger* f. 'mother-in-law' (= Sk. *śvaśrū*,
Gk. *hekhurá*, Lat. *socru-s*, OSl. *svekry*); along with ON *flá* from
flahan 'to skin animal' there is ON *flaga* weak f. 'layer' and
flagna 'to loosen (the skin from the meat)'; along with Gmc. *felhan*
'to hide, conceal' (Goth. *filhan*, ON *fela*, OHG *felahan*) there is

Goth. *fulgina-* 'hidden' and ON *fjalg-r* in compounds 'safe, well-kept'; etc. In the dental series we have, for example, Goth. *hinθan* 'to catch, capture', Swed. *hinna* strong verb, Dan. dial. *hinne* 'to get there on time, to leave time to' along with the related Gmc. *handu-* f. 'hand' (Goth. *handu*, ON *hönd*, OSax. *hand*, OE *hond*, OHG *hant*, hand); Gmc. *finθan* 'to find' (Goth. *finθan*, ON *finna*, OSax. *fīðan*, OHG *findan*) along with *fund-r*, stem *fundi-* m. 'assembly'; Goth. *fraθjan* 'to understand, be understanding' along with Gmc. *frōda-* 'understanding' (Goth. *froda-*, ON *frōð-r*, OSax. OE *frōd*, OHG *fruot*); Gmc. *līθan* 'to go' (Goth. *leiθan*, ON *līða*, OSax. *līðan*, OE *līðan*, OHG *līdan*) and *liθu-* m. 'member' (Goth. *liθu-*, ON *lið-r*, OE *lið*, OHG *lid*) along with Gmc. *laidjan* 'to lead' (ON *leiða*, OSax. *lēdian*, OE *lædan*, OHG *leittan*) and *laida-* f. 'way' (ON *leið*, OE *lād*); Goth. *soθa-* m. 'satiation', *ga-soθjan* 'satiated' along with Gmc. *sada-* 'satisfied' (Goth. *sada-*, ON *saδ-r*, OSax. *sad*, OHG *satt* = OSl. *sytŭ*; compare Lat. *satur*, *sat*, *satis*); etc. In the labial series *f* and *b* merged into a single sound in most of the Germanic languages through secondary sound shifts so that the original distinction was obliterated. From Gothic, which, like Old High German, kept the two sounds apart, there is the example *af-lif-nan* 'to be left over' along with *laiba-* f. 'remainder'.

In looking over these examples one might be tempted to explain the general split of the original voiceless stops as being a mere whim of the language, and to ascribe the appearance of the voiced stops where voiceless fricatives are to be expected as being due entirely to chance. After all, to consider a further striking example, the three similarly formed Sanskrit kinship terms *bhrātar*, *mātar*, *patar*, have the reflexes *brōθar*, *mōdar*, and *fadar* in Germanic, where it is not at all clear why *mōdar* and *fadar* do not follow the regular development of *brōθar*. Nevertheless, one cannot continue to attribute this to chance. Admittedly, comparative linguistics cannot completely deny the possibility of chance development, but chance developments en masse such as we have here, where the cases of irregular change in medial position are almost as frequent as the cases of regular change, it can and must not admit. There must, in such cases, exist a rule for the irregularities; the task is to find this rule.

Let us first make the phonetic facts clear. One can certainly assume that the Germanic voiceless fricatives arose directly from the Indo-European voiceless stops through a relaxing of the oral closure. On the other hand the Germanic voiced stops cannot have originated from the Indo-European voiceless stops through the addition of voicing, since this would involve a sound change going precisely counter to the main direction of the sound shift (which

yielded Germanic voiceless stops from IE voiced stops.) Therefore,
one must try to get indirectly from the voiceless stops to the
voiced stops. We first consider Scherer's explanation in his very
nice section on the sound shift (*History of the German Language*,
p. 82): "I assume that all the stops with irregular development
first became voiceless spirants according to the general rule, that
in the more frequently used words (such as *fadar*, *mōdar*) these spirants were voiced through the influence of voiced elements in the
environment, and that with the commencement of the third part of the
sound shift these spirants assumed the direction of all the remaining voiced spirants, thus becoming voiced affricates." If one wants
to maintain that, as in the above explanation, spirants (fricatives)
are replaced everywhere by the so-called affricates (Rumpelt, *German
Grammar* I, §27), one is free to do so. The decision to adopt this
explanation is in itself of small importance, and (especially for
our purposes) makes no real difference; it suffices that we have
ascertained that the irregular development was part of the regular
development but involved one additional step.[1] We can now proceed
to formulate the question about the _etymological_ explanation: _why_
did the sound shift tend to stop in some cases with the voiceless
fricatives, while in other cases it proceeded from there to the
voiced fricatives and then to the voiced stops?

  The only one who has tried to find an answer to this question (so
far as I know) is Scherer in the work cited above. He assumed that
the shift to voiced stops took place "in the frequently used words
(such as *fadar*, *mōdar*)", so that the less frequently used words
showed the regular shift. It is my belief that the distinguished
writer did not wish to attach much weight to this explanation, and
that he ventured it only as a conceivable possibility. As it turns
out, an inspection of the Germanic vocabulary does not lend support
to his assumption. Is it likely that *fadar* and *mōdar* were used more
frequently than *brōθar*? After all, in Ulfilas *mōdar* does not appear
at all (only *aiθei*) and *fadar* is used only once (elsewhere *atta* is
used), but there is no synonym to replace *brōθar*. Could *fehu-*, the
Germanic word meaning the epitome of material prosperity, cattle,
money, riches, and property have been a less frequent word than,
for example, *lagu-* 'lake' (ON *lǫg-r*, OE *lagu* = Lat. *lacu-s*)? Could
one believe that our Germanic ancestors used the numbers 4 and 100
(*fedvōr*, *hund*) more frequently than the number 10 (*tehan*)? More
examples of this kind could be cited; however, in what follows I
will be able to demonstrate even more convincingly the improbability
of this position.

  A comparison of a section of the Germanic vocabulary with comparable sections of the vocabularies of other Indo-European languages

with the goal of trying to find an etymological rule for the split
of Proto-Germanic voiceless fricatives into voiceless fricatives and
voiced stops can lead to no certain result, for precisely because
this split is seen so clearly in word formation, it is not enough to
compare words which have only a common <u>root</u> - what is needed is a
set of words which have root <u>and</u> affixes in common - this means that
there will not be sufficient material on which to build a reliable
explanation. Fortunately, however, the investigation can be shifted
to a considerably more limited area which will enable us to gain a
foothold for further investigation. Not enough attention has been
paid to the fact that <u>the split of Proto-Germanic voiceless fricatives can also be seen in the conjugation of certain verbs</u>.[2] For
example, in OE *līðe* 'navigo, proficiscor' has the participial form
lidan; obviously the same split occurs here as in *lið* 'member' and
lid 'vessel'. Up until now Germanic philology has hardly touched on
this fact. Yet the phenomenon is very interesting and is worthy of
further consideration since a change of root consonant in a conjugation is certainly not a common occurrence. Perhaps the reason that
this has not received more attention is the fact that Gothic, the
language usually used as a basis for comparison, does not have this
split in the conjugation. However, by collecting the relevant data,
it can be shown that the split was originally common to all Germanic
languages and thus, at one time, must have occurred in Gothic as
well. The Germanic voiceless fricatives and voiced stops which arose
from Indo-European voiceless stops are treated in the following manner in conjugation: voiceless fricatives appear in all the present
forms (infinitive, present indicative, subjunctive, imperative, and
participial) as well as in the singular forms of the preterite indicative, whereas voiced stops appear in all other verb forms. In the
following presentation I must ignore the development of the labials;
it was mentioned above that the split (into fricatives and stops) of
labials in word formation was almost completely obliterated through
a subsequent collapse of these sounds - there is hardly a trace remaining in the conjugation of this early split.

A. Verbs whose root ends in IE in *k* and in Germanic in *h(hv)* or *g*:

1. root *slah, slag* 'ferire'.[3]
   ON *slá, sló, slógum, sleginn.*
   OSax. *slahan, slōh, (slōg), slōgun, slagan.*
   OE *sleán, slōh, (slōg), slōgon, slägen.*
   OFris. *slā, slōch, slōgon, e-slein.*
   OHG *slahan, sluoh* (MHG *sluoc*), *sluogum, slagan.*
   OSax., OE *slōg,* MHG *sluoc* result from the influence of the
   plural forms, as is often the case below.

2. root θvah, θvag 'lavare'.

ON θvá, θvô, θvôgum, θveginn.

OSax. thuahan, (thuōg), [thuōgun, thuagan].

OE θveán, θvōh, θvōgon, θvägen

OHG dwahan, dwuoh (MHG dwuoc), dwuogum, dwagan.

3. root lah, lag 'vituperare'.

OSax. lahan, (lōg), [lōgun, lagan].

OE leán, lōh (lōg), lōgon, [lägen].

OHG lahan, (luog), luogum, [lagan].

4. root flah, flag 'excoriare'.

ON flá, flô, flôgum, fleginn.

5. root klah, klag 'fricare'.

ON klá, klô, klôgum, kleginn.

6. root vah, vag 'mentionem facere'.

OHG [ge-wahan], -wuoh, -wuogum, [-wagan].

7. root hlah, hlag 'ridere' makes its present forms with -ja-.

ON hlæja, hlô, hlôgum, hleginn.

OSax. ? [hlōh], hlōgun, hlagan.

OE hlehhan, hlyhhan, hlōh (hlōg), hlōgon, [hlägen].

OHG hlahhan, (hluoc) ? ?

8. root fah, fag 'laetari'.

OE ge-feón, -feah, -fægon, [-fegen].

In OHG ge-fehan, -fah, -fāhum, -fehan the distinction has been lost.[4]

9. root sahv, sagv 'videre'.

OSax. sehan, sah, sāgon sāuuun (sāhun), seuuan (sehan).

OE seón, seah, sægon sāvon, seven.

OFris. sia, (sag), sagen, sien.

OHG sehan, sah, (sāhum), sewan (sehan).

The v which only appears in the preterite forms, must also be looked upon as a kind of split.

ON sjá, sá, sáum, sénn do not have this split.

10. root falh, falg 'commendare, abscondere'.

ON fela, fal, (fálum), folginn.

OE feolan (felgan), fealh, fulgon, (fēlon, fælon), (folen, feolen).

In the preterite plural ON fulgum would be expected; fálum is formed by analogy with fela fal as if the verb belonged to the second ablaut-class (stela, stal, stálum); similarly the OFris. bi-fellan for *bi-felhan has shifted to the second ablaut-class.

OSax. *bi-felahan, -falah, -fulhun, -folhan* and OHG *felahan,*
falah, fuluhum, folohan do not have the split.

11. root *tih, tig* 'demonstrare, nuntiare'.
OSax. *tīhan, [tēh, tigun, tigan].*
OE *teón tīhan, tāh, [tigon], tigen.*
OHG *zīhan, zēh, zigum, zigan.*
ON *tjá* has become weak.

12. root θ*ih,* θ*ig* 'crescere, proficere'.
OSax. *thīhan, [thēh, thigun], thigan.*
OE θ*eon,* θ*īhan,* θ*āh (*θ*eáh),* θ*igon (*θ*ugon),* θ*egen (*θ*ogen).*
OHG *dīhan, dēh, digum, digan.*

13. root *sihv, sigv* 'colare, liquare'.
OE *seón, sāh, sigon, [sigen].*
OHG *sīhan, sēh, [sigum], sigan siwan (sihan).*

14. root *vrih, vrig* 'operire'.
OE *vreón, vrīhan, vrāh, vrigon, vrigen.*
OHG *(int-) rīhan, [-rēh], -rigum, -rigan.*

15. root *lihv, ligv* 'commodare'.
OSax. *(far)-līhan, [-lēh], -liuuum (-lihun), -liuuan.*
OE *līhan, lāh, [ligon, ligen].*
OHG *līhan, lēh, liwum, liwan (lihan).*
Compare no. 9- ON *ljá,* OFris. *līa* have become weak.

16. root *tuh, tug* 'trahere'.
ON --- --- --- *toginn*
OSax. *tiohan, tōh, tugun (tuhun), togan*
OE *tèón, teáh, tugon, togen.*
OFris. *tīa, tāch, tegon, tein.*
OHG *ziohan, zōh, zugum, zogan.*

17. root θ*luh,* θ*lug* 'fugere'.
OSax. *fliohan, flōh, [flugun, flogan].*
OE *fleón, fleáh, flugon, flogen.*
OFris. *flīa, ---, flegen, flain.*
OHG *fliohan, flōh, flugum, flogan.*

B. Verbs whose roots end in *t* in IE, and in θ, *d* in Gmc.
ON cannot be adduced for comparison here since θ and *d* collapsed into
a single sound medially. Also, in OSax., the two sounds had merged
into ð in the conjugations, whereas elsewhere this language kept the
sounds distinct. That, nevertheless, both languages had at one time
maintained the distinction in the conjugations even in the dentals
can be seen from ON *finna,* OSax. *fīðan.* In OHG, Gmc. θ in medial

position became *d* (in the Low Franconian Isidor it became *dh*), Gmc
d became *t* (in Isidor *d*).

1. root *kvaθ, kvad* 'dicere'.
   OE *cveðan, cväð, cvædon, cveden*.
   OHG *quedan, quad, quātum (quādum), quetan*.
   In Isidor *quhedhan (quhedan), quhādum, quhedan*.

2. root *fanθ, fand* 'invenire'.
   ON *finna, fann, fundum (funnum), fundinn (funninn)*.
   OSax. *fīdan (findan), (fand), fundun, fundan*.
   OHG *findan, fand, funtum (fundum), funtan (fundan)*.
   OE *findan,* OFris. *finda* with *d* throughout.

3. root *varθ, vard* 'fieri'.
   OE *veorðan, vearð, vurdon, vorden*.
   OFris. *wertha, warth, worden, worden*.
   OHG *werdan, ward, wurtum, wortan.* In Isidor *uuerdhan
   (uuerdan), (uuard), uurdum, uuordan*.

4. root *liθ, lid* 'ire, proficisci'.
   OE *līðan, lāð, [lidon] (liðon), liden (liðen)*.
   OHG *līdan, leid, litum, litan*.

5. root *sniθ, snid* 'secare'.
   OE *snīðan, snāð, snidon, sniden*.
   OFris. *snītha, snēth, sniden, snein (snithen)*.
   OHG *snīdan, sneid, snitum, snitan*.

6. root *vriθ, vrid* 'ligare, torquere'.
   OE *vrīðan, vrāð, [vridon] (vriðon), [vriden] (vriðen)*.
   OHG *rīdan, [reid, ritum, ritan] (ridan)*.

7. root *miθ, mid* 'evitare'.
   OE *mīdan, māð, [midon, miden] (miðen)*.
   OHG *mīdan, meid, mitum, mitan*.

8. root *skriθ, skrid* 'gradi'.
   OE *scrīðan, scrāð, scridon, [scriden] (scriðen)*.

9. root *suθ, sud* 'coquere'.
   OE *seóðan, seáð, sudon, soden*.
   OHG *siodan, (sōt), [sutum], sotan*.

10. root *hruθ, hrud* 'ornare'.
    OE *hreóðan, [hreáð, hrudon], hroden*.

The above verbs all belong to the various ablaut-classes; of the
verbs which in Germanic originally formed their preterites by reduplication there are only two that show the split, but these have
voiceless fricatives only in the present forms, while the preter-

ite singular is like the remaining preterite forms in having voiced
stops:

1. root *fanh, fang* 'capere'.

   ON *fá, fékk* (for **fénk, *féng), féngum, fenginn.*
   OSax. *fāhan, fēng, fēngun, fangan.*
   OE *fōn* (from **fōhan, *fonhan, *fanhan), fēng, fēngon, fangen.*
   OFris. *fā, fēng, fēngon, fangen fenszen.*
   OHG *fāhan, fiang, fiangum, fangan.*

2. root *hanh, hang* 'pendere'.

   ON *(hanga), hékk, héngum, hanginn.*
   OSax. [*hāhan, hēng, hēngun*], *hangan.*
   OE *hōn, hēng, hēngon, hangen.*
   OHG *hāhan, hiang, hiangum, hangan.*

It is certainly not possible to view all these cases as arising
separately within each individual language. It is inconceivable,
for example, that each of the five languages considered here could
have, independently of one another, replaced the *h* in the preterite
participle of *slahan* by *g*. The split shown in the conjugation must
therefore have already existed at a time when the five languages
still had a common development. Indeed even where this split is
only attested for one language, it must be viewed as having arisen
during such a period of common development, for a phenomenon which
occurs under such special conditions and which is based on such a
slight acoustic difference could hardly have given rise to analogical formations. But if the split in the conjugation is common to
the five languages, then it must have occurred at one time in Gothic
as well. This language <u>does</u> show the split in word formation, but
in conjugation, where the other Germanic languages have the split,
it has voiceless fricatives throughout:

> *slahan, sloh, slohum, slahans;*
> *leiθan, laiθ, liθum, liθans;*
> *vairθan, varθ, vaurθum, vaurθans;*
> *fāhan, fai-fāh, fai-fāhum, fāhans;* etc.

The more frequent present forms have thus prevailed over the preterite forms and have imposed upon them their root consonant. Here we
see an instance of the strong tendency of this language toward uniformity, a tendency which is in evidence elsewhere; for example *i*
and *u* in Gothic correspond to *e, i* and *o, u*, respectively, in other
Germanic languages. <u>The split in the conjugation thus was already
in existence in the Germanic proto-language.</u>

If, on the other hand, the split in the conjugation had its origin
in the same period during which the split in word-formation took

place, then it is self-evident that both of these phenomena are the manifestation of one and the same sound movement. Therefore, they must be treated alike, and a common explanation for them must be sought. In general, the following relations will hold:

$$\frac{\text{Gmc. } \textit{tehan}}{\text{Gmc. } \textit{tegu-}} = \frac{\textit{slahana-}\text{(inf. stem)}}{\textit{slagana-}\text{(pret.part.stem)}} = \frac{\textit{brōθar}}{\textit{mōdar}} = \frac{\textit{kveθana-}\text{(inf.)}}{\textit{kvedana-}\text{(part.)}}$$

An explanation which worked only for one or for the other case of the split (or only for isolated cases of splitting)[5] is evidently unlikely. Even if it were possible to get the above explanation of Scherer to work for the split in word-formation, it could never be used to explain the split in conjugation since one would then have to make the absurd claim that the plural forms of the preterite indicative, which have the voiced stops (OSax. *slōgun*), were more frequent than the plural forms of the present indicative, which have the voiceless fricatives (OSax. *slahad*), and that the preterite participle (OSax. *slagan*) was more frequent than the infinitive (OSax. *slahan*).

The regular occurrence of the split in the conjugation of the above verbs leads one to the conclusion that its cause must be sought in a <u>definite</u> <u>phonetic</u> <u>condition</u> <u>which</u> <u>varies</u> <u>with</u> <u>the</u> <u>conjugation</u>. Our search thus becomes somewhat more limited--the split took place <u>after</u> the sound shift had taken place and is thus specifically Germanic. On the other hand, the cause of the split must be older and could very well have been present in the IE proto-language. It follows that this cause must be sought in the linguistic stage which begins with the IE base forms and terminates with the base forms which can be reached in a comparison of the Germanic languages. Fortunately, the principle parts of the Germanic strong verbs are clear as far back as the IE proto-language. The IE conjugation makes use of the following four formative processes:

1. varying ending
2. varying root vowel
3. the employment or non-employment of augmentation and reduplication
4. varying accent

These devices and no others are used.

If one considers a series of Germanic base forms, e.g.

kveθana-	*kvaθ*	*kvādum*	*kvedana-*
slahana-	*slōh*	*slōgum*	*slagana-*
līθana-	*laiθ*	*lidum*	*lidana-*

43

it becomes immediately apparent that the phonetic basis for the
split cannot lie in the sound composition of the endings; the ending of the infinitive stem:

$kve\theta\text{-}ana\text{-}$ $slah\text{-}ana\text{-}$ $l\bar{\imath}\theta\text{-}ana\text{-},$

is the same as that of the participial stem:

$kved\text{-}ana\text{-}$ $slag\text{-}ana\text{-}$ $l\bar{\imath}d\text{-}ana\text{-},$

and still the split is there. Likewise, the basis for the split
cannot be sought in the vowel quantity of the root since voiceless
fricatives occur with both long and short root vowels:

$l\bar{\imath}\theta ana\text{-}, s l\bar{o}h; \; kve\theta ana\text{-}, kva\theta, slahana\text{-},$

as do voiced stops:

$sl\bar{o}gum; kvedana\text{-}, slagana\text{-},$

and these same relations of quantity occur also in IE. Finally, the
employment or non-employment of reduplication (augmented verb forms
were lost in Germanic) could not have brought about the split since,
on the one hand, we would have to have the same root consonant
throughout the entire preterite indicative, which is not the case,
and, on the other hand, we would have to give a special explanation
for the split in cases other than conjugation, since reduplication
is in general used solely in verbs.

There remains only one possible explanation. This is no desperate
hypothesis to which I must resort, all other attempts at explanation
having failed.   On the contrary, there are sober arguments which
force me to accept this remaining possibility: The split must be
based on the fourth formative device of conjugation--the varying IE
accent. This assumption is completely confirmed by a comparison of
Germanic verb forms with the corresponding Sanskrit forms. Where in
Sanskrit the accent falls on the root syllable, there is a root-
final voiceless fricative in Germanic; where in Sanskrit the accent
falls on the ending, there is a root-final voiced stop in Germanic.
In the following compilation I give, for each Sanskrit form, first
the etymologically corresponding Germanic paradigm and then a paradigm with the split. Since we are concerned here only with the
root-final sound, I give the Germanic forms with Gothic endings.

A. The Sk. accent is on the root--the Gmc. root-final sound is
a voiceless fricative.

    a. Sk. present indicative = Gmc. present indicative

sg.	1.	$bh\acute{e}d\bar{a}mi$	=	$b\bar{\imath}ta$	$l\bar{\imath}\theta a$
	2.	$bh\acute{e}dasi$	=	$b\bar{\imath}tis$	$l\bar{\imath}\theta is$
	3.	$bh\acute{e}dati$	=	$b\bar{\imath}ti\theta$	$l\bar{\imath}\theta i\theta$

44

pl.	1.	*bhédāmas*	=	*bītam*	*līθam*
	2.	*bhédatha*	=	*bītiθ*	*līθiθ*
	3.	*bhédanti*	=	*bītand*	*līθand*

b. Sk. present potential = Gmc. present subjunctive

sg.	1.	*bhédeyam*	=	*bītau*	*līθau*
	2.	*bhédes*	=	*bītais*	*līθais*
	3.	*bhédet*	=	*bītai*	*līθai*
pl.	1.	*bhédema*	=	*bītaima*	*līθaima*
	2.	*bhédeta*	=	*bītaiθ*	*līθaiθ*
	3.	*bhédeyus*	=	*bītaina*	*līθaina*

c. Sk. present imperative = Gmc present imperative

sg.	2.	*bhéda*	=	*bīt*	*līθ*
pl.	2.	*bhédata*	=	*bītiθ*	*līθiθ*

d. Sk. present active participle = Gmc. present active participle

bhédant-	=	*bītand-*	*līθand-*

e. Sk. verbal substantive = Gmc. infinitive

bhédana-	=	*bītan*	*līθan*

f. Sk. perfect indicative singular = Gmc. preterite indicative singular

1.	*bibhéda*	=	*bait*	*laiθ*
2.	*bibhéditha*	=	*baist*	*laist*[6]
3.	*bibhéda*	=	*bait*	*laiθ*

B. The Sk. accent is on the ending--the Gmc. root-final sound is a voiced stop.

a. Sk. perfect indicative plural = Gmc. preterite indicative plural

1.	*bibhidimá*	=	*bitum*	*lidum*
2.	*bibhidá*	=	*bituθ*	*liduθ*
3.	*bibhidús*	=	*bitun*	*lidun*

b. The Vedic forms (first recognized by Westergaard as perfect potential) *vavṛjyus, tuturyáma* = Gmc. preterite subjunctive

sg.	1.	*bibhidyám*	=	*bitjau*	*lidjau*
	2.	*bibhidyás*	=	*bitīs*	*lidīs*
	3.	*bibhidyát*	=	*biti*	*lidi*
pl.	1.	*bibhidyáma*	=	*bitīma*	*lidīma*
	2.	*bibhidyáta*	=	*bitīθ*	*lidīθ*
	3.	*bibhidyús*	=	*bitīna*	*lidīna*

45

c. Forms in *-ná-* in Sk. (usually called perfect passive
participle) = Gmc. preterite passive participle.

bhin-nâ for **bhid-nâ* = *bitana-*   *lidana-* [7]

Before I pursue further the rules which are apparent here, I must
make a short digression to discuss an alternation which, up until
now, has remained unclear but which can be explained in the present
connection. I refer to the alternation between *s* and *z* (*r*) in the
Germanic languages. Corresponding to IE *s* Gothic sometimes has *r*
and sometimes (but less frequently and never in initial position)
has *z*, which must be assumed to have the value of a voiced dental
fricative. To this latter sound there corresponds, in the remaining
Germanic languages, an *r*, which must be viewed as a further development. In every respect this split of original *s* into *s* and *z* (*r*)
in the Germanic languages is parallel to the split discussed above.
Thus we have voiced dental fricatives in Gmc. *auzan-* n. 'ear'
(ON *eyra*, OSax. *ōra*, OE *eáre*, OHG *ōra* = Lat. *auris* f. for **ausis*,
Lit. *ausì-s* f., OSl. *ucho*, stem *ušes-*); Gmc. *deuza-* n. 'animal'
(Goth. *diuza-*, ON *dýr*, OSax. *dior*, OE *deór*, OHG *tior*; from the root
dhus, which appears in OSl. in *dŭch-nǫ-ti*, *dyš-ati* 'to breathe',
duchŭ 'anima', *duša* 'soul'); [8] Gmc. *baza-* 'bare, naked' (ON *ber*, OSax.,
OE, OHG *bar* = OSl. *bosŭ*, Lit. *bása-s* 'barefoot'); etc. On the other
hand the voiceless fricatives have been retained in Gmc. *lausa-*
'gone, empty' (Goth. *lausa-*, ON *lauss*, OSax. *lōs*, OE *leás*, OHG *lōs*;
from a root *lus* in Goth. *fra-liusan* 'to lose'); Gmc. *mūs-*, *mūsi-* f.
'mouse' (ON *mūs* f., OE *mūs* f., OHG *mūs* f. = Sk. *mūsh-* *mūsha-* m.,
Gk. *mûs* *mu-ós*, Lat. *mūs* *mūri-s*, OSl. *myšĭ* f.); Gmc. *nasa-* f. 'nose'
(ON *nös*, OE *näse*, OHG *nasa* = Sk. *nāsā* f., Lat. *nāsu-s*, OSl. *nosŭ* m.,
Lit. *nósi-s* f.); etc.

The same split occurs in conjugation--one example should suffice:

ON	*kjŏsa, kaus, kurum kǫrum, korinn kǫrinn*
OSax.	*kiosan, cōs, curun, coran*
OE	*ceŏsan, ceás, curon, coren*
OFris.	*kiasa, kās, keron, keren*
OHG	*kiosan, kōs, kurum, koran*

Thus *s* and *z* (*r*) are distributed in conjugation in complete agreement with the distribution of *h*, *g* and *θ*, *d*.

Here, as elsewhere, Gothic does not have the split; i.e. the
voiceless fricatives of the present forms have prevailed everywhere,
as in

kiusan, friusan, fraliusan, driusan, visan, etc.

All this clearly shows that the split of *s* (giving *s* and *z* (*r*)) is
to be regarded as completely parallel to the split of the Proto-

Germanic voiceless fricatives (giving Germanic voiceless fricatives
and voiced stops). If the language's three voiceless fricatives--
h (Brücke's X^2), θ (Brücke's s^4), and f (Brücke's f^1)--are voiced
at a certain time and under certain conditions (that is, if they
become the sounds which Brücke writes as y^2, z^4, and w^1), then it is
almost inevitable that the language's fourth and last voiceless
fricative s (Brücke's s^3) must become voiced at the same time and
under the same conditions.[9] The cause of the split of s into s and
z (r) must therefore also be sought in earlier accentual conditions,
and we can add the two terms

$$= \frac{\text{Gmc. } m\bar{u}si\text{-}}{\text{Gmc. } deuza\text{-}} = \frac{keusana\text{-}}{kuzana\text{-}}$$

to the equation established on page 43.

If we consider the cases of divergence <u>outside</u> of the root syllable as well, then the entire range of the split can be formulated
in the following rule:

> <u>As the first step</u>, IE <u>k</u>, <u>t</u>, <u>p</u> became <u>h</u>, <u>θ</u>, <u>f in all environ-
> ments. These voiceless fricatives together with the voice-
> less fricative <u>s</u> inherited directly from IE were then voiced
> in medial voiced environments except when they were syllable-
> final in accented syllables, in which case they remained
> unvoiced</u>.

An imaginary IE word *$akasatam$ in Gmc. became first
*$ax^2as^3as^4am$ (using Brücke's notation), then became one of
*$\acute{a}x^2az^3az^4a(m)$, *$ay^2\acute{a}s^3az^4a(m)$, $ay^2az^3\acute{a}s^4a(m)$, *$ay^2az^3az^4\acute{a}(m)$
according to whether the accent fell on the first, second, third,
or fourth syllable. Later the new Germanic accentual system arose;
z^3 remained a fricative while the other voiced fricatives became
voiced stops, and IE *$akasatam$ would become Gothic *$ahazad(am)$,
*$agasad(am)$, *$agaza\theta(am)$, or *$agazad(am)$.

Physiologically, it is easy to see why voiceless fricatives in
accented syllables resisted the general tendency to become voiced.
For the older period of Germanic we must start with an accent which
was not <u>purely chromatic</u> as was the accent in Sanskrit and in the
classical languages, but which was somewhat <u>expiratory</u>[10] i.e.
characterized by greater activity of the expiratory muscles and
thus having a stronger accompanying burst of air) as in the modern
accentuation. The real difference between voiceless and voiced
consonants lies in the condition of the vocal cords (Brücke,
Grundzüge der Physiologie, p. 8.56). In voiceless consonants the
vocal cords are open wide--the breath stream from the chest cavity
is unrestricted and is therefore stronger than in voiced consonants,

and this stronger breath stream manifests itself in the stops through a more tense closure and a stronger release. In voiced consonants, however, the vocal cords are almost touching—the small glottis hinders the free passage of air, thus making the breath stream weaker, the closure more lax, and the release less energetic than in the voiceless consonants. Therefore, the expiratory accent and the voiceless consonants have in common a stronger breath stream. Thus the strong breath stream in accented syllables can prevent the vocal cords from being narrowed to a position for voicing as they were with a normal breath stream in unaccented syllables.

I hardly need to remark that we must not use here the modern syllable division fa-dar, fin-θan; all consonants following a vowel belong to the preceding syllable (fad-ar, finθ-an) as can be seen in the Germanic accent (the ON hendigar, assonance rhyme).

I have deduced my rule from the existence of the split in the conjugation, and, indeed, it can be seen above that it completely explains the root-final sounds in the conjugation. This, however, is not enough. If the rule is to have general validity, it must be able to explain the split in all the other cases as well—it must work for the root consonant in cases other than conjugation and it must work for endings (inflectional as well as derivational). I now shift my attention to this general test of the theory. Conscientiously, I will cite the isolated cases where the rule does not work. Again I must use Sanskrit as a basis for comparison—only rarely will I refer to Slavic and Lithuanian.

First of all the riddle of brōθar, mōdar, fadar can be solved. The Sk. accent is bhrā́tar-, but mātár-, pitár, and according to the rule we must have Gmc. brōθar opposed to mōdar, fadar. Other kinship terms can be cited:

Gmc. snuza f. 'daughter-in-law' (OHG snura, OE snóru f., ON snǫr f.), which corresponds exactly to the synonymous Sk. snushā́ (= Gk. nuó-s, Lat. nuru-s, OSl. snŭcha, Russian snochá).

Gmc. nefan- m. 'descendant, nephew' = Sk. nápāt-.

Gmc. svehra- m. 'father-in-law' (OE sveor, OHG swehur, MHG sweher, Goth. svaihran-) = Sk. śvā́śura- 'id.' (Gk. hekhuró-s Lat. socer, Lit. szészura-s, OSl. svekrŭ, Russian svjókor), while Gmc. svegrā f. 'mother-in-law' (OE sveger f., OHG swigar f.) goes back to Sk. śvaśrū́ f. 'mother-in-law' (Gk. hekhurá, Lat. socru-s, OSl. svekry, Russian svekróv' f.).

Of the numbers, Sk. daśan 'ten' and pañcan 'five' are paroxytones to which in Gmc. correspond tehan and fimf (Goth. fimf, ON fimm, OSax. fĩf, OE fĩf, OHG fimf, finf = Gk. pénte, pémpe, Lat. quinque, Lit. penkì, pènkios, OSl. pętĭ). On the other hand

Gmc. *fedvōr* 'four' and *hunda-* n. 'hundred' (Goth. *hunda-* n. ON *hund*,
OSax. *hund*, OHG *hunt*) = Sk. *catvā́ras* m., *catvā́ri* n., *catúr-* and
śatá- n. for **śántá-* (Gk. *he-kato-n*, Lat. *centu-m*, Lit.
szı̃mta-s, OSl. *sŭto*, Russian *sto* n.).

Gmc. *seban* 'seven' corresponds to Sk. *saptán*(Vedic; accented *sáptan*
in the classical language = Gk. *heptá*, Lat. *septem*).

Lit. *tū́kstanti-s* OSl. *tysǫšta*, *tysęšta* f. (for **tysantjā*), Russian
tы́sjača f. 'thousand' is Gmc. *θūsundja-* f. n. (Goth. *θūsundi* f.
θūsundja n. pl., ON *θúsund* f., OSax. *thūsint* n. pl., OE *θūsend*
n., OHG *dūsunt* n. pl.).

Gmc. *θridjan-* 'third' corresponds to Sk. *tṛtī́ya-*.

Gmc. *fedvōrθan-* 'fourth' (ON *fjórði*, OSax. *fiorðo*, OE *feóverða*,
feórða, OHG *viordo*) does not agree with Sk. *caturthá-* but possibly the accent in Gmc. *fedvṓrθan-* agreed with the accent of the
cardinals; compare Lit. *ketvir̃ta-s*, Russian *četvjórtyj*, Bulgarian *četvrъ̋ti*.

Other words which may be compared are:

Gmc. *fehu-* n. 'cattle' (Goth. *faihu* n., ON *fé*, OSax. *fehu*, OE *feó*,
OHG *fihu*) coincides completely with Sk. *páśu* n., 'id.' (this is
the Vedic accent; the masculine form *paśú-s* is oxytone; Lat.
pecu n.).

Gmc. *ehva-* m. 'horse' (ON *jó-r*, OE *eoh*, OSax. *ehu-skalk* 'groom') =
Sk. *áśva-* m. 'id.' (Gk. *hı̃ppo-s* Lat. *equu-s*).

Gmc. *volfa-* 'wolf' (Goth. *vulfa-* m., ON *ulf-r*, OSax. *uulf*, OE *vulf*,
OHG *wolf*; the *f* of the Germanic base form is assured by the
Goth. and OHG *f*) corresponds to Sk. *vṛ́ka-* m. 'id.' (Gk. *lúkho-s*,
Lat. *lupu-s*, Lit. *vil̃ka-s*, OSl. *vlъkŭ*, Russian *volk* gen. *vólka*).

Gmc. *angan-* m. 'bend, arrow head' corresponds to Sk. *aṅká-* m.

Gmc. *haidu-* m. appearance, nature, manner' (Goth. *haidu-* m., ON
heið-r, OE *hād*, OHG *heit* m.; compare (German) *Einheit*, *Gleich-
heit*, etc.) = Sk. *ketú-* m. 'luminous phenomenon, brightness,
clearness; appearance, shape, form'.

Gmc. *raθa-* n. 'wheel' (OHG *rad* n.) = Sk. *rátha-* m. 'cart' for **rata-*
(Lat. *rota*, Lit. *rãta-s*).

Gmc. *hardu-* 'hard, harsh' (Goth. *hardu-s*, ON *harð-r*, OSax. *hard*, OE
heard, OHG *hart*) = Gk. *kratú-s*.

Gmc. *anθara-* 'the other' (Goth. *anθar*, ON *annar-r*, OSax. *ōðar*, OE
ōðer, OHG *andar* = Sk. *ántara-* 'id.' (Lit. *àntra-s* 'id.').

Gmc. *undar-* adv. and prep. 'under' (Goth. *undar*, ON *undir*, OSax.
undar, OE *under*, OHG *untar*) = Sk. *antár* adv. 'within', prep.
'under' (Lat. *inter*, Oscan, Umbrian *anter*).

Gmc. *tanθu-*, *tanθ-* m. 'tooth' = Sk. *dánta-* m. 'id.'.

Gmc. *sanθa-* 'true' (ON *sann-r*, OSax. *sōð*, OE *sōð*) = Sk. *sánt-*, present participle of the root *as* 'esse' (Gk. *eónt-*, Lat. *praesent-*).

Gmc. *anadi-* f. 'duck' (ON *ǫnd*, OE *ened*, OHG *anut*) = Sk. *ātí-* f. 'a kind of water bird' (Gk. *nēssa*, Lat. *anati-*, Lit. *ánti-s* f. 'id.').

Gmc. *maθla-* n. 'speech' (Goth. *maθla-* n. 'meeting place', but *maθljan* 'speak'; ON *mál*, OE *mäðel*) = Sk. *mántra-* m. 'saying, agreement, counsel' (compare OSl. *moli-ti* 'ask, pray', Bohemian *modliti*, Polish *modlič* for **mot-liti* = Lit. *maldý-ti* 'ask', Goth. *maθljan* 'speak'; Polish *modly* f. pl. 'prayers', Lit. *maldà* f. prayer').

Gmc. *hleuθra-* n. 'the art of hearing' (OE *hleóðor*) - Sk. *śrótra-* n. 'the faculty of hearing, ear' (Avestan *śraothra-* n. 'hearing, letting hear, singing').

Gmc. θaθrō 'there' (Goth. θaθro, ON θaðra) = Sk. *tátra* 'id.'.

Gmc. *feθra* f. 'feather' (ON *fjöðr*, OSax. *feðara* weak f., OE *feðer* strong f., OHG *fedara*) = Sk. *pátra-*, *páttra-* m. and n. 'wing, feather' (Gk. *ptéro-n* OSl. *pero* n.).

Gmc. *rōθra-* m.n. 'oar' (ON *róðr* m., OHG *ruodar* n.) = Sk. *aritra-* m. 'oar', *áritra-* and *aritra-* n. 'rudder'.

Gmc. *nōsa* f. 'nose' (OE *nōsu* compare ON *nös* f., OE *näse* f., OHG *nasa* f.) = Sk. *nā́sā* f. 'id.' (Lat. *nāsu-s*, Lit. *nósi-s* f., OSl. *nosŭ* m.).

Gmc. *hazan-* m. 'hare' (ON *héri*, OE *hare*, OHG *haso*, in which *z* has gone back to *s*) = Sk. *śaśá-* m. for **śasá-* 'hare'.

Gmc. *fersna* f. 'heel' (Goth. *fairzna*, OE *fiersn*, OHG *fersna*) = Sk. *pā́rshni-* f. 'id.' (= Gk. *ptérna*).

Goth. *amsa-* m. 'shoulder' = Sk. *áṁsa-* m.n. 'id.' (Gk. *ōmo-s*, Lat. *umeru-s*).

I have noticed the following words where the rule does not work:

Gmc. *hvaθara-* 'uter' (Goth. *hvaθar*, ON *húar-r*, OSax. *hueðar*, OHG *hwedar*), but Sk. *katará-* 'id.' (Gk. *pótero-s*, Ionic *kótero-s*, Lit. *katrà-s*).

Gmc. *hersan-* m. 'head' (ON *hjarsi*, *hjassi*), but Sk. *śīrshán-* n. 'id.'

Gmc. *hvehvla-* n. 'wheel' (On *hjól*, OE *hveól*, *hveohl*), but Sk. *cakrá-* m.n. 'wagon wheel, ring' (= Gk. *kúklo-s*).

Gmc. *maisa-* m.f. 'sack, basket' (ON *meis-s*, OHG *meisa*), but Sk. *meshá-* m. 'ram, the fleece of the sheep and what is made from it.' (Lit. *maĩsza-s* 'large sack', OSl. *měchŭ* m. 'skin, leather bottle'; Bugge, *Zeitschrift* XX, p. 1).

Gmc. *fadi-* m. 'lord, husband', only as the last member of a compound (Goth. *fadi-* m.), but Sk. *páti-* m. 'id.' (Gk *pósi-s,* Lit. *pàti-s, pat-s).*

In the Sanskrit causatives the accent is on the ending: *bhāráya-, sādáya-, vedáya-,* etc. The Germanic causatives have this accentuation as well, as is apparent from the following examples.

Gmc. *hlōgjan* 'cause to laugh' (ON *hlœgja;* Goth. *uf-hlohjan* with *h* by analogy from the underlying verb), causative of *hlahjan* 'to laugh'.

Gmc. *hangjan* 'to hang' transitive (ON *hengja,* OHG *hengan, henkan),* causative of *hanhan* 'hang' intransitive.

Gmc. *laidjan* 'to lead' (ON *leiða,* OSax. *lēdian,* OE *lœdan,* OHG *leittan),* causative of *līθan* 'go'.

Gmc. *fra-vardjan* 'spoil (something)', causative of Goth. *fra-vairθan* 'go to ruin'.

Gmc. *sandjan* 'to send' (Goth. *sandjan,* ON *senda,* OSax. *sendian,* OHG *sentan;* compare Lit. *siunczù* 'I send'), causative of a lost verb *sinθan* 'to go', compare *sinθa-* m. 'trip, occasion' (Goth. *sinθa-,* ON *sinn* n., OSax. *sīð,* OHG *sind).*

Gmc. *nazjan* 'to rescue' (ON *nerian,* OE *nerjan,* OFris. *nera,* OHG *nerian;* Goth. again by analogy *nasjan),* causative of *nesan* 'to recover, grow well'.

Gmc. *laizjan* 'to teach' (ON *lœra,* OSax. *lērian,* OSax. *lœran,* OHG *lēran;* Goth. by analogy *laisjan),* causative of a verb *līsan* 'to know' which may be inferred from Goth. *lais* 'I know'.

On the other hand there are no Germanic causatives with *h, θ, s,* in root-final position, for *lausjan* 'to loosen, untie' (Goth. *lausjan,* ON *leysa* OSax., OHG *lōsian,* OE *lȳsan)* is not the causative of *leusan* 'to lose', but rather it is the denominative of *lausa-* 'loose , free'. We can thus take **satája-* (or, perhaps better **satíja-)* as the Proto-Germanic form of Sk. *sādáya-* 'to sit'. The new accentual principle gives *sátija-,* and then the (previously accented) vowel of the ending dropped, giving *satja-.* Moreover, observe the contrast between the causative form and the present form *-ja* which is clearly apparent in *hlōgjan* as opposed to *hlahjan-* the latter takes root accent (the fourth class in Sanskrit).

In Sanskrit the substantives which signify a feminine being were frequently formed with the suffix *-ī* from the corresponding masculine forms: *devá* m. 'god', *devī́* f. 'goddess'; *putrá-* m. 'son', *putrī́* f. daughter'; *meshá* m. 'ram', *meshī́* f. 'ewe'; *sūkará-* m. 'boar', *sūkarī́* f. 'sow'; *mátsya-* m. 'fish', f. *matsī́;* *śván-* m. 'dog', f. *śunī́;* *tákshan-* m. 'carpenter', *takshṇī́* f. 'wife of a carpenter';

dhártar- m. 'bearer, supporter', f. *-trí;́ bhártar-* m. 'supporter, provider', f. *-trí;́* etc. The feminine form is oxytone even when the masculine form is accented differently. It can be seen from the corresponding Greek forms that *-yá̄* must be taken as the IE form of this suffix:

> *sóteira* for **sóter-ya, tektaina* for **téktan-ya* = Sk. *takshṇí̄* for **takshan-yá̄.*

This feminine forming suffix is found, although less frequently, in Germanic; from θ*eva-* m. 'bondsman, servant' (Goth. θ*iu-s,* stem θ*iva-,* ΘEWAR in the oldest runes, OE θ*eóv*) we have θ*ivja-* f. '(female) slave, servant' (Goth. *Oivi,* stem θ*iuja-,* ON θ*ý̄,* gen. θ*ý̄jar,* OSax. *thiui,* OHG *diuwa*); along with *galtu-* m. 'gelded pig' (ON *gölt-r*) there is a *goltja* f. 'sow' (ON *gylt-r* f.). In this way ON *ylg-r* f. 'she wolf', stem *ylgja-* is explained as well; the Gmc. form is **volgja* the feminine form of *volfa-* m., which stands for **volhva-* just as *fimf* stands for **finhv.*[11] Thus Gmc. **volgja* agrees in its accent as well with the synonymous Sk. *vṛkí,́* just as **volhva* agrees with Sk. *vṛ́ka-.*

  Thus we see that the cases of split in places other than conjugation are handled very nicely by the above rule. It remains only for us to demonstrate the validity of the rule for the cases of split in endings. We have already met with such an example above in Gmc. θ*ū̄sundja-* --the Proto-Germanic accent falls on the first syllable of this word, so the *t* of the ending must appear as *d* in Germanic. Since the strong verbs in Germanic with only isolated exceptions go back to the first and fourth Sanskrit classes (the classes in which the accent falls on the root syllable), then we would expect Gmc. *d* to correspond to the *t* which frequently occurs in the IE conjugation endings. This is in fact what happens. Thus we have Gmc. *d* for IE *t* in the following endings:

Gmc. 3rd sg. pres. ind. *berid* (OSax. *-d,* OHG *-t,* Goth. *-*θ following
  the Goth. rule for final *-d* which also occurs here) = Sk.
  bhárati, Gk. *phérei,* Lat. *fert.*
Gmc. 2nd pl. pres. ind. *berid* (Goth. *-*θ for *-d* which also occurs;
  OHG *-t*) = Sk. *bháratha,* Gk. *phérete,* Lat. *fertis.*
Gmc. 2nd pl. pres. subj. *beraid* (Goth. *-*θ for *-d* which also occurs;
  OHG *-t*) = Sk. *bháreta,* Gk. *phéroite,* Lat. *ferātis.*
Gmc. 2nd pl. pres. imp. *berid* (Goth. *-*θ, *-d,* OSax. *-d,* OHG *-t*) =
  Sk. *bhárata,* Gk. *phérete,* Lat. *ferte.*
Gmc. 3rd pl. pres. ind. *berand* (Goth. *-nd,* OHG *-nt*) = Sk. *bháranti,*
  Gk. *phérousi,* Lat. *ferunt.*

Goth. 3rd sg. pres. ind. pass. *bairada* = Sk. *bhárate,* Gk. *phéretai.*

Goth. 3rd sg. pres. subj. pass. *bairaidau* = Sk. *bháreta,* Gk. *phéroito.*

Goth. 3rd pl. pres. ind. pass. *bairanda* = Sk. *bhárante,* Gk. *phérontai.*

Goth. 3rd pl. pres. subj. pass. *bairaindau* = Gk. *phérointo* (Sk. *bháreran*).

Goth. 3rd sg. imp. middle *bhairadau* (*atsteigadau* Matt. 27, 42) = Sk. *bháratām.*

Goth. 3rd pl. imper. middle *bhairandau* (*liugandau* I Cor. 7, 9) = Sk. *bhárantām.*

Gmc. pres. part. act. *berand* = Sk. *bhárant-,* Gk. *phéront-,* Lat. *ferent-.*

The *s* in the IE conjugation endings becomes *z* in Goth. 2nd sg. pres. ind. pass. *bairaza* = Sk. *bhárase,* Gk. *phérē;* in the subj. *bairaiza* = Gk. *phéroio* (Sk. *bhárethās).*

There are difficulties with the 2nd sg. pres. The 2nd sg. pres. ind. *bhárasi* in Sanskrit would, by our rule, lead to a Germanic base form *beriz.* ON *berr* presupposes such a base form; Goth. *bairis* could come from either *beriz* or *beris;* OSax., OHG *biris* could come only from *beris;* OE *byrest* and OFris. *berst* have an added *t* which is the result of a special development. The 2nd sg. pres. subj. *bháres* Gk. *phérois,* Lat. *ferās* would yield a Germanic base form *beraiz* which would also be presupposed by ON *berir,* OE and OFris. *bere;* again Goth. *bairais* could come from either *beraiz* or *berais,* but OSax. *beras* and OHG *berēs* only from *berais.* I shall attempt an explanation for these irregularities. At one time the base form *beriz* prevailed in all Germanic languages in the 2nd sg. pres. ind. In the separate development of Gothic the -*z* must appear as -*s.* In ON the -*z* stayed and became -*r* in a later development. In West-Germanic the -*z* should have dropped according to the rule for word-final sounds which operated in these languages; see Scherer, *Zur Geschichte der deutschen Sprache,* p. 97ff. One would thus expect a *beri or *ber in West-Germanic for Germanic *beriz;* this apocopated form was, however, too short for the language and could easily have been confused with other forms. Thus, <u>in the interest of clarity,</u> the language sought to preserve the fuller form. In doing this, OSax. and OHG unvoiced the -*z,* which was impossible in final position, while OE and OFris. changed the -*z* to -*s* by the addition of -*t* taken from the 2nd person preterite-present (OE θ*earf-t, vil-t,* OFris. *skal-t, wil-t*). Similarly, in the subjunctive forms, the base form *beraiz* to be posited becomes, by regular development, ON *berir,* Goth. *bairais,* OE, OFris. *bere,* while OSax. and OHG on the other hand took recourse to -*s.*

The ending -tá- of the perfect passive participle in Sanskrit corresponds in the Germanic weak verbs to the ending -da- of the preterite passive participle:

Goth. *tami-da* = Sk. *dami-tá*, Lat. *domi-tu-s;* Goth. *sati-da-* = Sk.
sādi-tá-; frijō-da-, habai-da, etc. Formed with the same
suffix are:

Goth. *munda-* 'believed', participle of *munan,* = Sk. *matá-* for
*mantá-.

Gmc. *kunda-* (Goth. *goda-kunda-* 'of good descent', OE *feorran-cund*
'come from afar') = Sk. *jātá-* 'born' for **jantá.*

Gmc. *hlūda-* 'sound' (OE *hlūd,* OHG *hlūt*) = Sk. *śrutá-* 'heard', Gk.
klutó-s, Lat. *(in)clutu-s.*

Gmc. *kalda-* 'cold' (Goth. *kalda-,* ON *kald-r,* OSax. *kald,* OE *ceald,*
OHG *calt*) from the root *kal,* ON *kala* strong verb 'freeze';
compare Lat. *gelu, gelidus, gelare.*

Gmc. *alda-* 'old' (OSax. *ald,* OE *eald,* OHG *alt*) - Lat. *altus,* compare *ad-ultu-s,* from the root *al* in ON *ala* = Lat. *alere.*

Gmc. *dauða-* 'died' (ON *dauð-r,* OSax. *dōd,* OE *deǎd,* OHG *tōt,* but
Goth. *dauθa-* with θ by analogy from the related substantive
Gmc. *dauθu-* m., Goth. *dauθu-,* ON *dauð-r,* OSax. *dōð* OE *deað,*
OHG *tōd*), from a root *dau,* ON *deyja,* OSax. *dōian* 'die'.

Here belongs as well the feminine Gmc. *θeuda* 'people' from the IE
root *tu* 'grow' = Lithuanian dialect *tautà,* Latvian *tauta,* Umbrian
tūtu.[12]

In Sanskrit the primary suffix *-ti-* forms feminine action nouns
which are sometimes paroxytone, sometimes oxytone: *gáti-* '(a) going'
from a root *gam* 'go', *sthíti-* '(a) standing' from a root *sthā* 'stant'
yutí '(a) joining' from a root *yu* 'hitch', *pītí-* '(a) drink' from a
root *pā* 'drink', *pūrtí-* 'filling, granting' from a root *pṛ* 'fill',
etc. Since the oxytone forms were earlier more widespread, one can
see that many of these forms which are oxytone in the Vedic language
are paroxytone in the later classical language; thus, for example,
kīrtí- '(a) mentioning', *ishtí-* '(an) impulse, wish', *paktí-* '(a)
cooking, digesting', *bhūtí-* '(a) vigorous existence, success', *matí-*
contemplation, opinion, insight', *rātí-* 'giving, gift', *vittí-* 'find,
discovery', *vītí-* 'pleasure', *vṛshtí-* 'rain', etc.; in the classic
language *kîrti-, îshti-, pâkti-,* etc. In Gmc. this suffix is *-θi-*
or *-di-.* It is rare in the form *-θi-:* Goth. *ga-qum-θi* f. 'assembly',
compare Sk. *gáti-* for **gámti-* mentioned above; Goth. *gabaurθi-* f.
'birth' (root *bar* 'bear, carry'). More frequently the suffix
appears in the form *-di-:* Goth. *ga-mun-di* f. 'memory' = Sk. *matí-*
for **manti* 'understanding, opinion', Gmc. *spōdi-* f. 'success, (a)
flourishing' (OSax. *spōd* OE *spēd,* OHG *spuot*) - Sk. *sphātí-*[13] '(a)

fattening, (a) flourishing', root *sphā, sphā-yati*, 'grow strong,
increase' = OSl. *spĕ-jetĭ* 'he has success' = Lit. *spê-ja* 'he has
time, opportunity' = OE *spē-v-eð* 'he succeeds in it'; Gmc. *sādi-* f.
'(a) sowing' (Goth. m. *mana-sedi-* 'crowd of people', ON *sáð*, OHG
sāt) from the root *sā* 'sow'; Gmc. *skordi-* f. '(a) shearing' (OHG
scurt 'tonsure'), root *skar* '(a) shearing', compare Gk. *karsi-s*
'(a) shearing', etc.

Sanskrit frequently forms abstract nouns from adjective stems by
means of the secondary suffix *-tā* f.; these nouns are accented on
the syllable preceding the suffix. Thus, for example, *śuklátā*
'whiteness' from *śúkla-* 'white', *āryátā* 'honorable behavior' from
ā́rya- 'Aryan, honorable', *nyūnátā* 'faulty condition' from *nyū́na-*
'faulty', *krūrátā* 'cruelty' from *krūrá-* 'cruel', *paṅgútā* 'lameness'
from *paṅgú-* 'lame', *pṛthútā* 'width' from *pṛthú-* 'wide', etc. The
Germanic forms in *-θa*, which correspond in every way to these Sanskrit forms, are extremely frequent; thus, for example, Gmc.
folliθa f. 'abundance' (OHG *fullida*) = Sk. *pūrṇátā* 'id.', from Gmc.
folla- 'full' (Goth. *fulla-*, ON *full-r*, OSax. *full*, OE *ful*, OHG *fol*)
= Sk. *pūrṇá-*, 'id.'; Goth. *gauriθa* f. 'grief' from Goth. *gaura-*
'grieved', which perhaps is to be tied in with Sk. *ghorátā* from
ghorá- 'dreadfulness'; Gmc. *hailiθa* f. 'health' (OHG *heilida*) from
haila- 'healthy, sound' (Goth. *haila-*, ON *heil-l*, OSax. *hēl*, OE *hāl*,
OHG *heil*), which would correspond to a Sk. **kalyátā* from *kalya-*
'sound, whole'; Gmc. *sāliθa* f. 'good fortune' (OSax. *sālða*, OE *sǽlð*,
OHG *sālida*) from *sāla-*, *sālja-* 'fortunate' (Goth. *sela-*, ON *sæl-l*,
OE *sēl*); Gmc. *deupiθa* f. 'depth' (Goth. *diupiθa*, ON *dýpt*) from
deupa- 'deep' (Goth. *diupa-*, ON *djúp-r*, OSax. *diop*, OE *deóp*, OHG
tiuf), etc.

The Gothic *θivadva-* n. 'servitude' from *θiva-* m. 'servant' corresponds to the frequent Sanskrit secondary formations with *-tva-*, as,
for example, *pitṛtvá-* n. 'fatherhood' from *pitár-* 'father'; *patitvá-*
n. 'married state' from *páti-* m. 'husband, lord'; *jñātitvá-* n. 'relatedness' from *jñā́ti-* m. 'relative'; *brahmaṇatvá-* n. 'the state of
being Brahman' from *brā́hmaṇá-* m. 'Brahman'. I do not know of the
feminine form of this suffix in Sanskrit, but it appears in Gothic
in *fijaθva* f. 'enmity' from *fijan* 'hate', *frijaθva* f. 'love' from
frijon 'love', *saliθva*, only f. pl. *saliθvos* 'lodging, inn' from
saljan 'to lodge'. This suffix apparently is needed in the formation of abstract nouns from verb stems--in this respect it is like
the corresponding OSl. suffix *tva-* f., for example in *žrŭ-tva* f.
'sacrifice' from a root *žrŭ*, inf. *žrĕ-ti* 'to sacrifice'; *bitva* f.
'battle' from *bi-ti* 'to beat'; *klętva* 'oath' from *klę-ti* 'to swear';
zętva 'harvest' from *zę-ti* 'to reap'; *molitva* 'prayer' from *molijti*
'to pray'; *lovitva* 'hunt, chase' from *lovi-ti* 'to hunt, chase';

selitva 'colony, dwelling' from *seli-ti sę* 'to settle, colonize'; compare *O ňekotorychŭ zakonachŭ Russkogo udarenija* Ja. Grota, St. Petersburg, (1858), p. 41 (off-print from the reports of the 2nd department of the academy, Vol. VII). The modern Slavic languages, which still preserve free accent, have the accent on the syllable preceding the suffix: Russian *žértva;* Russian *bȋtva;* Russian *kljátva* = Bulgarian *klétvŭ* = Serbian *klḗtva,* which comes by definite laws[14] from *klḗtva;* Russian *žátva* = Bulgarian *žétvŭ* = Serbian *žȅtva* for *žȅtva;* Russian *molȋtva* = Bulgarian *molítvŭ* = Serbian *mòlitva* for *molȋtva;* Russian *lovȋtva.* The θ in the Germanic form of the suffixes is in keeping with this accentuation; perhaps Goth. *saliθva* from *saljan* is from the same word as OSl. *selitva* from *seliti,* although the latter goes back to **sedlitva* from **sedliti* (Bohemian *sedliti,* Polish *siedlić*).

In Sanskrit the primary suffix *-as* forms neuter substantives which semantically are usually action nominals and which have the accent on the root syllable. Formations of this kind are found in all Indo-European languages; thus in Greek there are neutral substantives in *-es-,* nom. *-os* (always with the accent on the first syllable), and in Latin in *-or-,* *-er-,* nom. *-us:*

Sk. *jánas* = Gk. *génos* = Lat. *genus.*
Sk. *árśas* 'wound' = Gk. *hélkos* = Lat. *ulcus* 'ulcer, sore'.
Sk. *sádas* 'seat' = Gk. *hédos.*
Sk. *ándhas* 'herb' = Gk. *ánthos* 'flower'.
Sk. *vácas* 'word' = Gk. *épos.*
Sk. *śrávas* 'fame' = Gk. *kléos.*
Sk. *sáras* 'water' = Gk. *hélos* 'swamp'.
Sk. *mánas* 'spirit' = Gk. *ménos* 'courage, strength'.
Sk. *nábhas* 'cloud' = Gk. *néphos*
Sk. *rájas* 'dust, darkness' = G. *érebos* 'darkness of the underworlds'.
Sk. *yáśas* 'flame' = Lat. *decus.*
Sk. *ápas* 'work' = Lat. *opus.*
Sk. *rádhas* 'power, wealth' = Lat. *rōbur.*
Sk. *áyas* 'metal' = Lat. *aes.*

In agreement with the Sanskrit accentuation this suffix has the form *-ez(a)* in Germanic:

Gmc. *aiza-* n. for **ajez* 'metal' (Goth. *aiza-,* ON *eir,* OE *ær,* OHG *ēr*) = Sk. *áyas,* Lat. *aes.*
Gmc. *seteza-* n. 'seat' (ON *setr* n. 'stopping place', *sôlarsetr* n. 'setting of the sun') = Sk. *sádas,* Gk. *hédos.*
Gmc. *rekveza-* n. 'darkness' (Goth. *riqiza-,* ON *rökkr* n.) = Sk. *rájas,* Gk. *érebos.*

Gmc. *bareza-* n. 'barley' (ON *barr* n., Goth. in *bariz-eina-* adj. 'barley') = Lat. *far*, gen. *farr-is* 'spelt, wheat'.

Gmc. *hateza-* 'hate' (Goth. *hatiza-*, ON *hatr*).

Gmc. *faheza-* n. 'sheep' (ON *fǽr*, Old Swedish, Old Danish *fár*; see
   Steffensen in *Tidskrift for filologi*, new series, II, p. 70) =
   Lat. *pecus*, *oris* 'cattle'.

Here belongs Fick's connection of Gmc. *aruza-* n. 'scar' (ON *örr* n.)
with Sk. *árus* n. 'wound'.

   The Sanskrit comparison suffixes (comparative *īyaṁs-* and superla-
tive *ishṭha-*) require the accent on the stem syllable even when the
accent in the positive falls on the ending: *vára-* 'excellent',
váriyaṁs-, *várishṭha-*; *dīrghá-* 'long', *drā́ghīyaṁs-*, *drā́ghishṭha-*;
gurú- (Gk. *barús*), *gáriyams-*, *gárishṭha-*. As is well known, this
shift of accent also takes place in Greek: Gk. *hēdú* 'sweet' = Sk.
svādú-, comp. Gk. *hḗdion* = Sk. *svā́dīyaṁs-*, sup. Gk. *hḗdisto-* = Sk.
svā́dishṭha-; Gk. *elakhú-* 'light' = Sk. *laghú-*, comp. Gk. *élasson-*
= Sk. *lághīyaṁs-*, sup. Gk. *elákhisto-* = Sk. *lághishṭha-*; Gk. *kakó*
'bad', *kákion-*, *kákisto-*, etc. The accentuation of the modern
Slavic languages has this accent shift as well, so that the shift
must be considered as an IE phenomenon. In keeping with the root
accent in comparison which is seen in Sanskrit, Greek, and Slavic,
the comparative suffix appears in Germanic in the form *-izan-*,
-ōzan- (in the adverbial neutral forms as *-iz*, *ōz*):

Gmc. *batizan-* 'the better' (Goth. *batizan-*, ON *betri*, OSax. *betiro*,
   OE *betra*, OHG *beʒiro*).

Gmc. *blindōzan-* 'the blinder one' (Goth. *blindozan-*, ON *blindari*,
   OSax. *blindoro*, OE *blindra*, OHG *blindoro*).

Gmc. *batiz* adv. 'better' (ON *betr*, OSax. *bat*, *bet*, OE *bet*, OHG *baʒ*).

Gmc. *nāhviz*, *nāhvōz* adv. 'nearer' (Goth. *nehvis* for *nehviz*, ON *nǽrr*,
   OSax., OHG *nāhor*).

Gmc. *sīθōz* adv. 'later' (ON *sīðar*, OSax. *siðor*, OHG *sīdor*).

In Germanic *junga-* 'young' (Goth. *jugga-*, ON *ung-r*, OSax., OHG *jung*,
OE *geong* = Sk. *yuvaśá-* 'youthful', Lat. *juvencu-s*, base form
*yuvanka-), comp. Gmc. *junhizan-* (Goth. *jūhizan-* for **junhizan-*, ON
œri [according to Thorodd's account with a nasal *œ*] for **jōhizan-*,
*junhizan-), and sup. ON *œst-r* for **junhista* may reflect the accent
shift in Sk. *svādú-*, *svā́dīyaṁs-*, *svā́dishṭha-*, Gk. *hēdú-*, *hḗdion-*,
hḗdisto-. Then ON *yngri*, *yngstr*, OSax. *jungaro*, OE *geongra*, *gyngra*,
geongost, *gyngest*, OHG *jungiro*, etc., can be viewed as later analogical formations.

   Finally, what is the situation with the *s* which frequently appears
in Indo-European declension endings? For all originally oxytone and

monosyllabic stems our rule would lead us to expect the ending -*s* in
the nominative singular masculine: *jungás, daudás, hardús, haidús,
kū̃s* = Sk. *gaus* 'cow', *hvas* = Sk. *kas* 'who', etc.; for all other stems
the ending is -*z*: *vólfaz, ámsaz, máisaz, sánθaz, ánθaraz, dáuθuz,
êhuz,* etc. Similarly, in the genitive singular of feminine *a*-stems,
whether -*s* or -*z* occurs depends on the accentuation: *snuzôs, θeudôs,*
but *nôsōz, férsnōz, folliθ̄ōz, saliθvōz,* etc. Likewise, for the other
declension endings which contain IE *s*. However, Germanic has -*z*
everywhere:[15] nom. sg. m. *volfaz* (Goth. *vulfs* for **vulfz* by the
Gothic rule for final sounds, ON *ulfr*, oldest runes -*AR*; in the West
Germanic languages with the regular dropping of the -*z*: OSax. *uulf,*
OE *vulf*, OHG *wolf*); gen. sg. f. *gebōz* (Goth. *gibos* for **giboz* ON
gjafar, OSax. *gebo, geba,* OE *gife,* OHG *gebo*); nom. pl. m. *volfōz*
(Goth. *vulfos* for **vulfoz*, ON *ulfar*, OHG *wolfa*), etc. The language
required a unity in the inflectional endings. Where the phonetic
development would have destroyed this unity, there the language suspended the sound law and monopolized the most frequently occurring
ending (which, in the above cases, was the inflectional ending of
non-oxytone stems). Similarly, with the 3rd pl. ind. *sind* (Goth.,
OSax., OE *sind*, OHG *sint*): Sk. *sánti* gives Gmc. **sinθ* but elswhere
the 3rd pl. ind. ending was -*nd* which ending *sinθ* must come to have
as well.

We can now review in outline form the history of Germanic accentuation from the oldest Indo-European time to the present. The Indo-
European accent was in its essence a pure chromatic accent, in its
use an unlimited free accent. In this we must assume that we have
in the Sanskrit accentuation a rather accurate picture of the original IE accentuation (if we take into account the obviously non-
original *svarita* in Sanskrit). During the common IE language period
this accent had maintained its original character: the accent of
the classical languages guarantees that it remained purely chromatic;
the free accent of Lithuanian and several modern Slavic languages
guarantees that it nonetheless remained fully free (and did not have
a limited freedom as the accent in Greek may have). Only after
Germanic was cut off from its nearest neighbor, Slavic-Lithuanian,
and had begun its own separate existence, do we find the accent in
its essence somewhat altered--it had become expiratory (or perhaps
chromatic-expiratory since it kept its chromatic character). But
the second characteristic property of the Indo-European accent, its
freeness, was carried over with wonderful completeness into Proto-
Germanic. The subsequent general transition to bound accentuation
(root accent) was an analogical formation. The cases in which the
accent fell on the root syllable were already in the majority under
the old principle of accentuation; this root accent spread in

Germanic so that in the word forms where the ending was accented this accent was drawn back to the root syllable. The general prevalence of root accent in all living Germanic languages might lead one to believe that the transition to the new accentual principle was complete before Germanic split up into dialects. To argue against this position, however, we need only cite the pronominal forms *unsih, inan, imo, iru, ira*, which are often oxytonic in Old High German; this accentuation can hardly be explained as being anything but a remnant from the time of free accent, since the accent in the last four forms above corresponds in Sanskrit to the oxytonic forms *imám, asmaí, asyaí, asyás* (compare Scherer, Z. G., p. 152). We can thus assume that although at the time of the splitting up of Germanic into dialects the root accent was by far the most prevalent, some forms with the older accentuation still survived, and that only in the individual languages did these forms fall into line with the general accent shift.

Perhaps the result of my investigation will be considered quite surprising. Certainly it must seem strange that an accentual principle which vanished in the dim past nonetheless leaves its traces in the present day German verb forms, *ziehen gezogen, sieden gesotten, schneiden geschnitten*. Also, it must seem odd that it is the Germanic <u>consonants</u> which give us the key to the proethnic accentuation, even though people all along have been seeking in vain a key for this accentuation in the Germanic <u>vowels</u>. But even if my result is found to be surprising, I hope that it will not be looked upon as equally unlikely; one must recall the course taken in our investigation. Starting from an irregularity in the conjugation and carrying out an apogogic demonstration using methods acceptable even in rigorous mathematics, I arrived at an explanation which not only was completely satisfactory for every case at hand, but which also simultaneously showed that a series of phenomena which had previously been viewed as exceptional were actually an entirely organic product of the language development. Precisely the fact that this explanation gives a coherent account of the relation of several separate developments to each other and to the whole development serves as the best possible proof of the validity of my demonstration.

If my result is accepted by the critics, then we have in it a starting point for a further investigation of Proto-Germanic accentuation. Through it we will be able to approach more closely the important question of the origin of the ablaut phenomenon. I consider it to be a settled issue that the basic principle in Holtzmann's theory of ablaut, the assumption of a far-reaching effect that accentuation has on the vowels, holds true; however, the form in which Holtzmann presented his theory cannot be reconciled with what I have arrived at here and must be completely reformulated.

The most important new consequences of the above investigation are here summarized briefly:

(1) After the sound shift, Germanic still had the free Indo-European accent.

(2) The accent was no longer purely chromatic, as in Indo-European, but was expiratory as well.

(3) The fact that IE *k*, *t*, *p* in medial position occur in Germanic either as *h*, θ, *f* or as *g*, *d*, *b* is conditioned by the older accentuation.

(4) Likewise, the split of IE *s* into Germanic *s* and *z* in medial position depends on the earlier accentuation.

(5) Excluding the general lack of shift in certain consonant clusters, Grimm's Law has no frequently occurring exceptions.

Copenhagen, July 1875

Notes

[1]It is thus incorrect, for example, to speak of a split of IE *t* into Germanic θ and *d*; it was Germanic θ which split into θ and *d*.

[2]Cf. Braune's treatment "On the grammatical change in the German verbal inflection" in *Beiträge zur Gesch. d. deutschen Spr. und Lit.* by H. Paul and W. Braune, I, 513ff. (editor's footnote).

[3]The forms in ( ) are constructed on the basis of analogies; the forms in [ ] do not occur, or, more accurately, I cannot attest them.

[4]The ON adjective *feginn* 'happy' could, as far as its form goes, be the preterite passive participle of the root *fah fag* (cf. OE), but it is better to link it with the synonymous OSax. *fagan*, OE *fagen*; the umlaut then arises through the influence of the palatal (*k*, *g* with following *e*, *i*) as is often the case in ON: *lengi* adv. = OSax., OHG *lango*, OE *lange*; *degi* dat. sing. from *dag-r*; the participles *ekinn*, *tekinn*, *dreginn*, *sleginn*, *fenginn*, etc.

[5]This is true, for example, of Pauli's attempt (vol. XIV, p. 102, of this journal) to explain the *d* in *fadar*, *mōdar* as opposed to the θ in *brōθar* as being due to a folk-etymological form association with Gmc. *fōdjan* 'pascere' and *mōdi-* f. 'anger, courage'. Aside from the fact that it would take a very vivid popular language imagination to associate the concept of 'mother' with that of 'anger, courage', these explaining words themselves need an explanation, since *fōdjan* and *mōdi-* each have a *d* which comes from an IE *t*. Do we have to assume a folk-etymological explanation for these forms as well?

[6]The second person preterite indicative in the West Germanic languages (OSax. *biti*, *lidi*; OE *bite*, *lide*; OHG *bizi*, *lidi*) is a subjunctive form which has spread to the indicative = Goth. *biteis*, *liθeis*.

[7]Leo Meyer links the Germanic preterite passive with the Sk. forms in *-ānā-* with reduplication; thus *bitana-* = *bibhidānā-*. In these cases the voiced stop in *lidana-* also is in accord with the Sk. accent.

[8]The r which comes from z causes umlaut of the immediately preceding root vowel in ON (extremely rarely in Old Swedish and Old Danish): ker 'vessel', gær 'yesterday', dýr 'animal' dreyri 'blood', ber 'bare, naked', reyr 'reed', frörinn 'frozen', kýr 'cow', sýr 'sow'. Compare Bugge, Tidskrift for Philologi, VII, p. 320; Wimmer, Fornnordisk formlära (Lund, 1874) 12, fn. 2; Steffensen, Tidskrift, new series, II, p. 71.

[9]It would be tempting to draw the following further conclusion: if, at a certain time and under certain conditions, all Germanic voiceless fricatives became voiced, then all voiceless stops (k, t, p) must have also become voiced (g, d, b) at the same time and under the same conditions. However, as is well known, this did not occur. One might then conclude that the split took place at a time when the language did not yet have these sounds (k, t, p) in a voiced environment; i.e. before the last part of the sound shift (IE g, d, b, to k, t, p) had taken place. Such a conclusion is, however, illegitimate. Latin has a quite similar transition of proto-Latin: h, θ, f (from IE gh, dh, bh, Ascoli, Zeitschrift XVII, p. 241) which themselves became voiced in medial position in a voiced environment. Here s behaved like the other voiceless fricatives and became r. However, medial c, t, p were completely unaffected by this change.

[10]The accentuation in IE languages is two-fold in nature: (1) a syllable is brought into prominence by a greater tension in the vocal cords--the result is a higher tone contrasting with the lower tone of unaccented syllables. The accent in Sanskrit and in the classical languages was of this type, and this is the original meaning of the term accent, (Gk.) prosōdía. I call this accent chromatic. (2) A syllable is brought into prominence by greater activity in the expiratory muscles--the result is that the increased breath stream strengthens the voice and provides a relative forte contrasting with the piano of unaccented syllables. One can call this the expiratory accent. Brücke described it in his work: Die physiologischen Grundlagen der neuhochdeutschen Verskunst (Vienna, 1871), p. 2.

There is also a combination of the two accents in which the voice in the accented syllable is not only raised in pitch but also increased in intensity--in the above work (p. 3) Brücke shows how the expiratory accent tends more or less to give the effect of a chromatic accent as well. This accent must be called a chromatic-expiratory accent. Sk. mânas Gk. ménos have a purely chromatic accent on the first syllable--one can give them the musical notation ♪. The Serbian accusative vodu 'aquam' has a purely expiratory accent on the first syllable--in musical notation ♫ (Vuk Stefanović writes this accent as "). In the nominative of the same words, however, voda has a chromatic-expiratory accent which may be written ♫ (Vuk Stefanović writes `). When Brücke, loc. cit., maintains that 'it is not right for one to distinguish a word accent realized by a raising of the tone from a word accent realized by a strengthening of the tone", then I can no longer agree with the master of physiology. Whoever has heard the peculiar pronunciation of the Swedish words kalla, gata, ögon, syster, saker, and the like, must grant, first, that the syllables with expiratory accent are not necessarily higher on the tone scale than unaccented syllables and, second, that there can be a rise in tone (chromatic accent) along with but independently of the expiratory accent since, in these Swedish words, the expiratory accent falls on the root syllable while, on the final syllable, the voice is raised in pitch and is simultaneously decreased in expiratory strength ("hvarutí, om äan utan ljudvigt, rösten liksom svänger sig uppför", Rydqvist, Svenska språkets lagar IV, p. 211). Musically one could denote this pronunciation by ♪. Therefore, the cited words have, as it were, two accents--one purely expiratory on the root syllable and one purely chromatic on the final syllable. An old Greek ear would

hear only the last syllable as being accented (*kalla = khallá*). The
Swedish ear hears the accent only on the first syllable; this is why
native grammarians speak of a "low tone" ("låg ton") on this syllable
even though this is not strictly correct since this tone is not <u>below</u>
the normal speech tone--it is rather the same as the normal speech
tone while the final syllable is raised <u>above it</u>. Norwegian also has
this means of accentuation. In an article in *Christiania Videnskabs-
Selskabs Forhandlinger* (1874), Joh. Storm writes (p, 296) "En général
les syllabes atones ont ici un ton plus haut. Ceci est contraire à
l'usage de la plupart des langues européennes et montre que l'éléva-
tion de la voix (angl. *pitch*) et le renforcement ou l'appui (angl.
force) sont deux choses différentes, comme l'a très bien fait
ressortir M. Ellis dans son travail sur l'accent (*Transactions of the
Philological Society*, 1873-74, Part I, p. 133 ff)."

[11] The sound change χv-(χf) - f is known elsewhere. We find it, for
example, in the South Slavic languages: Bulgarian *falŭ* = Serbian
fala, OSl. *chvala* 'praise'; Bulgarian-Serbian *fat* 'a measure of
length' for *chvraate*; etc. Also in Lappish loanwords: *fadno* = ON
hvönn, *feres* = ON *hverr*, *fales* = ON *hvalr*; see Thomsen "Über den
Einfluss der germanischen Sprachen auf die finnisch-lappischen", p.
68.

[12] Gmc. *kunθa-* 'known', (Goth. *kunθa-*, ON *kunnar*, OSax. *kūđ*, OE *cūđ*,
OHG *kund*; preterite passive participle of *kunnan*) must not be viewed
as contradicting the rule. The facts concerning the phonetic characteristics of *nn* in certain roots are not clear. One recalls that
in these forms an *s* is often inserted in word formation as one likes
to say: OHG *cun-s-t*, Goth. *an-s-ti*, Goth. *ala-brun-s-ti*, German
gun-s-t, etc., and that the *nn* can change a following *d* = Sk. *dh*
into θ: Gmc. *unθa* (ON *unna*, OE *uðe*, OHG *onda*), preterite indicative
of *unnan* for **unnda*; Gmc. *kunθa* (Goth. *kunθa*, ON *kunna*, OE *cuðe*, OHG
conda), preterite indicative of *kunnan* for **kunn-da*. But if the
preterite indicative *kunθa* appears instead of the expected **kunnda*,
then the preterite passive participle *kunθa-* can also appear instead
of **kunnda-*.

[13] Accented in this way by Benfey, *Vollst. Gramm.*, p. 162 above; the
Petersburg dictionary does not indicate the accentuation for this
word.

[14] See. C. W. Smith, *De verbis imperfectivis et perfectivis in
lingvis Slavonicis* (University program, Copenhagen, 1875) p. 31f.

[15] In the genitive singular of masculine and neuter *a*-stems the endings in Germanic is *-s*, *volfas* (Goth. *vulfis*, ON *ulfs*, the oldest
runes *-AS*, OSax. *ullfes*, OE *vulfes*, OHG *wolfes*). The *-s* occurs here
since it was really *ss* and as such must keep its voiceless character
(IE *várkasya* = Gmc. **volf-asj*, **volf-ass*, *volfas*), see Ebel in
Zeitschrift, IV, p. 149 ff.

Abbreviations

Verner	This translation	Current name
adän. (altdänisch)	Old Danish	same
afries. (altfriesisch)	Old Frisian	same
ags. (angelsächsisch)	OE (Old English)	same
ahd. (althochdeutsch)	OHG (Old High German)	same
altind. (altindisch)	Sk. (Sanskrit)	same
an. (altnordisch)	ON (Old Norse)	same
as. (altsächsisch)	OSax. (Old Saxon)	same
aschwed. (altschwedisch)	Old Swedish	same
asl. (altslavisch)	OSl. (Old Slavic)	Old Church Slavonic
böhm. (böhmisch)	Bohemian	Czech
dän. (dänisch)	Danish	same
germ. (germanisch)	Gmc. (Germanic)	same
goth. (gotisch)	Goth. (Gothic)	same
idg. (indogermanisch)	IE (Indo-European	same
ion. (ionisch)	Ionic	same
lat. (latein)	Lat. (Latin)	same
lett. (lettisch)	Latvian	same
lit. (litauisch)	Lit. (Lithuanian)	same
mhd. (mittelhochdeutsch)	MHG (Middle High German)	same
osc. (oskisch)	Oscan	same
pol. (polnisch)	Polish	same
russ (russisch)	Russian	same
schwed. (schwedisch)	Swedish	same
sl. lit. (slavisch-litauisch)	Slavic-Lithuanian	Balto-Slavic
srb. (serbisch)	Serbian	same
umbr. (umbrisch)	Umbrian	same
ved. (vedisch)	Vedic	same
zend	Avestan	same

4   On Sound Alternation

NIKOLAI KRUSZEWSKI

Preface

This monograph is a slightly revised part of my larger work "On the
Question of the *guṇa*; An Investigation in the Domain of the Old
[Church] Slavic Vocalism" which appeared [in Russian] in the period-
ical *Russkiĭ Filologičeskiĭ Věstnikъ*, 1881, No. 1 [= pp. 1-109,
1880].

The German reader would certainly have found this publication much
more convincing had I selected German examples. To do so, however,
would have required complete competence in colloquial German, which
I cannot claim. I was therefore obliged to resort to examples from
Polish, my native language, and from Russian, in which I am fluent.
I have, as far as possible, included German examples, for which I am
much indebted to Dr. W. Radloff to whom I am also grateful for several suggestions concerning the work itself. I am similarly indebted to
Mr. [L. Z.] Kołmaczewski for making this German version possible.
Some of the ideas which serve as the basis of this research origin-
ated with my teacher, Professor J. Baudouin de Courtenay.

In the middle of the year 1880, when this study of linguistic laws
was already complete, I was still unfamiliar with Brugmann's *Ein-
leitung*, and with the work of [F.] Misteli and of [H.] Paul. After
I had the opportunity to acquaint myself with these works, I
attempted to clarify the relation between my own views and the views
of these authors. The appendix and the concluding diagrams contain
the results of this attempt.

Kazan, April 9/22, 1881

Original title: *Über die Lautabwechslung* (Kazan, 1881). Transl.
by Robert Austerlitz. [In this selection, palatals are marked with
a ´ and stress with ` . Thus, jĭmă = jĭmà; also the orthographic
forms of words are marked with a double underscore. Eds.]

Everyone will agree that the subject matter of linguistics must be those phenomena whose totality is called language, and that the object of this science must be the discovery of those laws which govern such phenomena. On the other hand, we would hardly arrive at this definition of linguistics and its aims merely by studying the works which have appeared under its aegis since the time of Bopp. We might, in that case, define linguistics as a science which attempts to clarify reciprocal relationships within the Indo-European language family and to reconstruct both the Indo-European proto-language and the proto-languages of its various sub-groups (Germanic, Slavic, etc.)

Needless to say, none of this can be considered science. Even if it could, one would still have first to admit that a science whose aim is to discover the laws which govern linguistic phenomena is both possible and necessary, and, secondly, that with the aid of such a science we are in a better position to clarify, among other things, the relationship of the Indo-European languages, and to reconstruct both the Indo-European proto-language and the original languages of its sub-groups.

It is not difficult to explain the reasons for the archaeological bias of present-day linguistics. The origins of such a bias must, of course, be sought among the humanities, namely, the historical and philological sciences. Specialists in the discipline of linguistics received their training in history and philology. They inevitably transferred their views, aspirations and methods to linguistics. The sole aim of their discipline was therefore the clarification of our view of the past.

One of the most important consequences of this relationship between linguist and linguistics is the neglect of modern languages, both now and in the past. If we wish to reconstruct the past, obviously the most important and most interesting matters for our consideration are those which immediately link us with the past. On the other hand, all recent events were disregarded since they were considered to be more remote from the past. If, however, our aim is not to reconstruct the past but, in general terms, to discover the laws which govern phenomena, then everything which is recent--everything, in fact, which happens before our eyes--acquires a special significance. It is either very difficult or completely impossible to discover such laws in what is dead or of the past. Under these circumstances we should not be surprised that linguistics is impoverished with regard to generalizations.

Let us first turn to morphology. What has been accomplished in this domain, other than an occasional ingenious discovery of facts about the past? Have many laws or generalizations been postulated?

Only two generalizations can be made about morphology: (1) morphological assimilation (which in all linguistic publications is, in my opinion, unscientifically presented as two different processes carrying the equally unscientific titles of "analogy" and "folk etymology") and (2) apocope of stems in favour of suffixes.[1] The first of these generalizations results primarily from a greater concern with modern than with ancient languages, and, at present, probably has more opponents than adherents among professional linguists. The second generalization, however, was posited by a member of the profession who is free of prejudice concerning modern languages;[2] it is also significant that no one has drawn his attention to this particular generalization. Let us note in passing that this generalization can very easily be enlarged and reformulated as the tendency on the part of morphological units[3] to absorb those units which precede them. This generalization is therefore one which can be converted into one of the most comprehensive generalizations of morphology.

The study of morphology is far less developed in linguistics than the study of phonetics. We might therefore expect to find a greater number of generalizations within phonetics. Phonetics, however, is superior only in that it treats more data and treats those data more adequately. Phonetics should, in fact, not pride itself on the merit of its own generalizations since it is unable even to answer simple questions such as the following: What do we understand by a phonetic law? How do we explain the fact that every phonetic law requires a large number of exceptions? How are we to conceive of the so-called "transition" of one sound to another if, as is so often the case, the two sounds are not [articulatorily] related or are related only very remotely?

Language occupies a completely isolated place in the realm of nature: it is a combination of physiological and acoustic phenomena governed by phonetic laws, and of unconscious and psychical phenomena governed by laws of an entirely different kind. This fact leads us to a most important question: What is the relation, in language in general and within phonetics in particular, between the physical principle and the unconscious and psychical principle? All of the questions which have been already posed are inseparable from this question.

We must, in the first place, realize that the classical languages which have been and which continue to be the concern of linguistics are completely unknown to us; we have access to them only through their literary heritage. Since phonetics is concerned not with signs but with the sounds which these signs represent, we have absolutely no immediate access to the phonetics of the classical languages. This means that we must determine every fact inductively. When we adopt this approach, the study of the phonetics of the classical languages begins to resemble astronomy: in phonetics, time is the factor which makes facts immediately inaccessible; in astronomy it is space.

Without undertaking a special investigation we cannot know what sounds are rendered by certain signs or, on the other hand, which sounds (or sound qualities) are not rendered at all. The orthography only gives us access to a limited number of phonetic phenomena while concealing from our vision an even greater number of such phenomena. In addition, the nature of the phenomena which are concealed by the orthography is such that they can throw light only on those phenomena which are not so concealed. One could even go so far as to say that what the orthography has preserved for us remains unintelligible, whereas what would have been intelligible, the orthography has concealed. In language, we are constantly dealing with sequences of indeterminate factors. Furthermore, language plays host to what in logic are called multiple causes: a sound can change (phonetically) as a result of the influence of factors which are combined with it (combinatory sound change), or it can change independently as a result of the lapse of time (spontaneous sound change). A sound may also be simultaneously subject to combinatory and spontaneous sound change. The presence of a certain sound within a word can also be due to diverse morphological factors. A sound therefore is often the product of processes of long duration, diverse in nature and great in number.

The factors which the orthography most commonly fails to articulate can be referred to as sound alternations or, more precisely, the alternation of a given sound with another sound (or sounds) or with zero.

Let *abc* represent a morphological unit (e.g. a root or a suffix) and the individual letters (or sounds) of this unit. The unit *abc* can appear in two forms:

(1) In the form *abc* when it occurs alone or in combination with a given morphological unit (*def*), e.g.

	German			Russian	
oks	Ochs	'ox'	*prok*	prokъ	'use, profit'
oks-n	Ochsen	'oxen'	*prok-u*	próku	S. Gen.

(2) In the form *zbc* (or *abz*), when it occurs in combination with a given morphological unit (*ghi*), e.g.,

ŏks-lein	Öchslein	*prŏč-nəj*	pročnyĭ
	'little ox'		'stable, lasting'

If we observe such a phenomenon often enough we are justified in considering it to be the alternation of sound *a* (or of *c*) with the sound *z*. Now, these alternations remain completely incomprehensible from every point of view.

[1] From the point of view of the <u>articulatory relationship</u> of two sounds which alternate with each other: Generally, one encounters statements to the effect that sound *a* (or *c*) <u>becomes</u> sound *z* or that *z* <u>becomes</u> *a* (or *c*). Such a formulation commonly results from articulatory considerations or from information about related languages. Often, however, the two sounds involved in the alternation resemble each other so little that the assumption of immediate transition from one sound to another defies common sense.

[2] From the point of view of the <u>causes</u> or <u>conditions</u> of the alternation: In most cases it is impossible to determine <u>what caused</u> a given alternation or <u>why</u> it was caused.

[3] From the point of view of the <u>necessity</u> of the alternation: One of a pair of alternating sounds may often belong to one grammatical category while the other member belongs to another grammatical category. In such cases we may regularly expect to find a more or less considerable number of exceptions. However, it may happen that while we can observe an alternation of sounds, we are unable to discern any regularity in it.

This matter can be clarified only if we focus our attention on a modern language such as German or Russian. In these we can clearly observe the operation of <u>three</u> principal categories of sound alternation.

The First Category
When Modern German *s* is followed by a vowel and, at the same time, preceded by a sonant or by zero, it necessarily becomes *z*. This sound change has absolutely no connection with morphology and occurs without exception in all positions where the conditions indicated above obtain: e.g., *S*eele, un*s*er, gewe*s*en but Hau*s*, Och*s*, i*s*t, etc. The law is also valid for foreign words, e.g., *S*imbirsk, Con*s*ervatoire (as heard in Strasbourg), Ar*s*enal.

Let us take an example from Russian. It is well known that the vowel *o* alternates with a vowel of uncertain quality which occupies an intermediate position between *a* and *o*. We shall write this vowel *ə*. The vowel *o* occurs when stressed; as soon as *o* precedes the stress it immediately becomes *ə* e.g., *vadá : vòdu* (<u>voda</u> 'water' : <u>vodu</u> sAcc.).

This phenomenon is general: in all existing words *o* will occur with stress and *ə* only preceding stress. If a new word is derived in Russian in which an originally stressed *o* loses its stress in that the stress moves towards the end of the word, the *o* immediately becomes *ə*. Such would be the case in the non-existent adjective *dal'evój* (from the noun *dòl'a* dolä 'fate'). Similarly, if a foreign word is introduced into Russian, any stressed o it may contain will become *ə* if the stress moves away from the o (toward the end of the word); e.g., the proper names *məd'èna, tənašèn* (Modena, Tomasenь).

The following is an example of consonantal alternation in Russian. Preceding the palatal vowels *e* and *i* we only find consonants which have palatal coloring (i.e. *mouillure* in French). *t*, for example, will generally occur before vowels other than *e* and *i*; before these it will occur as *t'*, e.g. *svèta* 'of the world': *na svèt'e* 'in the world', or the proper name *t'èxas* Texasь.

The sounds *o* and *t* cannot occur in Russian under this last set of conditions; only *ə* and *t'* can occur. This does not mean that a Russian cannot pronounce *o* or *t* under the converse conditions. It only means that he does not pronounce them. In other words, the appearance of *o* and *t* in the place of *ə* and *t'* is possible under these conditions only with the concurrent participation of the will. Since language belongs to that category of human functions which are devoid of the participation of the will, exceptions to such alternations are only possible under abnormal circumstances.

The minimal change in the original sounds which we have treated as our first category of alternations is a combinatory sound change and depends on articulatory, that is to say purely physical, causes. Alternations of this kind are of course completely unknown to us from the classical languages. The orthography indicates not only such minute changes as pertain to individual qualities of sound, but often such changes as occur when one sound is replaced by another which is completely different from it (regardless of what the causes for this may be), e.g. xodätь 'they go' instead of *xòd'ut*.

We can generalize the alternations we have just discussed by means of a formula, and thereby determine their characteristics. Let x represent the condition which governs the occurrence of sound *s* and let x_1 represent the condition which precludes the occurrence of *s* (a condition in fact, under which *s* must change into another sound). Let s_1 represent this second sound which is closely related to the first sound, *s*. We can therefore characterize the alternations of the first category as follows:

(1) The causes of the alternation are present and can be immediately identified. Whenever we encounter an alternation of the type $s : s_1$ we also encounter the alternation of phonetic factors or conditions $x : x_1$.

(2) <u>The</u> <u>alternation</u> <u>is</u> <u>general</u>. The alternation $s : s_1$ occurs everywhere, i.e. s and s_1 alternate in all words whenever the necessary conditions are present, regardless of the morphological categories to which the words in question belong.

(3) <u>The</u> <u>alternation</u> <u>is</u> <u>necessary</u>. Under the conditions $x : x_1$ the alternation $s : s_1$ must occur and admits of no exception; i.e. s cannot occur under x_1 and s_1 cannot occur under x.

(4) <u>The</u> <u>articulations</u> <u>of</u> <u>the</u> <u>sounds</u> <u>which</u> <u>participate</u> <u>in</u> <u>the</u> <u>alternations</u> <u>are</u> <u>closely</u> <u>related</u>. s and s_1 are closely related from the point of view of speech production or, more exactly, they are both modifications of one and the same sound.

If we wish to determine whether a given alternation is to be classified under the first category, we must consider the first three characteristics to be <u>decisive</u>. The fourth characteristic is less decisive, because in alternations of the first category s and s_1 are <u>by</u> <u>necessity</u> related articulatorily; in alternations of the second and third categories they <u>may</u> be closely related in this way. <u>Any</u> <u>one</u> of the first three characteristics is <u>sufficient</u> to classify a given alternation as belonging to the first category since <u>all</u> of the <u>four</u> characteristics are <u>inseparable</u>. In other words, all alternations of the first category are simultaneously identified by characteristics 1, 2, 3, and 4.

Since the sounds $s : s_1$ are merely modifications of one and the same sound we can call them divergents.[4] In so doing, we can designate the sound s (since it is original in relation to the sound s_1) as the <u>primary</u> <u>divergent</u> and designate s_1 as the <u>secondary</u> <u>divergent</u>.

The Second Category

Let us first consider an alternation such as that between <u>s</u> and <u>r</u> in Modern German, e.g. <u>war</u> : <u>gewesen</u>. Since cases of this kind are common, we have the right to assume that <u>r</u> and <u>s</u> often alternate. It would be futile to seek the cause of such an alternation only among instances as they <u>occur</u> in Modern German. The pair <u>war</u> : <u>gewesen</u> could possibly suggest the explanation that whereas <u>r</u> appears in final position, <u>s</u> appears in medial intervocalic position. The disadvantage of such an explanation (one which would disqualify it from serving as a rule) would reside in the many exceptions for which it would fail to account, e.g. such cases as <u>kiesen</u> : <u>erkoren</u> 'to choose [archaic] : chosen'. The causes or conditions of such an alternation can only be discovered by investigating the history of the language. Such an investigation of <u>s</u> : <u>r</u> leads us to the following conclusions:

(1) <u>s</u> is etymologically primary; <u>r</u> is secondary.

(2) In the course of a long combinatory-spontaneous process, inter-

vocalic s̲ gradually became r̲. In non-intervocalic position s̲ remained unchanged.

(3) All cases in which we find r̲ (i.e. etymological s̲) in positions other than intervocalic, as well as all cases of intervocalic s̲, can be considered later formations and can be explained as having arisen through secondary phonetic and morphological processes.

The Russian vocalism presents an analogous example in the alternation of u with o:

mùxa	:	*mòška*
muxa 'fly'	:	moška 'kind of mosquito'
gluxoĭ 'deaf'	:	gloxnutь 'to lose one's hearing'
suxoĭ 'dry'	:	soxnutь 'to dry (intrans.)'.

Again, the conditions which govern the alternation cannot be determined at first glance; furthermore, an historical investigation would be required to determine the conditions and causes which are operative here. In this case *mùxa : mòška* goes back to an original *má₂us-ā̃ : mus-i-kā̃* (> Old Church Slavic mouxa : *mŭšĭka). During the pre-Slavic period the stress weakened the vowel a_1. This weakening increased continually and resulted in the complete disappearance of the vowel. Therefore a root such as ma_1us can assume three different shapes: [i] ma_1us with stress, [ii] ma_2us with stress coupled with a condition unknown to us, and [iii] mus without stress. In the presence of the suffix -$kā̃$, which once bore stress, we would therefore be inclined to expect the root vowel o, just as we would expect the root vowel u in the presence of the suffix $ā̃$ which did not carry stress. Contrary to these expectations, however, we find many forms which have both the suffix -$kā̃$ and the root vowel u. For example, we find *mùška* muška 'little fly' by the side of *mòška* 'a kind of mosquito', as well as *dùška* duška 'darling', etc. This alternation (Modern German s̲ : r̲ and Russian $o : u$) is not motivated in such cases purely by articulatory factors (as was the alternation of the first category). It must be considered to be already partly connected with certain morphological categories.

This Russian example clearly indicates the extent to which various linguistic processes can confound original regularity.

(1) As a result of the spontaneous process, both of the alternating phonemes[5] can be subject to complete degeneration, e.g.

original $a_2u : u$ > Russian $u : o$.

(2) The alternation does not necessarily occur. Instead of two alternating sounds, only one of the two may occur, e.g.

muxa : *muška.*

Not only the conditioned factor but also the conditioning factor
can be subject to manifold and aberrant development.

(3) The alternation of two conditioning factors (or, more correctly,
of two factors which were once conditioning factors) can be absent.
In such a case, when two sounds alternate only one of the conditioning moments is present, e.g.

$$mùxa \quad : \quad mòška.$$

(4) The relation of the conditioning factors to the conditioned
ones can be reversed, e.g.

$$mà_2us\text{-}ā \quad : \quad mus\text{-}i\text{-}k\grave{\bar{a}}$$

and

$$suxòj \quad : \quad sòxnuť.$$

Note also the following:

(5) What we recognized as the original cause of the alternation
$u : o$ in Russian still motivates an alternation completely unlike
the alternation $u : o$. If we examine words such as $dǔšà$ duša 'soul'
(sNom.) and $dùšu$ dušu (sAcc.) we observe that the u which precedes
the stress is characterized physiologically by the almost complete
passivity of the lips. The acoustic effect of this u, albeit very
weak, approaches that of an a. We shall write it $ǔ$. The alternation
$u : ǔ$ is therefore caused by an alternation in stress. The same can
be observed in Modern German. At an earlier stage of German, a
final s (which was preceded by a vowel) changed to r if it was
followed by a vowel. The same condition in Modern German causes a
completely different change: The change from s to z (voiceless to
voiced), i.e. $s : z$.

If we take into account the fact that all the phonetic phenomena
of the classical languages were almost as complex as those we have
just considered, we shall be able to surmise the small degree to
which these phonetic phenomena are intelligible to us and to realize
how difficult it is to establish the laws which governed them.

Let us take another example from the consonantism of Russian.
Russian k, g alternate with $č$, $ž$. The conditions which govern this
alternation are not readily apparent and only an historical investigation will reveal that $č$ and $ž$ occur only before palatal vowels
(and k and g before other vowels). However, we do encounter such
forms as $rùki$ ruki 'hand' (p.Nom.), $bòɣi$ bogi 'gods', $ṕeḱi$ peki 'bake'
(s2 Imperat.). We shall find that the alternations $k : č$ and $g : ž$
still occur in conjugation, for example, while they can no longer be
found in declension. In general, sequences of k or g plus palatal
vowels and sequences of $č$ or $ž$ plus non-palatal vowels can be en-

countered throughout Russian. If the velar consonants k or g occur
in a new word before a palatal vowel, they do not become $\check{c}$ or $\check{z}$ but
$\acute{k}$ or $\acute{g}$, e.g. $k\grave{o}\check{s}kin$, $br\grave{a}\acute{g}in$ (Koškin, Bragin; family names). The
same holds for foreign words, e.g. $k\grave{i}sin\acute{g}en$, $\acute{g}e\partial gr\grave{a}\hat{f}ija$ (Kissingenъ,
geografïä).

Before enumerating the characteristics of the alternations which
we have discussed we must to some extent alter our symbols. In
alternations of the first category we used $s : s_1$ to indicate that
the sounds which were involved were closely related articulatorily.
In the second category, the sounds which alternate are not so closely related from the standpoint of articulation. They are no longer
modifications of the same sound but are completely different sounds.
We shall therefore use $s : z$ to indicate them.

Characteristics of alternations of the second category:

1. It is impossible to determine directly the causes (and conditions) of the alternation: in some cases it may not even be present.
Only an historical investigation will reveal the causes (or conditions) $x : x_1$ of the alternation $s : z$. Furthermore, the words
which display the alternation $s : z$ will not contain the factors
which historical study would reveal had motivated the alternation in
the first place.

2. The alternation is not a necessary one. The sound s may occur
under condition x_1 and z under x. (The formulation of this characteristic is only approximate: not s but s_1 is, in fact, possible
under condition x_1; cf. $d\check{u}\check{s}\grave{a}$, $k\grave{o}\check{s}\hat{k}in$, etc. Similarly, every exception to the rule s͟ : r͟ will necessarily be subordinate to the new
alternation s͟ : z͟, e.g. gewesen, lesen.) In such cases we will deal
not with alternations but with divergences of sounds. In other
words, what is an exception to the rule of correlation will necessarily obey the law of divergence which admits of no exceptions.

3. The alternation is not general. The alternation $s : z$ occurs
as partially coupled with certain morphological categories (which
we will represent by means of $f : f_1$).

4. The alternating sounds are remotely related to each other from
the standpoint of articulation. Alternating s and z are often
related [only] remotely to each other.

Of these four characteristics the first two are decisive. The
third is less decisive and the fourth still less so. The first and
second characteristics are inseparable.

The Third Category

Let us consider the vowel alternation in the Modern German noun
which occurs in conjunction with certain endings, such as

Haus : Häus-er, Häus-lein
Rad : Räd-er, Räd-lein
Loch : Löch-er, Löch-lein
Buch : Büch-er, Büch-lein .

The original cause of this alternation can only be determined historically. The alternation is by no means general throughout the language. Nevertheless, it is unavoidable in certain nouns and in these
cases occurs without exception. This fact becomes clear when we
consider artificial and comical nonce formations which do not occur
generally in the language, such as (Viennese)

Krach 'scandal, racket' : "Krächer", "Krächlein"
Abraham : "Abrahämer" [plural]

etc. It is the German *Sprachgefühl* which forces us to use forms of
one type and not of another. We cannot, therefore, speak of an alternation of the sounds a : ä, o : ö, u : ü, au : äu but must refer
to an alternation of forms, such as

$$\text{noun}\left\{\begin{array}{l}\underline{a}\\\underline{o}\\\underline{u}\\\underline{au}\end{array}\right. : \text{noun}\left\{\begin{array}{l}\underline{ä}\\\underline{ö}\\\underline{ü}\\\underline{äu}\end{array}\right. + \underline{\text{-er}}, \underline{\text{-lein}}.$$

The vowel alternation *o : a* in the following Russian verbs is of the
same kind:

stròjitʹ zəstràjivatʹ
stroitь 'to build' zastraivatь 'id. (iterative)'
bròśitʹ : zəbràsyvatʹ
brositь 'to throw' zabrasyvatь 'id. (iterative)'

The original cause of such alternations can be determined only
by historical research. (In this example it is completely unknown.)
Again, we cannot consider the alternation to be general in the
language since in Russian the alternation *a : o* is exceptional. The
alternation of these sounds, however, in the verbs *stròjitʹ :*
zəstràjivatʹ is inevitable and admits of no exception. By the side
of verbs of this type, this alternation is also characteristic of
such denominals as

əprəstəvəlòśitʹ əprəstəvəlàśivatʹ
oprostovolositь oprostovolašivatь
'to make a fool of 'id. (iterative)' from *vòlos*
someone' volos 'hair'

74

           nəmə zoľit́   *nəmə zaľivat́*

           namozolitь   :   namozalivatь
           'to cause corns'   'id. (iterative)'.

Another interesting pair is
           zəpədòzŕit́   *zəpədàzŕivat́*
                                   :
           zapodozritь   zapodazrivatь
           'to suspect'   'id. (iterative)'

where the alternation occurs in a syllable which was once a proclitic
(-podo-) but was later absorbed by the vestige of an old root (-zr-).
In other words, we encounter this alternation in a new (compound)
root, podozr.

     The alternation *o : a* would be inevitable even in a pair of
verbs which, at the present time, do not exist in the language, but
might for some reason be introduced.   If, for example, we were to
derive a verb *pòľit́* '[roughly] to divide into sexes' from the existing noun *pol* polь 'sex', then we would expect *zəpàľivat́* to correspond to *pòľit́* just as *zəstràjivat́* (see above) corresponds to
stròjit́.

     We are therefore dealing with an alternation of forms

           ...ò...´it́   :   ...à...´$i\atop y$vat́.

(The verb *zəpədàzŕivat́* by the side of *zəbràsyvat́* shows that the
type of the second correlative verb has not yet achieved independent
status since both *i* with the palatalization of the preceding consonant and *y* are possible.)

     The alternation *k : č* may serve as an example from the realm of
consonants. This alternation occurs in nouns and verbs as

           prəròk   *prəròčit́*
                                   :
           prorokь   proročitь
           'prophet'   'to prophesy'.

This type also admits of no exceptions. To every noun with a *k* in
final position must correspond a verb with *č* as the stem-final consonant. For example, the proper name *ľekòk* Lekokь could only have
a corresponding verb of this type *ľekòčit́*. This alternation is,
therefore, also an alternation of forms

           (noun) ...*k*   :   (verb) ...*čit́.*

and shares characteristics 1, 2, and 4 with the alternations of the
second category. The specific difference between categories II and
III resides in characteristics 3 and 5 which can be formulated as
follows:

3. The alternation of the sounds s : z is connected with the alternation of the grammatical categories f : f_1.

5. The appearance of the sound s in the form f_1 or that of the sound z in the form f is impossible.

We can designate the sounds which participate in alternations of the second and third categories as <u>correlatives</u>. The sound s would be the <u>primary</u> correlative and z the <u>secondary</u> correlative.

The following objection can be raised against these designations. The term <u>correlative</u> can be applied to each of two things which stand in a certain relation to each other. Therefore the sounds which we have designated <u>divergents</u> will also be correlatives. This objection is hardly justified since when we gave a name to the alternation of the sounds s : s_1, we not only considered the fact that they alternate but also their close phonetic similarity. When designating the alternation s : z we need consider nothing more than the fact that <u>they</u> <u>alternate</u> <u>with</u> <u>each</u> <u>other</u>.

All of the phenomena which we have been discussing result from physical processes called combinatory and spontaneous sound change, and from unconscious psychical processes which we shall not examine any further.

A given sound s is compatible with the condition x but not with the condition x_1. This condition affects the sound s, i.e. s undergoes a minor change: it changes into s_1. This is a case of combinatory change, which means that, in all words, combinations of the type s : x_1 disappear and only the combinations

$$s : x \quad \text{and} \quad s_1 : x_1$$

remain. The connection between s, and x_1 is a causal one, i.e. the condition x_1 changes the sound s into the sound s_1. (It should thus be clear why the alternation s : s_1 admits of no exception.) This constitutes the <u>first</u> stage for those words which display the combinations indicated above.

Sounds are also subject to spontaneous sound change. Such change especially affects those sounds which are already exposed to pressure. The sound s_1, which is in a continuous stage of change, thus becomes another sound, z:

$$s_1 \quad : \quad x_1$$
$$\downarrow$$
$$> z.$$

Words which were introduced after the first stage will therefore display the following combinations in this, their <u>second</u> stage:

$$(1) \qquad s : x, \quad z : x_1.$$

The connection between the condition x_1 and the sound z is no longer a causal one, i.e. this condition can not change the sound s into the sound z. The connection is now one of coexistence. Since the connection between the sounds s and z is no longer felt (because of what may be called the degeneration of z), and since the connection between z and the condition x is possible from the articulatory point of view, diverse unconscious and psychical processes can still bring about the connection

$$(2) \qquad z : x.$$

This state of affairs obtains only for words which were formed during the first stage. In these words, therefore, we can also see the beginnings of the connection between phonetic phenomena and morphological categories.

In words which are in the process of being formed during the second stage (as the result of various linguistic processes), combinations of the sound s with condition x_1 can again appear. The condition x_1 will again change s into s_1; that is, words which are formed during the second period will only be of the kind

$$(3) \qquad s : x, \qquad s_1 : x_1.$$

The correlatives s-x : z-x_1 are not constant for the following reasons:

(1) x_1 is incapable of effecting the occurrence of z. (Absence of an articulatory connection between the sound z and the condition x_1.)

(2) No connection is felt between the sounds s and z. (Absence of an articulatory connection between the sound s and the sound z.)

(3) The correlatives characterize only a few words. They specifically characterize only those words which arose during the first stage. (Absence of generality, in the sense that a given word is independent of a given morphological category.)

The irregularity which we seem to observe in the second stage is only an apparent one: the second stage may be regarded as transitional to the third stage.

A comparison may now be appropriate. If we look around us and observe innumerable human aspirations, desires, and events, we can only conclude that we are surrounded by chaos. If, however, we let these events follow their course and let them come to their conclusion, we shall see that everything that seemed chaotic and fortuitous falls into a magnificent constellation of order and regularity.

In a similar way, chaos, as we observe it in the domain of phonetic phenomena, is only temporary. Everything that was once, but is no longer, absolutely necessary from the articulatory point

of view is exposed to the effect of <u>unconscious</u> and <u>psychical</u> factors.
These factors stand either in a <u>destructive</u> or in a <u>reinforcing</u> relation to the correlatives. (Correlatives are those sounds which are
connected through coexistence.) Regardless of whether these factors
are destructive or reinforcing, they <u>strive</u> <u>to</u> <u>impose</u> <u>complete</u> <u>order</u>
<u>and</u> <u>simplicity</u> <u>on</u> <u>language</u>. This is their ultimate goal.

   1. If, in a given system of forms, some forms contain *z* and
others *s*, either the former assimilate (morphologically) to the
latter or the latter to the former. The present-tense paradigms of
the verbs *p'ekù* 'I bake' and *məgù* 'I can' in [a] standard Russian,
[b] a Russian dialect, and [c] Ukrainian may serve as examples:

	[a]		[b]
<u>peku</u>	*ṗekù*		*ṗekù*
<u>pečešь</u>	*ṗečðš*		*ṗeǩðš*
<u>pečetъ</u>	*ṗečðt*		*ṗeǩðt*
<u>pečemъ</u>	*ṗečðm*		*ṗeǩðm*
<u>pečete</u>	*ṗečðťe*		*ṗeǩoťe*
<u>pekutь</u>	*ṗekùt*		*ṗekùt*

	[a]		[c]
<u>mogu</u>	*məgù*		*možù*
<u>možešь</u>	*mðžeš*		*mðžeš*
<u>možetъ</u>	*mðžet*		*mðže*
<u>možemъ</u>	*mðžem*		*mðžemo*
<u>možete</u>	*mðžeťe*		*mðžete*
<u>mogutь</u>	*mðgut*		*mðžut*

Compare also:

Old High German	Middle High German	Modern German
[1] <u>lësan</u>		: <u>lese</u>
<u>las</u>		: <u>las</u>
<u>larun</u>		: <u>gelesen</u>
[2]	<u>verliuse</u>	: <u>verliere</u>
	<u>verlôs</u>	: <u>verlor</u>
	<u>verlorn</u>	: <u>verloren</u>.

   In the first of these cases, the primary correlative <u>s</u> has
everywhere displaced the secondary correlative <u>r</u>. In the second
case, the secondary correlative <u>r</u> nullified the primary correlative
<u>s</u>.

2. Let us present two more examples. The first is concerned with the study of function. Entire series of forms of this kind can be constructed. For example, the relation n between two sets of forms, f and f_1 remains constant, as in

f		f_1
stròjit'	:	*zəstràjivat'*
bròśit'	:	*zəbràsyvat'*
nəməzòlit'	:	*nəməzàlivat'*

etc.

Their relation (n) is the following: what occurs as an <u>iterative</u> under f_1 occurs as a <u>non-iterative</u> under f. If, by chance, a form under f contains the sound s and if the form under f_1 contains the sound z, then the feeling gradually arises that the sound s is inseparable from the form f and that the sound z is inseparable from the form f_1. In our [Russian] example the terms were

$$s = o \qquad\qquad z = a.$$

The sound o occurs as a skeletal part of the form f

$$...o...\acute{}\,it'$$

and the sound a as a skeletal part of the form f_1

$$...a...\,{\acute{}i \atop y}vat.$$

The unconscious and psychical principle thus came to the rescue of the alternation $o : a$ by endowing the alternation with a new function. Were it not for this function, the alternation would be destined to irrevocable extinction.

We may similarly compare the German forms

f		f_1
<u>Mann</u>	:	<u>Männer</u>
<u>Loch</u>	:	<u>Löcher</u>
<u>Buch</u>	:	<u>Bücher</u>

i.e.

$...\underline{V}...$	:	$...\underline{V}...\underline{er}$.

The second example is concerned with semasiology. A similar state of affairs can be observed in the words *mùxa* : *mòška*. The word *mùška* appeared at the same time as *mòška*. In terms of meaning, *mùška* is closer to *mùxa* 'fly' and, in fact, divests *mòška* of its original meaning 'small fly'. The word *mòška* found its sole salvation by acquiring a new function, namely, by acquiring a meaning which designated a completely different insect. All of this applies equally well to the corresponding Polish nouns, *mucha, meszka, muszka.*

The same obtains in the case of <u>verlieren</u> : <u>verliesen</u>. The word <u>verliesen</u> co-exists with <u>verlieren</u>, but only because <u>verliesen</u> does not mean 'to lose' but rather 'to loose (in a maritime sense)'.

I have attempted to present this generalization in its simplest form. I have excluded everything that could be removed without causing significant detriment. In doing so, I was guided by the following considerations.

1. If a generalization is proposed for the first time, it is advisable to present it in a simple, approximate form. The astronomer will thus use a circle to describe the trajectory of the planets, although he is well aware of the fact that their real orbit is an inexact ellipse rather than a circle.

2. There would be no great difficulties in developing a generalization and in incorporating in it all those facts which are relevant to it. Nevertheless, this would involve undertaking a special investigation which I am not in a position to do at this time.

3. The reader who summons the effort necessary to think his way into the generalization presented above will soon be convinced that reference to detail will enlarge, supplement, and improve it, rather than undermine its fundamental idea.

We must, in fact, indicate briefly <u>what</u> requires more complete consideration in our generalization.

We have already seen above that x, x_1 appear as the conditioning moments and s, s_1, z as their conditioned pendants. Of these five quantities I have taken into consideration only the s_1 and z. This means that x and x_1 and s still require discussion. The following are samples of the sort of problems which could be discussed:

1. <u>What</u> <u>can</u> <u>appear</u> as <u>the</u> <u>conditioning</u> <u>moment</u>? Obviously, a diversity of things: sound, stress, position within the word, etc.

2. <u>Classification</u> <u>of</u> <u>the</u> <u>conditioning</u> <u>moments</u>.

3. <u>The</u> <u>history</u> <u>of</u> <u>the</u> <u>conditioners</u> x and x_1.

4. <u>The</u> <u>history</u> <u>of</u> <u>the</u> <u>conditioned</u> <u>pendants</u> (s).

5. <u>Classification</u> <u>of</u> <u>the</u> <u>correlatives</u> <u>according</u> <u>to</u> <u>their</u> <u>reciprocal</u> <u>relations</u>.

Compare, e.g. Greek <u>pheúgo</u> : <u>éphugon</u>, Russian *vərətìt : vərɔ̆čat́* (<u>vorotit</u> 'to turn up[side down]', <u>voračat</u> 'to turn'), *rŭka : rŭ̆čka* (<u>ruka</u> 'hand', <u>rŭčka</u> dimin.). The original element in Greek <u>eu</u> : <u>u</u> is <u>eu</u> ; <u>u</u> arose as the result of loss of *e*. In Russian *ti : č̆, ti* is original, while *č̆* is the result of the gradual degeneration of the sequence *ti (ti > tj > č̆)*. *k* is original in *k : č̆; č̆* is developed from k through a change (palatalization) in this same k, by way of the degeneration of $\hat{k}$ into $\check{c}$.

I now intend to discuss the relation of my own opinions to those of the most recent school of linguistics. I must therefore repeat much of what has already been said.

I shall collapse the first two[6] of Brugmann's four well-known theses into one, without altering Brugmann's ideas:

> Every sound law must be conceived of as allowing
> no exceptions; everything that diverges from it
> must be assumed to be due to analogical formation.

The postulative form of this thesis permits the reader to reformulate it affirmatively as follows:

> All sound laws have exceptions which can be
> explained by analogy

or

> The effect of a sound law can be suspended by
> unconscious-psychical factors.

These theses however, give rise to serious difficulties. Since I do not wish to deal with them in detail here I shall only indicate the principal ones.

1. It is obvious that what is called a sound law is not strong enough to withstand the effect of unconscious psychical factors. When, we may ask, is the psychical factor (analogy) the stronger and when the physical factor (the sound law)? Our position becomes all the more difficult when we consider that even if the so-called "sound laws" are known to us, we are still--to be completely honest-- entirely ignorant of the laws which govern "analogy".

2. Which phonetic phenomena are generally called <u>sound</u> <u>laws</u>? Such phenomena as the change from k to $\check{c}$ in the Slavic languages or from s to r in the Germanic languages are generally called <u>sound</u> <u>laws.</u> Three main points must be distinguished.

(a) <u>The</u> <u>primary</u> <u>sound</u>: k or $\underline{s}$.

(b) <u>The</u> <u>cause</u> <u>of</u> <u>its</u> <u>change</u>: <u>the</u> <u>palatal</u> <u>vowel</u> <u>which</u> <u>follows</u> k <u>or</u> <u>intervocalic</u> <u>position</u> (<u>in</u> <u>the</u> <u>case</u> <u>of</u> <u>s</u>).

(c) <u>The</u> <u>secondary</u> <u>sound</u> <u>which</u> <u>arises</u> <u>from</u> <u>the</u> <u>primary</u> <u>sound</u> <u>as</u> <u>a</u> <u>result</u> <u>of</u> <u>the</u> <u>effect</u> <u>of</u> <u>the</u> <u>cause</u> <u>indicated</u> <u>under</u> <u>(b)</u>: $\check{c}$ or r.

[(b') The connection between secondary sound and the cause.] Have we the right to consider the palatal vowel (in Slavic $k > \check{c}$) or intervocalic position (in German $\underline{s} > r$) as the <u>cause</u> <u>which</u> <u>effects</u> <u>the</u> <u>change</u>?

(1)   Such "causes" are often not present in the case of ŏ̌ or *r*.

(2)   In a strict sense, these "causes" do not change *k* into ŏ̌ or
s̲ into *r*.

(3)   They change *k* and s̲ into something quite different from ŏ̌ and
r, namely into *ǩ* and *z*. Furthermore, we have no right to conceal
the fact that in these "exceptions to sound laws" we can recognize
an ideal instance of regularity (i.e. the divergences *k* : *ǩ* and
s : *z*).

(4)   Indeed, even in those cases in which the cause is close at
hand, its relation to the secondary sound (ŏ̌, *r*) is by nature such
that we can only state a case of coexistence of ŏ̌ with a palatal
vowel (or of intervocalic position with *r*). It is my opinion that
it would be unphilosophical to assign the name "law" to such a mere
coexistence.

[(c') The connection between the secondary sound and the primary
sound.] Usually the term "transition" (of sounds) is much misused.
Only a very few of the many vocal phenomena which are called "transitions" deserve this designation in a strictly scientific sense.
Let me restrict my examples to consonants. It is generally agreed
that the term consonant implies the production of a certain noise at
a specific place in the mouth. It is therefore evident that what
appears acoustically to be the transition of one sound into another
is, from the physiological point of view, a change in the place
where the noise is produced. That is why we can speak of a transition of *k* to *ť*, of *t* to ŏ́ and so on. On the other hand, we cannot
speak of a transition of *k* to *p* or *p* to *k* for the change in the
place of articulation of *p* and *k* cannot be conceived of as gradual,
once there is no trajectory between tongue and lips along which such
a place of articulation could progress. Nor can we call such a
phenomenon as Russian *jĭmă̌* : *jĭmě̌ńi* (imă̌ 'name' sNom. : imeni sGen.)
a transition from *a* coupled with the palatalization of the preceding
consonant to the syllable *ě̌n* (i.e. *'a* into *ě̌n*). Likewise in
Russian o̲l̲ : o̲l̲o̲ as in dolbitь 'to chisel, to hollow' : doloto
'chisel [noun]', or in *ě* : *oj* as in petь 'to sing' : poü 'I sing'.
The only designation appropriate to these phenomena is alternation:
this term alone covers all the relevant instances without suggesting
an a priori decision.

Let us once more consider the connection between the secondary
sound and the cause. While it is true that in a German word such
as erkoren the cause of the change of s̲ to *r* is still observable,
we have no right to say that this cause accounts for the change or,
more accurately, the cause initiates the first impetus, as a result
of which primary s̲ changes to *r*. These factors have, by now, begun
to lead to something else: the vowel which follows the s̲ changes

this s to z[7] as, for example, in _gewesen_. Some linguists (e.g. Curtius) have tried to differentiate between laws which operate today and those which have operated in the past in order to circumvent this difficulty. They said that a certain law was once operative in a given language but that it is now no longer operative, and that in its place there is now a new law. If we proceed in this manner we create a state of affairs which is unheard of in any science. A supposition according to which the same domain of observable data is regulated by different laws at different periods of time cannot be called scientific.

In my opinion, the theory whose broad outlines I have developed in this monograph eliminates all the difficulties indicated above. The reader, however, has had the opportunity to convince himself of the fact that my theory does not require the assumption of any hypotheses. It requires only facts which have already been developed and which are by now generally recognized in linguistics. _The entire theory rests only on the transfer of investigations from the sphere of macroscopic phonetic phenomena to the sphere of microscopic phonetic phenomena_. We can encounter sound laws in the strict sense only in the latter [microscopic] realm, where every cause will indeed be a real and efficient cause which would also rule out the possibility of an exception. It is only in this realm that an unequivocal answer to questions concerning the relationship between unconscious and psychical and physical factors can be given.

Sound change can be either combinatory or spontaneous. The boundary between these two cannot be drawn with certainty. Since the physiological properties of a single sound can be infinitely varied, depending on a diversity of instances, and since our range of acoustic perception covers a very narrow area, it is understandable that not every shade of phonation (or, more accurately, not every shade of a sound's physiological side) will be accompanied by a corresponding perceptual effect. I think it likely that only a combinatory process, i.e. only the accommodation of sounds, can allow for purely physiological changes in sound which lie outside the boundaries of our perceptual range. On the other hand, this combinatory process is linked to the spontaneous process. The feature which characterizes a sound's physiological properties gradually grows and begins to be realized acoustically. It begins to associate a certain coloring with a given sound. Within a period of time this coloring increases. I call this the _quantitative stage of change of the combinatory process_. The gradual increase in the sound's coloring ceases when the sound enters the domain of another sound. I call this the _qualitative stage of change of the combinatory process_. This, in general terms, is the

progress of sound change. It always begins with minimally and exclusively physiological changes which are occasioned by the accommodation of the sound to its conditions. It ends in complete
degeneration.

No one will dispute that these processes are purely physiological.
On the other hand, what is the relation between these and the un-
conscious-psychical factors? No psychical factor can prevent a
sound from accommodating itself to the conditions under which it
appears, that is, the combinatory process cannot be impeded by
"analogy". In the same way, no psychical factor can impede the
spontaneous factor <u>as long as it is at the quantitative stage of
mutation</u>: e.g. nothing can prevent Russian *t'* from palatalizing
still further, i.e. from changing still further to *t"*. This statement cannot be made of a spontaneous process once <u>it has reached
the qualitative stage of change</u>. Once the spontaneous process has
reached the point where a given sound of a word has begun to in-
fringe on (i.e. to degenerate acoustically into) the realm of
another sound, the presence of related groups of words can impede
this transition. Thus, the Russian post-linguals, for example, are
so strongly palatalized when they are followed by palatal vowels
that they are on the verge of becoming pre-linguals. We can thus
observe that, in the case of <u>isolated</u> words, such a transition has
already occurred:

t'ĭśt'	<u>kistь</u> 'hand'
ăvdŏťjă <u>Avdotьä</u>	<u>Evdokiä</u> (given name)
ăkăťjĕv <u>Akatьevь</u> (family name), from	<u>Akakiĭ</u> (given name)
ďĭŕă	<u>girä</u> (a weight)
ăńďĕl	<u>angelь</u> 'angel'
ďĕmĕnăźjă	<u>gimnaziä</u> 'secondary school'
ďĕmĕtŕja	<u>geometriä</u> 'geometry'.

Words which <u>belong to existing word families</u> have preserved their
[original] post-linguals up to this day:

> *ǩĭsləj* <u>kislyĭ</u> 'sour', cf. *kvas* <u>kvas</u> 'sourish malt
> beverage' *ǧĭbnut'* <u>gibnutь</u> 'to be destroyed', cf.
> *guǧĭt'* <u>gubitь</u> 'to ruin'.

The psychical factor does not obliterate the sound law in these
cases. It merely impedes its future progress: the *k̂* and *ĝ* of these
examples (<u>kislyĭ</u> and <u>gibnutь</u>) can resist transition into *t̂* and *d̂* only
for a certain period of time.

Are there sound laws which are operative at all periods and in all
languages? Without doubt, there are. We may make this a priori

assumption since it is impossible that language as such is anything
but regular. Palatal vowels will thus palatalize the consonants
which precede them at all times and in all languages though in differing degrees. In all languages and at all times stops in final
position are weaker than stops in initial position. Likewise,
vowels in stressed syllables are articulated more clearly and with
more energy than vowels in unstressed syllables in all languages and
at all times. Etc.

The fact that "one and the same sound" in different languages may
develop in different directions (e.g., Latin $s > r$ but Greek $s > \phi$)
does not, in any way, contradict what has been said above. It seems
to me that we are dealing with a misunderstanding which results from
confusing letters with sounds. We say "Latin s" and "Greek s" without realizing that a single symbol can represent two different
sounds.[8] A rule in formula form cannot be set up with so uncertain
a quantity as "s". In these cases only a well-defined s can play a
role. We must fashion our formulation as follows: "An s with
certain acoustic and psychological features which characterizes the
Latin sound gradually becomes r." If in this instance we were again
to abandon the macroscopic approach in favor of the microscopic one,
we would in all probability discover that those languages in which
we observe rhotacism (such as Latin, German, or Chuvash) have only
one and the same s and that this s is altogether different from the
s of those languages in which we do not observe rhotacism.

Let us now leave phenomena of a purely phonetic nature and consider
the phonetic phenomena connected with morphology. As we have seen
above, we also find that laws apply to such data without exception.
These laws, however, no longer belong to the physical domain but to
the psychical. We have seen above that departures from the law of
divergence are possible only when there is an effective participation
of the will. The same applies in the case of departures from the
law of morphological alternations. Every native speaker of German
will form the plural Muselmänner 'muslims' from the singular Muselman
(as in Ehemänner from Ehemann 'male spouse'). Only those Germans
who wish to indicate that they know that -man in Muselman has no
connection with the German word Mann 'male adult' will use another
plural, such as Muselmane 'muslims'.

The purpose of the following Tables 1 and 2 is to illustrate
graphically what has been presented above. The confines of the
rectangles contain pairs of correlative sounds from German and from
Slavic. Phonetics has, until now, been exclusively concerned with
such phenomena as are contained within the rectangles, at the expense
of all other phenomena. Phonetics has, until now, failed to indicate
both the paths which lead to this magic rectangle and those which
lead away from it.

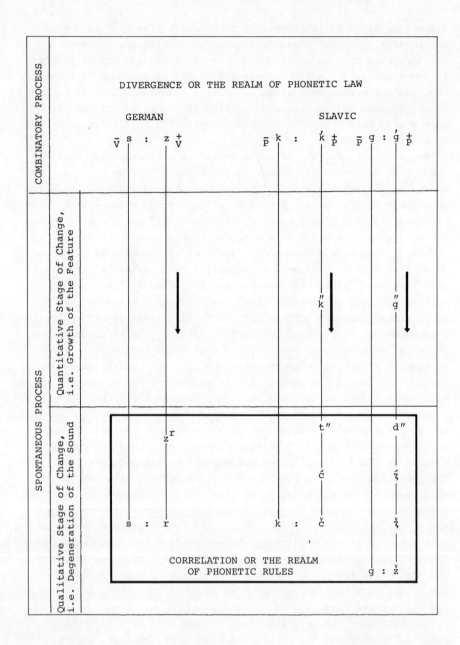

TABLE 1

THE REALM OF PHONETIC LAW. DIVERGENTS.[a]

LEXICON. IMMOBILE CORRELATIVES

verlor : verlieren	
las : lesen	$\frac{r}{z}$[b]
	$\frac{s}{z}$
mogu : mogi	$\frac{g}{\check{g}}$
možu : možešь	$\frac{\check{z}}{\check{z}}$
peku : peki	$\frac{k}{\check{k}}$
peki : peki	$\frac{k}{\check{k}}$

THE REALM OF PHONETIC RULES (TEMPORARY CORRELATIVES)

$k : \check{k}$
$\check{c} : \check{c}$
$u : o$
$\check{z} : \check{z}$
$g : \check{g}$
$r : \underline{\underline{z}}$
$s : \underline{\underline{z}}$
$v : \ddot{v}$

THE REALM OF MORPHOLOGICAL LAW (MOBILE CORRELATIVES)

...k : ...čitь
Noun   Verb   proročitь
prorokъ : proročitь
...ka : ...čka
Noun   Diminutive   ruka : ručka

...v... : ...v...er
Sg. noun   Pl. noun   Buch : Bücher

1. IN ROOTS (ROOT-CLEAVAGE)

konecь : načalo
pokoi : počivatь
verliesen : verlieren

2. IN WORDS[c] (WORD-CLEAVAGE)

muška : mȯška

ASSIMILATION
Destructive Effect of Morphological Factors

DIFFERENTIATION
Reinforcing Effect of Morphological Factors

TABLE 2

87

[In the upper third of the table, $\frac{}{v}$ and $\frac{+}{v}$ are to be read, respectively, as "not in intervocalic position" and "in intervocalic posi-
tion." Similarly, $\frac{-}{p}$ and $\frac{+}{p}$ are to be read: "preceding a non-palatal
vowel" and "preceding a palatal vowel."]

The symbol z^r represents an indeterminate phonetic series located
between z and r (more or less $\check{z}$, r without a trill, etc.). In fact,
the following conditions govern the change from etymological s to z:
s must be preceded by a vowel, by zero, or by r, l, m, or n; s must
be followed by a vowel. For this reason, my example may not seem
altogether appropriate, but at this moment I cannot think of a better
one.

' stands for palatalization and " for stronger palatalization.

I use $\hat{c}$ to transliterate Old Church Slavic ц which may be considered as being equivalent to a palatalized sequence ts. The voiced
counterpart of $\hat{c}$ is here written $\hat{\zeta}$ (OCS з).

$\check{\zeta}$ stands for $d\check{z}$. It is the [voiced] counterpart of $t\check{s}$ (OCS ч).
It ($\check{\zeta}$) represents OCS ж whose quality is, in fact, unknown to us and
which we may assume only as a hypothesis.

Notes to Table 2

a. From the historical point ov view, this is already a second
layer of divergents. The first, older layer of such divergents has
already changed into the correlatives contained in the rectangle by
way of the spontaneous process.

b. I am not in a position to decide whether there is an acoustically perceptible difference between r in word-final position and r
in medial intervocalic position.

c. The boundary between root-cleavage and word-cleavage is difficult to determine.

Appendix

On the "Palatalization" and "Dentalization" of the Old Slavic Post-
linguals.

It is well known that Old [Church] Slavic k̲, g̲, x̲ alternate with
either č̲, ž̲, š̲ or with c̲, z̲, s̲. Since, at least as far as I am aware,
there is no sufficient explanation of this phenomenon, so striking at
first glance, I shall now take the liberty of presenting my own explanation.

Let us consider the main occurrences of both subtypes of this alternation in connection with the question of the original of Slavic c̲, z̲,
s̲ in the first place.

I. Palatalization.

sVoc. of nouns ending in k̲, x̲, g̲; e.g., člověče 'human being', bože
'god', douše 'spirit'.

Some forms in the verbal paradigm; e.g. s2 pres. of verbs ending in
k, g, x: pečeši 'bake', žežeši 'burn', vrišeši 'tread'.

In derivation, e.g. člověčĭstvo 'humanity', božĭstvo 'divinity',
strašĭnŭ 'terrible'.

In roots; e.g. poučivati 'to repose' (cf. s2 imperat. pokoi),
načalo 'beginning' (cf. konĭcĭ 'end'), časŭ (< *čĕsŭ) 'hour', čеšę
'to comb' (cf. kosa 'head, hair'), ženę 'to strike' (cf. gnati).

II. Dentalization.

(a) pNom. of nouns ending in k̲, g̲, x̲; e.g. plŭci 'trumpet', drouzi
'other', strasi 'fear'.

pNom. of the pronoun kyi—cii.

Imperatives of verbs ending in k̲, g̲, x̲: tĭci 'run', žĭži, vrĭsi.

sLoc. and pLoc. of nouns ending in k̲, g̲, x̲; e.g. vlŭcě 'wolf',
nozě 'foot, leg', plŭcěxŭ, drouzěxŭ, strasěxŭ, člověčistě (-scě
'human').

(b) In verbs such as k̲l̲i̲c̲a̲t̲i̲ 'to shout', brącati 'to sound [trans.]'
dvizati 'to tarry', nasmisati 'to laugh at'.

In suffixes: otĭcĭ 'father', selĭce 'country-house', pŭtica 'bird',
kŭnązĭ 'prince'.

(c) In words such as zemlä 'earth, land', slama 'stalk' and so on,
in which the "dentals" correspond to original front *K*-sounds.

Let us now compare group (a) with the two other groups of so-called
dentals.

The causes of dentalization in the groups are different:

(a) The combinatory process is motivated by a following palatal
vowel.

(b) The combinatory process is motivated by a preceding palatal vowel.   (Cf. the German *ich*-Laut and *ach*-Laut.)

(c) Spontaneous process.

   Furthermore, group (c) is distinguished by the lack of an alternation while groups (a) and (b) regularly alternate with *K*-sounds even
where there is no motivation for dentalization (in the preceding or
in the following vowel).

   If we now compare group (a) with group I (with examples of palatalization) we find that the two correspond almost completely. The
reason for the change of the original *K*-sounds is the same in every
respect; furthermore, there is alternation with *K*-sounds both in
group (a) and in group I. The two groups only diverge in that we
observe palatalization not merely in forms which are intimately connected with their pendants, but also in pairs of forms whose connection is much weaker. On the other hand, we encounter dentalization
<u>exclusively</u> in forms which are intimately connected with each other.

   On the basis of what was said above, and especially because one
and the same cause cannot be said to account for two different results, the following explanation alone seems possible to me:

   During the prehistoric period, the original *K*-sounds always changed
into *č*-sounds before palatal vowels. The declensional forms and some
conjugational forms [then] assimilated to their pendants with *K*-forms,
i.e. the *č*-sounds again turned into *K̂*-sounds and these *K̂*-sounds
again spontaneously became *ĉ*-sounds.

   In Russian, the same process of assimilation of forms which contained dentals occurred a second time.

   The following is a graphic representation of one example:

           *k̂ešẽ : <u>kosa</u>   ::   *vlŭk̂i : <u>vlŭky</u>
              ↓   ↓
           *t̂ešẽ   ::   *<u>vlŭt̂i</u>
              ↓   ↓
           *ĉešẽ   ::   *<u>vlŭĉi</u>
              ↓   ↓
           <u>češẽ</u>   ::   *<u>vlŭči</u>
                                            ↘
                                        *<u>vlŭk̂i</u>
                                           ↓
                                        *<u>vlŭt̂i</u>
                                           ↓
                                         <u>vlŭci</u>

                                      ↘
                                       (<u>peki</u> : <u>pici</u>)
                                      [Russian] [OCS]

90

Or:

$$*\acute{k}\underset{\downarrow}{e\check{s}\check{e}} : \underline{kosa} \qquad :: \qquad *\underline{vl\breve{u}\acute{k}i}\underset{\downarrow}{} : \underline{vl\breve{u}ky}$$

$$*\acute{t}\underset{\downarrow}{e\check{s}\check{e}} \qquad :: \qquad *\underline{vl\breve{u}\acute{t}i}\underset{\downarrow}{}$$

$$*\acute{c}\underset{\downarrow}{e\check{s}\check{e}} \qquad :: \qquad *\underline{vl\breve{u}\acute{c}i}\underset{\rightarrow}{}$$

$$\underline{\check{c}e\check{s}\check{e}} \qquad\qquad\qquad *\underline{vl\breve{u}\acute{k}i}\underset{\downarrow}{}$$

$$*\underline{vl\breve{u}\acute{t}i}\underset{\downarrow}{}$$

$$\underline{vl\breve{u}ci}\underset{\rightarrow}{}$$

(peki : pici)

[Russian] [OCS]

Notes

[1] With regard to this generalization see my articles in the *Russkiĭ Filologičeskiĭ Věstnik* 1879 Nos. 3 and 4 and 1880 No. 3.

[2] It is Professor J. Baudouin de Courtenay's.

[3] I am inclined to assign the term confix to morphological units.

[4] This designation is Professor J. Baudouin de Courtenay's.

[5] I propose to use the term phoneme to designate the phonetic unit (i.e. what is phonetically indivisible) as opposed to the term sound which would designate the articulatory unit. The advantage and the inevitability of such a designation (and of such a concept) is obvious a priori. In order to render the term even more convincing, however, I wish to point out the following: The correlative of Greek *i* (in *élipon : leĭpō*) will be the sequence *ei*; the correlative of Russian *u* [= Old Church Slavic *ě*] (in *smuščénje* 'non-plussedness' : *śmatěn̂je* 'confusion' — smušenie : smätenie) will be coupled with the palatalization of the consonant which precedes it. The correspondent of Russian *olo* will be *ło* in Polish (cf. Russian golova : Polish głowa 'head'); similarly Russian *ml'* : Polish *m̂* (Russian zemlä : Polish ziemia 'earth'). The phonetic unit can therefore be equal to more than one sound, or even to a single sound coupled with the quality [here palatalization] of another sound.

[6] I shall not discuss the remaining theses since I myself have already, independently of Brugmann, proposed the thesis that the modern languages should serve as the point of departure for all study of language (see my *Zur Frage über den Guna*). The reader is already familiar with my rejection of the thesis concerning the reconstruction of proto-forms. The reconstruction of past linguistic phenomena is, in itself, not as important as is generally assumed. As is the case with all deduction, reconstruction will be possible only when the true laws of linguistic phenomena have been established by means of induction.

[7] When *s* is preceded by a sonant (such as a vowel, *r*, *l*, *m*, *n*, or φ).

[8] It is probable that these varieties of *s* are not even noticeably different from each other acoustically. Nevertheless, they are produced under the most diverse physiological conditions. We need only remind the reader that one and the same *s* may be pronounced while the speech organs are assuming a great variety of positions.

Section Two
Twentieth Century: Structuralism

Introduction

The papers in this section, like those in Section I, share the view
that phonological change is a change in sounds, i.e. phonemes, but
they differ from those in the first section by insisting that the
phonemes involved in a change must be treated in terms of the systems,
i.e. inventories, in which they participate. The schools represented
by the authors in Section II are, somewhat loosely, Geneva (de
Saussure), Prague (Jakobson), and American structuralism (Greenberg,
Hoenigswald). Martinet's views are best seen as a combination of
these three, though closest to the Prague School. The glaring absence of Hockett from this section has already been discussed.

The affinity of the excerpt from de Saussure's *Course* (1915) to
the Kruszewski selection has been mentioned. Spontaneous changes
are caused by factors within the phonemic system itself (= unconditioned change), whereas combinatory (= conditioned) changes result
from the presence of phonemes in the environment. De Saussure's
novel statement of Verner's Law proposes a spontaneous change of,
say, [θ] to [ð] non-initially, followed by the combinatory change of
[θ] to [θ] non-initially, where the spontaneous change was actually
impeded (i.e. prevented) by the stress on the preceding vowel. Sound
changes are seen as absolutely regular in the sense that all words
containing the same phoneme are identically altered; a sound change
affects sounds, not words.

The highly technical classification of phonological changes succinctly presented in Jakobson's paper (first published in German in
1931) is best summarized by these two important generalizations:
(1) "every modification must be treated as a function of the system
of which it is a part"; (2) "the spirit of equilibrium and the
simultaneous tendency toward its rupture constitute the indispensible
properties of that whole that is language."

Jakobson's view of linguistic change, as well as his terminology
(function, system, equilibrium), are very close to those expressed
by Martinet (1952), though the compensatory processes of phonologization (split) and dephonologization (merger) are cited as evidence

for stability by the former, for instability by the latter. Martinet's description of the process of sound change is parallel to those of Hockett (1965) and selections 1 and 2. A margin of security separates the normal ranges of dispersion (Hockett's density distribution, Gabelentz's circle) of phonemes. Each range has a center of gravity (Gabelentz uses the same term), rarely attained by speakers in actual performance. A sound shift occurs when the normal range of a phoneme is displaced (Hockett: when the local maxima drift). Martinet's basic theoretical concept is that of economy (principle of least effort), which states that "linguistic evolution [is] regulated by the permanent antimony between the expressive needs of man and his tendency to reduce his mental and physical exertions to a minimum". Martinet's concept of functional yield (or load) is discussed and rejected by King [10].

The main point of Hoenigswald's article (1964) is that the so-called 'minor' sound change processes are no different from any other kinds of sound change. They have sound-law character in that they are regular rather than sporadic, gradual rather than sudden. This paper, by showing, for example, that such 'sporadic' assimilations as *ds* to *ss* in Latin (*adsimilare* > *assimilare*) are every bit as phonologically statable as assimilatory changes universally given sound change status (e.g. umlaut), is another important contribution to the true understanding of regularity in sound change.

Greenberg's paper (1966) on phonological universals examines the mutual complementation of synchronic and diachronic universals. Thus, synchronic universals can be an index to diachronic universals. For example, the synchronic universals that all languages have oral vowels and that the presence of nasal vowels implies the presence of oral vowels (but not vice-versa) give rise to the diachronic universal that nasal vowels invariably originate from oral vowels. Conversely, two diachronic universals, (1) the origin theory of nasal vowels, and (2) the fact that the merger of nasal vowels is more frequent than and precedes that of oral vowels, lead to the synchronic universal that the number of nasal vowels is never greater than the number of oral vowels. The kind of universals proposed by Greenberg are typological, referring, in this case, to surface phonetic phenomena, based on the structuralist concept of change by sound; whereas Kiparsky's [11] universals, on the other hand, referring to relationships of rule order, are based on the generative concept of change by rule.

5   Phonetic Changes

FERDINAND DE SAUSSURE

1. *Their Absolute Regularity*

We saw earlier that a phonetic change affects not words but sounds.
What is transformed is a phoneme. This event, though isolated like
all other diachronic events, results in the identical alteration of
all words containing the same phoneme. It is in this sense that
phonetic changes are absolutely regular.

In German, every *ī* became *ei*, then *ai*: *wīn, trīben, līhen, zīt*
became *Wein, treiben, leihen, Zeit;* every *ū* became *au: hūs, zūn, rūch*
became *Haus, Zaun, Rauch;* in the same way *ü* changed to *eu: hüser* became *Häuser,* etc. On the contrary, the dipthong *ie* became *ī,* which
is still written *ie:* cf. *biegen, lieb, Tier.* In addition, every *uo*
became *ū: muot* became *Mut,* etc. Every *z* became *s* (written *ss*): *wazer* →
Wasser, fliezen → *fliessen,* etc. Every intervocalic *h* disappeared:
līhen, sehen → *leien, seen* (written *leihen, sehen*). Every *w* was
changed to labiodental *v* (written *w*): *wazer* → *waser (Wasser).*

In French, every palatalized *l* became *y: piller* 'pillar' and
b̦ouillir 'boil' are pronounced *piyę, buyir,* etc.

In Latin, what was once intervocalic *s* appears as *r* in another
period: **genesis, *asēna* → *generis, arēna,* etc.

Any phonetic change at all, when seen in its true light, would confirm the perfect regularity of these transformations.

2. *Conditioned Phonetic Changes*

The preceding examples have already shown that phonetic phenomena,
far from always being absolute, are more often linked to fixed conditions. Putting it another way, what is transformed is not the phonological species but the phoneme as it occurs under certain conditions
—its environment, accentuation, etc. For instance, *s* became *r* in
Latin only between vowels and in certain other positions; elsewhere
it remains (cf. *est, senex, equos).*

From *A Course in General Linguistics* (New York, 1959), 143-153.
Transl. by Wade Baskin. Reprinted by permission of the publishers,
Philosophical Library Inc.

Absolute changes are extremely rare. That changes often appear to be absolute is due to the obscure or extremely general nature of the conditions. In German, for example, *ī* became *ei*, *ai*, but only in a tonic syllable. Proto-Indo-European k_1 became *h* in Germanic (cf. Proto-Indo-European k_1olsom, Latin *collum*, German *Hals*), but the change did not occur after *s* (cf. Greek *skotos* and Gothic *skadus* 'shadow').

Besides, the classing of changes as absolute or conditioned is based on a superficial view of things. It is more logical, in line with the growing trend, to speak of *spontaneous* and *combinatory* phonetic phenomena. Changes are spontaneous when their cause is internal and combinatory when they result from the presence of one or more other phonemes. The passing of Proto-Indo-European *o* to Germanic *a* (cf. Gothic *skadus*, German *Hals*, etc.) is thus a spontaneous fact. Germanic consonantal mutations or *Lautverschiebungen* typify spontaneous change: Proto-Indo-European k_1 became *h* in Proto-Germanic (cf. Latin *collum* and Gothic *hals*) and Proto-Germanic *t*, which is preserved in English, became *z* (pronounced *ts*) in High German (cf. Gothic *taihun*, English *ten*, German *zehn*). Against this, the passing of Latin *ct*, *pt* to Italian *tt* (cf. *factum → fatto*, *captīvum → cattivo*) is a combinatory fact, for the first element was assimilated to the second. The German umlaut is also due to an external cause, the presence of *i* in the following syllable: while *gast* did not change, *gasti* became *gesti*, *Gäste*.

The result is not an issue in either case, and whether or not there is a change is of no importance. For instance, on comparing Gothic *fisks* with Latin *piscis* and Gothic *skadus* with Greek *skótos*, we observe in the first pair the persistence of *i* and in the second the passing of *o* to *a*. The first phoneme remained while the second one changed, but what matters is that each acted independently.

A combinatory phonetic fact is always conditioned, but a spontaneous fact is not necessarily absolute, for it may be conditioned negatively by the absence of certain forces of change. In this way Proto-Indo-European k_2 spontaneously became *qu* in Latin (cf. *quattuor*, *inquilīna*, etc.) but not, for instance, when followed by *o* or *u* (cf. *cottīdie*, *colō*, *secundus*, etc.) In the same way the persistence of Proto-Indo-European *i* in Gothic *fisks*, etc. is linked to a condition—the *i* could not be followed by *r* or *h*, for then it became *e*, written *ai* (cf. *wair →* Latin *vir* and *maihstus →* German *Mist*).

3. *Points on Method*

In devising formulas to express phonetic changes we must consider the preceding distinctions or risk presenting the facts incorrectly.

Here are some examples of inaccuracies.

According to the old formulation of Verner's law, "in Germanic every noninitial þ changed to ð if the accent came after it": cf. on the one hand *faþer → *faðer (German Vater), *liþumé → *liðumé (German litten), and on the other *þris (German drei), *broþer (German Bruder), *liþo (German leide), where þ remains. This formula gives the active role to accent and introduces a restrictive clause for initial þ. What actually happened is quite different. In Germanic, as in Latin, þ tended to sonorize spontaneously within a word; only the placing of the accent on the preceding vowel could prevent it. Everything is therefore reversed. The fact is spontaneous, not combinatory, and the accent is an obstacle rather than the precipitating cause. We should say: "Every internal þ became   unless the change was opposed by the placing of the accent on the preceding vowel."

In order to separate what is spontaneous from what is combinatory, we must analyze the stages of the transformation and not mistake the mediate result for the immediate one. It is wrong to explain rhotacization, for instance (cf. Latin *genesis → generis), by saying that s became r between two vowels, for s, having no laryngeal sound, could never become r directly. There are really two acts. First s became z through a combinatory change. Second, this sound was replaced by closely related r since z had not been retained in the sound system of Latin. The second change was spontaneous. It is therefore a serious mistake to consider the two dissimilar facts as a single phenomenon. The fault is on the one hand in mistaking the mediate result for the immediate one (s → r instead of z → r) and on the other, in regarding the total phenomenon as combinatory when this is true of only its first part. This is the same as saying that e became a before a nasal in French. The fact is that there were in succession a combinatory change—nasalization of e by n (cf. Latin ventum → French vēnt, Latin fēmina → French femə, fēmə) —and a spontaneous change of ē̃ to ã (cf. vãnt, fãmə, now vã, fãm). To raise the objection that the change could occur only before a nasal consonant would be pointless. The question is not why e was nasalized but only whether the transformation of ē̃ into ã is spontaneous or combinatory.

The most serious mistake in method that I can recall at this point—although it is not related to the principles stated above— is that of formulating a phonetic law in the present tense, as if the facts embraced by it existed once and for all instead of being born and dying within a span of time. The result is chaos, for in this way any chronological succession of events is lost sight of. I have already emphasized this point in analyzing the successive phenomena that explain the duality of tríkhos: thriksí. Whoever says "*s* became *r* in Latin" gives the impression that rhotacization is inherent in the nature of language and finds it difficult to account for exceptions like *causa, rīsus*, etc. Only the formula "intervocalic *s* became *r* in Latin" justifies our believing that *causa, rīsus*, etc. had no *s* at the moment when *s* became *r* and were sheltered from change. The fact is that speakers still said *caussa, rīssus*, etc. For a similar reason we must say "*ā* became *ē* in the Ionian dialect (cf. *mā́ter mḗter*, etc.), for otherwise we would not know what to make of forms like *pâsa, phāsi*, etc. (which were still *pansa, phansi*, etc. during the period of the change.)

4. *Causes of Phonetic Changes*

The search for the causes of phonetic changes is one of the most difficult problems of linguistics. Many explanations have been proposed, but none of them thoroughly illuminates the problem.

(1) One supposition is that racial predispositions trace beforehand the direction of phonetic changes. This raises a question of comparative anthropology: Does the phonational apparatus vary from one race to the next? No, scarcely more than from one individual to the next. A newborn Negro transplanted to France speaks French as well as a native Frenchman. Furthermore, expressions like "the Italian vocal apparatus" or "the mouth of Germanic speakers does not allow that" imply that a mere historical fact is a permanent characteristic. This is similar to the mistake of stating a phonetic law in the present tense. To pretend that the Ionian vocal apparatus finds long *ā* difficult and changes it to *ē* is just as erroneous as to say that *ă* "becomes" *ē* in Ionian.

The Ionian vocal apparatus had no aversion to *ā*, for this sound was used in certain instances. This is obviously an example, not of racial incapacity, but of a change in articulatory habits. In the same way Latin, which had not retained intervocalic *s* (**genesis → generis*), reintroduced it a short time later (cf. **rīssus → rīsus*). These changes do not indicate a permanent disposition of the Latin voice.

There is doubtless a general direction that phonetic phenomena follow during a particular period and within a specific nation. The monophthongizations of diphthongs in Modern French are manifestations of one and the same tendency, but we would find similar general currents in political history and never question their being merely historical without any direct influence of race.

(2) Phonetic changes have often been considered adaptations to conditions of soil and climate. Consonants abound in some northern languages while more vowels occur in certain southern languages, giving them their harmonious sound. Climate and living conditions

may well influence language, but the problem becomes complicated as soon as we enter into detail: beside the Scandinavian idioms with their many consonants are those of the Lapps and Finns, which are even more vocalic than Italian. We also notice that the accumulation of consonants in present-day German is in many instances a quite recent fact, due to the fall of posttonic vowels; that certain dialects of southern France are less opposed to consonantal clusters than the French of the north; that Serbian has as many consonantal clusters as Great Russian, etc.

(3) The cause of phonetic changes has also been ascribed to the law of least effort by which two articulations are replaced by one or a difficult articulation by an easier one. This idea, regardless of what is said about it, is worth examining. It may clarify the cause of phonetic changes or at least indicate the direction that the search for it must take.

The law of least effort seems to explain a certain number of cases: the passing of an occlusive to a spirant (Latin *habēre* → French *avoir* 'have'); the fall of great clusters of final syllables in many languages; phenomena relating to assimilation (e.g. *ly* → *ll* as in **alyos* → Greek *állos*, *tn* → *nn* as in **atnos* → Latin *annus*); the monophthongization of diphthongs, which is only another type of assimilation (e.g. *ai* → *e* as in French *maizõn* → *mezõ*, written *maison* 'house'), etc.

But we might mention just as many instances where exactly the opposite occurs. Against monophthongization, for example, we can set the change of German *ī*, *ū*, *ü*, to *ei*, *au*, *eu*. If the shortening of Slavic *ā*, *ē* to *ă*, *ĕ* is due to least effort then the reverse phenomenon offered by German (*fater* → *Vāter*, *geben* → *gēben*) must be due to greatest effort. If voicing is easier than nonvoicing (cf. *opera* → Provençal *obra*), the reverse must necessitate greater effort, and yet Spanish passed from *z* to *χ* (cf. *hiχo*, written *hijo*) and Germanic changed *b*, *d*, *g*, to *p*, *t*, *k*. If loss of aspiration (cf. Proto-Indo-European **bherō* → Germanic *beran*) is considered a lessening of effort, what is to be said of German, which inserts aspiration where it did not exist (*Tanne*, *Pute*, etc., pronounced *Thanne*, *Phute*)?

The foregoing remarks do not pretend to refute the proposed solution. In fact, we can scarcely determine what is easiest or most difficult for each language to pronounce. Shortening means less effort in the sense of duration, but it is equally true that long sounds allow careless pronunciation while short sounds require more care. Given different predispositions, we can therefore present two opposing facts from the same viewpoint. Thus where *k* became *tš* (cf. Latin *cēdere* → Italian *cedere*), there is apparently an increase in effort if we consider only the end terms of the change, but the impression would probably differ if we reconstructed the chain: k became palatalized $\acute{k}$ through assimilation to the following vowel; then $\acute{k}$ passed to ky; the pronunciation did not become more difficult; two tangled elements in $\acute{k}$ were clearly differentiated; then from ky speakers passed successively to ty, $t\chi$, $t\overset{v}{s}$, everywhere with less effort.

The law of least effort would require extensive study. It would be necessary to consider simultaneously the physiological viewpoint (the question of articulation) and the psychological viewpoint (the question of attention).

(4) An explanation that has been favored for several years attributes changes in pronunciation to our phonetic education during childhood. After much groping and many trials and corrections, the child succeeds in pronouncing what he hears around him; here would be the starting point of all changes; certain uncorrected inaccuracies would win out in the individual and become fixed in the generation that is growing up. Children often pronounce t for k, and our languages offer no corresponding phonetic change in their history. But this is not true of other deformations. In Paris, for instance, many children pronounce $fl'eur$ $(fleur$ 'flower') and $bl'anc$ $(blanc$ 'white') with palatalized l; now it was through a similar process that $florem$ became $fl'ore$, then $fiore$, in Italian.

The preceding observations deserve careful attention but leave the problem undented. Indeed, what prompts a generation to retain certain mistakes to the exclusion of others that are just as natural is not clear. From all appearances the choice of faulty pronunciations is completely arbitrary, and there is no obvious reason for it. Besides, why did the phenomenon break through at one time rather than another?

The same question applies to all the preceding causes of phonetic changes if they are accepted as real. Climatic influence, racial predisposition, and the tendency toward least effort are all permanent or lasting. Why do they act sporadically, sometimes on one point of the phonological system and sometimes on another? A historical event must have a determining cause, yet we are not told what chances in each instance to unleash a change whose general cause has existed for a long time. This is the most difficult point to explain.

(5) Phonetic changes are sometimes linked to the general state of the nation at a particular moment. Languages go through some periods that are more turbulent than others. There have been attempts to relate phonetic changes to turbulent periods in a nation's history and in this way to discover a link between political instability and linguistic instability; this done, some think that they can

apply conclusions concerning language in general to phonetic changes. They observe, for example, that the sharpest upheavals of Latin in its development into the Romance languages coincided with the highly disturbed period of invasions. Two distinctions will serve as guideposts:

(a) Political stability does not influence language in the same way as political instability; here there is no reciprocity. When a political equilibrium slows down the evolution of language, a positive though external cause is involved. But instability, which has the opposite effect, acts only negatively. Immobility—the relative fixation of an idiom—may have an external cause (the influence of a court, school, an academy, writing, etc.) which in turn is positively favored by social and political equilibrium. But if some external upheaval that has affected the equilibrium of the nation precipitates linguistic evolution, this is because language simply reverts back to its free state and follows its regular course. The immobility of Latin of the classical period is due to external facts; the changes that it later underwent, however, were self-generated in the absence of certain external conditions.

(b) Here we are dealing only with phonetic phenomena and not with every type of modification of language. Grammatical changes are obviously similar. Because they are always closely linked to thought, grammatical facts are more easily affected by the impact of external upheavals, which have a more immediate repercussion on the mind. But there is no solid basis for the belief that sudden evolutions of the sounds of an idiom correspond to turbulent periods in the history of a nation.

Still, it is impossible to cite a single period—even among those where language is in a deceptive state of immobility—that has witnessed no phonetic changes.

(6) The "linguistic substratum" has also been posited as the cause of phonetic changes. The absorption of an indigenous population by newcomers brings about certain changes. The difference between Provençal and French (*langue d'oc and language d'oïl*) would accordingly correspond to a different proportion of the autochthonous Celtic element in the two parts of Gaul. This theory has also been used to trace the dialectal differences of Italian and the influence of Ligurian, Etruscan, etc., depending on the region. But first, this hypothesis supposes circumstances that are rarely found. Second, one must be more specific: Did earlier populations introduce some of their own articulatory habits into the new language on adopting it? This is admissible and quite natural. But if the imponderable forces of race, etc. are called in anew, the pitfalls described earlier reappear.

(7) A final explanation—which scarcely merits the name—compares phonetic changes to changes in fashion. But no one has explained these changes. We know only that they depend on laws of imitation, which are the concern of the psychologist. This explanation, though it does not solve our problem, has the advantage of fitting it into another larger problem and positing a psychological basis for phonetic changes. But where is the starting point of imitation? That is the mystery, in phonetic changes as well as in changes of fashion.

5. *The Effect of Phonetic Changes Is Unlimited*

If we try to determine how far phonetic changes will go, we see immediately that they are unlimited and incalculable, i.e. we cannot foresee where they will stop. It is childish to think that the word can be changed only up to a certain point, as if there were something about it that could preserve it. Phonetic modifications derive their character from the arbitrariness of the linguistic sign [signifier], which is distinct from the signified.

We can easily observe that the sounds of a word have been affected at a certain moment and see the extent of the damage, but we cannot say beforehand how far the word has become or will become unrecognizable.

Like every word having the same ending, Proto-Indo-European *aiwom* (cf. Latin *aevom*) changed to *aiwan, *aiwa, *aiw* in Proto-Germanic; next, *aiw* became *ew* in Old High German, as did every word that contained the cluster *aiw*; then the change of final *w* to *o* resulted in *ēo*, which in turn passed to *eo, io* in accordance with other equally general rules; finally *io* became *ie, je*, giving Modern German *jē* (cf. das schönste, was ich *je* gesehen habe 'the prettiest that I have *ever* seen').

The modern word does not contain a single one of its original elements when considered from the viewpoint of the starting point and the end result. Each step, when viewed separately, is absolutely certain and regular and limited in its effect; viewed as a whole, however, the word gives the impression of an unlimited number of modifications. We might make the same observation about Latin *calidum* by first leaving out the transitional forms and comparing this form with Modern French *šǫ* (written *chaud* 'warm'), then retracing the steps: *calidum, calidu, caldu, cald, calt, tsalt, tsaut, šaut, šǫt, šǫ*. Compare also Vulgar Latin *waidanju → gẽ* (written *gain* 'gain'), *minus → mwẽ* (written *moins* 'less'), *hoc illi → wi* (written *oui* 'yes').

A phonetic change is also unlimited and incalculable in that it affects all types of signs, making no distinction between radicals, suffixes, etc. This must be true *a priori*, for if grammar interfered, the phonetic phenomenon would mingle with the synchronic fact, a thing that is radically impossible. It is in this sense that we can speak of the blind nature of the evolutions of sounds.

For instance, *s* fell in Greek after *n* not only in **khānses* 'geese', **menses* 'months' (giving *khênes*, *mênes*), where it had no grammatical value, but also in verbal forms like **etensa*, **ephansa*, etc. (giving *éteina*, *éphēna*, etc.), where it marked the aorist. In Middle High German the posttonic vowels *i, e, a, o* regularly became *e* (*gibil → Giebel, meistar → Meister*) even though the difference in timbre marked a number of inflectional endings; that is how the accusative singular *boton* and the genitive and dative singular *boten* merged into *boten*. Phonetic changes will thus cause a profound disturbance in the grammatical organism if they are not stopped by some barrier.

6   Principles of Historical Phonology

ROMAN JAKOBSON

It is understandable that at first the attention of phonologists was
concentrated principally on the primary concepts of the new discipline; on phonemes, their reciprocal relations and their distribution.
But as soon as these basic questions have been settled, one will have
to examine carefully phonological phenomena from the point of view of
space (that is, phonological geography) and from the point of view of
time (that is, historical phonology). Let us try to sketch, in a
preliminary essay, the fundamentals of historical phonology.[1]

I

In traditional historical phonology, it was characteristic to treat
phonetic changes in an isolated manner, without taking account of
the whole system that undergoes these modifications. This kind of
methodology went hand in hand with the world view that reigned at
that time; the creeping empiricism of the neogrammarians, which
viewed any system, and in particular the linguistic system, as a
mechanical whole (*Und-Verbindung*) and not at all as a formal unity
(*Gestalteinheit*), to use the terms of modern psychology.[2]

Phonology opposes to the isolating method of the neogrammarians an
integrating method. Every phonological fact is treated as a part of
the whole, which is related to other parts of higher levels. Thus
the first principle of historical phonology will be: *every modification must be treated as a function of the system of which it is a
part*. A phonological change can be understood only by elucidating
its role within the system of the language.

Once a phonological change has taken place, the following questions
must be asked: What exactly has been modified within the phonologi-

Originally published in German in *TCLP*, IV (Copenhagen, 1931). A
revised version appeared in the Appendices to N. S. Trubetzkoy's
Principes de Phonologie (Paris, 1949), translated by J. Cantineau.
The French version, on which the current translation by Alan R.
Keiler is based, was reprinted in Jakobson, *Selected Writings*, I
(Mouton, 1962), pp. 202-220.

cal system? Have certain phonological differences been lost, and if
so, which? Have new phonological differences been acquired, and
which? Or finally, if the inventory of phonological oppositions remains unchanged, has the structure of individual oppositions been
transformed? Or in other words, has the place of a specific opposition been changed, either in its reciprocal relations with other
oppositions, or in its differentiating ability? Every phonological
unit within a given system must be examined in its reciprocal relations with all other units of the system before and after the given
phonological change:

(Ex. 1) In White Russian t' changes to c' and similarly d' to ς'. If
we describe the change of t' to c', we must make clear first of all the
relations of the phoneme t' with the other phonemes of the system to
which it belonged, therefore with t, d, d', s, s', c, and so forth;
and secondly, the relations of the phoneme c' with the other phonemes
of the system in question, that is with the unchanged phonemes t, d,
s, s', c, and so forth, and with the newly created phoneme ς'.[3]

II

A phonological change need not necessarily involve a change in
function. It can simply augment the number and diversity of combinatory variants of a phoneme:

(Ex. 2) In many dialects of Russian ε changes to ρ (close e) before
a palatalized consonant.

(Ex. 3) The phoneme r is palatalized at the end of a word in certain Norwegian dialects.

Or on the contrary, one of the combinatory variants is generalized,
two variants combining into a single one:

(Ex. 4) In many southern dialects of Russian the unaccented a phoneme occurs as a before narrow accented vowels and as a mid-vowel
before open accented vowels. In a part of these dialects, the variant a was generalized later. The contemporary phonetic forms $m'ilá$,
$p'iták$, and so forth, attest to the fact that the phonetic form $vadá$
preceded the phonetic form $vadá$: the mid-vowel that appeared after
the palatalized consonant ended up by coalescing with the variant of
the phoneme i in the same position. A phonological mutation, therefore, took place here: the unaccented a phoneme was replaced in the
position indicated above by the unaccented i phoneme. Consequently,
the subsequent unification of the variants of the phoneme a could
not be extended to these cases.

(Ex. 5) In certain Slavic dialects, the voiced bilabial stop occurs
before a vowel as a labiodental v, and in all other positions, as
the bilabial w. But in the majority of Slavic dialects one of these
two variants (most often v) is found generalized.

Finally, the fundamental variant of a phoneme can be modified phonetically, the system of phonemes remaining identical and the relations between the given phoneme and all of the other phonemes unchanged: one must therefore consider such a change as extraphonological as well:

(Ex. 6) There are dialects of Russian which have an accented vocalic system with seven vowel phonemes. Certain of these dialects have the following system of accented vowels:

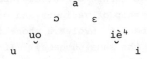

In the other dialects of the same type, instead of the close vowels uo, ie, one finds $o̦$, $e̦$, which seems a secondary phenomenon: $o̦$, $e̦$ have, in this system, the same place as uo, ie. Consequently, the replacement of one of the pairs of vowels by the other does not alter the phonological system.

III

In the case where a phonetic change is manifested in the phonological system, it can be regarded as the vehicle of a *phonological mutation* or a bundle of phonological mutations. We will use the term *mutation* in order to stress that phonological changes occur in leaps:

(Ex. 7) In Southern Russian unaccented o coalesces with a. Perhaps intermediate degrees existed: o was changed to a very open o and then to an a^o and finally into an a as it progressively lost its rounding. But from the phonological point of view, there are only two stages: 1. $o(o^a, a^o)$ is distinguished from a; and these are two different phonemes; 2. the implementation of o is no longer distinguished from a: the two phonemes have coalesced into one. There is no third alternative.

The formula for the phonological mutation is:

$$A : B > A_1 : B_1$$

One must distinguish two principal categories of mutations: one of the two relations (A : B or A_1 : B_1) is phonological or both of them are: A : B as well as A_1 : B_1 are different varieties of the same phonological relation. The first category is divided into two types: *the suppression of a phonological distinction can be called "dephonologization" (or "phonological devalorization") and the formation of a phonological distinction, "phonologization" (or "phonological valorization").* [5]

IV

Dephonologization: A and B are opposed phonologically, whereas there is no phonological difference between A_1 and B_1.

In analyzing dephonologization, one must ask the following questions: What is the nature of the phonological opposition A:B? Is it a disjunction or a correlation? If it is a correlation, does its loss represent one particular case of a more general process (that is, the loss of a correlation entirely), or does the correlation still exist? What is the nature of the extraphonological relation $A_1:B_1$? Is it a relationship of variants and of what kind: combinatory? stylistic? Or does it involve a phonetic identity (two exact realizations of one and the same phoneme)? If the relation $A_1:B_1$ is a relationship of extraphonological variants, A_1 is phonetically similar to A, and B_1 phonetically similar to B, and only the conditions by which each appears are changed. But if A_1 is phonetically similar to B_1, then either $A_1 \neq A$ and $B_1 \neq B$, that is, A and B have coalesced into a certain sound C which is distinguished phonetically both from A and B; or $A_1 \neq A$, but $B_1 = B$, that is, A > B. The classification of types of dephonologization must take into account the existing relationship between the phonemes before the mutation, of the relationship existing between the sounds as a result of the mutation, and the relationship that exists between each resulting sound and its prototype. Let us consider examples of dephonologization:

A disjunction results in a relationship of combinatory variants:

(Ex. 8) In some Russian dialects, two disjunct phonemes, unaccented *e* and unaccented *a*, change into combinatory variants of one and the same phoneme: after palatalized consonants, this phoneme is represented by *e*, after nonpalatalized consonants, by *a*. This dephonologization was accomplished in the following way: *a* became *e* after palatalized consonants (*p'atak p'eták, p'at'i p'et'i*), *e* became *a* after nonpalatalized consonants (*žen'ix žan'ix*).

A disjunction results in a relationship of combinatory stylistic variants:

(Ex. 9) The phonemes ʒ and *z* coalesced in the majority of Japanese dialects into one and the same phoneme: in initial position, after a nasal, this phoneme is realized by ʒ; between vowels in a careless style, by *z*; and in a more careful kind of speech by ʒ.[6]

A disjunction results in an identity (A > B):

(Ex. 10) Certain Polish dialects coalesced two series of consonants into a single series: (1) *š, ž, č, ǯ*; (2) *s, z, c, ʒ*: *š > s, ž > z, č > c, ǯ > ʒ*; therefore *š:s > s:s*, and so forth.

A disjunction results in identity (A > C, B > C):

(Ex. 11) In several northern and central Russian dialects, palatalized s' and z', as well as $š$ and $ž$, which had still not lost their palatalization coalesced into intermediate consonants, particularly the palatalized dorsals $ŝ$, $ẑ$.

A correlation results in a relation of combinatory variants (the correlation is suspended):

(Ex. 12) The pair $b:p$ and all of the other oppositions between voiced and voiceless stops lost in Chuvash their phonological character: between a voiced phoneme (that is, all the vowels and the voiced consonants) and a vowel, b and the other voiced consonants became generalized; in all other positions p and the other voiceless consonants were generalized.

A correlation results in an identity (the correlation is suspended: A > B):

(Ex. 13) In western Slovak, long $á$ coalesces with short a and all the other long vowels are similarly shortened: the correlation of vowel quantity was suspended.

(Ex. 14) In Common Slavic, aspirated consonants lose their aspiration and coalesce with the corresponding nonaspirate consonants.

A correlative pair results in an identity (the correlation is maintained A > B):

(Ex. 15) In some White Russian and Ukrainian dialects, the palatalized consonant r' became nonpalatalized r. The other pairs of consonants that make up the correlation of palatalization remained unchanged.

It is characteristic that in the suppression of correlations, it is ordinarily the marked correlative term that is suspended (see N.S. Trubetzkoy, *Die phonologischen Systeme*, p. 97): in example 13 the length of vowels, in example 14 the aspiration of consonants, in example 15 palatalized r'.

V

Phonologization: Between A and B there is no phonological difference, but between A_1 and B_1 such a difference exists. In analyzing phonologization, one must ask the following questions: Do A_1 and B_1 represent a disjunction or a correlation? If it is a correlation, then is the mutation under question only an enlargement of an already existing correlation, or is it part of a more general phenomenon— the formation of a new correlation? As far as the relation between A_1 and B_1 is concerned, Polivanov and van Ginneken consider the existence of extraphonological variants as an indispensable condition for phonologization. In effect, a relationship of identity between

A and B is apparently excluded. Consequently, from the phonetic point of view, $A_1 = A, B_1 = B$. Most often A and B are combinatory variants.

A combinatory variation results in a disjunction:

(Ex. 16) In Latvian k, g became c, $\check{z}$ before back vowels. The sounds k and c (or g and $\check{z}$) were combinatory variants of one and the same phoneme. After the passage of the diphthong ai to i in final syllables, k became possible in the same position where c appeared, that is k and c became disjunctive phonemes.[7]

A combinatory variation results in a correlation (a new correlation is formed):

(Ex. 17) In some Latvian dialects, dental consonants become palatalized before front vowels. These were combinatory variants of the dental phonemes, but since under certain conditions unaccented vowels disappeared, there was constituted a phonological opposition between the palatalized consonants that preceded them and the corresponding nonpalatalized consonants. Thus a correlation of consonantal palatalization was formed in these dialects.[8]

A combinatory variation results in a pair of correlative phonemes (the correlation already existed):

(Ex. 18) In Old Polabian, the phoneme χ was represented before certain vowels as a voiceless velar spirant χ, and before other vowels as a voiceless palatal spirant $\hat{\chi}$. These were two combinatory variants: they changed into two autonomous phonemes when the weak mid and low vowels coalesced, and there occurred a differentiation of words such as feminine $sau\underset{\wedge}{u}\chi a$—neuter $sau\hat{\chi}a$. The pair $\hat{\chi}$:χ was incorporated into the correlation of palatalization that already existed in Polabian.[9]

There are also examples of phonologization in which the relation A:B is one of stylistic variants. These variants can gradually become lexicalized. In other words, the affective variant of the phoneme can be solidified by words that are most often pronounced with an emotive nuance. These words form a particular stylistic level in the vocabulary of the language in question. Next the affective character gradually disappears in some of these words: the corresponding variant of the phoneme loses its emotional basis and is felt to be a specific phoneme:

(Ex. 19) Meillet points out the characteristic introduction of an expressive phenomenon in Latin—the gemination of consonants. Geminative consonants, which were foreign to the intellectual vocabulary of Indo-European, represent a common phenomenon in words that carry an affective nuance. They were solidified by these words; and when they had lost their sentimental value and were neutralized, the geminative consonants were conserved as specific phonemes.[10]

Similar examples where an emotive variant of a phoneme is transformed into an independent phoneme are relatively rare, but another
series of phenomena extensively utilized is related to it. When a
language borrows foreign words, it accommodates them to some extent
to its own system of phonemes, and partially retains the phonemes of
the foreign language. Words containing such phonemes are still felt
as foreign words, that is, belonging to a particular stylistic level.
But these words occasionally begin to enter the general vocabulary,
and the language thus becomes enriched with new phonemes whose foreign character is no longer felt. Foreign phonemes that the language
appropriates for itself most easily are those that become incorporated into already existing correlations.

(Ex. 20) Russian, like the other Slavic languages, borrowed a considerable number of foreign words containing the phoneme f. In those
cases where there was a tendency to completely Russify the borrowed
word having an f, this phoneme was replaced by xv, x or p. F was an
indication of the foreign character of a word, and sometimes it was
introduced into borrowed words where it had no place, for example,
kufárka instead of *kuxárka* 'cook', and so forth. But gradually a
portion of the words that retained f were assimilated to native
Russian words (*fonár'*, *lif*, *fîlin*, *Fêdja*, and so forth), and the
fundamental Russian archiphoneme $\boxed{v, v'}$ was enriched by two new
phonemes: $\boxed{\begin{array}{l} v, v' \\ f, f' \end{array}}$

VI

Alongside dephonologization and phonologization there exists still
another group of phonological mutations, that is, rephonologization
(or phonological revalorization): the transformation of a phonological distinction into a heterogeneous phonological distinction with
a different relation to the phonological system from the first. A
and B as well as A_1 and B_1 are opposed phonologically, but the phonological structure of these oppositions is different. In this re-
organization of the phonological structure resides the principal
difference between rephonologization and the cases cited above the
extraphonological sound changes (Ex. 5, 6).

There are three types of rephonologization: (I) The transformation
of a pair of correlative phonemes into a disjunctive pair; (II) the
transformation of a disjunction into a correlation; and (III) the
transformation of a pair belonging to a correlation into a pair belonging to another correlation. One must always consider whether
it is a question of (*a*) the outcome of a single pair of correlative
phonemes or (*b*) the correlation itself.

I *a*. A pair of correlative phonemes results in a disjunction (the correlation is maintained):

(Ex. 21) In Old Polish, palatalized *r'* became *ř*. The other pairs of the correlation of palatalization were conserved.

(Ex. 22) In the southern areas of the Slavic languages of the northwest and east, *g* became a spirant γ with the same point of articulation, and its relation with *k*, which was part of a correlation, became part of a disjunction.

I *b*. A pair of correlative phonemes results in a disjunction (the correlation is suspended):

(Ex. 23) In Italic, *bh* became *f*, and similarly each one of the other aspirated stops changed into a simple fricative, but all of these resulting phonemes coalesced to *f*, except *x*, which ended up as *h*.

(Ex. 24) In Old Czech, the correlation of consonantal palatalization was suspended. The palatalized sounds *s'*, *z'* lost their palatalization. The same thing happened in certain conditions to palatalized labials, which in other conditions were changed to the groups "nonpalatalized labial + j". The oppositions between the phonemes *t*, *d*, *n* and the corresponding palatalized phonemes were rephonologicized: these oppositions of correlative phonemes change into disjunctive localized differences between apical and palatal consonants (compare R. Jakobson, *Über die phonologischen Sprachbünde, TCLP, IV*).

II *a*. A disjunction results in a pair of correlative phonemes (the correlation already existed previously):

(Ex. 25) The Indo-European palatal *ĝ* ends up in Old Slavic as *z*, that is, it becomes the corresponding voiced sound of the phoneme *s*.

(Ex. 26) The change of *g* to γ, which is peculiar to a part of the Slavic languages (compare Ex. 22), furnished a voiced opposition for the phoneme *x*, which was disjunct with respect to *g*.

I know of no examples of the creation of a new correlation by a rephonologization of a disjunct pair (II *b*), nor of cases in which a pair of correlative phonemes becomes separated from an existing correlation and is joined to another correlation, that is, modifies its differentiating mark (III *a*).

III *b*. A correlation changes to another correlation. These kinds of mutations are of many different varieties.

(Ex. 27) According to the description of Meillet, a whole bundle of rephonologizations modified the consonantal correlations of Armenian.[11] The Indo-European opposition between voiced aspirated consonants and nonaspirated consonants ended up as an opposition between voiced and voiceless sounds, voiced aspirates ending up as

simple voiced sounds and the old simple voiced sounds as voiceless
ones. The Indo-European opposition between simple voiceless sounds
and aspirated sounds was replaced by a distinction of tense and lax
aspirated voiceless sounds: the tense aspirated voiceless sounds
coming from aspirated voiceless ones, the lax aspirated voiceless
sounds coming from simple voiceless sounds. It is characteristic
that the marked series of the correlation of aspirated consonants
has been replaced by a marked series of new correlations, (voiced
and tense consonants).

(Ex. 28) Certain Polish dialects replace the opposition of the
vowel a and $\overset{\circ}{a}$ by the opposition $\ddot{a}$ and a.[12] This modification of a
single pair of correlative phonemes attests to a change in the
differentiating particularity of an entire correlation: in the first
case, there exists the correlation of rounded and unrounded vowels,
in the second case a correlation of front and back vowels (compare
R. Jakobson, *Über die phonologischen Bünde, TCLP,* IV). All the
other oppositions of the correlation are capable of two interpretations: e-o, ρ-ρ, i-u. In these pairs one of the terms is opposed
phonologically to the other as a nonrounded vowel to a rounded
vowel, and at the same time as a front vowel to a back vowel.[13]

One must separate from the rephonologizations that we have just
discussed cases of the fusion of two existing correlations, that is,
cases where all of the existing pairs of a correlation end up by
coinciding with the existing pairs of another correlation, which is
a kind of dephonologization:

(Ex. 29) In Proto-Czech the opposition between long vowels with
rising pitch and long vowels with falling pitch is transformed into
an opposition between long and short vowels. Vowels with falling
pitch have been identified with short vowels (dephonologization).
It is characteristic that the unmarked series of the pitch correlation coincided with the equally unmarked series of the quantitative
correlation.

VII

*There are sound changes that modify not the inventory of phonemes
of a language but only its inventory of groups of phonemes.* As the
phonological structure of a language is characterized not only by
the repertory of phonemes, but also by the repertory of groups of
phonemes, a phonetic change that modifies admissible groups of
phonemes in a given language constitutes a phonological fact in the
same way as modifications of the inventory of phonemes. There are
two different kinds of these phonological mutations:

(Ex. 30) In several Russian dialects, the group "$\acute{e}$ + palatalized
consonant" was transformed into the group "$\acute{i}$ + palatalized conson-

ant". In this way, the relation between the above stated group and the old group "i + palatalized consonant" is dephonologized; the relation between the old group "$é$ + palatalized consonant" and, for example, "$ó$ + palatalized consonant" is rephonologized and the relation between the two combinatory variants of the phoneme $é$ (a close vowel before palatalized consonants and an open vowel in other positions) is phonologized. The repertory of phonemes is not modified, but a combination of phonemes has been lost in the language.

If the mutations of groups of phonemes do not by themselves modify the system of phonemes, they become evident, on the other hand, in the functioning of phonemes. The frequency of use of different phonemes is changed and eventually also the degree of their functional load.

(Ex. 31) The mutation considered in Ex. 30 represents an increase in the frequency of the phoneme i and a corresponding decrease in the frequency of the phoneme $é$. The functional load of the phonological difference $é$-i becomes less, because these phonemes could at one time be opposed to each other independently of what followed them. After this mutation, however, they can occur only when no palatalized consonant follows them. But $é$ appears in this position very rarely: $é$ has become $ó$ before nonpalatalized consonants, whereas in final position $é$ gave in some cases o, in some cases $á$; $é$, when not followed by a palatalized consonant, does not appear in these dialects except as the end result of the diphthong ie ("jat") .

It would be a dangerous simplification to overestimate the role of the statistical factor in language evolution, but we must not forget either that the dialectical law of the passage from quantity to quality is also important. The low frequency and the weak functional load of a phonological difference naturally favors its loss:

(Ex. 32) In the Serbian dialect reflected in the grammar of Brlić, the opposition of the two kinds of accent on a short syllable is only possible in an initial syllable after pause (compare R. Jakobson, *Die Betonung und ihre Rolle in der Wort- und Syntagmaphonologie TCLP*, IV). The limited use of this opposition was undoubtedly partly responsible for its suppression. As soon as such a suppression took place, it served to set in motion a whole accentual evolution in many Serbian dialects.

VIII

All of the cases of phonological mutations that we have examined are characterized by a common factor: All the terms of these mutations are equal with respect to their phonological character. If A and B are phonemes, A_1 and B_1 are also; if A and B are groups of phonemes, A_1 and B_1 are groups of phonemes to the same extent. But

it is not of the least importance from the point of view of historical phonology that there exist mutations in which the resultant A₁
is not similar, as far as its phonological character is concerned,
to its prototype A.

I. *A phoneme splits into a group of phonemes.* Consequently the
distinction between two phonemes changes into a distinction between
a group of phonemes and a phoneme (rephonologization):

(Ex. 33) The long phoneme *ie̯* (= long "jaťˮ) changes, in a part of
the Serbo-Croatian dialects, into a dissyllabic group of two phonemes
i + e. In the place of the disjunction *i̯e—i*, and so forth, there
appears an opposition between the group of phonemes "*i + e*" and the
phoneme *i*, and so forth.

(Ex. 34) In Ukrainian the palatalized labials change before *á* into
the groups "labial + *j*"; *p':p* (a pair of correlative phonemes) becomes
pj:p (relation between a group of phonemes and a phoneme); *p':j* (disjunction) becomes *pj:j*.

The difference between·a phoneme and a group of phonemes can change
into an identity of two groups of phonemes (dephonologization):

(Ex. 35) In Ukrainian the group *pj* which comes from *p'* (compare
Ex. 34) coincided with the old group "*p + j*". One should compare,
for example, *pjat'* (from *p'at'*) and *pjanyj* (with old *pj*).

A transformation can occur from a combinatory variation into a significant difference between a group of phonemes and a phoneme (phonologization):

(Ex. 36) *p'* before *i* and *p'* before *a* (compare Ex. 34) in Ukrainian
were originally combinatory variants of one and the same phoneme *p'*
(the degree of palatalization was different according to the following vowel). With the change of *p'* before *a* to *pj*, the relation
between the two variants becomes phonological.

II. *A group of phonemes is transformed into a phoneme.* There are
two possibilities:

(a) The result of the transformation produces a phoneme that already existed in the system:

(Ex. 37) In the Slavic languages of the east and southwest, the
group *dl* changed to *l*. This result is identical to one of the phonemes of the original group. On the one hand, there is here a dephonologization, that is, *dl:l* becomes *l:l*, and on the other hand a
rephonologization, that is, *dl:n* becomes *l:n*, and so forth.

(Ex. 38) In Latin the group *dw* became *b* initially. The result is
not identical to any of the phonemes of the original group. The
relation of *dw* to *b* is dephonologized, and its relation with the
other phonemes is rephonologized.

(b) The result of the transformation constitutes a phoneme that was until then unknown in the system:

(Ex. 39) In Serbo-Croatian the groups *tj*, *dj* became *ć*, *đ* (palatal stops). This process characterizes a rephonologization of the relation between *tj*, *dj*, and all the other phonemes existing in the language.

(Ex. 40) In Kirghiz, after the merging of the old long and short vowels, new long vowels appeared as a result of a contraction of groups of phonemes: in *ēr* 'addle' (distinct from *er* 'man') compare Uzbek *egær* 'saddle'; or, for example, Kirghiz *tō* 'mountain' from *taw* coming from $*t^a\chi$.[14] These contractions produced in this case a new correlation of phonemes.

(Ex. 41) The transformation in French of the group of phonemes "vowel + *n*" into nasal vowels introduced a correlation of nasality for the vowels into the phonological system.

(Ex. 42) In certain Chinese dialects a transformation of the groups "vowel + stop" into vowels with glottal stop (according to the Chinese terminology: the fifth tone of the vowels) produced a new prosodic correlation.

The numerous mutations of the type *dl* becoming *l* (compare Ex. 37) represent a reduction of a group of phonemes to a single phoneme. The transformation of a phoneme to zero can be limited to specific groups of phonemes, but it can also be more general. This is a particular case of the same type of mutation.

(Ex. 43) Certain Serbo-Croatian dialects lose the laryngeal phoneme *h* (from Old Slavic *x*). It disappears in all positions. This is a particular case of the tendency that is manifested in these dialects to divide all of the fricatives into pairs of voiced and voiceless ones.

The inverse phenomenon evidently does not exist, that is, a phonetic zero cannot under any circumstances change into a phoneme.

IX

When one discovers the existence of a great many mutations that occurred at the same time, one must analyze the entire bundle of these mutations as a whole. The connection existing among these mutations is not due to chance: they are intimately tied together. The laws that preside among their reciprocal relations must be clarified. One of these laws, very fruitful for the elaboration of the principles of historical phonology, was established by Polivanov: phonologizations "never occur without being accompanied by another innovation"; "in an overwhelming number of cases a divergence (= phonologization) is accompanied by some conversion (= dephonologization) and is found to be dictated by it".[15] Here it is a question of the phonologization of combinatory variants, and in a sense the law is indeed without exception. Such a combination of phonologization and dephonologization must be considered, from the point of view of the mutations of groups of phonemes, as a rephonologization. A difference is replaced by another difference, and this complex of mutations is only distinguished from rephonologization in a single way: in the rephonologization of phonemes, the implementations of the phonological opposition remain the representatives of the same phonemes that before the mutation were opposed phonologically. On the other hand, in the "rephonologization of groups of phonemes" the differentiating aspect of the groups of phonemes remain, but the differentiating function passes from certain phonemes to others, for example, to the neighboring phonemes of the same groups of phonemes:

(Ex. 44) In certain Chinese dialects, the voiced and voiceless consonants merge. The voicing correlation of consonants is replaced by a correlation of pitch of the following vowels: low tone of the vowel is substituted for the voiced feature of the preceding consonant; rising pitch corresponds on the contrary to the voiceless character of the consonant in question.[16] The difference in pitch, at first a combinatory variation, became a correlative property.

(Ex. 45) In the Ukrainian dialects of the northwest, from which is descended the dialect of the parish of Kornicy of the old government of Sedlec,[17] the phoneme $\acute{a}$ occurred after palatalized consonants as a diphthong ia (a combinatory variant). The subsequent palatalization of r rendered the opposition ia-$\acute{a}$ phonological after r, and consequently ia becomes an independent phoneme. The scheme of this mutation would be in phonological transcription:

$$r'\acute{a}{:}r\acute{a} \; > \; ri\underline{a}{:}r\acute{a} \quad [18]$$

X

Contrary to the phonologization of combinatory variants, the phonologization of stylistic variants is not tied to a dephonologization (see Exs. 19,20). In other words, *there do not exist, in the framework of a system belonging to a single style of language, phonologizations that are not compensated for by dephonologizations*. The tendency to multiply phonological differences is foreign to a "specific functional dialect"; such an isolated phonologization is possible only as a result of the reciprocal reaction of two different functional dialects (of two styles of language). The phonologization of a phonemic difference is here compensated for by the loss of its stylistic value. A *permutation of functions* takes place in this case.

As far as I can see, dephonologization is also based on a permutation of functions, particularly in those cases where dephonologization is not tied to any other mutation. Dephonologization can be a generalization of a phenomenon that originally constituted a specific peculiarity of a style of a particular language, for example, careless and hasty discourse. A phenomenon that signals a specific style of language, an oratorical nuance that is particularly emotional, can then be transported into a style of speaking that does not include this nuance, and be thus transformed into a kind of linguistic norm:

(Ex. 46) As the Russian grammarians of the eighteenth century attest, the educated classes of Moscow still conserved in their speech the diphthong *i̯e* ("jat́ ") as a specific phoneme, but in careless and hurried discourse it was already becoming merged with *ê*. Dialectologists observe a similar phenomenon: a removal of the differences between *i̯e* and *ê*, *u̯o* and *ô* into "allegro" kinds of speech in the Russian dialects that conserve in principle the differences between these phonemes.[19] This is the first stage in the loss of a differentiation; the second stage would be the displacement of relations between the careless style and careful style of speech.

(Ex. 47) The confusion of unstressed *e* and unstressed *i*, which I was witness to in the dialect of Moscow, was realized at first only in deliberate and careless discourse. The difference between the two phonemes was still felt as normal, but the following generation generalized the "allegro" style of unaccented vocalism as a linguistic norm.[20]

If one puts aside reciprocal relations of different styles of language, one notices that the tendency not only of multiplication, but also of diminution of phonological differences, is foreign to languages. *Within the framework of an isolated functional dialect, one cannot speak either of an increase or a reduction of a phonological system, but only of a restructuring, that is, of its rephonologization.*

XI

We have already indicated that it is only by means of an "integrating method" that it is possible to describe a phonological change. One must investigate what the phonological differences are, which ones have undergone the modification, what differences remain unchanged, and in what manner the functional load and utilization of all these phonemes were changed. In addition, one must consider the sound change in terms of relationships to the sound systems of different functions. But the description of mutations does not yet exhaust historical phonology. We still have the task of interpreting these mutations.

A description furnishes the data concerning two linguistic situations, the period before and after the change, and allows us to

investigate the direction and meaning of this change. As soon as
this question is posed, we pass from the terrain of diachrony to that
of synchrony. A mutation can be the object of a synchronic investigation in the same way as invariable linguistic elements are. It
would be a grave fault to consider static and synchrony as synonymous. The static viewpoint is a fiction: it is only a scientific
procedure to help us; it is not a particular aspect of the way things
are. We can consider the perception of a film not only diachronically, but also synchronically: the synchronic aspect of a film is not
identical with an isolated image extracted from a filmstrip. The
perception of movement is already present in the synchronic aspect.
The same is true for language. The work of Ferd. de Saussure spares
us from having to prove that a consideration of language from the
point of view of synchrony is a teleological mode of understanding.
*When we consider a linguistic mutation within the context of lin-
guistic synchrony, we bring it into the sphere of teleological problems.* It follows necessarily that the problem of finality can be
applied to a chain of successive mutations, that is, to diachronic
linguistics. It is, in effect, the logical end result of the work
of the neogrammarians, begun several decades ago, at least in the
sense that they made the first effort to emancipate linguistics from
the methodology of the natural sciences, which reigned at their time,
and in particular from the quasi-Darwinistic clichés propagated by
Schleicher and his disciples.

If a rupture in the equilibrium of a system precedes a given
mutation, and if a suppression of disequilibrium results from this
mutation, we have no trouble in discovering the function of this
mutation: its task is to reestablish the equilibrium. However,
when a mutation reestablishes the equilibrium in one point of the
system, it can disturb the equilibrium at other points and consequently provoke the necessity for a new mutation. In this way, a
whole series of stabilizing mutations is often produced.

(Ex. 48) The loss of the reduced vowels (weak "jers") in the
Slavic languages brought about a correlation of palatalization for
consonants. All of the Slavic languages have a tendency to dis-
associate the palatalization correlation of consonants from the
pitch correlation of vowels by suppressing one of the two oppositions. The Slavic languages that have suppressed the pitch correlation (that is, the opposition of rising and falling pitch) in favor
of a correlation of palatalization have been spared having to give
up either the autonomous differences of vocalic quantity or a free
accent, since these two correlations are ordinarily incompatible in
a language that does not have a pitch correlation. Certain Slavic
languages have taken the first alternative; others, the second.[21]

But it would be a mistake to limit the spirit of each phonological mutation to the reestablishment of equilibrium. If the phonological system of a learned language normally tends toward equilibrium, the rupture of the equilibrium, on the contrary, forms a constitutive element of the emotional and poetic language. This is why a static phonological description sins the least amount against reality in those cases where the object of this description is a system of learned language.

The expressive capacity of affective discourse is obtained by means of a great exploitation of extraphonological phonetic differences existing in the language in question, but for the highest degree of affectivity, discourse has need of more efficacious procedures and does not stop even before the deformation of the phonological structure: for example, different phonemes merge, phonemes whose articulation is modified with a view toward overcoming the automatism of indifferent discourse; or emphasis goes as far as a violation of existing prosodic correlations; or finally, certain phonemes are "swallowed up" because of the acceleration of tempo. This is all given favor by the fact that in affective language, information gives way to emotivity, and hence the phonological value of certain phonological differences becomes attenuated. Similarly, the poetic function forces the language to overcome the automatism and imperceptibility of the word—and this also goes as far as displacements in the phonological structure.

(Ex. 49) B. Miletić notes that in Štokavian, under the influence of emphasis, "falling" pitch of short vowels changes into a "rising" pitch.[22]

(Ex. 50) Sometimes the loss of phonological differences serves to satisfy aesthetic needs: for example, the Russian dialect of Kolyma is characterized by a tendency to replace the phonemes r, l and in particular palatalized r', l' by the phoneme j. This pronunciation is designated there by the term *sladkoglasie* 'honeyed speech'; and according to one investigator, the majority of the population can easily articulate, without any difficulty, palatalized r', l' and so forth but think that such a pronunciation is ugly.[23]

The different functions of language are intimately bound up with each other, and the permutation of functions is permanent. The spirit of equilibrium and simultaneous tendency toward its rupture constitute the indispensible properties of that whole that is language.

The joining together of the static and the dynamic is one of the most fundamental dialectic paradoxes that determine the spirit of language. One cannot conceive of the dialectic of linguistic development without referring to this antinomy. Attempts to identify

synchrony, static, and the domain of application of *teleology* on the
one hand and, on the other, *diachrony, dynamic,* and the sphere of
mechanical causality illegitimately narrow down the frame of synchrony, make of historical linguistics a conglomerate of disparate
facts, and create the superficial and harmful illusion of an abyss
between the problems of synchrony and diachrony.

Notes

[1]The way in which historical phonology was born will not be
examined here.

[2]Compare, for example, K. Koffka, *Psychologie. Die Philosophie in
ihren Einzelgebieten* (Berlin, 1925), pp. 531 ff: "The condition under
which one can understand an identity, and in general a relation, is
for two terms to be not simply juxtaposed, but entering as parties
into a form. As they were formerly isolated with respect to each
other, they are now tied to each other and can reciprocally influence
each other."

[3]In order to interpret phonologically a sound change, it is necessary to know in an exact way the phonological system of the given
language and also its evolution. This is why I draw most of my
examples from the history of the Slavic languages, because their
phonological evolution is particularly well-known to me.

[4]*u͈ǫ* comes from *o* with rising pitch, *i͈ę* from the Proto-Slavic diphthong *ě* ("*jat´*").

[5]
I find the terms "phonologization" and "dephonologization" more
appropriate than the terms "divergence" and "convergence" that E.
Polivanov used in his noteworthy studies on dephonologization ("Iz
teorii fonetičnogo Instituta v čest' prof. A. E. Šmidta," Taškent,
1923, pp. 106-115, and "Faktory fonetičeskoj èvoljucii jazyka, kak
trudovogo processa," *Učenye zapiski Instituta jazyka, literatury,
III,* pp. 20-42), because in scientific language the latter are
usually bound up with another meaning. Thus in biology, convergence
is used to describe the acquisition of similar traits by different
organisms, without bothering to find out whether it is a question of
related or nonrelated organisms (cf. e.g. L. Berg, *Nomogenez,* Pb.,
1922, chap. 18). Similarly in linguistics one designates by the
term convergence similar phenomena in the independent development of
different languages (cf. Meillet, "Convergence des développements
linguistiques", *Linguistique historique et linguistique générale,*
Paris, 1921, pp. 61 ff).

[6]
Polivanov, "Faktory . . . ", p. 35.

[7]See J. Endzelin, *Lettische Grammatik* (Heidelberg, 1923), p. 89.

[8]See Endzelin, p. 90.

[9]N. Trubetzkoy, *Polabische Studien* (Wien, 1929), pp. 91 ff., 38 ff.
123.

[10]*Esquisse d'une histoire de la langue latine* (Paris, 1928), pp.
166 ff.

[11]See A. Meillet, *Esquisse d'une grammaire comparée de l'arménien
classique* (Vienna, 1903), pp. 7 ff., and *Les dialectes indo-européens*
(Paris, 1922), chaps. X, XI, XIII.

[12]See K. Nitsch, "Dyalekty jezyka polskiego", *Encyklopedya Polska,
III,* Dzial III, Cześć II, p. 264.

[13] This example is equally instructive from another point of view, e.g., the pair i-u remained unchanged (A_1 = A, B_1 = B), and the conditions under which the two phonemes exist are not changed. Nevertheless, the replacement of the pair a-$\overset{\circ}{a}$ by the pair $\ddot{a}$-a suffices to bring about, because of the structural laws of the system, a rephonologization of all of the other pairs.

[14] Polivanov, *Vvedenie v jazykoznanie* (Leningrad, 1928), p. 196.

[15] "Faktory. . .", p. 38.

[16] See B. Karlgren, *Études sur la phonologie chinoise* (Stockholm, 1915), chaps. 14, 16.

[17] See N. Jančuk, "Kornickij govor b. Konstantinovskogo uezda Sedleckoj gub." *Trudy post. komissii po dialektologii russkogo jazyka* IX, pp. 13 ff.

[18] See also examples 16-18, which are typical cases of the rephonologization of phonemes. It is thus that in example 16 the relation i:ai is dephonologized, in example 17 ti:t # > t' #: t #, etc. (# = phonological zero).

[19] See N. Durnovo, *Dialektologičeskie razyskanija v oblasti velikorusskix govorov*, I, 2e liv. (1918), pp. 53ff.

[20] In *Remarques sur l'évolution du russe* (Prague, 1929, pp. 48ff.) I interpret the fall of the weak semivowels of Slavic as a generalization of the careless style of speech.

[21] I described this cycle of phenomena more thoroughly in *Remarques sur l'évolution phonologique du russe*, *TCLP*, II (Prague, 1929).

[22] *O srbo-chrvatských intonacich v nářeči štokavském* (Prague, 1926), pp. 13-14, 20.

[23] V. Bogorz, "Oblastonoj slovar' kolymskogo russkogo narečija", *Sb. otd. rus. jaz. slov. IAN*, XVIII (4), p. 7.

7   Function, Structure, and Sound Change

ANDRÉ MARTINET

I. *Introduction*

Today, just as twenty years ago, many linguists would be tempted to
agree unreservedly with Leonard Bloomfield that "the causes of sound
change are unknown".[1] Not a few would infer from this statement
that any research aimed at determining such causes is inevitably
doomed to failure. Scholars who regard linguistics, primarily and
even exclusively, as a descriptive discipline both on the synchronic
plane and in evolutionary matters will most naturally be tempted to
favor these views since they afford a justification for their reluc-
tance to go beyond mere statements of directly observable facts,
such as "English *p* and *b* are distinct phonemes" or French *u* ([ü])
corresponds to Latin *ū*". The modern followers of the neogrammarians
who are ready to reckon with mutual influence in the spoken chain,
but who ignore and would deny the fact that the nature of a given
phoneme depends on that of its neighbors in the pattern will find
themselves in agreement with those phonemicists who conceive of
"structure" as resulting from combinatory latitudes of distinctive
units in the chain rather than as based upon the latter's partial
phonic identities and differences. Whoever sees in a phonemic
pattern nothing but a convenient way of summarizing the behavior of
segments in the utterance is hardly prepared to conceive of it as a
dynamic reality. The componential analysis of phonemes, which is
the first step toward the setting up of a pattern based upon phonic
identities and differences, is still often looked upon as an amusing
but impractical refinement of more traditional methods, and its wide
implications are rarely perceived. Yet it is felt by an increasing
number of structurally minded linguists[2] that it paves the way toward
a better understanding of phonetic evolution.

From *Word* 8 (1952), 1-32. Reprinted by permission of André Martinet and the Johnson Reprint Corporation.

What would seem to prevent a general acceptance of diachronic phonemics as a legitimate discipline is not only the wide-spread feeling that linguistics would jeopardize its hard-won scientific character by venturing beyond the limits of pure description, but also an
irrational conviction that there should be one and only one answer
to the question: Why do sounds change? and that a principle of explanation which can be shown not to account *in toto* for any change
chosen at random is *ipso facto* to be rejected as invalid. This conviction is so ingrained that, in the case of conditioned sound
changes, some linguists would probably reject the view that well-
known conditioning factors afford a partial answer to the question.
In Old English, intervocalic *s* as in *ćéosan* is found to have been
shifted to [z] whereas *s* has been preserved as [s] elsewhere. We
know for sure that intervocalic position was instrumental in the
change. But, of course, intervocalic position was not enough, since
Old Icelandic has preserved a voiceless *s* in *kjósa*, and hundreds of
easily accessible languages show no sign of voicing their intervocalic sibilants. The unknown reason, or reasons, which let Old
English *s* become a prey to its vocalic environment are, in the
opinion of some, the only elements of the case that deserve the name
of "cause." And yet, can we not imagine that the voicing in question
may have resulted from a concurrence of phonetic circumstances, one
of which (intervocalic position) we know, and the others (nature of
the accent or various other prosodic features) we are not well
enough informed to recognize? All of these would be of a similar
nature, and if we should have to distinguish among them, the distinctions would not be made because they are of intrinsically different nature, but exclusively on the basis of what we happen to
know about the one or the others. It is methodologically unsound to
assume anything about the importance or lack of importance of un-
identified factors. Above all we have no right to postulate that
these should all be of one and the same type, and that, short of the
identification of some sort of ever present *deus ex machina*, any
theory of the causes of sound change has to be resolutely brushed
aside. Bloomfield's sweeping statement that the causes of sound
change are unknown should be replaced by the one that some of the
causes are still either unknown or difficult to identify or to
verify. This could by no means be interpreted as an invitation to
restrict linguistic activities to descriptive practices, but on the
contrary might incite the reader to investigate the possibilities
of reducing the domain of the unknown.

So far external factors of sound change, among which interdialectal
and interlinguistic influences stand in the foreground, have been
the object of much theorizing but of little factual observation.

Among internal factors only those that can be found in the spoken chain and account for allophonic differences, have been submitted by phoneticians to a more or less exhaustive examination. It remains to investigate to what extent the coexistence in the pattern of a number of phonemic units can account for their synchronic nature and diachronic comportment. We know that an [s], when placed in a given context in the utterance, may develop in a certain way. We have to determine what we can expect from /s/ when placed in the frame of a given pattern.

The problem of the causes of sound change would remain one of the central problems of linguistic science even if we should refuse to consider linguistics as an historical discipline, because we shall not fully know what language is and how it works before we have determined why languages change. No one would maintain that morphology, syntax, and lexicon change irrespective of the communicative needs of the speakers. It remains to be seen whether this is true or not of phonology. If it can be shown that phonetic evolution is not as "blind" as some of our predecessors meant it to be, we shall be able to discover not all but some of the so-far unknown factors of phonological evolution.

We shall, in what follows, center our attention on "regular" sound changes, the type whereby all the performances of a given phoneme, everywhere or in a well defined context, are eventually affected. There are sporadic sound changes of many kinds, some of which may be due to causes similar to those which may be adduced or supposed for "regular" changes. But it is felt that the consideration of sporadic changes would needlessly complicate our research. It should further be stressed once more that we are ultimately concerned here with the behavior of speakers keeping distinct or merging various phonemes of a pattern and not at all with what has normally been so far the practically exclusive preoccupation of historical phoneticians, namely the mutual influencing of successive phonemes in the spoken chain. In phonemic terms, our predecessors were intent upon accounting for the appearance of combinatory variants or allophones. By now, it should be a well established fact that one and the same phoneme when appearing in different contexts may be submitted to divergent treatments, and this should need no further emphasizing. In the frame of the present exposition, it is completely immaterial whether a change affects a phoneme in all contexts or only in phonemically well defined ones, whether what is eventually merged or kept distinct is two phonemes or two combinatory variants of different phonemes. We know that combinatory factors of sound change play a considerable role, but if we want to be able to identify functional and structural factors, we have to concentrate upon them and keep the former out of our

field of vision as far as this is practicable. In order to simplify
the exposition, it is therefore advisable not to stress at every
turn the existence of allophonic deviations, and to establish the
following convention: unless otherwise stated, what will be said of
phonemes applies equally to those allophones whose phonic evolution
happens to be deviating. In theoretical discussions, it will look
as if we were always operating with phonemes whose unity is never
endangered. But illustrations will show that allophones are also
involved. Allophones will usually be presented in the form of a
cluster of phonemes: the front allophones of a /k/ will appear as
/ki/, /ke/, or both /ki/ and /ke/. In other words we no longer deal
with a single phoneme /k/ but the phoneme clusters /ki/, /ke/. In
view of the fact that phoneme clusters often coalesce into single
phonemes in the course of phonological evolution and would seem frequently to exert an influence upon the pattern behavior of single
phonemes, the use of clusters instead of allophones will actually
result in a simplification. We can accordingly reword what we said
about our statements applying to allophones as well as to phonemes:
unless otherwise stated, what we say about phonemes applies to
larger phonemic units as well.

II *Function*

It is an obvious fact that the pronunciation of a given phoneme in
one and the same word by a given speaker varies from one utterance
to another. The variation is normally imperceptible, but strictly
speaking, no two pronunciations can be exactly alike. Under certain
conditions the variation may be more considerable. In any case, we
have to reckon with a range of possible dispersion even in the speech
of one person and still more so probably if we consider all the
speakers of a given community. The existence of such a range of
dispersion is of course obvious if we consider a phoneme with important allophonic variations, i.e. a phonemic unit whose actual
performances are largely dependent on the context as is the case for
instance with English /k/ whose range of dispersion covers a large
part of the palato-velar area, or with Russian /a/ which varies,
depending on context, from [æ] to [a]. But what is stressed here
is not the dispersion resulting from combinatory variation, but that
which may affect a phoneme in a well characterized context.

Some scholars have been tempted to interpret de Saussure's statement that a linguistic "value" is everything that the other "values"
of the same system are not[3] in the sense that this range of dispersion of every phoneme is limited only by those of other phonemes.
This is certainly not universally true. It is probably meaningless
to try to imagine whether [ɸeil] would, by English speakers, be in-

terpreted as *pale* or as *fail*, because [φ] is a normal rendering of
neither /p/ nor /f/, and if, under most unusual circumstances, any
one said [φeil], the interpretation as *pale*, *pail*, or *fail* would depend
on the context. In the frame of a homogeneous speech community
it is probable that the normal range of dispersion of every phoneme
in a given context will not be contiguous to those of its neighbors,
but that there will be a margin of security in the form of a sort of
no man's land. We speak here of "normal" range because it is a well
known fact that, under unusual circumstances such as severe intoxi-
cation, neighboring phonemes of the pattern may be completely merged.
It is then clear that the minor evil consisting in an impingement
upon the margin of security must also occur in "abnormal" circumstances. Abnormal circumstances of the kind considered here are not
likely to affect the articulation of a single phoneme only, but that
of most, if not all, of the phonemes of the pattern, and this in itself will be a perceptible mark of their abnormality. Hearers will
unconsciously make allowances for it, discount deviations, or rely
more heavily on context and situation in their interpretation of
what they hear. Among "abnormal" circumstances we might also include
the cases where the language is spoken by a foreigner who has not
achieved a complete mastery of the phonetics of the language. Here
again allowances will be made.

For a full understanding of what will follow, one should remember
that, on all occasions, it is far easier for man not to be than to
be accurate; as Jerspersen puts it[4] "it requires less effort to chip
wood than to operate for cataract;" the main difficulty for children
in learning to speak, or to write or to draw, for that matter, is
not to produce sounds, bars, or curves, but to hit upon the right
sound, bar, or curve asked for at a given instant by the necessities
of communication. This applies to adults' phonemes as well. For
each one of them, in a given context at least, there must be an
optimum which we might call the center of gravity of every range of
dispersion, but actual performances will normally fall somewhat off
the mark. In the normal practice of speech, some of them are even
likely to fall very far off it. If too dangerously near the center
of gravity of some other phoneme, they may be corrected, and, in any
case, will not be imitated. If unusually aberrant, slightly beyond
the normal range of dispersion, but not in a direction where misunderstanding might arise, they would in no way threaten to impair
mutual understanding. If not, in themselves, imposing any strain
on the organs, they might well end up as establishing a legitimate
extension of the acceptable range.

We shall reckon with a sound shift as soon as the normal range of
a phoneme (in a given context—from now on this shall be understood)

is being ever so little displaced in one direction or another, whereby the margin of security which separates it from its neighbors increases or decreases. We do not choose to discuss at once the
possible causes of such a shift, but rather try to determine how it
may affect other phonemic units of the pattern. Let us call A the
phoneme whose normal range is being displaced, B the one separated
from A by an increasing margin, C the one separated from A by a decreasing margin. The dynamic situation will thus look as follows:

$$B \quad A \rightarrow \quad C$$

If, as the saying goes, "phonetic laws work blindly" i.e. irrespective of communicative needs, the outcome of this situation will
necessarily be a merger of A and C unless, for some mysterious reason,
the trend is stopped or reversed. If it is found that B and C begin
to shift in the same direction as A, so that the situation becomes

$$B \rightarrow \quad A \rightarrow \quad C \rightarrow$$

it will be assumed that the same unknown reason is affecting the
three units equally. As a rule, in such a case, it will be difficult
to prove that A actually began to shift before B and C did, and, if
this could be shown, one could probably argue that, for some unknown
reason, A was more susceptible to being shifted and therefore yielded
to the push before the two others. If one is not inclined to be
economical, one could of course also assume three different causes
for the different shifts.

  The basic assumption of functionalists in such matters is that
sound shifts do not proceed irrespective or communicative needs, and
that one of the factors which may determine their direction and even
their appearance is the basic necessity of securing mutual understanding through the preservation of useful phonemic oppositions.
Lest we should give the impression that we are dealing with some sort
of linguistic providence, we shall have to present a fairly detailed
analysis of how we may conceive the working of the various observable
phenomena.

  Let us revert to the afore-mentioned situation where A is drifting
toward C and away from B, and concentrate our attention first on the
possible ensuing comportments of B: (1) the normal range of B may
remain what it was before A began to shift, or it may happen to start
drifting in any direction but toward A; in this case, we shall assume
that the shift of A exerts no influence, or at least no direct influence, on the comportment of B; (2) the normal range of B will
begin to shift in the direction of A, thus

$$B \rightarrow \quad A \rightarrow$$

If it can be shown that the shift of A actually preceeded that of B, and/or that the shifts of A and B can not be ascribed too well to the same general phonetic trend such as a general tendency toward aperture, closure, or other, so that the situation would more adequately be represented as

$$B \rightarrow \quad A \uparrow$$

functionalists will assume that B has, as it were, "taken advantage" of the space left vacant by the drifting away of A. In fact, the chances are that B is environed by other phonemes and separated from them by margins of security which we may assume, for simplicity's sake, to have been just as wide as the one which originally separated B from A. At that time, any random deviation of B out of its normal range and in the direction of any one of its neighbors was not likely to be imitated since it would have tended to conflict with communicative needs. When, however A started to shift away from B, chance deviations out of the normal range of B and in the direction of the receding A would no longer conflict with communicative needs; from that time on, B was contained on all sides except in the direction of A, and the center of gravity of its range naturally began to shift away from the sections of the field where it could not expand. What will often happen in such cases is that one of B's neighbors will in turn take advantage of the space left vacant by B so that a sort of chain reaction will be set in motion which may eventually affect an important section of the pattern.

At this stage of the exposition, it is not easy to present illustrations taken from actual languages, because every shift considered will involve the play of certain internal factors which have not so far been presented and discussed. Yet, in a few cases, such factors may be temporarily discounted without distorting the facts, although it will become clear at a later stage that the proof of the coherence of the shifts presented can only be administered if all factors are taken into consideration.

A comparison of the phonemic pattern of the Hauteville dialect[5] with those of vernaculars spoken in the same region shows that, at about the same time, the following shifts must have taken place: (1) /ẽ/, from Lat. ĭn, > /ɛ̃/ (lowering); (2) /ɛ̃/, chiefly from Lat. en, = /ɛ/ (denasalization); (3) /ɛ/, from Lat. ĭ,ē, > /a/ (lowering and retraction); (4) /a/, chiefly from Lat. a in open syllables, > /ɔ/ (raising and rounding). Since there was previously no /ɔ/ in the pattern, none of these four shifts has resulted in any phonemic merger. Schematically the process can be represented as follows

$$ẽ \rightarrow \quad ɛ̃ \rightarrow \quad ɛ \rightarrow \quad a \rightarrow$$

There has been no wholesale lowering in the front series since /i/
and /e/ are intact, no wholesale raising in the back series since
/u/ and /o/ have not moved, no wholesale denasalization since /ã/
and /ɔ̃/ remain by the side of the new /ɛ̃/. Therefore the whole shift
can not be accounted for as resulting from one and the same general
phonetic trend. Taken one by one, each of the first three shifts
should have resulted in a merger. As a matter of fact, every one of
the four phonemes involved has kept clear of the others. Since the
margin of security between the old /a/ and /o/ was twice as wide as
every one of the others in the vocalic pattern, it seems most likely
that /a/ was the first to start moving. Today all margins of security have approximately the same width and no shift is in progress.
It seems difficult to escape the conclusion that some necessity of
preserving existing phonemic distinctions has been at work throughout
the process.

Another illustration is afforded by the Portuguese dialect of São
Miguel in the Azores.[6] A comparison with standard Portuguese shows
that /u/ has been shifted to /ü/, /o/ has passed to /u/, /ɔ/ has
been raised toward /o/ without always reaching it, /a/ has assumed a
back value "tending toward open ó." This description of the shift
is not exhaustive; some features of it, which would only assume full
significance at a later stage of this study, have been left out.
The powerful influence of standard Portuguese has obviously exerted
some disturbing influence. It seems clear, however, that /u/ took
the lead in its shift toward /ü/, /o/ soon followed, /ɔ/ began its
shift with a certain delay, and /a/ was last to move. Schematically
the process could be represented as follows:

$$a \longrightarrow ɔ \longrightarrow o \longrightarrow u \longrightarrow$$

The shift of /u/ to /ü/ raises a problem which we are not yet ready
to tackle.[7] Let it suffice to say that it may have resulted from a
pressure exerted upon /u/ by its partners of the back series. It
should only be stressed here that if three of the particular shifts
involved can be described as raisings, the /u/ > /ü/-shift is of a
totally different phonetic nature, and yet a causal connection between the fronting and the raisings can hardly be denied.

Let us now direct our attention to the possible comportment of C,
the phoneme toward which the range of dispersion of A is moving for
reasons so far unknown. The range of C may well not move away from
invading A, and a phonemic confusion will take place. The undeniable
frequency of such mergers is sometimes held as a powerful argument
against the assumption that the preservation of phonemic distinctions
is a factor of phonological evolution. Since phonemes, by definition,

serve to distinguish between words and forms, any phonemic merger
will inescapably involve confusions detrimental to the normal functioning of the language, and yet mergers do take place.

In a number of cases it might be argued that C is, as it were, at
the end of its tether, that its performance represents an extreme
phonetic possibility as when it is an /i/ badly pressed by an invading /e/ with surrounding diphthongs which block all way of escape.
An objection would be: how is it that these circumstances have not,
from the start, prevented the range of /e/ from moving into the
margin of security separating it from /i/? But of course the unknown
reasons pushing /e/ upward may simply be more powerful than the
functional factors working for conservation. This does not mean that
the latter do not exist. It must be stressed over and over again
that no one has ever pretended that internal phonemic factors are
the only ones or even necessarily the most potent. What we have to
show is not that these factors explain all features of phonological
evolution, but that there are cases where no understanding can be
reached unless they are duly taken into account.

It will be seen that both the articulatory and acoustic nature of
the distinctive features involved may be a factor of some importance
in the fate of an opposition. But, at this stage, the problem which
shall detain us is whether the relative importance of the opposition
in the satisfaction of communicative needs plays a role or not in
its own elimination or preservation. The question to be answered is
whether, everything else being equal, a phonemic opposition which
serves to keep distinct hundreds of most frequent and useful words
will not offer a more successful resistance to elimination than one
which only serves a useful purpose in a very few instances. What
makes this answer particularly difficult is that we know, thus far,
so little that is definite about other factors involved. The first
step we have to take in order to bring some clarity into the affair
is to investigate whether and how the distinctive importance of a
phonemic opposition can be evaluated.

The functional importance of a phonemic opposition is often called
its functional yield or burden (Fr. *rendement fonctionnel*, German
funktionelle Belastung). There is no complete agreement as to what
this term is meant to cover. In its simplest somewhat unsophisti-
cated acceptation, it refers to the number of lexical pairs which
would be complete homonyms if it were not that one word of the pair
presents one member A of the opposition where the other shows the
other member B: the pair *pack-back* is part of the functional yield
of the /p/-/b/ opposition in English, and so are *repel-rebel*, *cap-
cab* and hosts of others. The number of such /p/-/b/ pairs being
considerable, it is said that the functional yield of the /p/-/b/

opposition is high. If we try to do the same with, say the English
/θ/-/ð/ opposition, we shall find only a few pairs like *thigh-thy,
mouth* n.-*mouth* v.; it will be said that the functional yield of this
opposition is low. Provided we consider a given dictionary as fully
representative of the lexicon of the language under consideration, it
is possible to make exhaustive lists for every one of the phonemic
oppositions, although in practice only those would be considered that
involve phonemes which componential analysis has shown to be minimally distinct: In English /s/-/š/ and /s/-/z/ would be included in the
research, but not /s/-/ž/ or /š/-/z/. Thereby vague labelings like
"high," "medium," "low" can be advantageously replaced by exact numerical ratings.

    It is of course easy to point out the drawbacks of such a method as
a tool for determining the actual number of cases where a given phonemically distinctive feature is by itself the sole element which
prevents misunderstanding, as the degree of vocalic aperture would
be if *give me a pen!* were uttered in a situation which did not give
any clues as to whether a *pen* or a *pin* is wanted. In order to be
fully valid, any rating of the functional yield of an opposition
should be based upon a frequency rating of such linguistic situations
as the one just mentioned. Since such a count is practically impossible, one might be content with a listing of those lexical pairs
that could be conceived of as likely ever to give rise to such in-
determinacy as illustrated above by *pen* and *pin*. But, in order to
avoid subjective decisions, one would probably have to be satisfied
with the exclusion of only such pairs as involve words belonging to
different parts of speech and therefore not likely ever to appear in
the same grammatical context. In that case, among the pairs cited
above *pack-back, repel-rebel, cap-cab* would pass muster, but *thigh-
thy* and *mouth* n.-*mouth* v. would be rejected. Yet, even then, some
complications might arise: the minimally distinct Fr. pair *poignée
poignet* will never give rise to conflict as long as the two words
are used in the singular since, in that case, the difference of
gender will show up one way or another and would tell which is which
even if the /e/-/ɛ/ opposition happened to be blurred; but in the
plural (*les poignées-les poignets*) the vocalic opposition might have
to bear all the distinctive burden. Furthermore this type of evaluation would completely disregard the essential factor of frequency
and would give equal rating to *prig-brig* (Thorndike frequency levels
19 and 16 respectively) and *pack-back* (2 and 1). In view of all the
difficulties involved, it is perhaps just as indicative in most
cases and certainly incomparably simpler to determine the lexical
frequency of every phoneme involved, assuming that the more frequent
a phoneme is, the more likely it is that it will have to assume

clearly distinctive functions. Lexical frequency is probably preferable to actual frequency in texts or utterance because it is not
exceptional that a phoneme such as English /ð/, which enters into
the minimally differentiated pair /θ/-/ð/ with a very low functional
yield, appears very frequently in texts or utterances. There might
however be cases where a lexically very frequent phoneme is less
frequent in speech than some other one with lower lexical frequency,
if for instance the former appears mostly in learned, the latter in
everyday lexical items. In such a case, the conclusions derived
from a lexical count would have to be tempered by reference to the
actual situation in speech. Generally, the method would have to be
adapted to the language under consideration.

From what precedes, it is clear that the functional yield of an
opposition can only be evaluated with any degree of accuracy if we
deal with linguistic stages for which fairly exhaustive word lists
are available. This circumstance makes it practically impossible to
check the validity of the functional assumption in the case of prehistoric sound shifts. It would seem, for instance, that the merger
of *o, and *a in Slavic, Baltic, and Germanic is in some way connected with a relative rarity of *a (from *a or *ə) in these languages where *ə is dropped in second medial syllables, and vocalic
sonants universally develop high vowels. But since we do not know
the lexicon of Slavic, Baltic, and Germanic at the time when they
merged *o and *a, we can hardly go beyond vague assumptions. Even
in the case of early Romance, our fairly exhaustive knowledge of
Classical Latin vocabulary gives us an imperfect picture of the
lexical resources of the vulgar language from which we would have
to start. In the case of certain mergers taking place in modern
cultural languages for which full data are available, the functional
yield has been found to be extremely low: the Parisian French
merger of /ɛ̃/ and /œ̃/ which is in full swing, practically never
results in any homonymic conflict, and the lexical frequency of /œ̃/
is of the lowest.[8] The same could be said of the merger of /ñ/ and
/ni/ which seems to be gaining ground,[9] and of the earlier confusion
of /lʸ/ and /y/. In the same language, the old distinction between
long and short /i/, /ü/, /u/, /e/ whose function was practically
restricted to distinguishing between masculine and feminine words is
now practically eliminated among Parisians.[10] Since gender in French
is usually expressed in accompanying articles or pronouns, the
actual yield of these oppositions was very low, and this circumstance
may well have been instrumental in the merger. It is interesting to
notice that, to this day, French speakers have not found a universally accepted solution for the irritating problem resulting from
the homonymy of *l'amie, l'ami, mon amie, mon ami.*[11] If low func-

tional yield is accepted as a factor of the merger, we shall have
to conclude that even one very useful pair is not enough for preserving a phonemic opposition.

The actual importance of functional yield in the preservation of
phonemic oppositions can not be assessed on the basis of the limited
information available to date. It will have to be tentatively considered as one of the internal factors of phonological evolution,
and the possible extent of its influence will have to be evaluated
wherever feasible. The problem will have to be reconsidered when we
possess a large body of relevant data. It should however be pointed
out immediately that (1) two neighboring phonemes will not necessarily tend to merge simply because the functional yield of their opposition is practically nil: /š/ and /ž/ in English are not found to
approach each other in spite of the exceptionally low yield of their
opposition; (2) semantic extension, word composition, and morphological reshuffling frequently afford easy solutions to the problems
which may arise when a functionally important opposition is being
threatened by the drifting together of two phonemes: as soon as the
margin of security is invaded and danger of misunderstanding arises,
speakers will be induced to give preference to such alternative
words, phrases, or forms as will remove all ambiguity.

We now revert again to our theoretical example of a phoneme A
drifting in the direction of a phoneme C, but this time we shall
assume that C, instead of awaiting the impending merger, recedes before the invader preserving all the time a margin of security between
A and itself. This type of assumption conflicts of course with the
traditional views concerning the "blindness" of "phonetic laws."
Yet it is not too difficult to understand how a phoneme can yield
under the pressure of one of its neighbors. As soon as the margin
of security separating A from C is invaded by the former, any performance of C that falls too close to that margin will incur the
danger of being misinterpreted and will therefore be disfavored.
Thereby the center of gravity of the range of C will be displaced
away from A. It may be that, in so doing, C will exert upon one of
its other neighbors the kind of pressure that A is exerting upon it,
and that neighbor will in its turn be shifted further, away from invading C. We shall thus observe a chain of reactions similar to the
ones we have noticed in the case considered above of A and B.

In practice, it may often be difficult to tell whether we have to
do with a B → A → chain, or drag-chain, or an A → C → chain, or
push-chain. Even in the B → A → type, there is some amount of
pressure from such neighbors of B as are not included in the diagram.
In order to simplify the exposition, we have purposely refused to
investigate factors acting upon A and determining the drift of its

range. But among them may, in the case of B → A → , figure a pressure exerted by B and its neighbors. We have, in the case of Hauteville, suggested the existence of what amounts to a tendency toward
equidistance between the phonemes of the same pattern or, in other
terms, toward equalization of the mutual pressures. Hauteville's
/a/ passing to /ɔ/ would result from this equalizing tendency. São
Miguel's /u/ > /ü/ would result from a pressure exerted upon /u/ by
the other three back phonemes of a series where margins of security
are, by nature, narrower than in the corresponding front series. We
thus probably have to reckon with pressure everywhere, so that the
suggested distinction between drag and push would often be blurred.
We may say that, in some cases, the move of the leading phoneme is
one which our phonetic and phonemic experience would lead us to expect, and in others, that it is the move of the last phoneme which
would seem to make more sense. What we have called A is the first
phoneme in the former case and the last phoneme in the latter. Now
A was the phoneme whose move we took for granted all the time, so
that our final judgment in such matters will depend on our interpretation of such factors as we have not so far investigated, or as
will ultimately remain out of the frame of this study.

The difficulty of deciding which unit is leading the shift may be
illustrated by the following example: (1) Italian *qui* is derived
from eccv[m]hīc and generally, in the traditional vocabulary, /kwí/
should result from Lat. dissyllabic /ku + í/ or /ko + í/; (2) *chi*/ki/
is from Lat. qvi, qvis, and generally, /ki/ derives from Lat. /kwi/;
(3) *ci*- /či/ as in *città* is from Lat. *ci*- /ki/ as in cīvitātem;
three phonemic units have thus been kept distinct although the articulation of every one has changed. The whole shift can be schematized as follows:

$$\text{kuí} \rightarrow \text{kwi} \rightarrow \text{ki} \rightarrow \text{či}$$

Since palatalization of dorsals before front vowels is a most frequent phenomenon, we might be tempted to call this a drag shift:
/ki/ was first palatalized, then /kwi/ could be reduced to /ki/, and
/kuí/ could become a monosyllabic /kwi/. But we could also start
from /kuí/ and argue that since hiatuses in general were being widely reduced in Imperial Latin, /kuí/ would tend to pass to /kwi/ and
thereby exert a pressure on former /kwi/'s. These in turn would
press upon /ki/'s with the result that they would be articulated
farther forward in the mouth and become palatalized. This whole
shift can not have been general in the Romania: qvi must still have
been something like /kwi/ pretty late in northern Gallo-Romance since
the purely French palatalization, which is found to affect /ki/ in
Germanic loans as in *échine* from *skīna, leaves the dorsal intact in

the reflex of qvi; only the palatalization in ci- must have spread
out of its original domain to the provinces with the well known exceptions of Sardinia and Dalmatia. This latter account of the shift
is highly satisfactory in as much as it ties up neatly with what is
universally recognized to have been the fundamental trends of Vulgar
Latin phonological evolution: the tendency to eliminate hiatuses
obviously resulted from the development of stress accent; the resistance of individual phonemes or clusters must have been negligible in comparison with such a powerful irreversible trend; /kuí/
had to become /kwi/ and actually did everywhere. But was the functional yield of the /kuí/-/kwi/ opposition so important that /kwi/
had to recede before the invader? Many Latin speakers in northern
Gaul and elsewhere just let the two groups merge. Could we not
think that if the merger did not take place in central Italy, it
was because Latin speakers there had already palatalized ci and considerably weakened the /w/ of qvi thus making room for /kuí/? On
the other hand, it can not be argued that a push shift is to be discounted here on the ground that there are so many known cases of
palatalization of dorsals which certainly do not result from a
pressure upon /ki/ exerted by /kwi/ and /kuí/. There is no valid
reason for assuming that the ultimate cause of such a palatalization
is necessarily the same in all cases. What is needed here, as elsewhere, is a large body of tentative functional and structural explanations for the most varied cases of the type of phenomenon
under consideration, and a set purpose never to let one's self be
deterred from causal research by the complexity of the problems.

III. *Structure*
We have, in what precedes, been generally considering the problem
of sound change as if every phoneme were characterized by one specific articulatory feature, entirely different from that of every
other phoneme of the language. In fact this would seem to be the
exception rather than the rule. The articulation of the majority
of consonants in most languages implies the combination of two or
more characteristic features, every one of which is to be found in
some other phoneme or phonemes of the language. These features may
be defined in articulatory or acoustic terms. We shall here as a
rule operate with articulatory data, since they are more readily
available and better known. A feature is said to be characteristic
in this connection if it is phonemically distinctive. In a language
like English, the lungs play a role in the production of every
single phoneme, and practically the same role; therefore the pul-
monic articulation is never characteristic and never distinctive.
On the contrary, the bilabial articulation characterizes three

134

phonemes /p/, /b/, and /m/ and is distinctive since it keeps these
phonemes apart from e.g. /t/, /d/, and /n/ respectively. The occlusive nature of these bilabials is not characteristic or distinctive
since English bilabials are always articulated as stops. Instrumental research may show that the bilabial articulation is not quite
the same for /p/, /b/, and /m/, nor is the apical articulation quite
of the same type for /t/, /d/, and /n/, but whatever difference may
be found could, in the case of English, easily be shown to result
from such concomitant (glottal or nasal) articulations as distinguish
/p/ from /b/ or from /m/, /t/ from /d/ or from /n/, and so forth.
We have thus to do with an automatic deviation with no distinctive
significance and comparable to the one which makes the /k/ of /ki/
different from that of /ka/. A number of consonantal phonemes
characterized by one and the same articulation will be said to form
a "series" if their other characteristic articulations can be
located at different points along the air channel. Thus in English
/p/, /t/, /č/, /k/, all characterized by the same glottal articulation but distinguished by the region where the stoppage takes place,
will form a series, and so will /b/, /d/, /ǧ/, /g/.

A number of phonemes characterized by one and the same articulation at a given point of the air channel, but distinguished from one
another by some other distinctive articulation will be said to form
an "order." Thus in English /p/, /b/, /m/, will form a labial order,
/t/, /d/, /n/ an apical order, and so forth. In regard to vowels,
it seems more advantageous to label as "series" a number of phonemes
characterized by the same type of resonance cavities, but distinguished by different degrees of oral aperture, and as "order" a
number of phonemes characterized by the same degree of aperture but
distinguished by different types of resonance cavities. In English,
/i/, /e/, /æ/ form a front series; /i/, /u/ a high order. In such
matters /y/ and /w/ are often advantageously grouped with the vowels
and may form a special order if they are phonemically distinct from
/i/ and /u/.

It should be pointed out that both series and orders are opposi-
tional in nature just like any other phonemic entity. Just as a
phoneme as such presupposes other phonemes, a series presupposes one
or more other series, an order, one or more other orders. A language whose consonantal inventory was restricted to /p/, /t/, /ṭ/,
/c/, /k/, /q/ would not present any consonantal series because its
six phonemes would have no distinctive features in common. A language with /p/, /t/, /k/, /m/, /n/, /ŋ/ would present two series, one
of non-nasals and one of nasals, and three orders, labial, apical,
and dorsal. Series and orders presuppose a larger unit grouping
them into a whole, namely, the "correlation," which includes two

parallel series and a number of coupled phonemes belonging to the
same orders. The six phonemes of our second theoretical example
would form the following correlation:

$$
\begin{array}{ccc}
p & t & k \\
m & n & \eta
\end{array}
$$

Strictly speaking, a phoneme which phonetically would seem to belong
to one series, is actually no member of that series and of the
correlation to which that series belongs if it has no correspondent
in the other series: if a language had only the five consonants
/p/, /t/, /k/, /m/, /n/—and no /ŋ/—/k/, in the theory, would not
belong to the non-nasal series comprising /p/ and /t/ since the
absence of nasality is not distinctive in combination with dorsal
articulation. In a language where there is only one lateral phoneme
/l/ articulated with the tongue tip in the same position as that of
/t/, /d/, /n/, it could not be said to belong to the apical order
because the apical articulation is not distinctive in combination
with laterality. In diachronic phonemic practice, it will however
be found convenient to include a phoneme in a series even when it
has no counterpart in the parallel series, or in an order even when
it has no counterpart in parallel orders, if its general phonic
behavior (allophonic deviations, distribution, etc.) is similar to
that of the phonemes of that series or of that order. In the case
presented above of a language with /p/, /t/, /k/, /m/, /n/, it would
probably be advisable to include /k/ in the non-nasal series. But
there might not exist the same reasons in our second theoretical
example for placing /l/ in the apical order.
   The relationships existing between phonemes of the same order are
usually rather different from those between phonemes of the same
series. In the former case they would seem generaly to be bilateral,
whereas in a series they would be multilateral. In other words,
phonemes of the same order would form a binary opposition or, if
there are more than two of them, a complex of binary oppositions.
On the contrary, all phonemes of a series would stand in the same
relation to one another. If a language has, among other phonemes,
/p/, /b/, /m/, /t/, /d/, /n/, they will form three series, and an
order of labials, an order of apicals and so forth. Thence:

$$
\begin{array}{ccc}
p & t & \ldots \\
b & d & \ldots \\
m & n & \ldots
\end{array}
$$

The /m/ and /n/ phonemes are likely to be normally voiced, but
occasionally unvoiced without losing their identity; /p/ will be
defined as unvoiced (in opposition to /b/), non-nasal (in opposition

to /m/), labial (in opposition to /t/ and others); /b/ will be defined as voiced (in opposition to /p/), non-nasal (in opposition to
/m/), labial (in opposition to /d/ and others); /m/ will be defined
as nasal (in opposition to /p/ and /b/) and labial (in opposition to
/n/ and others). It is clear that /p/ and /b/ have two characteristics in common, non-nasality and labiality, which they are the
only ones to share. They are said to form a bilateral opposition,
and, as one unit, they enter into another bilateral opposition with
/m/. One can also say that /p/ and /b/ stand in exclusive relation,
since they are the only phonemes to share the distinctive features
of labiality and non-nasality.

The relation between the different phonemes of a series (or the
different pairs of a correlation) seems to be of a different nature.
Theoretically at least, every one of them is opposed exactly in the
same way to any one of the others.

This will explain why a correlation, the simplest coherent partial
pattern, consists of an indefinite number of orders but of only two
series of phonemes standing in a one-to-one exclusive relation, the
same for all pairs.

Two or more parallel correlations form what is called a "bundle."
A bundle can be made up of three series, as in the case of

```
p   t . . .
b   d . . .
m   n . . .
```

presented above; of four series grouped in various ways, as for instance in a language combining phonemically voice and aspiration
and presenting e.g. the four labials /p/, /b/, /ph/, /bh/; of five
series or more.

In practice however, there would seem to be exceptions to this
clear-cut opposition between bilaterality inside orders, and multi-
laterality characteristic of series: a labial order consisting of
/p'/, /p/, and /p'/ might be more naturally conceived of as a triad
than as a combination of two binary oppositions. In many languages
two orders of hissing and hushing sibilants seem to stand in particularly close relation since they appear in partial complementary
distribution.[12] In the case of vocalic patterns, three vowels of
the same order such as /i/, /ü/, /u/ form a triad, and to present
them in the frame of two binary oppositions would certainly distort
reality. On the other hand, phonemes of the same series such as
/i/ and /e/ or /e/ and /ε/ are found in certain languages to be in
partial complementary distribution.

These facts and a number of theoretical considerations have induced
some scholars to attempt a reduction of all phonemic oppositions to
the type we have seen to prevail inside orders.[13] It has for instance been suggested that the phonemes of consonantal series actually form a more closely knit pattern than the one which is suggested
by a linear presentation. The oppositions in such a series should
result from combinations of acute or grave quality with two different
degrees of "compactness." Thereby a close parallelism could be
established with vocalic patterns, and a considerable reduction in
the number of distinctive features would be achieved.

We can not enter here into a discussion of the advantages or dis-
advantages of such a method in synchronic studies. In diachronic
matters it would seem so far that not too much is gained by departing from a linear conception of the relations between the consonantal
phonemes of varying degrees of articulatory depth. In a pattern with
the four phonemes /p/, /t/, /c/, and /k/, /p/ would share with /k/
the distinctive feature of graveness, and /p/-/k/ would be parallel
to /t/-/c/. Yet it is found that, diachronically, passages from
the /c/ type to the /t/ type are quite frequent, and so are shifts
from /k/ to /c/, but /p/ and /k/ are kept well apart. The frequent
shift of [k^w] to [p] can not be adduced to support a close kinship
of /p/ and /k/, because [k^w] combines a dorsal and a labial articulation and [p] can only result from a hardening of the latter and a
release of the former. Generally, a diachronic approach requires a
greater concern with phonetic reality than is possible when we are
bent upon reducing the number of distinctive features to a minimum.
Even in a language like French where /k/ has no exact fricative
counterpart /x/, and /š/ no occlusive partner /č/, /š/ can not be
said to be the fricative or continuant counterpart of /k/ because it
can not be maintained that a velar fricative normally tends toward
a hushing articulation as a result of its fricative nature.[14] Two
phonemes can only be said to belong to the same order if they both
present the local characteristic articulation in exactly the same
form or in forms which deviate from each other only through features
which can be fully accounted for as due to the synchronic influence
of a concomitant articulation: in Arabic the tongue-tip articulation
of "emphatic" /ṭ/ takes place much farther back than that of "non-
emphatic" /t/, but the two phonemes still belong to the same order,
because the retracted articulation of /ṭ/ is readily accounted for
as resulting from the concomitant velar or pharyngeal articulation
which is the permanent characteristic of modern Arabic "emphasis."
On the contrary, in a language where /t/ has the normal apical articulation, and /s/ is predorsal, we have no right to include the two
of them in the same "dental" order, because we do not see why a tense

fricative counterpart of /t/ should have a predorsal and not the same apical articulation. It may, in certain cases, be difficult to decide whether two phonemes belong to the same order or not, and we have in practice to reckon with borderline cases, but phonologists should be warned against identifying orders as defined above with the traditional loose grouping of the phonemes of a language into the ready-made classes of labials, labiodentals, dentals, palatals, and velars.

All this does not mean that a componential analysis of phonemes that strives at maximal reduction of the number of distinctive features and eventually reveals unheeded connections between the seemingly most remote sections of the pattern, may not have to play a role in diachronic considerations: /k/ and /a/, for instance— which are described as "compact" as opposed to /t/ and /p/, /i/ and /u/—will often evince parallel evolutionary trends, as when they tend toward [e] and [æ] i.e. a more "acute" pronunciation, a phenomenon which we find for instance in Anglo-Frisian and Old French. This might mean that, in such cases, the palatalization of dorsals before front vowels is not entirely conditioned by the quality of the following vowel as usually assumed, but also by a general fronting of all dorsal consonantal articulations whereby post-velars become velars, velars become post-palatals, and so forth. This "acutization" would of course still have to be explained, but it is scientifically preferable to operate with one unknown cause than with several, one for each of the individual changes. It is a fact however that a presentation of the pattern in terms of orders, series, correlations, and bundles, with its concomitant insistance on the details of phonetic reality, is as a rule more revealing of evolutionary probabilities.

Since most phonemes actually result from combinations of distinctive articulations, we may expect that in many cases a change in the performance of a phoneme will result from a modification of only one of these articulations. If a /t/, characterized by a certain apical and a certain glottal articulation, is found to change, it may be that only the nature of its apical articulation is affected, or only that of its glottal distinctive feature. A change in the apical articulation, as for instance a retraction of the tip of the tongue from the upper teeth toward the alveolas, if it is not in some way connected with the glottal behavior characteristic of /t/ and the other phonemes of the same series, will probably affect not only /t/, but all the other phonemes of the apical order, e.g. /d/ and /n/. Similarly, a change in the glottal articulation which characterizes /t/ as opposed to /d/ will affect not only /t/ but all the phonemes of the voiceless series, e.g. /p/ and /k/. In other words, it may

be expected that every distinctive articulation will change irrespective of the other articulations with which it may combine in order
to form individual phonemes. This is what we actually find in the
most varied languages: as a rule, when in a given language /t/ is
being "aspirated," it is found that other phonemes of the voiceless
stop series are also being "aspirated," which means that the glottal
articulation is shifted irrespective of the oral articulations with
which it combines. If /d/ is being unvoiced, /b/ and /g/ will
probably be unvoiced too. If /k/ is palatalized in certain conditions, /g/ is likely to be palatalized in the same conditions, and
the difference in glottal articulation between /k/ and /g/ will not
determine a different treatment. All this is of course well-known
and it is felt that what would need investigation are the cases in
which one phoneme of a given series shows a specific treatment of
its glottal articulation, or one phoneme of a given order presents
a shift of its local oral articulation which is not being shared by
the other phonemes of the order.

All this has obviously an important bearing upon our present research. If, as we have assumed, the functional yield of an opposition is one of the factors in its preservation or elimination, it is
clear that the opposition of two articulatory features which serve
to keep distinct not merely two isolated phonemes, but two large
series or orders will, everything else being equal, be far more
resistant. We have seen that the actual yield of the English /θ/-
/ð/ opposition is extremely low. But this is not what really
counts: the feature of voice supplemented by concomitant differences in articulatory strength, which distinguishes /ð/ from /θ/ is
also the one which distinguishes /v/ from /f/, /z/ from /s/, /ž/
from /š/, /č/ from /ǧ/ and helps to keep /b/ apart from /p/, /d/
apart from /t/, /g/ apart from /k/. The functional yield of the
opposition of voice to its absence is in English tremendous, and
contributes to the stability of a large section of the consonantal
pattern. All this does not mean of course that the phonetic nature
of such an opposition is not likely to change in the course of time,
but that if a change takes place, it is less likely to result in a
merger than if the opposition were limited to a single pair.

Apart from the stabilizing influence exerted by the high functional yield of correlated oppositions, we probably have to reckon with
a further factor of stability resulting from the mere frequency of
the articulations characteristic of series and orders. Linguistic
features which recur frequently in the chain are likely to be
learned earlier and remembered better than those which appear less
often. This is obvious in the case of morphological and lexical
elements and syntactic patterns, and should apply to phonemic items

as well. Although we still lack a large body of scientifically observed data relating to the acquisition by children of the most
varied phonemic patterns, it would seem that in general correlated
oppositions are acquired earlier than non-correlated ones. Here
again, stability does not mean resistance to change, since perfect
imitation on the part of the child should not prevent sound change
from taking place, and should only prevent mergers.

If it is true that such oppositions as are integrated in a correlation or a bundle of correlations are *ipso facto* more stable than
the ones between non-correlated phonemes or between a correlated
phoneme and a non-correlated one, it will mean that phonemes outside
of the integrated pattern will vary much more freely. If for simplicity's sake we assume complete fixity for correlated phonemes,
and incessant erratic wanderings for non-correlated ones, we shall
come to the conclusion that, at some time or other, every one of the
latter will, just by mere chance, assume a phonetic shape which will
make it the correlative partner of some other. Let us, for instance,
assume the following correlation:

$$
\begin{array}{ccc}
f & s & \check{s} \\
v & z & \check{z}
\end{array}
$$

plus a /x/, theoretically no part of the correlation since it has no
voiced partner, but behaving exactly like /f/, /s/, and /š/. There
is in the same language a trilled phoneme /r/, normally voiced,
which is not integrated because it has no voiceless counterpart,
whose articulation has been shifting around, and whose range of dispersion includes some non-trilled performances. A day may come when
it will assume a post-velar fricative articulation which will make
it the voiced partner of /x/. It will be integrated in the correlation which will henceforward appear as

$$
\begin{array}{cccc}
f & s & \check{s} & x \\
v & z & \check{z} & \gamma
\end{array}
$$

and that will be the end of its erratic wanderings. As a matter of
fact, there certainly is more to this than pure chance, and we have
to reckon with some amount of attraction on the part of the integrated pattern. Let us assume that the /r/ phoneme was at some time
a uvular trill. Pure least effort would probably result in weakening certain of its performances to sheer friction. But friction at
the uvular level would not be so very different, both articulatorily
and acoustically, from the post-velar friction characteristic of /x/.
Since the performances of /r/ are normally voiced, there is no functional resistance against a merger of the two fricative articulations.

The oral articulation of /x/ will exert an attraction on that of /r/ or maybe the reverse. This means that, at a certain point of time, speakers will no longer take the trouble to keep apart two minimally distinct articulations whose distinction does not serve any useful purpose. Attraction thus amounts to confusion of two neighboring articulations that have been allowed to drift closer and closer because their difference is never distinctive, since they characterize only such phonemes as are sufficiently distinguished by means of other features.

This attraction exerted by a closely knit pattern on marginal phonemes has been referred to as the filling of "holes in the pattern"[15] (Fr. "cases vides,"[16] Sp. "casillas vacías"[17]). This phrase is undoubtedly picturesque, but it is apt to deter linguists from a painstaking analysis of the successive processes involved. "Paper phonetics" has been severely and justly criticized. Juggling with the symbols of phonemic charts would be equally dangerous and reprehensible. Isolated phonemes do not rush into structural gaps unless they are close enough to be attracted, and whether they are attracted depends on a variety of factors which always deserve careful investigation. Furthermore, we shall see below that what looks like a hole on the chart does not necessarily correspond to a linguistically favorable combination of articulations. Yet it can not be denied that phonemes in groups tend to impose their articulatory types upon isolated phonemes.[18]

In dealing with pattern attraction, it is often tempting to oppose integrated to non-integrated phonemes, but it is more accurate to work with various degrees of structural integration. We have first of all to take into consideration phonemes whose phonic make-up and general behavior are that of an existing series, but which lack the partners that would integrate them in a correlation, e.g. /k/ in a language with /p/, /t/, /k/, /m/, /n/, but no /ŋ/. In such a case we might say that /k/ is ready for integration through the filling of the [ŋ] gap. In a pattern like

$$
\begin{array}{ccc}
p & t & k \\
b & d & \\
m & n & ŋ
\end{array}
$$

/k/ is undoubtedly integrated, but less so than /p/ or /t/. It is clear of course that we could not speak of "holes in the pattern" unless we reckoned with /k/, in the two preceding examples, as somehow integrated. In a language where an apical /l/ is the only lateral, it may be both theoretically and practically advisable not to place it in the same order as /t/, /d/, or /n/, and to consider

it as non-integrated. But that language may present geminate consonants whose frequency is comparable to that of their simple partners
in intervocalic position. Although, in a descriptive study, these
geminates would still be analyzed as successions of two single consonants—so that geminated *t* would be /tt/, geminated *l* /ll/, and
so forth—they would, on account of their frequency, play a functional role similar to that of single phonemes. We would be justified
in speaking of a correlation opposing a series of single and one of
geminated consonants; /l/ and /ll/ would thus be integrated into a
correlation just as /t/ and /tt/ and /n/ and /nn/. But of course
/t/ and /n/ would remain more fully integrated than /l/ because they
would belong to other correlations than only that of gemination.

The theory of pattern attraction could accordingly be summarized
by stating that the phonemes of a pattern tend to be as fully integrated as conflicting factors make it possible. This means that
filling of holes may involve phonemes which already had some degree
of integration, but which, through the process, will emerge as more
fully integrated. Let us revert to the above-sketched Hauteville
shift as a good illustration of this kind of process.

Both before and after the shift, the normal length vocalic phonemes
of Hauteville can be ordered into three series characterized as
front-retracted (/i/ type), front-rounded (/ü/ type), back-rounded
(/u/ type), with four orders (or degrees of aperture) which we can
designate as 1, 2, 3, and 4. The fourth order presents only one
phoneme, /a/, in which front-back and retracted-rounded oppositions
are neutralized. All these phonemes further enter a correlation
composed of one nasalized and one non-nasalized series. The phonemes
of the nasalized series are fewer than those of the non-nasalized
one, which is frequently the case in similar patterns. Only the
more open orders present nasal phonemes. This results from the
fact that nasal articulation is detrimental to the clarity of the
concomitant oral articulation since it implies that part of the air
escapes through the nose and is thus lost for the oral cavity proper.
Yet the wider the oral aperture, the more air will flow through it,
so that open nasal vowels are likely to be more distinct than close
ones. This may account for a frequently observed tendency for nasal
vowel phonemes to become more and more open.

Before the shift, the two patterns, oral and nasal, must have been

1	i		ü		u		
2		e	ö	o		ẽ		
3		ɛ				ɛ̃		ɔ̃
4			a			ã		

There are two gaps in oral order no. 3, to wit [œ] and [ɔ]. The

143

[œ] gap is not rare in such patterns and may be easily accounted
for: for a relatively large degree of aperture, it is more difficult
to distinguish between retraction and protrusion of the lips. The
comparative rarity of /œ/ as a distinct phoneme is thus due to the
same articulatory and acoustic factors as those that determine the
frequency of a single phoneme for order no. 4. There are thus only
two oral phonemes for the whole of the two most open orders. Since
the opposition of /ɛ/ to /a/ is one not only of aperture but also of
depth, it is understandable that speakers should have tended to
neglect the difference between apertures 3 and 4, which was irrelevant in the rest of the oral pattern, and to stress the difference
between front and back articulation, which was largely supported
elsewhere. In the process /a/ passed from middle to back. The result was first an oral pattern with only three degrees of aperture

```
1     i     ü        u
2        e     ö     o

3           æ     a
```

where the margin of security was wider between 2 and 3 than between
1 and 2,

The original nasal pattern had one more phoneme at the front than
at the back; among nasal phonemes, /ɛ̃/ was less fully integrated
than /ɛ̃/ or /ɔ̃/ since it was the only unit to combine nasality with
aperture no. 2. We have seen that speakers would tend to open nasal
vowels, and therefore /ẽ/ was exerting a pressure downward. In the
frame of the nasal pattern, /ɛ̃/ could not become more open without
threatening to impinge upon the domain of /ã/, which in its turn
could hardly shift toward the back because of the proximity of /ɔ̃/;
/ɛ̃/ was thus squeezed between the gradually opening /ẽ/ and the
resistance of its more open and back congeners. Random weakly nasalized deviations of /ɛ̃/ were apt to be favored since there no longer
was any /ɛ̃/ in the pattern. Eventually /ɛ̃/ was totally denasalized,
and /ẽ/ could occupy its former position. The resulting situation
is actually attested in dialects spoken a few miles from Hauteville
where the pattern may be represented as follows:

```
1      i            ü              u
2         e           ö         o
3   (ɛ̃>)       ɛ          [ɔ]       (ẽ>)   ɛ̃    ɔ̃
4           æ    a                    ã
```

Here, a fourth degree of aperture has reassumed phonemic relevance,
but only in the front series; at the back, aperture no. 3 is only

144

represented by contextual variants of the /a/ phoneme. At Hauteville
all the allophones of /a/ have passed to [ɔ], and /æ/ has shifted
back to middle position, hence:

1	i	ü		u		
2	e	ö	o			
3		ɛ	ɔ			ɛ̃	ɔ̃
4		a				ã

a pattern which shows much more complete integration than the original one.

A few very natural objections to the structural approach could be
raised at this point: How is it that after so many millennia of un-
interrupted speech practice, patterns should still be in need of
structural integration? What has been called the original Hauteville
pattern was of course "original" only in the sense that we chose to
make it the starting point of our research. But, just like any other
Romance pattern, it was nothing but one of the numerous avatars of
the Latin vocalic pattern, a pattern which may have enjoyed at some
period a fair degree of integration. We have of course to assume
that the trend toward structural integration is at work all the time.
But how can we explain that there should always be grist for its
mill? Why could phonemic patterns not reach perfect stability? Or
do we mean that the beautifully balanced modern Hauteville pattern
has reached such a stage of perfection that it would last forever if
the dialect itself were not doomed to disappear in the course of the
next sixty years?

These are many questions which require separate answers. First,
what we have presented of the modern Hauteville pattern looks perfectly harmonious, but so much harmony may actually involve some
strain on the physiological latitudes: the usage of certain speakers would seem to indicate that the back series, with its four
phonemes, is somewhat too crowded, and this could be a germ of instability. [19] Second, we have left out the short vowel phonemes
whose pattern shows clear signs of disintegration, [20] and if the
dialect were to live, we or our successors might probably witness a
total reshuffling of the vocalic pattern which might be necessitated
by a dephonemicization of quantitative differences. Completely
harmonious patterns are probably never reached, and even if one were
found which would seem to stand close to structural perfection, it
would be at the service of a language which, like all languages,
would be used for the expression of changing needs. These needs,
acting through syntax, lexicon, morphology, tempo, intonation, and
others, would ultimately manage to destroy the beautiful, phono-

logical balance. Third, languages do not evolve in ivory towers.
The Hauteville dialect for instance has, for centuries, been spoken
by an increasing number of bilinguals whose medium of inter-regional
communication and intellectual expression is French. Before that
time, it was a local variety of a larger dialectal unit whose most
prominent and prestige-endowed users were bilinguals, also with
French as a medium of wider communication. Even before French was
actually spoken in the region by the leaders of the community, a
number of linguistic features of all sorts, phonological as well as
others, must have seeped through chains of contiguous forms of speech
all the way from Northern France, politically dominant since the rise
of the Frankish empire. Dominant cultural languages do not necessarily preserve the integrity of their patterns better than local patois
when they spread over large heterogeneous areas and become the linguistic mediums of whole nations.

All this accounts for the never-ceasing phonological fermentation
that can be observed practically everywhere. There will always be
holes in patterns and phonemes moving in to fill them. New series
and new orders will appear, resulting either from general reshufflings or from the coalescence of successive phonemes of the spoken
chain, the result of new accentual conditions, articulatory imita-
tions, etc. These new series and orders will not always be complete
from the start; for some time there will remain gaps which ensuing
generations may fill through either sound change or borrowings.

The creation of a hushing order in early Castilian affords an interesting illustration of the ways through which a new phonemic type
can expand by convergence of the most varied elements:[21] the first
hushing units must have resulted from the coalescence of apical
articulations with neighboring newly evolved Romance [i̯], hence
word-medial /č/ and /š/; the corresponding holes in the word-initial
pattern must have been filled mainly by borrowings from neighboring
dialects. Word-initially the voiced hushing phoneme (probably [ǧ])
was normally a reflex of Vulgar Latin yod, but intervocalic yod was
never modified, and the corresponding hole in the word-medial pattern
was filled by early Romance /l^y/ passing to [ž]. This rather start-
ling treatment can be understood only if we keep in mind that geminated (at that time probably just strong) l was tending toward its
modern [l^y] reflex, and was exerting a pressure upon earlier /l^y/.

This Castilian process further affords a welcome illustration of
what we might call the action of a phonemic catalyst. We have so far
assumed that functional yield, even if it were practically nil, would
act as a deterrent against merger. But if the opposition in question
is between a fully integrated phoneme and one that is not, or upon
which some phonemic pressure is being exerted, a minimal functional

yield will not act as a deterrent and, on the contrary, an articulatory attraction is likely to take place. In simpler, less technical terms, if a well-integrated phoneme is extremely rare, it may attract a not so well integrated neighboring unit. In the case of early Castilian there must have been a few words in which the [zi̯] cluster was preserved, having escaped the metathesis whereby basium became *beso*; these rare [zi̯] clusters naturally yielded [ž] as in *frijuelo* from phaseolum.[22] This new /ž/ phoneme occurring word medially was well integrated in an order which presented, further, word medial /č/ and /š/. But the instances of this phoneme were so few as to exclude any homonymic conflict if what had been /l^y/ merged with it; /l^y/, which was being unintegrated by the pressure of a former /ll/, must have been attracted by /ž/. Attraction, as we have presented it before, results from the confusion of two articulations when concomitant articulations suffice to preserve phonemic identity. In the case of a catalyst we have the confusion of two characteristic articulations when this does not actually result in confusion of words and forms. Functionally the two phenomena are quite parallel. They both result in articulatory economy without any impairing of communication.

IV. *Inertia and Asymmetry*

The most serious resistance to phonemic integration stems from the limitations set up by human physiology to the combination of the most varied articulations. The articulations themselves may conflict if they involve neighboring organs. But, more often, the incompatibility will be acoustic, i.e. hearers will find it difficult to perceive a difference between various combinations of the same type, at least in ordinary speech conditions.

We have, in what precedes, indicated in several occasions how some physiological necessities may counteract phonemic integration. We have pointed out that vocalic correlations are quite generally much better represented in the higher than in the lower orders: /œ/ as a phoneme is probably rarer than /ö/ or /ü/; patterns with three series (e.g. of the /i/, /ü/, and /u/ types) practically never keep these three series distinct for the lower order, which is easily accounted for by pointing out that, with maximally open jaws, the lips will be automatically retracted, and that it will become difficult to distinguish between a front and a back oral cavity. The difference of aperture between [o] and [u] will be smaller than that between [e] and [i], although it corresponds to the same maxillary angle. From the point of view of the speaker who has to control the play of his muscles, the proportion [o]:[u] = [e]:[i] will be correct; but acoustically the distinction between [e] and [i] will

be clearer than that between [o] and [u]. For the same number of
phonemes in the front and in the back series the margins of security
will be narrower at the back than at the front, and this may partially account for diverging comportments of the two series. We have
also seen that concomitant nasalization affects the clarity of
vocalic articulations, which means that there are articulatory combinations which are acoustically good, and others which are not so
good.

If phonemes were not of phonic nature but resulted e.g. from combinations of flags, if /p/ for instance, instead of being, say,
voiceless and bilabial, was performed by stringing the Stars and
Stripes and the Union Jack along the same line, /t/ by combining the
Stars and Stripes with the French Tricolor, /d/ by adding to the
latter the Danish Dannebrog, and so forth, any combination of two
flags would be just as good as any other. We can not combine voiced
and voiceless articulation, but we could combine the Stars and
Stripes with the Dannebrog. Furthermore, if in order to make morphemes or words, we should produce a succession of different flag
combinations, any combination could follow any other, so that a word
could easily be composed of /ptd/ if the respective units involved
were performed as described above. Not so of course with distinctive units performed as sounds. The vowel-consonant dichotomy,
with its syllabic corollary is imposed upon us by the nature of the
so-called speech organs. The vocalic and consonantal patterns may
overlap in certain languages, but they are always organized according to two different models. Even if we should agree with Jakobson
that, in human speech generally, the coordinates are the same for
vowels and consonants, we would find, in individual languages, no
constant parallelism between the two patterns. Czech would have a
quadrangular consonantal system and a triangular vocalic one:

```
          t    p    i       u
          c    k         a
```

and Finnish just the reverse:

```
     t       p    i    u
        k         æ    ɑ
```

The necessity of alternating, in the spoken chain, between closed
and open articulatory complexes, which naturally result from the
combination of different types of articulation, opposes the integration of all the phonemes of a language into one closely-knit
pattern: the opposition of voice to its absence plays a great role
in consonantal matters; with vowels, on the contrary, voice is

almost indispensable and therefore phonemically irrelevant. Some
distinctive features can be found to characterize both vowels and
consonants, but not too easily in the same language. Palatalization
of consonants and front vowel articulation may be conceived as the
same feature, with whatever actual difference that may exist being
determined by concomitant vocalic or consonantal features; but where,
as in Russian, we might believe that the two coexist, more careful
observation will often show that if consonants enter a correlation
of palatalization, the vowel series will actually be distinguished
by the play of the lips: Russian /i/ is frequently pronounced far
back in the mouth, and /u/ may, in certain contexts, be performed
as [ü].

The case of nasality is interesting since it will combine with
both consonantal and vocalic articulations, but not equally favor-
ably with all consonants and all vowels: most languages distinguish
/b/ and/or /p/ from /m/, /d/ and/or /t/ from /n/; /ñ/ is probably
about as frequent as its non-nasal counterparts /ɟ/ and /c/, but
/ŋ/ as a distinct phoneme is rarer than /g/ and /k/, which may be
due to a tendency of the two velar articulations to conflict. Nasal
fricatives as distinct phonemes are extremely rare since friction
requires a pressure which can not be obtained if the air is allowed
to flow unhindered through the nose. The rarity of liquid nasals
can be accounted for in very much the same way. We have already
seen that, for similar reasons, nasality combines better with open
than with closed vocalic articulations; but, in any case, nasal
vowels are never so clear as oral ones, and this should account for
their relative infrequency and instability as phonemic units. With
stop articulations, experience shows that nasalization as such is
easily perceived, but, unless [m] and [n] are clearly exploded, the
place of oral occlusion can be identified only with difficulty, as
shown by the frequent neutralization of nasal consonants in syllable
final position where they are assimilated to the following consonant
and, if word final, merged into [n] or [ŋ].[23]

All this means of course that there will be gaps in patterns which
are not likely ever to be filled, or if they are, only as a result
of a fairly exceptional concurrence of circumstances. The phonemes
characterized by acoustically or articulatorily unfavorable combinations will, everything else being equal, be less stable than others
combining features with a high degree of compatibility. Orders and
correlations will tend to expand as far as human physiology, and
certain conditions inherent to the specific language, will permit.
To an original /m, n/ nasal series a /ñ/ is added in Vulgar Latin
when a palatal order is formed. In Germanic a tendency to simplify
the clusters of nasal and homorganic oral stop (cf. the discrepancy

between the spelling and the pronunciation of Eng. *lamb, comb;*
Danish has gone farthest with its mute *d* in *land*) has resulted in the
phonemicization of the dorsal nasal [ŋ]; the same phenomenon is found
in Sanskrit as a result of the reduction of all final consonant
clusters to one phoneme, hence /n/ + dorsal > /ŋ/. A general weakening of implosion is likely to yield a whole pattern of nasal vowels.
In all these cases, we can hardly speak of filling of holes since the
appearance of the new phoneme or phonemes is obviously determined by
trends which have nothing to do with pattern attraction. In most of
these shifts the main factor probably was least effort, which was
allowed to play in certain domains where communicative needs offered
little resistance and in the frame of certain prosodic situations
involving a specific nature of accent and a given pattern of syllabi-
fication.

Linguistic evolution in general can be conceived of as regulated
by the permanent antinomy between the expressive needs of man and his
tendency to reduce his mental and physical exertions to a minimum.
On the plane of words and signs, every language community will have
to strike a balance between an expressive trend toward more numerous,
more specific, and less frequent units, and natural inertia which
favors fewer, more general, and frequent ones. Inertia will be
there all the time, but expressive needs will change, and the nature
of the balance will vary in the course of time. Uneconomical expansion, i.e. one which would entail more exertion than the community
would deem worth while, will be checked. Inertia, when felt to be
excessive, i.e. detrimental to what is felt to be the legitimate
interests of the community, will be censored and punished. Linguistic behavior will thus be regulated by what Zipf has called the
"Principle of least effort,"[24] a phrase which we would rather replace
by the simple word "economy."[25]

Linguistic economy is ultimately responsible for the very existence
of phonemic articulation: the inertia of the organs involved in the
production and reception of speech phenomena makes it impossible for
any normal human vocal language to afford a specific homogeneous and
distinctive phonic product for every linguistic sign. Yet communication requires distinct expression for each. A satisfactory balance
is reached by limiting to a few dozens the number of specific and
distinctive expressive units, the phonemes, and by combining them
successively into distinct signifiers. Economy is further achieved
by making these units result from combinations of non-successive
phonic features, but of course only such combinations as will best
serve communicative purposes. We find here an antinomy between what
we have called the trend toward phonemic integration and the inertia
and asymmetry of the organs opposing the inclusion of all phonemes

into a theoretically perfect, immutable pattern. When a vocalic
pattern presents four phonemically relevant degrees of aperture in
the front series, phonemic integration will tend to preserve or produce four relevant degrees of aperture in the back series. When the
vocalic structure of Classical Latin with its three relevant degrees
of aperture eked out by a quantitative distinction was, by elimination of the latter, reorganized into a four order pattern, in most
of the Romania the reshuffling followed the same procedure in the
front and at the back. But for the same number of phonemes in the
two series the asymmetry of the organs entailed narrower margins of
security in the back series. The mutual pressure could be relieved
by diphthongization of the phonemes of one order or more. But in
such a case diphthongization resulting from a gradual increase or
decrease of the maxillary angle in the course of the articulation of
the vowel would not be restricted to the back series but would ex-
tend to all the vowels of the same order: where ϱ became uo, ε would
become ie, and pattern symmetry would be preserved. A tendency to
merge orders 2 and 3 might also affect equally the front and back
series. If on the contrary the pressure was relieved by gradual
fronting of /u/, the back series would from then on only distinguish
between three orders and the pattern remain asymmetrical.[26]

The effect of the asymmetry of speech organs is also clear in the
case of consonant patterns, not only when we think of the obvious
restrictions to the spread of various correlations, but also in the
course of certain wholesale mutations when it is found that some
orders proceed more rapidly than others. An articulatory weakening
will as a rule decisively affect bilabials before the other orders:
/p/ is frequently weakened to [h] or zero where /t/ and /k/ are preserved. A shift affecting strongly articulated consonants is likely
to act more rapidly on the phonemes of the apical order, as seen for
instance in Modern Danish where, of the three energetically articulated aspirates, /t/ is the first to show unmistakable signs of
affrication.[27]

A full awareness of the existence of this asymmetry will, in many
cases, help to account for such changes as seem only to affect a
single phoneme. It will make clear that this seemingly isolated
change is, in fact, the outcome of a general trend, variously warped
by specific conditions, hastened if these are favorable, delayed if
they are not: a general articulatory strengthening acting upon a
series of spirants may change a [þ] into [t], but will never change
an [f] into a stop, and will simply make the articulation of [s]
more energetic; [γ] may remain a spirant when [đ] is made an occlusive, whereas [b] becomes a stop in strong (e.g. initial) positions
but remains a spirant elsewhere.[28]

In combination with the various factors considered above, asymmetry should go a long way toward accounting for most of the phenomena which could be described as local modifications or reorganizations of phonemic patterns. When, in such matters, we find two sections of the same language community striking out into different phonological paths, we shall find, as a rule, that both courses had their functional, structural, and physiological justifications, and that the factors responsible for the divergence must have been such imponderables as will always escape scientific scrutiny when human behavior is involved.

V. *Prosody and Non-Phonemic Pressure*

Still largely unexplained remain such changes as affect whole orders, series, correlations, bundles, and even the system, both vocalic and consonantal, in its entirety. When investigating these, all the previously discussed factors should be kept in mind. It will be found that the direction and amplitude of every one of them is, as a rule, largely dependent on the nature and diachronic comportment of the structural environment. The behavior of orders and series will be reminiscent of the one we have ascertained above in the case of our three phonemes A, B, and C, and this is easily understandable since the whole of an order or of a series differs from the whole of another order or series in exactly the same way as we assumed A differed from B or from C. Orders and series will merge, just like phonemes, but in most well-documented cases we shall find that, for classes as well as for individual phonemes, a relatively low functional yield may have played a role. But if we can thus account for some of the modalities of these changes, we have so far no way of telling what started them.

Among the possible factors in such changes we shall distinguish between internal and external ones. By internal factors, we mean here the influences exerted upon the pattern of phonemes by those sections of the linguistic structure we have not so far considered, namely the complex of prosodic, "suprasegmental," features, and the system or systems of meaningful elements. Among external factors, we should distinguish between the influences exerted by other linguistic structures, those of other dialects of the same language or of other languages, and the fairly mysterious non-linguistic factors whose importance may well have been grossly exaggerated by our predecessors. We can not deal here with the influence of other linguistic structures.[29] Let it suffice to say that they would deserve to be taken into consideration far more than has generally been done so far.

One would have a right to object to our separating, in the present survey, prosodic from phonematic features. It can indeed not be denied that, at least in some languages, suprasegmental features can be arranged into patterns very similar to those we have established for phonemes. For instance, the tones of many south-eastern Asiatic languages could be grouped into orders and series just like the phonemes of the same languages. Most of what we have said above about the comportment of phoneme patterns would apply just as well to such tone patterns. The function of these tones is distinctive like that of phonemes, and the mutual diachronic relations they entertain with the phoneme patterns must be of the same type as those between different sections of such patterns. Accent, which can be defined as prominence given to one syllable in the word, or whatever meaningful unit has prosodic relevance, may at times assume some distinctive function, particularly when it is found to appear in two or more phonemically distinct types. These two or more distinct types may pattern in very much the same way as tones proper, their difference being generally one of pitch or melody. In so far as they exert distinctive function, prosodic features have, from a diachronic standpoint, to be considered together with the purely distinctive features we find combined into phonemes. They form with vowels and consonants three natural classes of distinctive units. We have, in what precedes, pointed to a definite tendency to avoid the use, in the same language, of certain features for both consonants and vowels. In a similar way, it is found that, for instance, prosodic intensity, if distinctive, usually excludes phonemically relevant vocalic intensity manifested under the form of quantity.[30]

Yet the basic function of accent as such is not distinctive. When its place in the unit it characterizes is not predetermined by the phonematic make-up of that unit, it may occasionally evince some sort of distinctive power (cf. e.g. Sp. *côrtes-cortés*). But this is normally a by-product. Accent is really there to characterize and localize the word (or a certain type of morpheme or phrase) in the spoken context. If the localization is approximate, its function has been called culminative. If it is accurate, its function is demarcative. The true function of accent is less clear in languages where it is a traditional feature than where a new accentual pattern is being developed at the expense of tradition. In contemporary French, for instance, the weak traditional phrase-final accent seems to be increasingly overshadowed by what has been called the accent of insistence. This accent has two concurrent forms, an emotional and an intellectual one. The former is usually characterized by stressing and lengthening of the first consonant of the word, the latter by some prominence given to the first syllable. Formally, the two varieties are clearly distinct only in words beginning with a vowel (*im´possible* vs. *´impossible*), and, even then, emotional accent can be heard on the first syllable (*c´est ´impossible*).[31] In what could be dubbed "didactic style," first syllable prominence is widely prevalent and its function is clearly demarcative; by setting individual words apart from the context, it gives a bolder relief to the successive articulations of thought. The functional difference between phonemes and such an accent is obvious: phonemes contribute only indirectly to the expression of the semantic contents of language, and therefore the expressive needs of man will as a rule affect phonemes only through devious channels; this still optional accent is an immediate reflex of these expressive needs; its intensity will vary from one utterance to another and mirror exactly the communicative purposes of the speaker. Such an accent is linguistic in the narrow sense of the word because its existence is determined by an inherited convention, but its arbitrariness is highly limited in the sense that, once it has been accepted in principle by a community, the details of its actual use will be regulated by what we may call psychological factors. Even when such an accent has been stabilized and has ceased to be optional, it will be liable to various degrees of intensity whereby meaning will be conveyed directly from speaker to hearer.

What has just been said about accent applies largely to all the prosodic features grouped under the heading of intonation. In many languages, an utterance final melodic rise is the functional equivalent of an interrogative morpheme such as Fr. *est-ce que*, Russian *li*, Lat. *-ne*. Once tone, as automatic accompaniment of every syllable or mora, and occasional phonemically distinctive uses of accents have been discounted, prosodic features may be said to belong to the same linguistic plane as meaningful units, and, just like them, to be liable to be directly affected by communicative needs. But the physical nature of their performances is such as to exert a deep influence on those of the phonematic units of the spoken chain.

This is of course clear in the case of stress accent, which, when particularly strong, is known to play havoc with inflexional endings[32] if it does not happen to bear on them, and which must also be ultimately responsible for the most revolutionary reshufflings of phoneme patterns. The umlaut phenomenon illustrates most clearly how processes that originally affect phonemic units in the spoken chain, lead eventually to a reorganization of the phoneme pattern. The prominence of a syllable can only be achieved at the expense of the other syllables of the word; as stress increases in one part of the word, the other parts become more weakly articulated, hence blurring of vocalic distinction and, frequently, syncope. This, in

itself, does not affect the inventory of the phonemes, only their
distribution. In many cases, this would be expected to result in
the elimination of a large number of useful distinctions; OHG *scóno*
and *scóni* would have merged into *scōn*, if speakers had not unconsciously favored in the second form such deviations of /ō/ as were
determined by a tendency to anticipate the front articulation of /i/;
hence, of course, the eventual split of /ō/ into /ō/ and /ȫ/ attested
in German *schon* and *schön*. This shows how the phoneme pattern can
be made to expand when the average number of phonemes per word is
diminishing, and how, more generally, demarcative needs can enlarge
the phoneme inventory and lead to a reshaping of the system.

But of course the well-known umlaut process is only one way, among
many others, whereby prosodic non-distinctive features can affect
the phoneme pattern. This, a central problem of diachronic linguistics, should receive far more attention than has been granted to it
so far, since prosodic features are the most normal channel through
which the varying communicative needs of speech communities can influence the pattern of distinctive features. As factors of phonological changes, prosodic features are extremely powerful precisely
because they are immediate responses to the needs of expression. The
speaker of Modern French who makes an extensive use of optional
initial accent is prompted to do so by a desire to make his statements as clear and convincing as possible. How could he imagine
that he may be paving the way toward the establishment of initial
stress as an automatic feature of the language, which may eventually
result in blurrings, mergers and syncopes? We do not mean hereby
that the phonetic trends launched by, say, a strong stress accent
will develop blindly, ruthlessly destroying any piece of linguistic
machinery that happens to be in their way. If the vocalism of unstressed endings plays in the economy of the language too important
a role to be wiped out, speakers may be induced to save some of
their articulatory energy for the final syllable of every word.
When, as it seems, prehistoric Latin developed a word initial stress,
wide-spread blurring of vocalic timbres took place in medial syllables, but final syllables, in which lay the expression of most
morphological categories, were hardly affected. At a much later
period, when the language had extensively weakened its adverbs into
mere grammatical tools, a new onslaught of prosodic intensity resulted in the wholesale massacre of a declensional pattern which by
that time must have become a burden rather than a real help.

In this rapid survey of the ways through which communicative needs
may influence the phoneme pattern, we should of course mention again
the assumed role of the functional yield of oppositions. But, by
the side of this conservative action, it would remain to be seen

whether the necessities of expression could not, in some cases, be directly instrumental in enlarging some sections of the phoneme pattern. If some phonemically relevant feature, say, glottalization, happened to be the frequent mark of a morphological or lexical category, could it not be imagined that speakers would be tempted to combine it with new articulations and extend it beyond those sections of the phoneme pattern where we would normally expect to find it? The example we have to offer does not illustrate exactly this type of action, but rather the extension of a correlation beyond its expected range under the pressure of an all-pervading pattern of morphophonemic alternations; most Breton consonants may be grouped into two series of strong and weak units; weak stops are voiced and their strong counterparts are generally voiceless; the strong member of phonetically voiced pairs often evinces a tendency to devoicing, a tendency fully developed in Welsh. This strong-weak opposition frequently coincides with the morphophonemic pattern of "lenited" versus "non-lenited" consonants; /b/ for instance is the phonemic weak counterpart of /p/ and also, in the morphology, the "lenited" equivalent of it. Since, however, [b] could also be the "non-lenited" counterpart of /v/, a tendency has been at work to distinguish phonemically between morphologically "strong" [b] alternating with /v/ and morphologically weak [b] alternating with /p/. As a result, we have today to reckon with two b phonemes: a strong b transcribed /bb/ which Breton speakers tend to unvoice and which they have in consequence some difficulty in keeping apart from /p/, and a weak fully voiced /b/. The distinction is widely neutralized, or rather it has only got a foothold in a very specific position, namely word initially within an utterance if the last phoneme of the preceding word is a vowel.[33]

This last illustration and the preceding suggestions should by no means be conceived of as exhausting all possibilities of direct diachronic influence of one of the linguistic planes upon the other. Neither in this final section nor in the previous parts of this study has there been any attempt at being exhaustive. A complete functional and structural theory of phonological evolution will have to be based upon a much larger body of structurally sifted material than is available to date. The justification for the sketchy and tentative outline which has been presented here is that it may incite diachronically inclined linguists to utilize in their investigations some of the conclusions arrived at after two decades of phonemic research.

Notes

[1]*Language* (New York, 1933), 385.

[2]A bibliography will be found in A. G. Haudricourt & A. G. Juilland, *Essai pour une histoire structurale du phonétisme français* (Paris, 1949), 119-120; see, *ibid.*, ix-xiv and 1-13. Later contributions will be cited in the course of this paper.

[3]*Cours de linguistique générale* (Paris, 1931), 162.

[4]*Language, Its Nature, Development, and Origin* (London, 1922), 263.

[5]As presented in A. Martinet, "Description phonologique du parler franco-provençal d'Hauteville (Savoie)," *Revue de linguistique romane* 15, 1-86; see, in particular 2-3.

[6]Cf. F. M. Rogers, "Insular Portuguese Pronunciation: Porto Santo and Eastern Azores," *Hispanic Review* 16. 1-32, in particular 13.

[7]The problem is dealt with by Haudricourt-Juilland, *op. cit.*, 100-113.

[8]Lip-rounding, which distinguishes /œ̃/ from /ɛ̃/, is an unstable feature in the case of such very open articulations. The same is true of course for /ɔ̃/ which we might expect to merge with /ã/ in forms of speech where /œ̃/ merges with /ɛ̃/ (actually [æ̃]). But the functional yield of the /ɔ̃/-/ã/ opposition is very high in French, and the merger is only attested in such northern Gallo-Romance dialects (and the corresponding local forms of Standard French) as have kept *en* phonemically distinct from *an* so that the frequency of /ã/ (= *an*) is much lower than in the standard language.

[9]Cf. A. Martinet, *La prononciation du français contemporain* (Paris, 1945), 170-173.

[10]*Ibid.*, 94-109.

[11]The language affords no easy solution by means of composition, such as exists in English: *boyfriend, girlfriend;* most French speakers will pronounce the *-e* of *amie*, which results in a phonemically exceptional combination, phonetically [a'mi'ə] or [a'mi'œ].

[12]As for instance in German.

[13]Roman Jakobson was the first scholar to advocate such a reduction: see *Proceedings of the Third Intern. Congress of Phon. Sciences* (Ghent, 1939), 34-41, and *Kindersprache, Aphasie und allgemeine Lautgesetze, Språkvetenskapliga sällskapets förhandlingar* 1940-1942 (Uppsala, 1941), 52-77. It was applied by J.P. Soffietti in his *Phonemic Analysis of the Word in Turinese* (New York, 1949), and by Roman Jakobson and J. Lotz in Notes on the French Phonemic Pattern, *Word* 5, 151-158. The latest exposition of the procedure is to be found in *Preliminaries to Speech Analysis, The Distinctive Features and their Correlates*, Technical Report No. 13, January 1952, Acoustics Laboratory, Massachusetts Institute of Technology, by Roman Jakobson, C.G.M. Fant, and M. Halle.

[14]In such a case, it would of course be redundant to state that such an opposition as /š/-/k/ is one of hush-friction vs. velarity-plosion, and descriptive economy is achieved by reducing it to friction vs. plosion (or continuant vs. interrupted; cf. *Preliminaries to Speech Analysis*, 6 and 21) because the hush-velarity opposition can thus be eliminated. But it should be clear that descriptive economy is achieved here through blurring the actual synchronic relationship between two phonemic units. Descriptive economy does not necessarily do full justice to functional and structural reality.

[15] The term is found in K. L. Pike's *Phonemics* (Ann Arbor, 1947), 117b.

[16] Probably used for the first time by this author in "La phonologie synchronique et diachronique," *Conférences de l'Institut de linguistique de l'Université de Paris* (1938) 6, 53.

[17] See Alarcos Llorach, *Fonología española* (Madrid, 1950), 80-81.

[18] For a detailed analysis of a clear case of pattern attraction, see A. Martinet, "The Unvoicing of Old Spanish Sibilants," *Romance Philology* 5, 139. In his pioneering article "Phonetic and Phonemic Change," *Language* 12, 15-22, A. A. Hill uses the term "phonemic attraction" for a different phenomenon resulting in partial or total phonemic confusion; cf. 21.

[19] "Description phonologique. . . ," 36 and 38.

[20] Cf., *ibid.*, what is said, pp. 44 and 56, about a tendency toward making *e* the phonemic equivalent of zero.

[21] See "The Unvoicing of Old Spanish Sibilants," 135-136, 140-141.

[22] See Vicente García de Diego, *Gramática histórica española* (Madrid, 1951), 103.

[23] For a general survey of the restrictions imposed upon the expansion of correlations by the inertia and assymetry of speech organs, see A. Martinet, "Rôle de la corrélation dans la phonologie diachronique," *TCLP* 8, 273-288.

[24] *Human Behavior and the Principle of Least Effort* (Cambridge, Mass., 1949), 56-133.

[25] "La double articulation linguistique," *TCLC* 5, 34.

[26] See Haudricourt-Juilland, 17-58, 98-113.

[27] Cf. Henrik Abraham, *Etudes phonétiques sur les tendances évolutives des occlusives germaniques* (Aarhus, 1949), 108.

[28] Cf. e.g. A. Martinet, "Some Problems of Italic Consonantism," *Word* 6, 35-41.

[29] Cf. "The Unvoicing of Old Spanish Sibilants," generally, and 152-156 in particular.

[30] See, e.g. N.S. Trubetzkoy, *Grundzüge der Phonologie* (Prague, 1939), 180, or *Principes de phonologie* (Paris, 1949), 215.

[31] See J. Marouzeau, "Quelques aspects du relief dans l'énoncé," *Le français moderne* 13, 165-168, with references to former contributions by the same author.

[32] It is clear of course that the energy with which stressed syllables are pronounced varies greatly from one language to another. Stress is, for instance, decidedly weaker in Spanish than in Italian, and probably weaker in standard Italian than in standard German. Some languages, like German, show close contact of stressed short vowels and following consonants; others have loose contact in such cases. When Bloomfield writes, *Language*, 385: "many languages with strong word stress do not weaken the unstressed vowels" and cites among them Italian, Spanish, Czech, and Polish, he obviously wants to convince his readers that stress as such can not be held entirely responsible for vowel blurring. But his examples do not carry conviction: neither Czech nor Polish accent can be said to be particularly energetic; in standard Castilian, accent is uncommonly weak. In such matters, it is particularly important to distinguish between the successive stages of the same language. It is commonly

assumed that "Germanic accent" is vowel-blurring. But it remains to be proved that, e.g. in contemporary English and German, absence of stress is actually conducive to the blurring of vocalic distinctions. For Standard German, at least, this seems highly doubtful.

[33] See F. Falc'hun, *Le système consonantique du breton* (Rennes, 1951), 63-65.

8 Graduality, Sporadicity, and the Minor Sound Change Processes

HENRY M. HOENIGSWALD

Our traditional treatment surrounds the so-called minor sound change processes, or their purported instances, with an aura of special importance; first, by setting them off from other, presumably "major" processes, and then by hinting mysteriously that the minor ones somehow represent borderline phenomena of a kind which suggests that there is more beyond, and that their exploration will widen the theoretical basis for our existing treatment of change--giving us, perhaps, an entirely new framework for entirely new and deeper insights. This sounds reasonable because it would not be for the first time in the history of scholarship that such a thing should come to pass.

Perhaps we should first ask just what our assertions on linguistic change are like in general. One style is that of *typological* comparison. For instance, it may be asserted that the earlier state of a language has a three-number system (singular, plural, dual), while the later stage, by comparison, has a two-number system. Or, to turn from grammar to our present concern, phonology: it may be said that an earlier stage has a three-vowel system while a later stage has a five-vowel one. Note that the "comparison" we find here is the kind that might be made between any two or more languages but is here specifically applied to two languages defined not only as "related" but as related in the particular manner to which we refer as "descent from an ancestor language." Note further that "comparison" here carries its everyday, almost non-technical meaning, in contrast to the specific sense which the word "comparative" has acquired during five generations of historical linguistics.

Second style states what would be called correspondences in the case of languages that are merely related, and what we shall specifically call *replacements* in the case of ancestor-and-descendant

From *Phonetica* 11 (1964), 202-215. Reprinted by permission of Henry M. Hoenigswald and S. Karger AG.

languages. These statements of replacement are not comparisons at all; if the expression be allowed, they rather describe bits of translation from stage to stage. Some of these translations recur in such a manner that we have to formulate them phrase-by-phrase, word-by-word, stem-by-stem, ending-by-ending — or, to use the general term, morph-by-morph; for instance, as we go from older English to modern English *egg* replaces *ey, conscience* replaces *inwit*; in French *cheval, un cheval,* and *le cheval* all replace the Latin word for 'horse' depending on differences in meaning and in surroundings. Other replacements are more regular than that—that is, they can be stated in terms of phoneme sequences, phonemes, or distinctive components. These are, of course, our familiar "sound laws". Thus an IE "*p*" is replaced by a Germanic "*p*" after "*s*" (or, if we prefer, IE "*sp*" is replaced by Gc "*sp*"). IE "*p*" is replaced by a Germanic "*f*" otherwise. This reminds us that the formulation of a number of interlocking replacements leads to the recognition of *replacement patterns:* entities (for instance, phonemes) merge, or split, or do neither.

This leaves us with the third style of assertion. This third style represents a return to the principle of common-sense comparison; but this time the comparison is, so to speak, derivative and subordinated to the second style, since it is restricted to the two partners involved in a replacement. In those cases where the replacement happens to be a sound change (rather than some kind of morphemic change) the framework for the comparison is usually one of two things: it is either (a) a *phonetic* framework (sounds are declared to 'become' palatalized; 'lose' their lip rounding; 'suffer loss'; 'remain unchanged'—and what not). Or else the framework may be (b) a *typological* one (for instance, it may be asserted that the topmost vowel of a five-vowel system translates into—i.e. 'becomes'—the second highest front vowel in a seven-vowel system. This is, of course, particulatly striking if the two vowels are what is called "phonetically the same").

Of these three styles of statement, style number one has a recent flavor as the history of linguistics goes. It is the hallmark of structuralism in historical linguistics.

Number two, on the other hand, is an old classic. It embodies the paradox at which we have already hinted: while it is precisely that style which does not aim at true comparison, it nevertheless has come to constitute the very essence of the so-called "comparative" method when applied to sister languages and hence of just about all that is valuable in etymology, language classification and reconstruction. It can be shown that the matching-operations of the CM, while complex and sophisticated, are essentially performed on purely style-II premises.

Style number three, as indicated, is a mixed bag, since it may utilize all kinds of properties provided they go beyond the defining relationship of replacement itself. In the domain of sound change, however, the overwhelming majority of familiar examples will match the two partners, the replaced phone and the replacing phone, from a phonetic point of view. The prevailing framework for the classification of sound changes is precisely this; any textbook of linguistics illustrates it. The fullest, most ambitious, and most important elaboration of this approach is probably Maurice Grammont's *Traité de phonétique*.

There is a special reason why Grammont's book has served as a point of departure for discussions of the minor sound change processes in particular. Dissimilation was one of Grammont's earliest scholarly interests; he returned to it in his later book in a strikingly elaborate fashion. In the interval, Karl Brugmann had written a monograph on dissimilatory changes. There is a much-read article by Roland Kent on the relationship between assimilation and dissimilation. These and many other writings have created something like a vulgate which found its way into our textbooks, and is apparently part of orthodox teaching. According to a recent author, namely Charles F. Hockett, there are three "mechanisms" of change: sound change, borrowing, and analogical creation. They are said to be capable of bringing about every kind of "phylogenetic change" described (i.e. every kind of difference in structure). 'However, not all known changes in the "design of languages" can be ascribed to just these three mechanisms. [This is where the 'minor mechanisms' come in of which it is said that they are] more closely allied to analogy than to borrowing or sound change.' Hockett then proceeds to name them, and a motley list they are: contamination and metanalysis; methathesis and haplology. A few paragraphs further on we read this "*Assimilation* makes one part of an utterance more like some nearby point in phonemic shape. When the two parts are adjacent, this may occur gradually, as a part of sound change [!]. But in *distant assimilation* other material intervenes." Then H. cites Lt. qu*inque* after *quattuor*; and (Gmc.) E. *four* after *five*. "We assume that the reshapings . . . were relatively sudden, and that they occurred in the context of counting. Contamination [already mentioned above] may well be a special variety of distant

162

assimilation." Hockett then concludes by saying "*dissimilation* works in just the opposite way," and he quotes the instance of *peregrinus* which becomes Ital. *pellegrino*.

The usual train of thought is, then, roughly this:[1] There are *unconditional* sound changes and *conditioned* sound changes. Unconditional sound changes are typically *regular* and *gradual*. Most conditioned sound changes are also regular and gradual. In addition conditioned changes are very largely *assimilatory* in nature. The assimilation in question is an assimilation to a nearest segment of sound—it is *contact* assimilation; and what is more, it is, typically, an assimilation to the nearest following segment: it is *regressive* (anticipatory). But then there are some conditioned changes which are different in all or some of the following ways:

(1) they are *sporadic* rather than regular,

(2) they are *sudden* rather than gradual,

(3) they are sometimes *dissimilatory*, although assimilatory changes likewise occur and are to be classified here, due to their associations with the other features that we are listing,

(4) these sporadic, sudden dissimilations or assimilations are *distantly* conditioned rather than conditioned in contact,

(5) they are not infrequently progressive, or else they are *reciprocal*—in other words, they are instances of lag or of metathesis, as the case may be, rather than instances of anticipation, and finally

(6) certain particular sounds or sound configuration are said to be more subject to these procceses than others: liquids and nasals for example; geminates are presumably prone to dissimilatory simplification; syllables are lost haplologically, etc.

There is usually also the hint that some of these minor change processes have a way of paralleling individual lapses—which is of course not the same thing as saying that they must originate in individual lapses.

To begin with the first property: what is sporadic sound change? What in fact is "regular" sound change? In a sense, as we know, this is only a matter of definition. As changes are described some replacements are stateable in unconditioned form for stretches other than whole morphs or multiples of morphs ("Lt. *h* to late Lt. zero"; "Lt. ClV to It. CiV"). Others require the listing of morphs ("Lt. *domus* to It. *casa*"). The former are regular sound changes. The others are not sound changes. This might well be the meaning of the

not unfamiliar pronouncement that there "is no" sporadic sound change.
Actually, of course, that pronouncement means a little more. It implies the claim that where morph listing is necessary, but where the
phonemic shape of the replacing and the replaced morph are not *randomly* different (as they are, say, in the pair *domus—casa*!)—we
must go on looking for proof that the replacing form is one of two
things. *Either* it must be a dialect borrowing and therefore related
to the replaced form. Thus *porridge* for *pottage* is surely not just
a 'sporadic change' or a vague indication that the pronunciation of
intervocalic *t* threatened to get out of hand at one point (as has
been said); rather it is the more concrete and specific phenomenon
called a dialect borrowing, with all the implied obligation for us
to study the geography and the chronology of the matter in detail.
The *other* recognized alternative for phonemically non-random, yet
irregular replacements is of course that of a morph being replaced
by a fellow-allomorph (as when *roofs* replaces *rooves*). Since many
allomorphs are morphophonemically related rather than suppletive,
this will once again create borderline cases in which morphs must be
listed, but in which some phonemic recurrence exists nevertheless
between replaced and replacing morph. Of course, these two alter-
natives are simply Bloomfield's famous 'residues': some *borrowing*
and all of *'analogic change'*—it is really quite unnecessary to say
much about them, except to conclude that a sporadic sound change
seems to be one whose irregularity cannot be explained in either of
these two ways. It is further claimed, and this brings us back to
our list, that such intermediate instances rarely occur except in
the presence of traits (2) to (6), that is, except as "minor sound
changes."

Now let us look at trait (2). Minor sound changes are said to be
non-gradual. Here we are concerned with presumable "stages" through
which the dissimilated, assimilated, metathesized or lost phones
pass; and note that we are not, at the moment, concerned with the
fact that the conditioning takes place over a distance. (This
needs saying because words like 'discontinuous', 'leaping', 'salta-
tory' are bandied about ambiguously in the literature.) The minor
changes, allegedly, do not (as the saying goes) go forward in small,
imperceptible steps, but take place suddenly. Many authors have
also pointed out that the result of some or most minor change processes is never a "new phoneme" (whatever that may mean), implying
that existing phonemes are here exchanged in some discrete, ready-
made way—very much, in fact, as morphs are exchanged in analogic
change, borrowing, etc.

Now, it is customary to emphasize a certain trait which would indeed seem seriously to set apart all sound changes from the other

change mechanisms: lack of awareness on the part of the speaker.
We must remember what weight classical linguistics had given to
awareness; and since it is surely difficult to imagine a speaker
discoursing about an ongoing sound change, it was by no means un-
reasonable to think of sound change as gradual and *hence* imperceptible. The "sounds," the ranges of articulation, the statistical
"maxima" of these ranges become more and more similar to each other
in a non-distinctive way until, presumably, the harm is done, and
the speakers (who would never have dreamed of dropping a given
phonemic contrast of their own free will) are insidiously trapped—
this seems to be the picture. So far as I know it has always been
an entirely speculative picture whose best feature is a surface
plausibility which it once possessed but does not possess any more.
Are there any data that would bear it out?

On the whole it seems that what close-range and fine-meshed observation of dialect areas (such as the atlases very occasionally
enable us to make) establishes, is an altogether different kind of
graduality—if we want to call it that at all. It is a quasi-
graduality of small but discrete steps, in which dialect borrowings,
with sound substitution, accumulate, until, under conditions of
"total" borrowing or of unlearning and relearning, they take on the
characteristics of sound change. There is, secondly, the further
type of quasi-graduality, quite poorly understood in detail, whereby a sound change first becomes regular for a specific conditioning,
only to attract to itself more and more allophones of the disinte-
grating phoneme. The history of /w/ (digamma) in Greek is a good
specimen. Viewed on a sweeping scale, across a vast gap in time,
/w/ simply disappears completely—that is: unconditionally. But we
know the language well enough to see that it first went out before
consonants, then after consonants, then before some and finally
before all vowels word-initially. We can also see that several
dialects went through the stages of this sequence at different times.
In addition, its ultimate consummation is in part a matter of certain dialects becoming extinct. It is a little difficult to imagine
the statistical centers of the measurement ranges for these various
/w/'s simply slipping into inaudibility. Rather, we have an impression that in more and more neighboring areas there were more and
more opportunities for more and more positional allophones of /w/
to behave somewhat like this:

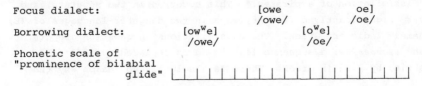

Focus dialect:		[owe /owe/	oe] /oe/
Borrowing dialect:	[ow^{w}e] /owe/	[o^{w}e] /oe/	
Phonetic scale of "prominence of bilabial glide"			

where both the /owe/ and the /oe/ are picked up by the borrowers as
their /oe/, so that the absolute extent of the physical distance between the contrasting articulations in either one isolated dialect
(not necessarily only spatial dialects are involved) is not at all
the point. Surely, also, a merger said currently to be in progress,
that of [ɛ̃] with [œ̃] in certain types of French is not, essentially,
a gradual unrounding, "by imperceptible steps," but by all accounts
something quite different; something in which the total vowel typology of the language and its dialects is involved, and where the
phonemic contrasts function as such, and as wholes.

Consequently one might say that it does not matter much whether or
not there exist some types of change (such as many typical dissimilations or metatheses) which could not have occurred gradually for
the good reason that the articulators in question are not connected
by an anatomical continuum. This, after all, is also true of many a
simple and phonemically unimportant alteration like the change from
lingual to uvular *r* in many parts of Europe—I do not know whether
anybody has ever for that reason bothered to classify this alteration as another example of "minor sound change." On the other hand,
quite a few sound changes which are distantly conditioned (4), and
some of which are dissimilatory (3) in character, are both quite
"regular" (that is: non-sporadic) and also perfectly amenable to the
idea of gradual shift—if there were any reason to attach central
importance to phonetic graduality! For instance, take the ordinary
umlaut of the several Germanic languages: phonetically one would
have to classify umlaut as a case of regressive, distant assimilation. If we wish, we may imagine that the coming-into-existence of
the front rounded "*ü*" was a gradual matter, although of course the
decisive event is not *that*, but rather the merger of the determining
factor in what had been the conditioning vowel of the following
syllable—that is, the decisive event is not the assimilation at all.
Also, umlaut is certainly amenable to treatment as a "regular" sound
change, as all students of Germanic know. Since this syndrome is
not untypical among the languages of the world, some scholars will
then turn around and say that the distant conditioning from vowel to
vowel is a somewhat different affair and more like contact assimilation—in other words, not a minor change process but an ordinary one.
This seems arbitrary.

Or take Grassmann's law, so-called. It is also referred to as the
"dissimilation of aspirates." This occurred in two separate, and
very significantly different, ways in two daughter-languages of IE,
namely Indic and Greek. The dissimilations in question are *distant*
and *regressive:* a sequence like *bh-dh* is replaced by *b-dh* in Sanskrit; by *p-th* in Greek. There is absolutely no reason why the

champions of graduality could not have this deaspiration occur in a perfectly gradual manner. And the same could be said for a great many other examples.

However, these cases bring us back to the matter of regularity vs. sporadicity. Umlaut and Grassmann's law are "regular"—they are shining examples of regularity. But perhaps they are exceptions; perhaps they could be eliminated by a suitably revised definition. Therefore we would have to examine other, clearer, and more extreme specimens for sporadicity. It does not appear that anybody has done this in the real sense of the word—not even Grammont who had his own axe to grind and whose writings only contain hints on this particular point. It would be necessary, in principle, to go through the 19th century literature on IE and Romance and Semitic phonology (to name only the more thoroughly cultivated fields), and sift the original collections of material, bringing them up to date at the same time. At the moment we can rely only on some random observations of our own, and, of course, on the recent useful monograph by R. Posner on Consonant Dissimilation in the Romance Languages.

Take "syllabic dissimilation" or "haplology." This is one of the purer "minor change processes"—probably one that is quite difficult to imagine as being phonetically gradual. It is frequent, as it happens, in Greek, and also in Latin where we have such examples as *stipendium* from *sti-pi-pendium*, *nutricem* from *nu-tri-tricem*; or in Greek *hē-(mi)-médimnos*, *am-(phi)-phoreús*. In spite of what is usually implied about these haplologies, I see no reason not to ascribe "regularity," i.e. sound-law character, to them. On the Greek side, I cannot find an important number of instances in which open syllables in the interior of a word are allowed to begin with the same consonant—except in cases of members of inflectional paradigms (say like *patē-téos* from *patéō*). Such exceptions mean very little if we consider the notorious strength of analogical regularization within verb paradigms. It is quite true that the instances of haplology are *also* morphemically complex—they seem to be mostly compounds, with the compounding seam passing between the inducing and the induced (i.e. the lost) consonant. Established compounds are just as notoriously much less exposed to analogy and much more to the normal obscuration of their etymology that goes hand in hand with separate semantic development. As a matter of fact, there *are* a few doubles like *hemimédimnos* (alongside *hēmédimnos*!) in which the compound is made up anew. All this is worth mentioning because it illustrates the fact that we cannot expect much in the way of crucial material that is derivationally simple and thus absolutely immune to possible analogical influences. Consequently, the cases in which the minor change process—in this instance, the haplology—has occurred, could well be even fewer than they actually are in Greek; so long as all the *counter*examples (i.e. the examples in which haplology did not occur and which thereby keep the haplology "sporadic"!) are complex, there are no grounds for saying that haplology is not a regular sound change. (The conditioning for this sound change must of course be carefully specified.)

Or take another case, also familiar to the classicist. The Latin adjective suffix *-alis* appears as *-aris* if the preceding stem has an *l* (and if certain other phonological provisos are met). Again we are sometimes told that this is not ordinary sound change. But it is quite plain that the suffix is fundamentally *-alis* (with *-l*), since *-aris* has no acceptable separate etymology, it is also plain that the change is in fact a dissimilatory, progressive, distantly conditioned, and nevertheless *regular* sound change. The situation is similar to the preceding: there are no good *counter*examples. On the other hand there are parallel cases, involving other suffixes which point to the same state of affairs. By and large, *l-l* does not occur; where we would expect it to arise we find *l-r* instead. The old standby, Lt. *peregrinus* to It. *pellegrino* had also better be considered the outcome of a sound change, with its regressive opera- tion yet to be accounted for. Rather than quote extensively from Mrs. Posner, let us only call attention to the many times in which she names "lexical and grammatical" factors as being needed to inter- pret restored, that is seemingly undissimilated, forms. I will add another standby, the so-called "mamilla"-law in Latin: if a long or checked (and therefore accented!) penult vowel is preceded by a geminate, this geminate is simplified (*canna*, but *canalis*; *omitto* instead of *ommitto*; and for that matter *mamilla* alongside *mamma*). Again, it is in the nature of things that not many *counter*examples can be expected such that they would at the same time be morphologi- cally unanalyzable; but the fact is that they do not in any real sense exist.

This list could be extended quite a bit. It is remarkable both for its strength (which is on the negative side: there is no compul- sion to consider the sound change irregular), and for its weaknesses (it is hard to find morphologically isolated instances). Perhaps this is also the time to recall Brugmann's observation, alluded to earlier, to the effect that dissimilations do not seem to "add en- tirely new sounds;" that is, no new phonemes. This would be remark- able only if it is taken to mean that the dissimilating factor never becomes itself obscured, thus making the dissimilated item distinc- tive. Otherwise, a dissimilation, like any other sound change, may do one of three things in the replacement pattern. It may be (1) a subphonemic, non-distinctive dissimilation, that is, the dissimilated

168

phone may not be altered "far enough"—to use the vocabulary of
gradualism—to merge with any other phone. In this case it will of
course not create a new sound; that is, it will not create another
phoneme for the repertory. The altered phone will remain a positional variant and no more. However that may be, there is the second
possibility (2) that the dissimilated phone will merge with another
phone—for instance, that l will become r, in an environment where
r already occurs. In this event (which seems to be common enough),
again no "new sound" is added to the stock of phonemes. Finally,
(3) the dissimilation may operate in a gap, as it were. It may
create a phone which is similar to phones of another phoneme which,
however, does not happen to occur in that particular environment.
In other words the dissimilation has the effect of splitting the
phoneme by reassignment rather than by outright merger. Once again,
this will not add anything to the *inventory*, but in a sense it adds
to the second phoneme what it detracts from the first. The available descriptions of sound changes often neglect these things much
to the detriment of our understanding of the facts. Thus it turns
out that the Greek variety of "Grassmann's law" necessarily produces
dissimilations of this third type while the Sanskrit counterpart
does not. When an early-Greek *thuphlós* 'blind' goes to *tuphlós*, as
it does in written standard Attic, this form and all the other dissimilated forms like it have very little opportunity of becoming
homonymous with anything since sequences like *t-ph* (i.e. IE *t-bh*)
had had no place in the IE root structure. Hence, in a sense, the
dissimilation is "only phonetic." At *all* times we may think of the
aspiration as occurring over the entire complex *t-p*. This should
be kept in mind by those who explain occasional local epigraphic
spellings like *thuphlós* as super-added assimilations, thus giving
the unwary reader the confusing idea that two opposed principles are
arbitrarily resorted to and that there is no coherent design in
phonological developments like these.

Let us look also briefly at the Latin numeral 'five' and the
Germanic numeral 'four' since they are paraded so prominently whenever talk turns to the minor sound changes. In fact they are harm-
less and should be discarded from any special context. The first of
the two is surely unsuitable: *p-qu* is distant-assimilated to *qu-qu*
(quinque) in Latin (perhaps in Italic in general) and in Celtic in
all cases in which the sequence is known to exist. There are only
three such: the word for 'five', the word for 'cook', and the name
of the tree called *quercus*—but there are no counterinstances, and
regularity is beyond the slightest doubt. We are not quite as lucky
in Germanic, but at least we know that the sporadicity of the

change: k^w to f in the word for 'four' has nothing to do with counting, since a handful of non-numerals (like *wolf*) have the same odd f.

This sketch is only meant as the expression of a solid negative conviction to the effect that the so-called minor processes offer no more difficulty to normal, orthodox interpretation than the so-called major processes. There are a good many loose ends in that sector, too; and yet we feel quite rightly that these uncleaned-up corners, so far from being fatal to our general assumptions, simply call for more knowledge of dialect-geographical data; of unrecorded intonations, etc. I cannot see, upon reflection, and upon reading Mrs. Posner, that the minor change processes raise insoluble problems, or even special problems about our fundamental assumptions. On the contrary, they illustrate and confirm the play of these assumptions in the presence of particular circumstances. For instance, rather than say that there are maverick processes in which sporadicity and distant conditioning are alarmingly combined, it could be, that distance conditioning produces the appearance of sporadicity, simply by leaving so much more scope for morpheme-boundaries to intervene, and hence for analogic change to operate. In other words, property number (1) could turn out to be determined by property (4). And distant conditioning, in turn, may or may not be frequent as languages go, but none of our fundamental assumptions exclude distant conditioning.

Here, I think, is the crux of the matter. What makes a change either major or minor is the typology of the language, or of the area to which the language belongs. In quite a few languages of Europe and Western Asia, a prohibition against recurrent identical liquids (to quote that special case) is apparently a reasonably stable phonemic trait. Modern English is after all part of this area: it has been remarked that with onomatopoetic words (i.e. in a particularly creative and native part of the vocabulary) we have such items as *crackle prattle flitter flicker clatter*—but characteristically *cracker* only with a morpheme boundary (and, I suppose, *fritter* as a loanword?). If we choose to speak in this style, we may say that the dissimilations of liquid against liquid, so frequent in European diachronic history evidently *serve this persistent sychronic trait*. Let a form with the disfavored sound sequence threaten to arise—from a new construction, from borrowing, from a loss of juncture or pause—and it will be dissimilated away in the fashion which has been so well classified and studied by our authors.

It may even be that the synchronic traits thus served are universal or nearly universal traits, common to all speech. We do not know enough typology at the moment to be very sure about something

of this sort. We may be a good deal surer about anything else, however—namely, that the minor sound change process does not lead a
separate existence as a specifically diachronic universal; that it
does not compromise our general ideas of change. It would not be
surprising if the exact opposite turned out to be true.[2]

Notes

[1]See Brugmann, *Abh. Sächs. Ges. Wiss. Phil.-Hist. Kl.* 27: 139-178;
Kent, *Lg.* 12: 245 ff.; Hockett, *A Course in Modern Linguistics*,
387 ff.

[2]See now K. Togeby, *Romance Philology* 17: 642-667.

9 Synchronic and Diachronic Universals in Phonology

JOSEPH H. GREENBERG

1. In spite of the influential Saussurean dichotomy of synchronic
and diachronic studies, it has in fact not been possible to keep
these two main aspects of linguistics in hermetically sealed compart-
ments. The aim of this paper is to explore the theoretical relations
between phenomena in the two fields in the context of the current
interest in universals. The examples cited are not intended to be
conclusive and are meant only as illustrations.

It is also not within the scope of this paper to present a detailed
historical account. My indebtedness to others who have worked in
this area should be evident; but three lines of previous investigation should not go unmentioned. The first of these is the work of
Bonfante, Hoenigswald, Marchand, Chafe, and others on internal reconstruction, a method by which synchronic data regarding morphophonemic alternations lead to diachronic conclusions about earlier sound
changes.[1] The second is the emphasis of Jakobson on the importance
of synchronic universals in testing the validity of reconstructed
phonological systems.[2] The third is the work of Martinet, which not
only calls attention to the importance of synchronic structure in
understanding sound change, but also contains numerous observations
regarding factors in diachronic phonology which are implicitly equivalent in some instances to universals of change.[3]

2.1 Very nearly all the language universals specifically proposed
so far in the literature have been synchronic. However, Ferguson in
his paper on nasals has offered two (those which he numbers 14 and
15) which are diachronic.[4] The first of these asserts that nasal
vowels "apart from borrowings and analogical formations, always
result from the loss of a primary nasal consonant." The second, in
parallel fashion, states that nasal syllabic phonemes, apart from
borrowings and analogical formations, always result from the loss
of a vowel. It is the first of these which interests us here.

From *Language* 42 (1966), 508-517. Reprinted by permission of
Joseph H. Greenberg and the Linguistic Society of America.

In Ferguson's statement regarding the origin of nasality in vowels from a primary nasal consonant, nothing is said about the position of the nasal consonant in relation to the nasal vowel which develops. The following appears to be the typical if not the exclusive sequence of events: $VN > \tilde{V}N > \tilde{V}$. Usually, though not always, the nasal consonant is in the same syllable as the preceding vowel.

Both of Ferguson's generalizations may be regarded as examples of a particular class of diachronic universals which we will call theories of exclusive relative origin. They are theories of relative origin because they indicate the manner in which nasal vowels, or syllabic nasals, have arisen again and again at different times and places. They are exclusive because they assert that the phenomenon in question arises in only one way. This implies that it is also possible to have theories in which a certain phenomenon arises in more than one way; such a theory, as will be indicated later, also has a certain value.

Theories of exclusive relative origin are of universal scope in that they refer to sequences of events which are of potential occurrence in languages of any chronologic period or linguistic stock. They are empirical in that we understand what kind of evidence would constitute an exception. Nothing is asserted about the length of time in which the change is accomplished. Indeed it would not be an exception in the above instance if the sequence VN either remained or developed into something other than a nasal vowel. What is asserted is that if we investigate a language at time t_2 and it has nasal vowels, then either at some earlier time t_1 it had VN from which the nasal vowels developed or as far as we can go back it already had the nasal vowels. The only evidence that will refute the thesis is a nasal vowel that can be shown to have arisen in some other manner.[5]

2.2 Taking Ferguson's theory of the origin of nasal vowels as an example, the relation between such diachronic universals and synchronic typologies not only has inherent interest but will help to uncover other types of diachronic universals.

The appropriate synchronic typology will evidently be one in which languages are classified by two criteria, the presence or absence of nasal vowels and the presence or absence of oral vowels. There will then be four logically possible typological classes of languages: (1) oral and nasal vowels both present; (2) oral vowels present but nasal vowels absent; (3) nasal vowels present but oral vowels absent; and (4) oral and nasal vowels both absent. Taken in the context of this classification, Ferguson's generalization states that languages

of type 1 arise from languages of type 2 in a particular and specified manner.

Of the four classes just defined, as far as our present knowledge
goes, classes 3 and 4 are empty. The absence of empirical exemplification of one or more logically possible classes can be, as usual,
restated in terms of universals. We have the unrestricted universal
that all languages have oral vowels and the implicational universal
that the presence of nasal vowels in a language implies the presence
of oral vowels but not vice versa.[6]

Generalizing from a thesis like Ferguson's, we can ask, regarding
any given set of typological classes generated by a synchronic typological criterion, what potential diachronic relations exist for
every pair of typological classes and in either direction. Thus,
given four classes, we consider the relation of class 1 to class 2,
class 1 to class 3, and so on (six pairs); and for each pair we seek
to specify the various ways, if any, by which the first type of the
pair can develop into the second or the second into the first.

This information can be set forth in what I will call a state-
process diagram. Using the numbering assigned earlier for the language types in the classification based on presence or absence of
oral and nasal vowels, and using arrows to indicate the existence of
at least one known process of change in the appropriate direction,
we have the situation in Figure 1.

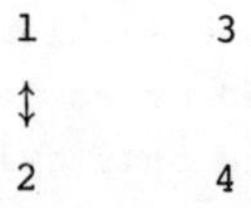

       1   3

       ↕

       2   4

              Figure 1

According to this diagram, a language of type 2 (with oral vowels
only) can change into a language of type 1 (with both nasal and oral
vowels). Such a change is implied by Ferguson's universal 14 already discussed. Further, languages of type 1 can change into languages of type 2. This involves loss of nasal vowels but retention
of oral vowels.

There is probably a single diachronic process involved here, loss
of nasality producing merger with corresponding oral vowels wherever
two vowels differ only in the presence and absence of nasality.

It is implicit in Figure 1 that no processes are known by which a
language of type 1 or type 2 can change to the nonexistent type 3
or type 4. If the synchronic universals mentioned above are valid,

this is a natural consequence. If it were not, types might come into existence which are not found in actuality. This leads to certain diachronic universals. Thus the nonoccurrence of the change of type *1 → 3 means that a language with both oral and nasal vowels may lose the latter but not the former. Again, the nonoccurrence of *1 → 4 excludes the possibility of losing both oral and nasal vowels and so having no vowel, of *2 → 3 that a language with oral vowels only should change them all to the corresponding nasals, and of *2 → 4 that a language with oral vowels only could lose them and thereby have no vowels. Statements of the kind just cited may be considered diachronic universals which exemplify other types than theories of relative origin.

2.3 The chain of reasoning of the previous section which draws consequences from Figure 1 may be considered a specific application of the general principle described by J. J. Jenkins, C. E. Osgood and myself—namely, that no diachronic change gives rise to a synchronically nonexistent type.[7] The converse does not necessarily hold; it is at least conceivable that a type may exist which is not produced by any known diachronic process if a language is created de novo, as possibly with Creoles or with the one or more original languages of mankind.

The diachronic universals cited by way of example in the preceding portions of §2 are for the moment considered sufficient exemplification both of their existence and their typological variety. This topic will be considered more systematically in a later section.

3.1 By the explanation of a universal I will mean its logical deduction from some more inclusive principle. This other principle, in turn, is not necessarily ultimate and will itself usually demand an explanation. Nevertheless it may be considered explanatory of the more restricted generalization, since the latter no longer requires a special answer and the whole question has, as it were, been shifted to a higher level.

With Ferguson's set of universals regarding nasals still serving as examples, the attempt will be made to furnish a deductive explanation of certain synchronic universals in which diachronic universals figure, though not always exclusively, among the premises of the argument.

3.2 One of Ferguson's synchronic universals about nasals (his No. 12) is that the text frequency of nasal vowels is always less than that of oral vowels. It is this universal which will be deduced from his diachronic universal (No. 14), already considered, regarding the origin of nasal vowels. If nasalized vowels arise from

earlier sequences of vowel and nasal consonant, then after this has
occurred the total frequency of nasal vowels compared to that of
oral vowels should parallel the earlier relative frequency of oral
vowels followed by nasal consonant compared to those in which oral
vowels are not so followed. That the total frequency of vowels
followed by anything except nasals should be greater than that of
vowels followed by nasals seems a priori highly plausible as a synchronic generalization. If we assume that fluctuations due to ob-
solescences, new coinages, borrowings, analogical formations and
other diachronic processes exercise a basically random effect, it
follows that Ferguson's synchronic universal regarding the greater
frequency of oral vowels compared to nasal vowels will be deducible
from his diachronic universal regarding the origin of nasal vowels
and the synchronic frequency hypothesis regarding the greater frequency of vowels not followed by nasals compared with the frequency
of vowels followed by nasals.

A test of this theory as applied to Latin and French is contained
in Table 1 below. In the first row is the proportional frequency of
vowels followed by tautosyllabic nasals and those not followed by
tautosyllabic nasals in Classical Latin, since this is basically
the origin of nasal vowels in French. The second row contains the
relative frequency of nasal and oral vowels in French. These figures
are based on samples of 1000 vowels.[8]

	Nasal	Oral
Latin	14.7	85.3
French	16.3	83.7

Table 1

3.3 Another instance of a synchronic universal in Ferguson's list
which can be deduced from other universals, and which has the same
diachronic universal regarding the origin of nasal vowels as a basic
premise, is his universal No. 11. This states that the number of
nasal vowels is never greater than the number of oral vowels.

The most frequent case will presumably be one in which, before
the development of nasal vowels, the set of vowels which occurs with
following nasals will be identical with the set that occurs in all
other environments. If this is so, then, to begin with, each oral
vowel will be matched by a corresponding nasal vowel which only differs from it in nasality. Hence the number of oral vowels will be
equal to the number of nasal vowels.

It will sometimes be the case that the set of vowels followed by
a nasal consonant is smaller than the set of vowels in other environ-

ments. This will be true if there are cases of neutralization of
quality before nasal consonants, or if there is a greater variety
of vowels in open syllables while, as is often the case, vowels become nasalized only in closed syllables. For example, in Classical
Arabic both short and long vowels are found in open syllabels but
only short vowels in closed syllables, including, of course, syllables with tautosyllabic nasals.

I do not know of any cases in which there is greater variety of
vowels before nasal consonants than in other environments. If this
observation is correct, then at the time when nasal vowels arise
they are the same in number as oral vowels or fewer, but never
greater. To this we may add a further diachronic factor, namely
that merger among nasal vowels seems to occur more often than among
oral vowels. This may be stated as a diachronic universal, to the
effect that merger between any pair of nasal vowels always precedes
merger of the corresponding pair of oral vowels if the latter occurs
at all. From this it will follow that there is a mechanism for decreasing the number of nasal vowels relative to the number of oral
vowels. To summarize, the synchronic universal that the number of
nasal vowels is never greater than the number of oral vowels is deduced from two diachronic universals, the origin theory of nasal
vowels and the preferential merger of nasal vowels, and one synchronic universal regarding the smaller or at most equal number of
distinct vowels followed by nasals as compared to the number of
vowels in other environments.

The merging of nasal vowels has a further predictable synchronic
effect which is verified. Although the overall frequency of nasal
vowels always seems to be much smaller than the overall frequency
of oral vowels, the coalescence of certain nasal vowels obviously
increases the individual frequency of the vowel which results from
the merger. It therefore happens, though infrequently, that a
particular nasal vowel may have a greater frequency than its oral
partner.[9]

3.4 The relation between oral and nasal vowels is, in certain re-
pects, similar to that between other categories of sounds. It may
be considered hierarchical in that the oral vowel is basic. This
relationship can be described in Prague terms, by now traditional,
as that between unmarked (basic) and marked terms. Thus in the
present context oral constitutes the unmarked and nasal the marked
category. Similar hierarchies occur in relation to grammatical and
semantic categories, but we shall be concerned here only with
phonology.

Four types of synchronic universals may be cited in which the unmarked category always figures as the implied member of an implicational statement. They will be stated here in the highly generalized
terminology of marked and unmarked, terms which may be considered
variables for which such pairs as nasal vowel : oral vowel, glotta-
lized consonant : unglottalized consonant can be substituted. The
four types, as will be evident, are not logically independent. The
stronger types, which assert more, imply the truth of the weaker
statements but not conversely. By substituting values for actual
variables, specific universals result. Not all of these turn out to
be true without exception. The extent to which the highly general
principles of the marked-unmarked hierarchy are valid varies with
each specific instance. What is relevant to the present circumstance
is that the degree to which these relations hold is at least partly
explicable by diachronic factors.

Consider the four following classes of synchronic universals.
(a) The presence of the marked category implies the presence of the
unmarked category. (b) The number of distinct phonemes of the marked
category is never greater than that of the unmarked category. (c)
The total text frequency of occurrences of all phonemes of the
marked category is always smaller than that of the unmarked category.
(d) Any particular phoneme of a marked category is less frequent
than a corresponding member of an unmarked category.

Of these statements d is strongest and a is weakest, but b and c
are logically independent of each other. The hierarchy of truth
implications among the four types of statements is shown in Figure 2
where $x \rightarrow y$ means that if x holds y must hold also, but not conversely.

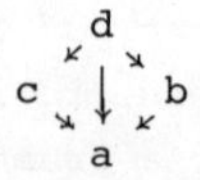

$$
\begin{array}{ccc}
 & d & \\
\nearrow & \downarrow & \searrow \\
c & & b \\
\searrow & \downarrow & \swarrow \\
 & a &
\end{array}
$$

Figure 2

From the available evidence, it appears that statement of types
a, b, c, are valid for nasal and oral vowels and that of type d
almost always. A general relation of the unmarked-marked types also
holds in regard to long vowels (marked) vs. short vowels (unmarked).
But statements of types b and d definitely do not hold universally.
There are certainly languages with more long vowels than short,
while there are apparently no languages with more nasal than oral
vowels.

The difference between these two instances of marked-unmarked relation is explicable in terms of diachronic theories of relative origin. There is a great variety of diachronic processes by which systems of contrasting vowel length arise; and for some of these it is by no means necessary that the number of long vowels should be fewer in number than the number of short vowels. For example, in languages which have syllabic types with initial vowels along with the type (universally present) consisting of consonant and vowel, there will be occurrences of hiatus, i.e. of vowel sequences in which each vowel forms a separate syllable. If these are contracted and the contract product is longer than an original single vowel, as it often is, the number of long vowels may be greater than the number of short vowels even though the frequency of hiatus itself may be relatively low, so that the text frequencies of the short vowels will still be greater than that of the long vowels. Consider the following simple model. In stage 1 three vowels a, i, u occur, with heterosyllabic vowel sequences and no length distinctions; in stage 2, as the result of contractions (a-a > a:, i-i > i:, u-u > u:, a-i > e:, i-a > $ɛ$:, a-u > o:, u-a > $ɔ$:, i-u > $ü$:, u-i > $ü$:) we have more long vowels than short. Even with an initially equal number of short and long vowels, additional long vowels may be developed from diphthongs, e.g. in some forms of modern Arabic. Where length develops from the loss of a syllable-closing consonant, the situation more closely parallels that of oral and nasal vowels.

This suggests not only that differences in the strength of the marked and unmarked opposition can be at least partly explained in terms of diachronic universals, but that individual cases with different origins will show different characteristics. Thus a language in which vowel length has arisen by vowel contraction will show different characteristics from one in which it has resulted from consonant loss. We may expect then that languages which belong to the same typological classes on very general criteria may by more specific criteria show similarity or difference, depending on whether the more general phenomenon arises by the same diachronic process or not. For example, there is a large class of languages in which there are word-initial consonant clusters with a maximum length of two. Such a feature may arise in at least two ways, by loss of a vowel in initial open syllable or by a morphological process of prefixing. In the former case, exemplied by Maltese Arabic, a large proportion of possible clusters occur. In the latter, as in most Mayan languages, only clusters with certain initials occur, e.g. s, $š$, h, and y in Tzeltal. It seems plausible and worth investigating that the distribution of languages among the logically possible subtypes may be largely explicable on diachronic grounds.

4.1 So far in the discussion I have adduced certain statements as examples of diachronic universals in phonology, without attempting to classify them or put them into a general framework such as has been described for synchronic universals. The following will be taken as representative examples. All except the last, which was proposed by G. Bonfante,[10] have been mentioned in the previous discussion.

1. Nasalized vowels always arise from a sequence of vowel and nasal consonant (exclusive origin).

2. A merger of oral vowels always presupposes the merger of the corresponding nasal vowels if they exist (preferential merger).

3. If nasal and oral vowels merge unconditionally, the phonetic result is always an oral vowel (direction of unconditioned merger).

4. Of the two vowels i and $\ddot{u}$, i may originate from $\ddot{u}$ but not $\ddot{u}$ from i (unidirectional change).

These examples represent a single subtype of diachronic phonologic universals in that they are all based on unconditional sound change.

The following proposal may be offered. If we assume that whenever a sound change occurs the old form exists alongside the new as a dialectal, diaphonemic, or individual style or free variant (all of which will be for the moment subsumed under free variation), then we should find free variation reflecting possible diachronic changes (although by the accidents of our knowledge or the relative rarity of the change it may not), but not variation resulting from changes forbidden by diachronic generalization. In this way it should be possible to map every phonological diachronic universal into a corresponding synchronic one involving free variation, thus providing a method for classification and for the investigation of all logical possibilities.

4.2 Let us consider the first example of §4.1 as representing theories of exclusive origin. In the most general terms we have a certain phoneme or phoneme set with a common feature b which has arisen from some previous phoneme or phoneme set or sequences of phonemes of a particular type a. At the time that the change is occurring, we assume, a is in free alternation with b. Now if by a theory of exclusive origin b can arise only from a, then b can never be in free alternation with anything but a. Hence we have the synchronic implicational universal regarding free alternation, that if b alternates freely at all, then a is always the alternating partner. If the theory is not one of exclusive origin, then a in the statement above is replaced by a finite disjunction—say, c or d or e.

Note that this free variation will be, on the basis of stricter types of phonemic theory, morphological. Suppose that $\tilde{a}n$, $\tilde{a}m$ and $\tilde{a}\eta$

are all in free variation with $\tilde{a}$. Then all morphemes which originally had $\tilde{a}n$ etc. will have alternants with $\tilde{a}$ which occur in exactly the same environments, i.e. are found only in the same allomorphs. In this, the temporally shallowest form of reconstruction, the free variants in $\tilde{a}n$, $\tilde{a}m$ and $\tilde{a}\eta$ are reconstructed as the earlier form, prior to the appearance of free variation with $\tilde{a}$, by the general rule that if a phoneme is in morphophonemic alternation with zero the phoneme which is earlier is the one which is not zero.

For the second example, preferential merger, if we generalize our symbolism so that the preferentially merged set (e.g. the nasal vowels) are denoted by a_1, a_2, etc., and the corresponding members of the other set by b_1, b_2, etc., we may assert a synchronic universal of the following type. Free variation between b_i and b_j implies free variation between a_i and a_j. If the diachronic generalization about the set b_1, b_2 as the marked member (where a marked-unmarked relation obtains) turns out to be valid, then of course the synchronic generalization can be correspondingly extended.

The third generalization in §4.1 concerns the direction of unconditioned mergers. This again is possibly generalizable in terms of marked and unmarked features: the result of an unconditional merger is always the unmarked phoneme or set of phonemes. If this were not so, there would be languages with the marked feature but without the corresponding unmarked, and so even the weakest type of sychronic generalization discussed in §3.4 (type 2) would not hold.

Again generalizing our symbolism, suppose that when phonemes of set a merge unconditionally with set b the resulting phonemes always belong to set a. Then at the time the merger is taking place there should be free variation between a_1 and b_1, a_2 and b_2, etc., but there should also be nonalternating instances of original members of set a. These would then be two sets of morphophonemes, $a_1 \backsim b_1$ and nonalternating a_1. Once more there would be morphological free variation, and $a_1 \backsim b_1$ could be internally reconstructed as originally nonalternating b_1.

The last instance is that of unidirectional change. Bonfante's example might be restated in the form: $\ddot{u}$ is a possible source for i but i is not a possible source for $\ddot{u}$. There are two cases, depending on whether the language previously had an i with which $\ddot{u}$ merges (the usual, perhaps the only situation) or previously had no i. In the former case we have free alternation between i and $\ddot{u}$, as well as a non-alternating i representing the old i. The synchronic universal which applies here is that where we have i and $\ddot{u}$ in unconditioned free variation, we never have a nonalternating $\ddot{u}$. Again, it is clear that the earlier state is reconstructible.

If there was no previous i, the free unconditioned alternation of

$\ddot{u}$ and i still implies that a nonalternating $\ddot{u}$ cannot exist; but now the reconstruction of $\ddot{u} \backsim i$ as an earlier $\ddot{u}$ is not justifiable except on the basis of collateral historical information regarding this change in other cases.

4.3   Another possible assumption leads to a set of synchronic universals paralleling those relating to free unconditional variation; this has to do with style variation. The common lento-allegro dichotomy no doubt oversimplifies the facts, but no other data are available. An examination of phonemic analyses in the literature using this distinction suggests very strongly the hypothesis that the lento form is always the earlier form and the allegro the later. A very instructive example which will be merely alluded to here is Bloch's description of the distribution of voiced and voiceless vowels in Japanese.[11] If we assume that change first occurs in the allegro style and will show free variation in its first stage, then the most recent changes will be reflected in this manner. In the next stage the innovation invades the lento style, where it occurs as a free variant; but in the allegro style the new form is now exclusive. The last stage, with the change fully accomplished, shows the new form as the exclusive variant in both styles.

Thus in Japanese, as reported by Bloch, the vowels of minimum aperture i and u are voiceless in the environment of certain voiceless consonants in allegro speech, but still in free variation with voiced vowels in lento speech.

4.4   The four examples of diachronic universals cited in §4.1 have in common that the changes are unconditional. In analogous fashion, universals of conditioned sound change are reflected in universals of allophonic conditioned variation which is presumably also free in its initial stages. This matter will not be pursued here in detail, but the example of voiceless vowels mentioned in §4.3 may serve as illustration.

A still incomplete review of the occurrence of voiceless vowels reported from 16 languages shows consistency in a number of respects. One of these is that vowels of minimum aperture have a greater tendency to become voiceless than lower vowels. This can be subsumed in an allophonic implicational universal which is valid in at least these 16 cases: if a language has voiceless allophones of low vowels, it always has voiceless allophones of high vowels. To take one example: Campa, an Arawakan language, has four vowel phonemes, i, e, o, and a. Of these only i has a voiceless free variant and only in final position. Style variants show the same phenomenon. In Japanese the vowels a, e, and o have voiceless variants which are less frequent than voiced in certain environments and only in allegro style whereas, as I have mentioned, i and u have exclusively voiceless forms in these environments in allegro and free variation between voiced and voiceless in lento. Further, in certain environments, including word final, reconstructible i and u are lost as such but show up as length in the previous consonant, while a, e, and o survive.

This example suggests that at least in certain cases of vowel loss known only from documentary sources, the vowels may first have gone through a voiceless stage. Again, the existence of $s \backsim h$ free variations in certain contemporary languages, and the apparent absence of alternations between s and zero, suggest that in historic cases where s becomes zero it first goes through an h stage. Alternations between h and zero are fairly common in existing languages, but of course by no means all of these result from an earlier s.

4.5 The example of voiceless vowels suggests a kind of dynamically oriented typological comparison as a possible source of illumination for interrelated synchronic and diachronic phenomena. In such a comparison I would include all languages exhibiting a certain phonetic characteristic, say voiceless vowels. The term 'phonetic' is used advisedly, since it will be valuable to include instances where the phenomenon is allophonic as well as those where it is phonemic and participates in morphophonemic alternations. Thus, diachronic preferences for particular types of conditional changes as against others will appear in the earliest stages as conditioned free variation in allegro style, later as conditioned unfree variation, and still later, if the positional allophone becomes phonemic, as a morphophonemic alternation.

The method is therefore like that of producing a moving picture from successive still shots obtained from languages at various stages of the development that interests us.

5. This paper has been concerned with phonology, and that only within the restricted area of conditioned and unconditioned regular sound change. Clearly much of what has been said will also apply not only to other phonological processes, such as distance dissimilation in relation to the canonical form of morphemes, but also to change in other aspects of language.

If what I have discussed here in tentative terms is enough to demonstrate certain rather neglected areas in which synchronic and diachronic studies can be fruitfully related, this paper will have accomplished its purpose.

[1]For internal reconstruction, see W. L. Chafe, "Internal reconstruction in Seneca," *Lg*. 35, 477-95 (1959); J. W. Marchand, "Internal reconstruction of phonemic split," *Lg*. 32, 245-53 (1956); and the references to the earlier literature in these articles.

[2]See particularly R. Jakobson, "Typological studies and their contribution to historical comparative linguistics," reprinted in *Roman Jakobson: Selected writings I: Phonological studies*, 523-32 (The Hague, 1962).

[3]A. Martinet, *Économie des changements phonétiques: Traité de phonologie diachronique* (Bern, 1955). Note that though the causes of particular phonological tendencies, which figure importantly in Martinet's exposition, are not discussed in this paper, I consider them an entirely legitimate area of inquiry.

[4]C. A. Ferguson, "Assumptions about nasals: A sample study in phonological universals," in *Universals of language*, 42-47, ed. J. H. Greenberg (Cambridge, 1963).

[5]It should be noted that statements regarding the origin of nasal vowels made here are subject to the reserve expressed in Ferguson's paper regarding the possible origin of a nasal vowel in Iroquoian languages by spontaneous nasalization of an oral vowel.

[6]Of course, where an unrestricted universal holds, any statement may figure as implicans. For example, if a language has a case system, it has oral vowels. Such implications as the present one might, however, be said to 'make sense' because of the phonetic similarity of oral and nasal vowels. But of course similarity is a vague concept. It seems more satisfactory to state as a further connection between synchronic and diachronic studies that there is a sufficient reason to make an implicational statement in which the implicandum is an unrestricted universal if there is an attested case of diachronic change connecting the states described in the implicans and the implicandum.

[7]J. H. Greenberg, C. E. Osgood, and J. J. Jenkins, "Memorandum concerning language universals," in J. H. Greenberg, ed., op cit., 255-64, especially 261-62.

[8]The figures for French are taken from A. Valdman, "Les bases statistiques de l'antériorité articulatoire du français," *Le français moderne* 27, 102-10 (1959), based on a sample of 12,144 vowels. Those from Latin derive from a personal count of the first 1,000 vowels from Cicero's *Letters to Atticus*, Book III, Letters 1, 3, 5, 7 and 9.

[9]This is true for several pairs in French as reported in A. Valdman.

[10]G. Bonfante, "Reconstruction and linguistic method, part I," *Word* 1, 83-94 (1945), 91.

[11]B. Bloch, "Studies in Colloquial Japanese IV. Phonemics", *Lg*. 26, 86-125 (1950).

Section Three
Twentieth Century: Generative Theory, Sociolinguistics, and Other Recent Contributions

Introduction

It is well-known by now that the 1960's bore witness to a theoretical and methodological upheaval in linguistics. Trends in this period were primarily derived from a revolutionary new approach to the structure of language, generative grammar. Noam Chomsky, the founder and developer of generative grammar, initially concentrated his efforts on English syntax and, to a somewhat lesser extent, phonology, and it was in these areas that the majority of research during the early sixties was carried out. It was only a matter of time, however—and it proved to be a short time indeed—before this new approach to language structure was found to be applicable and useful for language evolution as well, and in the process the model itself gained in sophistication, technique, and explanatory power, not to mention popularity.

As has been traditional and customary in historical linguistics, the first breakthroughs using the generative model came in the area of phonology. Kiparsky's seminal dissertation "Phonological Change" (M.I.T. 1965) provided the groundwork for a host of important studies throughout the late sixties and into the seventies, many of which tested and elaborated the basic premises of generative grammar as a useful diachronic theory. Given the traditional generative proposition that a language is a finite system of rules which speakers apply to produce an infinity of utterances, and, further, that the phonology of a language is structured very much like the syntax, with rules for deriving surface forms from abstract underlying ones, the "natural" conclusion of the generative-oriented analyst is that changes in a language reflect changes in the rules themselves. It is the fundamental premise of generative-historical linguistics that "sound change is rule change," or, as Postal has phrased it (1968: 270): ". . . what really changes is not sounds, but grammars." This statement more than any other draws the theoretical demarcation between the first four papers in this section and those in sections I and II. This more abstract, mentalistic approach to phonological change stands in emphatic contrast to the formulations of the structuralist school (especially as presented by Hockett 1965 which, as mentioned in the introduction to section II, the author was unwilling to release for reprinting), which by and large viewed sound change as the result of random articulatory errors. While structuralism insisted that sound change was primarily physical in nature, and is thus proper to the study of speech (performance), generative grammar argues that sound change is essentially mentalistic in nature, and its investigation should proceed from a study of the language system itself (competence). So, just as synchronic generative grammar dominated American linguistics throughout the 1960's and early 1970's, this model has also provided the theoretical and methodological foundation for the majority of work done on diachronic phonology in the past decade.

In "Functional Load and Sound Change" (1967), Robert D. King rejects Martinet's concept of functional yield (cf. selection 7). Martinet has claimed that functional load, which is a measure of the frequency with which two phonemes contrast in all possible environments, thereby helping to keep utterances apart, is a factor of prime importance in all sound change. In his paper, King adduces evidence from Germanic which indicates that functional load is a negligible factor in the motivation and direction of a sound change. King claims that, contrary to Martinet's assumptions, the speaker of a language has no ability to consciously avoid possible linguistic changes, and in the process refutes Martinet's claim that there is an interdependence between sound change and communicative needs.

Both excerpts [11] by Paul Kiparsky are concerned with the question of the order of rules in generative historical phonology. His "Linguistic Universals and Linguistic Change" (1968) has been the starting point for many a historical linguist who has attempted to relate the problems of linguistic change to the adequacy of linguistic theory. The sections which we reprint here, which deal with rule reordering and its unidirectional tendency, provide a significant statement on the nature of grammatical rules and the effects that their order has on the grammar of a language.

In the excerpt from "Historical Linguistics" (1971), Kiparsky addresses the problem of the feeding and bleeding order of rules, and their effects on the direction of reordering. Kiparsky here introduces the notion of rule opacity. Through this concept he attempts to explain non-automatic alternations and surface contradictions of phonological rules. Kiparsky claims that the more opaque a rule is, the harder that rule is to learn. This leads him to the general principle that rules tend to be ordered so as to become maximally transparent, and thus maximally applicable. Eventually, this leads to an overall simplification of the grammar.

William S-Y. Wang [12] advances the hypothesis that many seeming irregularities in sound change can be viewed as the result of two (or more?) sound changes competing with each other through time. Wang claims: "Two sound changes are intersecting if and only if the period of operation of one is partly or wholly concurrent with the period of operation of the other," and a sound change is regular "if no other changes compete against it." Wang proposes that the operation of a sound change must be viewed in the dimension of time (in terms of its spread throughout the possible set of relevant morphemes in the lexicon) along three parameters: the phonetic (sound X to Y); the lexical (from morpheme to morpheme in the vocabulary); and the social (from speaker to speaker in the same dialect). He claims that when two competing sound changes intersect in time, a residue may result, thus opening the possibility that a sound change may not complete its course. The longer sound changes operate, the more likely it becomes that they will intersect, compete, and leave a residue. In this way we may recognize incomplete sound changes as a cause of splits.

In his contribution, "Phonetic Analogy and Conceptual Analogy" [13], Theo Vennemann rejects the popular transformational notion that all analogical change can be accounted for within the grammar of a language, as well as the pre-transformational notion that it can be accounted for within the output of the grammar. He achieves this by establishing a distinction between phonetic analogy, which he maintains as proper to the internal structure of the grammar, and conceptual analogy, which he claims is motivated by irregularities in the output of the grammar. His study thus supports in part the formulations of Kiparsky and King (1968) in that it describes phonetic analogy as grammar change, but agrees with the precepts of pre-transformational linguistics, especially the work of Humboldt, by describing conceptual analogy as a result of irregularities in language itself.

In a volatile field such as linguistics, the stunning successes of today frequently become the historical oddities of tomorrow. Just as 'traditional' generative grammar (as best exemplified by Chomsky 1965) has been assaulted from a variety of angles, so diachronic generative linguistics has come under attack from several different quarters as well. Some new developments, for example Natural Phonology, can be viewed as theoretical descendants of traditional generative grammar, and are perhaps best thought of as evolution within the generative paradigm rather than revolution against it. Other developments, however, are far less easily reconciled with the traditional generative approach to diachronic phonology.

Three papers representing anti-generative views are included in this section. These are, first, Labov's "On the Use of the Present to Explain the Past" [14], which, in the tradition of Labov's pioneering work in sociolinguistics, rejects the notion that speech communities are homogeneous, and proposes instead that they embody orderly heterogeneity. Sociolinguistics attempts to balance the frequently opposed synchronic and diachronic aspects of language by showing that synchronic alternation among speakers, frequently dismissed by linguists as "mere stylistic variation," is in fact indicative of diachronic change in progress.

Labov examines the Early Modern English merger of words orthographically represented by *ea* (e.g. *meat, meal*) with words which are reflexes of words containing Middle English *a* (e.g. *great, break*), as well as the later separation of the *ea*-words which were to merge with words containing reflexes of Middle English *e* (e.g. *meet, seed*). Labov claims that general principles of phonetic and sociolinguistic research are needed to explore fruitfully the problems of historical linguistics. He observes that through an examination of the written records of grammarians, schoolmasters, and orthoëpists of the 16th century, the systematic variations, asymmetrical word classes, regional dialects, and class stratification of this period can all be identified as contributing factors in this merger and later split.

Labov cites compelling evidence from current sociolinguistic studies of sound change in process to support his claim that this merger/split, which has been the source of a protracted controversy in the history of English, was actually the result of such non-linguistic factors as opposing social values and the migration into London of a large Southeastern population. Labov finds that by appealing to our knowledge and understanding of the present, "we should have no hesitation in projecting this understanding to past events which are no longer accessible to direct observation."

Also included in this section is Henning Andersen's "Abductive and Deductive Change" [15], which, by examining a highly irregular and unexpected sound change in a Czech dialect, suggests an attractive and sociolinguistically sensitive alternative to the generative notion of spontaneous "change by rule." Andersen accomplishes this by using the well-established philosophical concepts of <u>abduction</u> and <u>deduction</u>. He suggests that there is a goal-directed, cyclical application of abductive and deductive processes involved in the construction of grammars by speakers of a language. He distinguishes several types of changes, including evolutive and adaptive changes, and in the process makes a significant contribution to our understanding of internally motivated sound changes, and those induced from without.

Finally, there is a significant and controversial paper by Raimo Anttila, one of the prime critics of the generative movement, entitled "Formalization as Degeneration in Historical Linguistics" [16]. In this paper Anttila seeks to trace the development and rise of the generative model as the standard theoretical paradigm for nearly a decade. He argues, quite forcefully, the reader will notice, that the generative movement has been a "social" rather than a "scientific" revolution, and that the generativists have repeatedly proffered elaborate descriptions and called them explanations. The attack is sharp; we will leave the issue for the reader to decide.

References

Chomsky, Noam. 1965 *Aspects of the Theory of Syntax* (Cambridge: MIT Press).

Hockett, Charles. 1965 "Sound Change." *Language* 41, 185-204.

King, Robert. 1968 *Historical Linguistics and Generative Grammar* (Englewood Cliffs: Prentice Hall).

Postal, Paul. 1968 *Aspects of Phonological Theory* (New York: Harper and Row).

10 Functional Load and Sound Change

ROBERT D. KING

The idea that functional load offers a tool of potentially great explanatory power in diachronic linguistics is shared by a number of contemporary
linguists, particularly those influenced at first or second hand by Prague.
It is the purpose of the present paper to investigate the hypothesis that
functional load plays a significant role in sound change. I will attempt
to demonstrate that functional load, if it is a factor in sound change at
all, is one of the least important of those we know anything about, and
that it is best disregarded in discussions centering on the cause and
direction of phonological change.

This paper is divided as follows. I begin with a brief inquiry into
the genesis and development of the various conjectures associated
with functional load, particularly those conjectures which occur in
the work of André Martinet. On the basis of this I formulate three
clearly testable hypotheses relating functional load to sound change.
Next I analyze three historical Germanic languages where functional
load can be evaluated in its effect on a number of phonological
changes, from which I draw my negative conclusions about the relevance of functional load to the causality and direction of sound
change. The final section of the paper is a discussion of what I regard as the inherent implausibility of any theory which purposes to
make sound change a function of statistical data on low-level phonological units. The Appendix contains the relevant statistical data
on the languages analyzed.[1]

1.1 *The Concept*
The term <u>functional</u> <u>load</u> is customarily used in linguistics to describe the extent and degree of contrast between linguistic units,
usually phonemes. In its simplest expression, functional load is a
measure of the number of minimal pairs which can be found for a given
opposition. More generally, in phonology, it is a measure of the
work which two phonemes (or a distinctive feature) do in keeping
utterances apart—in other words, a gauge of the frequency with
which two phonemes contrast in all possible environments.

From *Language* 43 (1967), 831–852. Reprinted by permission of
Robert D. King and the Linguistic Society of America.

Like much else which is commonly regarded as characteristic of
Prague Circle linguistic thought, functional load, or something very
similar to it, had found inchoate expression well before the Prague
Circle began its work in the late 1920's. The French dialect geo-
grapher Jules Gilliéron, basing his theories on the rich finds of
the *Atlas linguistique*, had worked under the assumption that language
had in itself various therapeutic devices for counteracting the
effects of regular sound laws. One of the most important of these
devices was the avoidance of homonymy (Gilliéron 1918:14). His concept was not, of course, the same thing as functional load, but it
was close. The crucial point is that sound change in Gilliéron's
view was restrained (though to an unstated and indefinite degree)
by the communicative function of language. This kind of interlocking
of sound laws (structure) and the communicative needs of the speaker
(function) was ready-made for inclusion into the thinking which went
on in Prague during the interwar period, and it is in the work of
the Prague Circle that we find the first relatively clear statement
of what functional load is.

The "Projet de terminologie phonologique standardisée" (Cercle
Linguistique de Prague, 1931:309-23) has the following entry:
"Rendement fonctionnel—Degré d'utilisation d'une opposition phonologique pour la différenciation des diverses significations des mots
dans une langue donnée." Credit is usually given to the founder of
the Prague Circle, Vilém Mathesius, for being the first to publish
on functional load (Vachek 1966:65). Actually, Mathesius did not
use the term in either of his two early articles concerned with the
degree of utilization of phonemic oppositions (1929, 1931), using
instead circumlocutions such as "valeur fonctionnelle," "l'utilisation fonctionnelle," and "Grad der Ausnützung von phonologischen
Einheiten." It is, however, clear that he was dealing with the concept of functional load, even if he did not use the specific French
or German term. Aside from the minor question of what terms Mathesius did or did not use, it is of more importance in the present
paper to observe that he regarded functional load as a purely descriptive device—as one part of a complete phonological description
of a language along with the roster of phonemes, phonemic variants,
distinctive features, and the rest (Mathesius 1931:148). He did not
attempt to establish a causal relationship between functional load
and the probability that a given phonological opposition might be
destroyed in sound change, at least not in his published articles to
which I have had access. It seems clear, however, that most linguists of the Prague Circle considered functional load as something
more than an item of description, as something which might serve as
a key in unraveling the causes of sound change.

Bohumil Trnka (1931) speaks of the "prophylactic tendency" in language to avoid the occurrence of excessive homonymy by means of phonemic change. Roman Jakobson (1931:259) points out that a small functional load favors the loss of an opposition. Trubetzkoy has, on the whole, very little to say about functional load. His *Anleitung* (1935) contains not a single reference to it; in the *Grundzüge* (1939) there are only a few statements dealing with functional load as a descriptive device of synchronic phonology, and nothing about the potentialities of functional load as a tool of diachronic study.

We see from this brief historical inquiry that the Prague Circle, for all its apparently considerable theoretical concern with functional load,[2] did little with it, either in synchronic or diachronic linguistics. The concept remained vague ("degré d'utilisation"); it was never operationally defined or used in practice; and the man whose name comes most easily to mind when the Prague School is mentioned—Trubetzkoy—had next to nothing to say about it. When one reads those members of the Prague Circle who wrote specifically about functional load, Mathesius and Trnka, it is not certain whether they regarded functional load as a simple adding up of near-homonyms à la Gilliéron, as some mathematical function of the relative frequencies of the phonemes or distinctive features involved, or as something yet more complex. (This massive unclarity continues to exist today in the thinking of a great many linguists concerned with functional load.) As for the role of functional load in sound change, the pronouncements remained programmatic; and no concrete instances of the effect of functional load on a sound change were discussed by a member of the Prague Circle during its classical period in any publication available to me.[3]

Thus, although functional load is felt, by most linguists acquainted with the term, to be characteristic of the Prague Circle approach to phonology, the truth of the matter is that, in the task of shaping functional load into a viable tool of either synchronic or diachronic phonology, Prague did not get much beyond Gilliéron's concept of the clash of homonyms. And, after all, one did not have to be a member of the Prague Circle to suggest that Gilliéron's ideas might be fruitfully incorporated into historical discussions based on the emerging concept of the phoneme.[4]

1.2 *Martinet.*

This brings us to André Martinet and his development of the notion of functional load as a discussable factor in sound change. In spite of the seductive plausibility of Gilliéron's teleological theory that language strives to avoid homonymy, mergers do occur—frequently, and often on a large scale. It is clear that the somewhat

primitive notions of the French dialectologist would need much re-
fining if they were to be salvaged at all as parts of a comprehensive theory of sound change. The salvage job, as it were, was undertaken by Martinet who, in his first published article in 1933, made
copious use of the concept of functional load in describing French
phonology. Furthermore, in publications dating back to 1938, Martinet has cogently and persistently argued that functional load has
rich yet unexplored possibilities for the linguist who attempts to
plumb the causality of sound change.[5] His contribution, as we shall
see, goes beyond the Prague Circle in its ambitiousness and scope.

  Martinet's initial assumption as what he calls a "functionalist"
is that sound changes do not proceed independently of man's need to
communicate: "Le postulat de base des fonctionalistes, en la matière,
est que les changements phonétiques ne se produisent pas sans égards
aux besoins de la communication, et qu'un des facteurs qui peut
déterminer leur direction, et même leur apparition, est la nécessité
foncière d'assurer la compréhension mutuelle en conservant les oppositions phonologiques utiles" (1955:49). Economy leads the speaker
to be careless in his speech, says Martinet;[6] but the requirement
that communication must be maintained places a constraint on how
careless a speaker can become. Generally speaking, the limit is the
necessity of making oneself understood—i.e. of communicating.
According to Martinet, then, the causes of sound change are to be
found in the interplay and interrelationships among a number of different factors: structure, or the relations between units in a linguistic system; function, or man's need to communicate with others;
inertia, or the tendency toward least effort; and the natural limitations of the speech organs.

  Given Martinet's initial hypothesis that sound changes do not
operate independently of communicative needs, it is but a short step
to his conjecture about functional load: ". . . toutes choses égales
d'ailleurs, une opposition phonologique qui sert à maintenir dis-
tincts des centaines de mots parmi les plus fréquents et les plus
utiles n'opposera-t-elle pas une résistance plus efficace à l'élimi-
nation que celle qui ne rend de service que dans un très petit
nombre de cas?" (1955:54). Thus, the requirement that communicative
needs must be satisfied should help prevent the merger of two phonemes whose opposition bears a high functional load, while such a
therapeutic factor need not assert itself to prevent the eradication
of an opposition whose functional load is very small.

  It is important to remember that this is an hypothesis, not a
statement of empirical findings. Martinet himself gives no evidence
to support it, and the evidence which others have produced is very
slight. The most that can be said for the hypothesis, a priori, is

that it seems compatible with Martinet's fundamental assumption about the interdependence of sound change and communication. Functional load is an example par excellence of a functional factor in sound change, as function is understood by Martinet. Given the assumption that communication must be maintained, and given the fact that sounds change, it simply seems indisputably true that sounds should change in a way which does the least damage to communication; and this implies that oppositions with low functional loads should be destroyed in preference to those which carry a high functional load. Doubts about the obviousness of this chain of reasoning have been expressed, for example by Hoenigswald (1960:79-82), but so far no evidence in refutation and little in support has been furnished.[7]

With this background presented, we can proceed to the statement of definite hypotheses linking functional load in various ways to sound change. Martinet's conjecture about functional load is subject to two interpretations, and in practice both interpretations have emerged. I state them formally as hypotheses: the weak point hypothesis and the least resistance hypothesis. I shall also formulate a third hypothesis, the frequency hypothesis, on the basis of further considerations.

The weak point hypothesis states that, if all else is equal, sound change is more likely to start with oppositions bearing low functional loads than within oppositions bearing high functional loads; or, in the case of a single phoneme, a phoneme of low frequency of occurrence is more likely to be affected by sound change than is a high-frequency phoneme.

A recent example of the use of this hypothesis is given by N.C.W. Spence (1965:4), writing on Vulgar Latin: "Functionally, the oppositions [in Classical Latin] between *ae* and *ĕ* between *oe* and *ē* and between *oe* and *ae* seem to have been of little importance; therefore, since their functional yield was low, the two diphthongs constituted a weak point in the system, which could be simplified at their expense without significantly impairing communication." As we see from this example, the weak point hypothesis has to do with the causality of sound change—why it gets started in the first place. It provides a way of searching for 'weak points' in the system, points from which phonological realignment might start. The least resistance hypothesis, on the other hand, leaves untouched the question of the causality of sound change. It is predicated on the assumption that change is about to take place, and it predicts the direction of that change, as follows:

The least resistance hypothesis states that, if all else is equal, and if (for whatever reason) there is a tendency for a phoneme x to merge with either of the two phonemes y or z, then that merger will occur for which the functional load of the merged opposition is smaller: i.e. x > y if L(x,y) is smaller than L(x,z), and x > z if L(x,z) is smaller than L(x,y), where L(x,y) designates the functional load of the opposition x ≠ y, and > designates merger. Several applications of this hypothesis are found in Benediktsson (1959), and I shall discuss these in detail in §3.1

There is still a third hypothesis which may be derived from Martinet's speculations. Let us suppose that an opposition x ≠ y is destroyed by merger, and that the merger could have taken either of the two forms x > y or y > x. From Martinet's principle that communication must be minimally disrupted during sound change, it follows that the direction of the merger would be dictated by the relative frequency of occurrence of the two phonemes x and y; i.e. that phoneme with the smaller relative frequency should disappear in the merger. One would expect, from a social point of view, that communication would be best maintained when merger takes the form of destroying the less frequent member of the merging opposition. We thus arrive at the following:

The frequency hypothesis states that, if an opposition x ≠ y is destroyed by merger, then that phoneme will disappear in the merger for which the relative frequency of occurrence is smaller: i.e. x > y if the relative frequency of x is smaller than that of y, and y > x if the relative frequency of y is smaller than that of x. It is this hypothesis that lies at the base of the investigations carried out by Diver on Old Bulgarian *št* and Abernathy on the Slavic *yers*.

2. *The Measure of Functional Load.*

I have given elsewhere (King 1965) a detailed motivation, formulation, and evaluation of the measure of functional load used in the present investigation. In particular, I show that this measure derives easily from Martinet's statements concerning what should go into a formula for functional load, that the definition of functional load used here conforms to the specifications enumerated by Wang and Thatcher (1962:10-12), and that functional load indices obtained with the present formula correlate well with those obtained by application of the information-theoretical formulation proposed by Hockett (1955:216-7) and corrected by Wang and Thatcher (17, fn. 7). (See now also Hockett 1966, for further efforts toward quantification of functional load.) In this section I wish only to describe in general terms what is measured by the formula for functional load used here.

The formula applies to oppositions between pairs of phonemes, e.g. English /p ≠ b/, though it can be used to derive an estimate of the

functional load of a distinctive feature. The present formula is
the product of two factors: the first measures the global text frequencies of the two phonemes involved; the second measures the degree
to which they contrast in all possible environments, where environment means, roughly speaking, one phoneme to the left and right.
This formula requires an input text of several thousand phonemes,
the reliability obtained in the computation of functional load indices being proportional to the length of the input text provided.
In this investigation the calculations were carried out on the IBM
7040.

The functional load indices obtained with this formula are always
greater than or equal to zero. A functional load of zero means
either that the phonemes are in complementary distribution (i.e. do
not contrast) or that one of the two phonemes does not occur in the
input text. The majority of functional loads in the languages investigated thus far have a magnitude ranging between 0.500 and 5.000,
though both smaller and larger functional loads are not infrequently
obtained. Like all statistics, these functional load indices are
subject to sampling error—i.e. they vary in magnitude according to
the sample of input text chosen. However, the input texts used in
the current investigation were sufficiently large to minimize the
effect of sampling fluctuation.[8]

3. *Functional Load in Sound Change*.
The performance of the functional load hypotheses stated earlier
(§1.2) are here investigated in four cases from historical Germanic:
Old Icelandic to Modern Icelandic, Old Saxon to Middle Low German,
Middle High German to Modern German, and Middle High German to
certain modern Yiddish dialects.

3.1. *The Icelandic Evidence*.
The vowel system of Icelandic at a time somewhat later than that
described in the First grammatical treatise was as follows:[9]

Short Vowels				Long Vowels			Diphthongs
i	y		u	i:	y:	u:	ei
e	ø		o	e:	ø:	o:	ey
		a	ǫ	ę:		a:	au

Of the changes which this vowel system subsequently underwent,
the ones of interest here may be summarized as follows, the changes
being given in chronological order as far as we are able to determine: (1) /ǫ > ø/ (merger); (2) /ø: > ę:/ (merger); (3) /au > ø^1/
(development of a new diphthong); (4) /e:/ > [e^1], /ę:/ > [a^1],

/o:/ > [o^u], /a:/ > [a^u] (allophonic diphthongization); (5) /y > i/
(merger); (6) /y: > i:/ (merger); (7) /ey > ei/ (merger). There
were further shifts in the vowel system (for example, the fronting
of /u/ to /y/ and the change in the oppositions /i ≠ i:/ and
/u ≠ u:/ from a correlation of length to one of quality), but I ignore these changes here since I see no reasonable way to bring functional load to bear on them.

3.11. /ǫ > ø/. This merger is especially interesting because
scholars have disagreed, in discussing it, on the relevance of functional load. Steblin-Kamenskij (1958:79) has asserted that the
merger of /ǫ/ and /ø/ was caused by the low functional load of the
opposition. Benediktsson disagrees, calling attention to the fact
that /ø/ may well have been a comparatively rare phoneme in Old Icelandic, but that there was a considerable number of minimal pairs
with /ǫ/ and /ø/. Benediktsson (298, fn. 20) concludes: "The hypothesis that the cause of the merger of /ø/ and /ǫ/ was the exceptionally low functional yield of this opposition is therefore not convincing."

The present investigation discloses the following functional loads
for oppositions between /ǫ/ and the other phonemes with which it
might be expected to merge:[10]

$$L(ǫ,a) = 6.721 \qquad L(ǫ,o) = 1.173$$
$$L(ǫ,ø) = 0.191 \qquad L(ǫ,u) = 1.131$$

We see that the functional load of the opposition /ǫ ≠ ø/ is, in
fact, much smaller than the others. Benediktsson, in spite of the
minimal pairs he gives, seems to be wrong on this point, and the
least resistance hypothesis holds up very well in this case—i.e. of
the oppositions which might likely have been destroyed by loss of
/ǫ/, that opposition is destroyed which has the lowest functional
load. The weak point hypothesis is also supported by the fact that
a functional load of 0.191 is quite low for Icelandic, as we see by
examining the Icelandic data in the Appendix; we are therefore not
surprised (under the terms of this hypothesis) to find that phonological realignment has started within this opposition.

The frequency hypothesis, on the other hand, is not supported by
the data in this case. The relative frequency of /ø/ is 0.201 and
that of /ǫ/ is 1.360 (both expressed as percentages). Thus /ǫ/ is
roughly six times more frequent than /ø/, and the frequency hypothesis would predict that this merger should have taken the form
/ø > ǫ/. One could argue, as a follower of Martinet doubtless would,
that /ǫ/, with no low-front vowel to oppose it, represented an un-
economic articulation which had to disappear; and that here the

structural factors prevailed over the functional ones. In either
case, the functional criterion of relative frequency is of no observable importance.

3.12. /ø: > ę:/. This merger, by which /ø:/ is not only unrounded
but also lowered, is unusual from the point of view of the general
Germanic patterns. There are cases in Icelandic and elsewhere of
simple unrounding unaccompanied by lowering, so that /ø: > e:/ would
be a more familiar phonemenon. Benediktsson's argument is that the
structural factor involved was the tendency to reduce the number of
tonality features characterizing /ø:/—it was front and rounded, and
by its merger with /ę:/ it became front with the redundant feature
of unroundedness. Merger with /e:/ would not have accomplished this;
/ø:/ would thereby have become front, but unroundedness would then
have been a distinctive feature.

   Let us examine the functional load data for minimally different
oppositions with /ø:/ as one member:

   L(ø:, ę:) = 0.087   L(ø:, y:) = 0.041   L(ø:, u:) = 0.041
   L(ø:, a:) = 0.139   L(ø:, e:) = 0.062   L(ø:, i:) = 0.170
                 L(ø:, o:) = 0.237

We note first of all that most of the functional load indices are
very small—only three of the seven are greater than 0.100. The
differences between indices as small as this may well be due to sampling fluctuation and not indicative of real differences in functional load. Tentatively accepting them as reliable, however, we see
that the functional load of the phonetically most likely merger
(/ø: > ę:/)is smaller than the functional load of the opposition
which was actually destroyed (/ø: ≠ e:/), and that the functional
load of the opposition /o: ≠ y:/, also a potential candidate for
obliteration, was lower than either. The functional load of the
opposition /ø: ≠ o:/ is the highest of all, which might explain why
that merger did not take place; but that sort of change is unusual
in Germanic in any case; front rounded vowels generally lose their
roundness, not their frontness, during change. Also, we will see
in §3.15 that a functional load many times larger than that of
/ø: ≠ o:/ is destroyed in the merger /y > i/, so that it would be
rash to suggest that the functional load of the opposition /ø: ≠ o:/
had anything to do with its resistance to merger.

   In this case, therefore, the least resistance hypothesis does not
correctly predict the direction of the merger (although the functional load indices involved were so small as to make this conclusion statistically shaky). The weak point hypothesis is supported,
since the functional load of the opposition /ø: ≠ ę:/ is extremely

small. The relative frequency of /ø:/ is 0.166, that of /ę:/ is 0.660, so that the less frequent member of the opposition disappears in merger, which is in accord with the frequency hypothesis.

3.13. /au > $ø^i$/. Concerning this development, Benediktsson (299) says: ". . . the diphthong /au/ approached the OIcel., diphthong /ey/ which presumably was phonetically similar to Mod. Icel. /öi/. . . . But the merger of these two diphthongs was avoided by the further development of /ey/ [i.e. /ey/ merged with /ei/]." Since no merger is involved in this change, there is no possibility of testing the hypotheses of least resistance or frequency. We may, nevertheless, examine the functional load data and the relative frequency data in an effort to determine whether the cause and form of this change are explained by low functional importance. The relative frequency of /au/ is 0.469. This is not excessively low: the relative frequency of /ø/, which did not disappear, is 0.201. The functional load of the opposition /au $\neq$ ey/ is trivially small, 0.075, so that the merger of the two (possible on the basis of Benediktsson's observation that /ey/ and /$ø^i$/ from /au/ were phonetically similar) would have erased an unimportant opposition of trifling functional load. I conclude, therefore, that the functional data (by which I mean functional load and relative frequency) explain nothing about this change—neither its cause, nor its form, nor why /$ø^i$/ did not merge with /ey/.

3.14. /e:/ > [e^i], /ę:/ > [a^i], /o:/ > [o^u], /a:/ > [a^u]. Here, as in the change /au > $ø^i$/, we are not dealing with mergers, so that we cannot test either the least resistance hypothesis or the frequency hypothesis. However, we can test the weak point hypothesis by seeing whether low frequency of occurrence can be made to account for this set of changes which have no readily obvious structural cause (i.e. there is no apparent asymmetry in the subset of long vowels to account for the diphthongization of the non-high long vowels).

The relative frequencies of the four phonemes which undergo change[11] are:

freq(e:) = 0.474   freq(ę:) = 0.826
freq(o:) = 0.963   freq(a:) = 1.981

It is obvious that the cause of this set of changes cannot be found in low frequency. All four phonemes are more frequent than /ø/, which has remained in the vowel system of Icelandic down to the present; three of them (/ę: o: a:/) are more frequent than /u:/ (relative frequency = 0.665), which likewise has remained in the vowel system to the present; and /a:/ has a fairly high frequency of occurrence—higher, for example, than /i:/ (= 1.242) and /ei/ (= 1.237), neither of which has been shifted out of the system by sound change.[12]

Two of these changes, viz. /e:/ > [e^1] and /a:/ > [a^u], might be expected to have resulted in merger with the previously existing diphthongs /ei/ and /au/.[13] These mergers did not occur, so that it is relevant to ask whether their non-occurrence might not be due to high, merger-inhibiting functional loads. The indices involved are L(e:, ei) = 0.700 and L(a:, au) = 0.895. These functional loads are not trivially small, though they are small in comparison with numerous other functional loads of vowel oppositions in Icelandic; and in particular both are much smaller than the functional load of the opposition /y $\neq$ i/(= 6.481), which was destroyed by merger (§3.15). I conclude, therefore, that functional load is of no use in explaining the non-occurrence of either of these mergers.

3.15. /y > i/. Benediktsson (299), adhering to the logic of his principle that the changes in the Icelandic vowel system are to be explained by the tendency to lose the second tonality feature, argues that /y/ should have merged with /u/, not /i/. This did not occur, and Benediktsson (311) suggests that the high functional load of /u $\neq$ y/ prevented the expected merger.

The present investigation gives the following data for the oppositions involved: L(y,i) = 6.481, L(y,u) = 1.442. These figures are in disagreement with Benediktsson's feeling for the relative magnitudes of the functional loads. The functional load of /y $\neq$ i/ is more than four times as great as that of /y $\neq$ u/, and the difference is definitely significant (i.e. not due to sampling error). This is evidence against the least resistance hypothesis (which would predict the merger /y > u/) and against the weak point hypothesis (since 6.481 is a large functional load). On the other hand, the frequency hypothesis is supported by the form of this merger, since the frequency of /y/, which disappears in the merger, is 0.748, and this is lower than the frequency of /i/, which is 7.380. If one accepts Benediktsson's argument that the merger /y > u/ is structurally more favored (which I do not), then there are strong structural and functional grounds for that merger, and it becomes very difficult within the Martinet framework to explain why it did not occur.

3.16. /y: > i:/. The functional load indices pertinent here are: L(y:, i:) = 0.111, L(y:, u:) = 0.174. Neither opposition carries a very high functional load, which is to be expected because of the relatively small frequencies of the three phonemes involved, and it is not certain whether the observed difference is real or due to sampling fluctuation. If we accept the difference as real, then the least resistance hypothesis correctly predicts the direction of merger. The functional load of the merged opposition /y: ≠ i:/ is small, but not trivially small: the functional load of /y: ≠ ø:/ was much smaller, namely 0.041, so that functionally the merger /y: > ø:/ would have been favored over either /y: > i:/ or /y: > u:/, yet this merger did not occur. Thus the weak point hypothesis is at best only slightly supported by the data of this merger. However, the frequency hypothesis is supported by the relative frequency data: freq(i:) = 1.242, freq(y:) = 0.245, so that the less frequent member of the opposition disappears in the merger.

3.17. /ey > ei/. The relative frequency of /ei/ is 1.237 and that of /ey/ is 0.196. Since /ey/ disappears in the merger, the frequency hypothesis correctly predicts the form of the merger. It is not clear how one should test the least resistance hypothesis here, since we are not sufficiently aware of the possibilities of development of /ey/. If we assume, as it seems plausible to do, that /ey/ could equally well have merged with /ei/ or /e:/, then we find that this merger does not follow the path of least functional resistance. The relevant indices are L(ey, ei) = 0.107 and L(ey, e:) = 0.052, so that the least resistance hypothesis predicts the wrong merger. The weak point hypothesis is supported quite well by the data: the relative frequency of /ey/ and the functional load of /ey ≠ ei/ are both very small, so that, under the terms of this hypothesis, one is not surprised to find sound change affecting /ey/ and the opposition /ey ≠ ei/.

3.2. *The Old Saxon Evidence.*
Old Saxon is not as useful as Icelandic for investigating the relationships between functional load and sound change. Icelandic has had a plethora of mergers in its history, and it is only to mergers that two of the hypotheses apply. If we view Middle Low German as the continuation of Old Saxon (which is customarily done, though the diverse changes between the two require caution in using the formula OS > MLG), we must conclude that most of the developments which carry us from Old Saxon to Middle Low German were not mergers. Nevertheless, the merger þ > d in late Old Saxon does permit us to raise the question of the relevance of functional load to sound change.

3.21. /þ > d/. This same merger took place in early Old High German, though there the structural and phonetic reasons seem to be stronger than in Old Saxon. The tongue-tip region of the stops and fricatives of Germanic was crowded: the sounds /t d þ s z/ were all formed with the tip of the tongue against the teeth or the alveolar ridge. The "marge de sécurité," to use Martinet's phrase, of each dental consonant was presumably great enough for effective and consistent differentiation; modern English, after all, has all of these plus /ð/, and there does not seem to be any general tendency to thin out the tongue-tip consonants in English. The Old High German consonant shift, however, produced two new consonants in the dental region, the affricate /t^s/ and the dorsal sibilant /z/ (Joos 1952). At this point the pressure for merger must have been very great, so that we are not surprised to find /þ > d/, doubtless via [ð]. This particular form of the merger was favored in Old High German by the fact that there was a hole in the pattern, earlier /d/ (< PGmc. *ð) having shifted to /t/.

It would not be wise to attribute the cause of the /þ > d/ merger to the Old High German consonant shift alone, for /þ/ dropped out of the system in many other dialects as well: in Low German and continental Scandinavian, for example. The merger did not occur in English, so there is no overwhelming structural reason for the change. Let us now examine Old Saxon and see whether the merger can be explained on the basis of low functional load or low frequency.

First, we observe that the frequencies of the tongue-tip consonants were all high in comparison with other Old Saxon consonants. We have, in percentages:

freq(þ) = 4.554	freq(d) = 5.683
freq(t) = 4.000	freq(s) = 5.901

The frequencies of the other consonants, excluding nasals and resonants, were considerably smaller.[14] There is, therefore, no reason to regard /þ/ as a weak point in the system, particularly susceptible to sound change.

Let us investigate the functional load data for oppositions between /þ/ and phonemes with which it might be expected to merge. Here we must take account of the general continental West Germanic lenition of the voiceless spirants, which led in Old High German from /þ/ through /ð/ to /d/, parallel except for the occlusion to the development of /f/ (often spelled u in Old High German documents) and /s/ (cf. modern German). For Old Saxon this indicated a pronunciation [ð], and if this were going to merge with anything, it would be with the voiced or lenis allophones of /s/ or with /d/. The relevant functional load indices, therefore, are L(þ, s) = 27.048, L(þ, d) = 9.740. The least resistance hypothesis correctly predicts the merger /þ > d/, and, as we see from the relative frequencies given above,

the frequency hypothesis correctly predicts the surviving member of
the opposition, viz. /d/. However, the weak point hypothesis comes
off very badly in this merger. Both from the point of view of relative frequency (the frequency of /þ/ is very high for a consonant)
and of functional load (the functional load of /þ ≠ d/ is very
high for a consonantal opposition in Old Saxon), there is nothing
which marks the phoneme /þ/ or the opposition /þ ≠ d/ as especially
suitable candidates for obliteration.[15]

3.3. *Middle High German to Modern German.*

The Middle High German vowel system offers some opportunity for testing the various hypotheses associated with functional load. For the
time being, I shall limit my investigation to developments in the
standard language, and reference will be made to the situation in
the dialects only when reliable and pertinent data are available.

Let us diagram the vowel system of Classical Middle High German:

Short Vowels			Long Vowels			Diphthongs		
i	ü	u	i:	ü:	u:	iə	uə	üə
e	ö	o	e:	ö:	o:	ei	ou	öi
ɛ			æ:		a:			
æ		a						

The changes which take us from this vowel system to that of Modern
Standard German are:[16] (1) /æ > ɛ/ (merger); (2) /e > ɛ/ (merger);
(3) /æ: > e:/ (merger); (4) /iə uə üə/ > /i: u: ü:/ (creation of
long, more open high vowels); (5) /i: u: ü:/ > /ei ou öi/ (merger);
(6) /ei ou öi/ > /ai au oi/ (allophonic changes in the first element
of the diphthongs). There was also some rounding (MHG *helle* > NHG
Hölle) and isolated unrounding (MHG *küssen* > NHG *Kissen*), but these
changes are not subject to ready application of any of the functional
load hypotheses and will be ignored here.

3.31. /æ > ɛ/. The low-front /æ/ is an extremely rare phoneme in
Middle High German. Its relative frequency in the text sample used
here is 0.023, or slightly more than two occurrences per ten thousand
phonemes. It is thus in line with the weak point hypothesis that
/æ/ should disappear from the system. If we suppose that /æ/ could
have merged with /ɛ/, /e/, or /a/, then the relevant functional load
indices are:

$$L(æ, ɛ) = 0.004 \quad L(æ, a) = 0.040 \quad L(æ, e) = 0.005$$

All three indices are trivially small, especially the two for
/æ ≠ ɛ/ and /æ ≠ e/, and it is not certain whether the small
difference in their sizes is significant or whether it is the result

of sampling fluctuation (and therefore not significant). If the differences can be trusted, then the least resistance hypothesis correctly predicts that /æ/ merged with /ɛ/ instead of /e/ or /a/, and it is in accord with the weak point hypothesis that change occurs within an opposition bearing so small a functional load as /æ ≠ ɛ/. Finally, the frequency hypothesis is supported by the evidence of this merger, since /ɛ/ is decidedly more frequent than /æ/, in percentages 4.132 against 0.023.

3.32. /e > ɛ/. The data given in the Appendix must be adjusted in order to take account of the prior merger of /æ/ and /ɛ/, which swells slightly the frequency of /ɛ/ and the functional loads of oppositions containing /ɛ/ as one member. The relative frequency of /ɛ/ is, upon recalculation, equal to freq(ɛ) + freq(æ) = 4.132 + 0.023 = 4.155. The functional load of /e ≠ ɛ/ is L(e, ɛ) + L(e, æ) = 1.995 + 0.005 = 2.000.[17]

Thus the functional load of the opposition destroyed by the merger /e > ɛ/ was 2.000. This is not a small functional load: it is much larger than the functional loads involved in the merger /æ > ɛ/; it is also much larger than the functional loads of numerous other vocalic oppositions in Middle High German which were not merged, e.g. L(i, ü) = 1.671, L(e, ö) = 0.010, L(ɛ, ö) = 0.069, L(ü, ö) = 0.022, L(i:, ü:) = 1.175, and L(e:, ö:) = 0.011. Also, the relative frequency of /e/ is not excessively low: it is 0.649, which is larger than the frequencies of other vowel phonemes which did not undergo merger, e.g. /ü/ (0.454), /ö/ (0.074), /e:/ (0.417), and /ö:/ (0.111). I conclude that the weak point hypothesis is not verified in this case.

As for the direction by which /e/ merged out of existence, it seems equally likely, on the grounds of phonetic proximity, that /e/ could have merged with /ɛ/ or /i/ (I disregard the possibility of /e > ö/, since that kind of development is rare, perhaps non-existent, as a regular phonetic change in German dialects). The functional load of /e ≠ ɛ/ is 2.000, and that of /e ≠ i/ is 1.963, so the least resistance hypothesis does not predict the correct direction of the change. The frequency hypothesis is supported here since the less frequent member of the opposition disappears: freq(e) = 0.649, freq(ɛ) = 4.155.

The overriding symmetry factor in this merger, as well as in /æ > ɛ/ and /æ: > e:/, was the trend to reduce to one the number of e-phonemes in the front series of vowels, opposed to a single /o/ or /o:/ in the back series. The opposition /æ ≠ ɛ/ was of little functional importance (since it had a very low functional load), and hence according to the weak point hypothesis could be disposed of without endangering communication; but if so, the opposition /ɛ ≠ e/ with its medium (certainly not trivial) functional load should have offered more resistance to merger. There is no evidence that this was so in the Middle German dialects which have given us Modern Standard German.

In Upper German dialects, on the other hand, we do find indications of differential treatment of the two oppositions. In Northern Switzerland it is possible to distinguish four regions according to the reflexes of MHG /e ɛ æ/. [18] (1) the East, with /e ≠ ɛ ≠ æ/ still maintained; (2) the North, with /e ≠ ɛ/ (/æ > ɛ/); (3) the West, with /ɛ ≠ æ/ (/e > ɛ/); (4) the Center, with /e ≠ æ/ (/ɛ > æ/). We see that, on the whole, the opposition /ɛ ≠ æ/ is more often destroyed than /e ≠ ɛ/, which is what we would expect from the disparity in the functional loads (0.004 vs. 1.995). But majority votes of this sort are notoriously bad practice, in linguistics and elsewhere. The indisputable facts remain that, in spite of the great disparity in functional load indices and frequencies of occurrence, no merger of any of the e-phonemes occurred in the East, the functionally less likely merger occurred in the West, and a merger occurred in the Center which is badly at odds with the frequency hypothesis, viz. /ɛ > æ/, though /ɛ/ is many times more frequent than /æ/.

This is bad predicting; a set of good hypotheses should explain things better than that. I am forced to conclude, at least as regards the set of facts just presented, that functional load gives no new insight, no new tool for exploring the complexity of sound change.

3.33. /æ: > e:/. Assuming on the grounds of phonetic similarity that /æ:/ could have merged with either /e:/ or /a:/, the functional loads of the pertinent oppositions are L(æ:, e:) = 0.093, L(æ:, a:) = 0.368. We observe that the least resistance hypothesis correctly predicts the direction of the merger. The frequency of /æ:/ is 0.482, that of /e:/ is 0.417; the more frequent member of the pair disappears in the merger, which is contrary to the frequency hypothesis. The weak point hypothesis is supported to the extent that L(æ:, e:) = 0.093 is rather small for a functional load of vocalic oppositions in Middle High German, though the frequency of /æ:/ itself is not excessively small.

3.34. /iə uə üə/ > /i: u: ü:/. Moulton (1961:32) suggests that /iə uə üə/ first became long, open vowels in contrast with old /i: u: ü:/, later being raised when the original, close vowels diphthongized. Since no merger is involved, we can examine only the weak point hypothesis to see whether functional load offers an explanation of why the change occurred in the first place or why the merger with old /i: u: ü:/ was averted.

The relative frequencies of the three in-gliding diphthongs are:

$$\text{freq(iə)} = 1.451 \quad \text{freq(uə)} = 0.543 \quad \text{freq(üə)} = 0.148$$

The frequencies of /iə/ and /uə/ are not excessively low: /e:/ and /ö:/ were less frequent (respectively 0.417 and 0.111), and they did not change. The frequency of /üə/ is low, though not as low as /ö:/. I see no reason, therefore, to suppose that low frequency had anything to do with the instability of the in-gliding diphthongs.

We might also seek an explanation for the non-occurrence of the possible mergers /iə uə üə/ > /i: u: ü:/ in high functional loads. The relevant indices are:

$$L(\text{iə, i:}) = 2.765 \quad L(\text{uə, u:}) = 0.078 \quad L(\text{üə, ü:}) = 0.020$$

The functional load of /iə ≠ i:/ is rather high, the functional loads of the other two oppositions are trivially small. According to one of the standard handbooks, Paul and Mitzka (1960, §44), the monophthongization of /uə/ and /üə/ preceded that of /iə/ by a century or so. If this is true, the reason perhaps lies in the considerable difference between the functional loads of /uə ≠ u:/ and /üə ≠ ü:/ (both less than 0.100) and that of /iə ≠ i:/. (Based on what we now know about the behavior of natural classes, I suspect that all three changes occurred at the same time and that the orthographic representation of /iə > i:/ lagged behind the representation of the other two mergers: the orthography of much used phonemes is generally apt to be conservative.)

In any case, there is no compelling functional reason against the mergers /uə > u:/ and /üə > ü:/. The functional load of /iə ≠ i:/ is of medium size, which might explain why that merger did not take place. As it stands, the functional data permit an explanation of why the merger /iə > i:/ did not occur, but they do not explain why the mergers /uə > u:/ and /üə > ü:/ were avoided.

3.35. /i: u: ü:/ > /ei ou öi/. Since this diphthongization did not take place in a number of High German dialects, especially Alemannic, we must assume that there was no overriding structural reason for its occurrence. Let us now see whether the functional data suggest an explanation for the cause or direction of this set of changes.

The relative frequencies of the three long high vowels are:

$$\text{freq(i:)} = 1.790 \quad \text{freq(u:)} = 0.311 \quad \text{freq(ü:)} = 0.779$$

These frequencies are not low; as was shown in §3.32, other phonemes had lower frequencies and were not 'weak points' in the system, i.e. did not undergo change.

The functional loads of the oppositions destroyed are:

$$L(i:, ei) = 1.265 \quad L(u:, ou) = 0.275 \quad L(ü:, oi) = 0.094$$

The functional load of /ü: ≠ öi/ is trivially small; the functional load of /i: ≠ ei/ and /u: ≠ ou/ are not. I conclude on the basis of the functional data that there is no reason why the phonemes /i: u: ü:/ should have been diphthongized out of the system of long vowels, and that there is no reason to suppose that the oppositions /i: ≠ ei/ and /u: ≠ ou/ were functionally 'weak'. The weak point hypothesis is, therefore, not supported by the data associated with this set of changes.

If one accepts Moulton's assumption that the reflexes of /iǝ uǝ üǝ/ were long open monophthongs, it seems likely that /i: u: ü:/ could have merged as easily with them as with the up-gliding diphthongs. The relevant functional load indices for the possible mergers are:

$$L(i:, ei) = 1.265 \quad L(u:, ou) = 0.275 \quad L(ü:, öi) = 0.094$$
$$L(i:, iǝ) - 2.765 \quad L(u:, uǝ) = 0.078 \quad L(ü:, üǝ) = 0.020$$

We note that the least resistance hypothesis correctly predicts that the opposition /i: ≠ ei/ should be lost in preference to /i: ≠ iǝ/, but it wrongly predicts the direction of merger in the other two instances.

Finally, let us determine whether the frequency hypothesis correctly predicts which member of the merged oppositions survives. The relevant frequencies are:

$$freq(i:) = 1.790 \quad freq(u:) = 0.311 \quad freq(ü:) = 0.779$$
$$freq(ei) = 1.039 \quad freq(ou) = 0.288 \quad freq(öi) = 0.134$$

As we observe, in each case the more frequent member of the opposition is lost, so that the frequency hypothesis makes the wrong prediction in every instance.

3.36. /ei ou öi/ > /ai au oi/. No merger is involved in this set of allophonic changes, and there is no likely merger which might be investigated in relation to functional load. There seems to be no good way to bring functional load or relative frequency to bear on these changes, and I shall not discuss them here.

3.4. *The Yiddish Evidence.*
Four long and short high-front and high-back vowels are reconstructed for proto-Yiddish.[19] /i i: u u:/. In Southern Yiddish the back series merged with the front series, and in Northeastern Yiddish the long vowels merged with the corresponding short ones. Thus we have:

> Southern Yiddish: /u: > i:/, /u > i/
> Northeastern Yiddish: /u: > u/, /i: > i/

There are, in addition, two areas in North Central Poland and the Northern Ukraine where all four vowels have merged into /i/.

It is apparent that the functional loads of the oppositions destroyed in these changes must have been very great. To determine exactly how great, we would need a text sample of proto-Yiddish, and, of course there is no such text available. However, in lieu of this, it may be possible to derive a serviceable estimate of some of these functional loads from the Middle High German data already available. I am naturally aware of the problems surrounding the relationship of Middle High German to Yiddish, and I do not wish to suggest that there is some direct lineal development from Classical Middle High German to Yiddish which justifies the derivation of statistical data on Yiddish dialects from like data in Middle High German. I justify my attempt at such a derivation on the grounds that there is no other way at all of obtaining an estimate; it is also of more than usual interest in a study devoted to functional load and sound change to investigate the magnitudes of the functional loads lost in these cases of 'massive merger', even though our tools are imperfect and even suspect. Having stated such caveats, let us investigate the matter.

By extension of a method employed earlier (§3.32, fn. 17), we can obtain a rough idea of the size of the functional load involved in the merger of Southern Yiddish /u > i/. One of the sources of proto-Yiddish */i/ was MHG /ü/, the other was MHG /i/, so that the opposition /ü $\neq$ i/ was lost in 'going' from Middle High German to proto-Yiddish. The Southern Yiddish merger /u > i/ causes the loss of a second opposition, which from the perspective of Middle High German represents the loss of the two oppositions /u $\neq$ i/ and /u $\neq$ ü/. Thus the Southern Yiddish merger /u > i/ must involve a loss of functional load approximately equal to L(ü, i) + L(u, i) + L(u, ü) = 1.671 + 11.560 + 0.501 = 13.732.

Unfortunately, this is the only functional load which can be computed even approximately from the existing Middle High German data. The other mergers in Southern and Northeastern Yiddish all affect proto-Yiddish long vowels (*u:, *i:) whose sources are mixed, and it would be hazardous to attempt the derivation of functional data on these vowels from assumed Middle High German etyma (cf. Weinreich, p. 67, for some of the difficulties).

Thus, if we accept the figure of 13.732 as even approximately accurate, it is clear that this merger affected a highly useful opposition in the functional sense. The mergers in Northeastern Yiddish affected oppositions whose functional loads were probably less high, for these mergers resulted in the loss of the correlation of vowel length. Length, as a distinctive feature, did not carry a high functional load in Middle High German: of the eight vowel pairs in which length was distinctive, only three were greater than one— L(i, i:) = 5.157, L(ɛ, e:) = 1.639, and L(a, a:) = 2.202. All the others range from small to trivially small—L(o, o:) = 0.574, L(u, u:) = 0.093, L(ü, ü:) = 0.089, L(ö, ö:) = 0.002, and L(æ, æ:) = 0.002. The arithmetic mean of these functional loads is 1.220. It is not probable that the functional load of vowel length was greater than this in proto-Yiddish. In the Yiddish dialects of North Central Poland and the Northern Ukraine, where all four high proto-Yiddish vowels have merged into /i/, the functional load of the oppositions destroyed must have been considerably larger than the provisional functional load of 13.732 lost in the merger of Southern Yiddish /u > i/.

It is clear from the Yiddish evidence presented here that oppositions bearing very high functional loads can be erased by sound change. We do not know how high these functional loads were, but they were certainly higher than any encountered elsewhere in our investigation. This is evidence that oppositions with high functional loads are not necessarily more resistant to merger than those carrying low functional loads, which of course is the heart of what is generally known as the 'functional load hypothesis' and which I here have formulated as the weak point hypothesis.

4. *Summary of the Evidence.*
It should be clear from the discussion which accompanied the presentation of data that none of the hypotheses stated in §1.2 stands up very well in confrontation with empirical findings from the Germanic languages studied here. This conclusion can be supported more precisely by tabulating the number of instances in which one of the three hypotheses is supported or rejected by the data in a particular case of sound change. These results are shown in Table 1. Instances of uncertain significance for the least resistance hypothesis (i.e. cases in which an observed difference of magnitude may have been due to sampling error) are not included, and the Yiddish evidence against the weak point hypothesis is disregarded. Sound changes affecting a natural class are treated as separate changes, e.g. MHG /i: u: ü:/ > /ei ou öi/ is counted as three separate changes.

We see that the weak point hypothesis and the least resistance hypothesis were wrong more often than not, and that the frequency hypothesis was wrong in almost half the cases. I conclude that, on the basis of the evidence assembled here, these hypotheses must be regarded as untenable. In extenuation, it should be pointed out that Martinet, although an enthusiastic adherent of the notion that functional load plays a rôle in sound change, never said more than that functional load could tentatively be considered as one of the factors in sound change (Martinet 1955:58). In this investigation, though I was primarily concerned with functional load and relative frequency, relevant structural and phonetic data have been introduced when it was possible to do so, but the conclusion remains the same: functional load and relative frequency seem to be largely irrelevant in sound change. This is clear from the table, and the conclusion is strengthened by the supplementary arguments developed in §§3.13, 3.14, 3.32, 3.34, and 3.4.

	Supported	Rejected
Weak point hypothesis	8	13
Least resistance hypothesis	4	5
Frequency hypothesis	7	6

<u>Performance of the Functional Load Hypotheses</u>

There seems to be no getting around the fact that functional load, if it is a factor in sound change at all, is one of the least important. Any hypothesis which predicts less than half the facts is not much use as an hypothesis, and the functional load hypotheses stated here seem to be precisely of that sort.

For practical purposes, perhaps the most important result is that we need not be unduly concerned about how to account for sound changes which have happened and yet resulted in considerable loss of functional load. Rather than regarding these as puzzling anomalies which need to be carefully scrutinized for special circumstances which would explain the merger of a highly loaded opposition, we can simply accept them as no more contrary than any other sound change.

5. *Final Considerations*.

There are many objections which can be leveled against the procedure employed in the present investigation. Of the numerous criticisms which an active imagination can anticipate, one seems particularly likely: that this study suffers from a narrow-minded concept of the relationship between sound change and the maintenance of communication. Language has in it, so this argument would go, manifold devices for carrying on its business of communication, and the informational value of phonological oppositions is only one of these devices, perhaps not even a very important one. Distinctiveness lost at the phonological level might be assumed without interruption of communication by higher-level markers in morphology and syntax. This is presumably what happened in those numerous cases in Germanic where the unstressed vowels all merged into schwa—with no break in communication potential, so far as we know.

I hasten to agree with my imaginary Devil's Advocate. Language is terribly complicated, and the present investigation was (intentionally) so conducted as to ignore great parts of this complexity without rendering the results trivial. I simply took what the most explicit writers on functional load had to say, translated it into testable hypotheses, and found these hypotheses wanting. It may well be that a more grandiose scheme, based on better and more complete knowledge of what communication in language really is, would find that functional load is, after all, a useful tool in seeking answers to the 'why' of sound change.

But it will not be easy to come by this more grandiose scheme. I most emphatically do not feel that information theory will show us the direction. The advantages hitherto gained from the application of information theory to linguistics have not exceeded our fondest dreams, even though information theory has from its inception been very much concerned with language. Furthermore, it has been found (King 1965) that functional load formulas based on information theory provide functional load indices which agree very well with the indices obtained by application of a simpler version of the formula used here, which did not make use of information theory. This is a predictable outcome, since any formulation of functional load ultimately is some function of the conditional probabilities of phonemes or phoneme sequences, given a set of environments.

In particular, I do not feel that information theory worked into a formula for calculating functional loads between taxonomic phonemic oppositions will help shape functional load into a more useful concept. Let us examine this point more closely. From the point of view of taxonomic phonemics, /ə/ is unquestionably present in the phonemic inventory of English, as is well known. But it is not at all likely that /ə/ would be present in the set of systematic phonemes of the complete, fully explicit grammar of English. Chomsky and Halle (1965:125) discuss the merits of adding to the grammar of English a rule of the shape

$$u \rightarrow \partial / \_\_CC\#$$

in order to account for [ləmp], [təsk], etc. The derivation of [ə] from /u/ effects other simplifications in the grammar of English: e.g. it permits roundness to coincide with gravity for vowel specifications, and it provides a natural way of accounting for vowel alternations of the type *reduce/reduction*.

The point of this example is to demonstrate that the /ə/ arrived at in a taxonomic phonemic analysis of English is not posited as a systematic phoneme in English—the introduction of [ə] is predicted by the operation of morphophonemic rules in the grammar. It follows from the basic notion of information theory that the amount of information conveyed by [ə] in English is precisely equal to zero; in other words, [ə] does not work in distinguishing utterances in English except at a very low phonetic level. Hence the functional loads of oppositions containing [ə] are zero in English.

This brings up the difficult question of just what functional load ought to measure. Should we measure the functional loads of subsets of the classificatory distinctive features? Or of certain phonological rules (if it makes any sense to talk about the functional load of rules)? Or is it even possible to define functional load in a way which makes it linguistically (and psychologically) relevant? I do not know the answer to any of these questions, nor do I have very clear ideas about what questions to ask. I wish only to stress the point that it is not easy to devise a measure of functional load which is useful and intuitively sound.

The present investigation has operated on the basis of functional load as calculated between taxonomic phonemes. All previous theorizing on the role of functional load in sound change has taken place within the framework of taxonomic phonemics,[20] and the performance of a particular theory can be tested fairly only within the framework intended by its adherents. My negative results must then to this extent be taken as preliminary.

One final point. The theory of therapeutic sound change as developed especially in Prague School linguistics is predicated on the assumption that the speaker, or at any rate some higher linguistic consciousness, is aware of certain informational indices in his language—relative frequencies of phonemes, functional loads of oppositions, etc.—and that the speaker (or his higher consciousness, whatever it is) possesses the ability to act on this knowledge to avert possible linguistic changes. I know of no empirical findings which support this assumption. I think, therefore, that concrete evidence of the soundness of such an assumption should precede further speculations on the nature of therapeutic sound change.

Appendix

I present here the data drawn upon in the preceding discussion. I have omitted the data on Old Saxon since only one change in Old Saxon was discussed, and the pertinent data for that change were given in analyzing it.

Several comments on the presentation of data may be useful in finding information in the following lists. First, in searching for the functional load of an opposition x ≠ y, it should be remembered that $L(x, y) = L(y, x)$; i.e., the functional load of an opposition is independent of the order of the two members. Second, functional loads are presented by beginning with phonemes in minimal contrast with /i/, then with /e/, then with /a/, and so on, moving counterclockwise and inward around the vowel chart.

Old Icelandic

OPP	LOAD	OPP	LOAD	OPP	LOAD	OPP	LOAD
i,y	6.481	ǫ,ø	0.191	e:,o:	0.445	a:,o:	0.612
i,u	17.505	ǫ,u	4.933	e;,ø:	0.062	a:,au	0.895
i,e	14.339	o,ø	0.495	e:,ę:	0.285	o:,u:	0.240
i,i:	3.413	o,o:	2.394	e:,a:	0.275	o:,ø:	0.237
e,ø	0.579	u,y	1.442	e:,ei	0.700	o:,au	0.375
e,o	15.363	u,ø	0.480	e:,ey	0.052	u:,y:	0.174
e,a	24.117	u,u:	1.053	e:,au	0.170	u:,ø:	0.041
e,e:	0.749	y,ø	0.563	ę:,a:	0.381	y:,ø:	0.041
a,ǫ	6.721	y,y:	0.570	ę:,ø:	0.087	ø:,ei	0.150
a,ø	1.377	ø,ø:	0.037	ę:,ei	0.530	ei,ey	0.107
a,a:	11.023	i:,u:	0.100	ę:,ey	0.082	au,ei	0.342
ǫ,o	1.173	i:,y:	0.111	ę:,au	0.108	au,ey	0.075
ǫ,u	1.131	i:,e:	0.181	a:,ø	0.139	au,ø:	0.139
ǫ,y	0.941	i:,ø:	0.170				

Middle High German

OPP	LOAD	OPP	LOAD	OPP	LOAD	OPP	LOAD
i,ü	1.671	ε,æ	0.004	o,o:	0.574	æ:,a:	0.368
i,u	11.560	ε,a	15.907	u,ü	0.501	a:,o:	1.391
i,e	1.963	ε,ə	22.143	u,u:	0.093	a:,ö:	0.107
i,ε	14.047	ε,e:	1.639	ü,ö	0.022	o:,u:	0.127
i,i:	5.157	ε,æ	2.078	ü,ü:	0.089	o:,ö:	0.032
e,ö	0.010	æ,ö	0.011	ö,ö:	0.002	u:,ü:	0.163
e,o	0.871	æ,a	0.040	i:,ü:	1.175	u:,ou	0.275
e,ε	1.995	æ,e:	0.001	i:,u:	0.152	u:,uə	0.078
e,æ	0.005	æ,æ:	0.002	i:,e:	0.129	ü:,ö:	0.014
e,a	2.457	a,o	6.860	i:,ei	1.265	ü:,öi	0.094
e,e:	0.117	a,ö	0.148	i:,iə	2.765	ü:,üə	0.020
e,æ:	0.233	a,a:	2.202	e:,ö:	0.011	ei,iə	0.485
ε,ö	0.069	o,u	1.976	e:,o:	0.053	ou,uə	0.056
ε,o	8.605	o,ö	0.095	e:,æ:	0.093	öi,üə	0.006

Notes

[1] I wish to thank Martin Joos , Warren Cowgill, and William S.-Y. Wang for their criticism of the dissertation from which the present paper has emerged. I wish also to thank the University of Texas Research Institute for financial aid which enabled me to carry out certain improvements in the computer aspects of this investigation. For the mathematical formulation of the measure of functional load employed here, see my paper, "A proposed measure for functional load," to appear in *Studia linguistica*. Complete frequency and functional load data on the languages investigated will also appear in that paper.

[2] See, for example, the lengthy discussion by Vachek (1966:64 f.)

[3] But see Vachek (1964) for a discussion from a later period of the history of English /h/.

[4] See, e.g. the brief but interesting comments by Hill (1936:22). Sapir had earlier made (1921:194) some observations on the tendency of sounds to drift through merger into (statistically) more favored positions.

[5] The earliest article I know of Martinet's which relates functional load to sound change is that of 1938. The idea is developed further in 1952. I have taken Martinet (1955) as the most definitive statement of his ideas.

[6] By economy he means Zipf's "principle of least effort" (cf. Martinet 1955:94).

[7] To the best of my knowledge, there are only two studies in which a numerical measure (as opposed to an impressionistic one based on minimal pairs) of functional load has been used in the discussion of sound change. Diver (1955) investigates the changes $ti > \check{s}t$ and $di > \check{z}d$ in Old Bulgarian and obtains findings in agreement with the functional load hypothesis. Abernathy 1963 discusses the fall of the *yers* in Slavic in the light of functional load and finds that functional load offers a solution to otherwise puzzling developments.

[8] Detailed information on the texts and phonemicizations used can be found in King 1965. A cautionary note: statistical data given there will not necessarily agree with the figures presented here, since a larger number of environments and larger input texts (approximately 20,000 phonemes for each language) have been used in obtaining the present findings.

[9] I follow here the summary of developments given by Benediktsson. He attempts to show that all the changes to be discussed are the result of an asymmetry in the ordering of the distinctive features of the vowel subsystems. The trend in the language, according to Benediktsson, is to reduce to two the number of distinctive features which differentiate the vowels: round vs. non-round, low vs. non-low. I am not convinced by this argument, which I regard as tautological; but Benediktsson's presentation of the data of the changes is very useful for present purposes, the more so since he brings functional load into the discussion at various points.

[10] Presumably any sound can change into any other sound. Austin 1957 suggests that this must take place one distinctive feature at a time: in Austin's metaphor, sound change is always the rook's move, never the bishop's. This is questionable as a language universal. However, following this rule of thumb which, in Germanic at least, is borne out in a great many cases, we can narrow down the variability of sound change to a degree sufficient for the present investigation. For example, given the fact that /ǫ/ is going to disappear from the system via merger, we would expect to find it merging with another short vowel which differs from /ǫ/ by one, or at most two, distinctive features, hence with /a/, /o/, /ø/, or /u/, not with /e/, /i/, or /y/.

[11] The relative frequency of /ę:/ is obtained by adding the frequencies for /ę:/ and /ø:/.

[12] Changes have occurred, e.g. the nature of the oppositions /i:≠ i/ and /u: ≠ u/ has changed from length to quality. My point, however, is that there were several phonemes considerably less frequent than /e: ę: o: a:/ which, unlike these, were not diphthongized or otherwise pushed out of the system by vowel change. Thus the dependence between low frequency and susceptibility to sound change predicted by the weak point hypothesis is not indicated by these data.

[13] The chronology of the changes /au > o^i/ and /a:/ > [a^u] relative to one another is not entirely certain. Benediktsson (299) says: "Long /a:/, as it developed a diphthongal glide, also tended to merge with one of the original diphthongs, viz. /au/, but this merger was avoided by a change of original /au/, which has given Mod. Icel. /öi/." Whatever the relative chronology, it seems fair to raise the question of whether functional load was a factor which may have inhibited or favored the merger.

[14] The other [— vocalic, +consonantal] segments in Old Saxon had frequencies less than 3.000, and most were smaller than 1.000 (cf. King 1965).

[15] One should not neglect the possibility that the Old Saxon change of /þ/ to /d/ was due to the linguistic encroachment of the more prestigious Old High German. But this does not alter the fact that an opposition bearing a high functional load was destroyed, whatever the cause.

[16] I follow here the analysis of Moulton (1961:31-3). On the disconcerting sequence of changed 4 and 5, see §3.34.

[17] After the merger /ε > æ/, the functional load borne by the opposition /e ≠ æ/ is the sum of the loads carried by the two earlier oppositions /e ≠ ε/ and /e ≠ æ/. A rigorous proof that functional loads can be added in this fashion has been worked out (King 1965:124-5).

[18] I take my data from Moulton (1960), an excellent study which provides evidence for the testing of many linguistic hypotheses.

[19] Cf. Weinreich (1960). In what follows I take data from Herzog (1965:163 f.) This information was brought to my attention in a paper given by Uriel Weinreich, Marvin I. Herzog, and William Labov on "Empirical foundations for a theory of language change: stimuli and constraints from structure and society," delivered at the Symposium on Historical Linguistics at the University of Texas, 29-30 April 1966.

[20] Martinet's concept of phonology looks taxonomic to me (cf. Postal 1966).

References

Abernathy, Robert. 1963 "Some theories of Slavic linguistic evolution," *American contributions to the Fifth International Congress of Slavists,* 1, 7-26 (The Hague, Mouton).

Austin, William. 1957 "Criteria for phonetic similarity," *Lg.* 33, 538-43.

Benediktsson, Hreinn. 1959 "The vowel system of Icelandic: a survey of its history," *Word* 15, 282-312.

Cercle Linguistique de Prague. 1931 "Réunion phonologique internationale . . . " *(Travaux,* 4).

Chomsky, Noam, and Morris Halle. 1965 "Some controversial questions in phonological theory," *Journal of Linguistics* 1, 97-138.

Diver, William. 1955 "The problem of Old Bulgarian št," *Word* 11, 228-36.

Gilliéron, Jules. 1918 *Genéalogie des mots qui designent l'abeille* (Paris: Champion).

Herzog, Marvin I. 1965 *The Yiddish language in Northern Poland (Indiana University Research Center in Anthropology, Folklore, and Linguistics,* Publ. 37) (Bloomington).

Hill, Archibald A. 1936 "Phonetic and phonemic change," *Lg.* 12, 15-22.

Hockett, Charles. 1955 *A manual of phonology (Indiana University Publications in Anthropology and Linguistics, Memoir 11)* (Baltimore).

_____. 1966 *The quantification of functional load: a linguistic problem (Rand Corporation memorandum* RM-5168-PR) (Santa Monica, Calif.).

Hoenigswald, Henry. 1960 *Language change and linguistic reconstruction* (Chicago: University of Chicago Press).

Jakobson, Roman. 1931 "Prinzipien der historischen Phonologie," *Travaux du Cercle Linguistique de Prague* 4, 247-67.

Joos, Martin. 1952 "The medieval sibilants," *Lg.* 27, 222-31.

King, Robert D. 1965 "Functional load: its measure and its role in sound change," Madison, University of Wisconsin dissertation.

Martinet, André. 1933 "Remarques sur le système phonologique du français," *Bulletin de la Société de Linguistique de Paris* 34, 191-202.

_____. 1938 "La phonologie," *Le Français Moderne* 6, 131-46.

_____. 1952 "Function, structure, and sound change," *Word* 8, 1-32.

_____. 1955 *Économie des changements phonétiques* (Bern, Francke).

Mathesius, Vilém. 1929 "La structure phonologique du lexique du tchèque moderne," *Travaux du Cercle Linguistique de Prague* 1, 67-84.

_____. 1931 "Zum Problem der Belastungs- und Kombinationsfähigkeit der Phoneme," *Travaux du Cercle Linguistique de Prague* 4, 148-52.

Moulton, William G. 1960 "The short vowel systems of Northern Switzerland," *Word* 16, 155-82.

_____. 1961 "Zur Geschichte des deutschen Vokalsystems," *Beiträge zur Geschichte der Deutschen Sprache und Literatur* 83, 1-35.

Paul, Hermann, and Walther Mitzka. 1960 *Mittelhochdeutsche Grammatik,* 18th ed. (Tübingen: Niemeyer).

Postal, Paul M. 1966 Review of *Elements of general linguistics,* by André Martinet, *Foundations of Language* 2, 151-86.

Sapir, Edward. 1921 *Language* (New York: Harcourt Brace).

Spence, N. C. W. 1965 "Quantity and quality in the vowel system of Vulgar Latin," *Word* 21, 1-18.

Steblin-Kamenskij, M. I. 1958 "A contribution to the history of the Old Icelandic vowel system," *Časopis pro Moderní Filologii* 40, 79-82.

Trnka, Bohumil. 1931 "Bemerkungen zur Homonymie," *Travaux du Cercle Linguistique de Prague* 4, 152-6.

Trubetzkoy, N. 1935 *Anleitung zu phonologischen Beschreibungen* (Brno: Cercle Linguistique de Prague).

_____. 1939 *Grundzüge der Phonologie (Travaux du Cercle Linguistique de Prague*, 7).

Vachek, Josef. 1964 "On peripheral phonemes of modern English," *Brno Studies in English* 4, 7-109.

_____. 1966 *The linguistic school of Prague* (Bloomington: Indiana University Press).

Wang, William S.-Y., and James W. Thatcher. 1962 *The measurement of functional load (Communication Sciences Laboratory*, Report No. 8) (Ann Arbor: University of Michigan).

Weinreich, Max. 1960 "The system of Yiddish proto-vowels," *Yidishe Sprakh* 20, 65-71.

11   Rule Reordering

PAUL KIPARSKY

Reordering as Simplification

Reordering resembles simplification both in the negative property
that rule addition miserably fails to do justice to it and in the
positive property of its driftlike character. I shall now claim
that reordering is in fact a special case of simplification, and
that the direction of reordering is predicted by general principles
which assign certain types of order a higher value than others. If
this can be established, then current phonological theory, which
does not distinguish different kinds of linear order, is wrong and
must be revised to account for this asymmetry.

To be convinced that reordering is a one-way affair, much as other
simplification is, it is enough to examine the individual examples.
For instance, many Swiss dialects have put the umlaut rule (3) after
o > *ɔ* (Rule 4), but none of these have made the reverse switch, and
we could not easily imagine it taking place. And a dialect of
Finnish in which *tie* from *teɣe* > *tee* becomes *tee* again but *vie* from
vee retains the diphthong, that is, a dialect in which dipthongiza-
tion reverts to its original position before the loss of medial
voiced continuants (which I will now call γ > ɸ for short) is inconceivable. The question is how this asymmetry, intuitively evident
enough in each particular case, can be given a general characterization.

Of the various functional relationships that can hold between two
rules, two are of relevance here. One way in which two rules, *A* and
B, can be functionally related is that the application of *A* creates
representations to which *B* is applicable. That is, the application
of *A* converts forms to which *B* cannot apply into forms to which *B*
can apply; schematically:

$$\text{A.} \quad [\ \ ] > [\varphi]$$
$$\text{B.} \quad [\varphi] > [\ \ ]$$

Such a relationship holds for example between $\gamma > \varphi$ (*teγe > tee*) and
diphthongization (*tee > tie*) in our Finnish example. If the rules
are applied in that order, $\gamma > \varphi$ supplies a set of new cases (namely
those derived from *eγe*) to which diphthongization can apply. In a
situation, call *A* a <u>feeding</u> <u>rule</u> relative to *B* (for example, $\gamma > \varphi$
is a feeding rule relative to diphthongization). Call this relation-
ship between rules a <u>feeding</u> <u>relationship</u> (for example, $\gamma > \varphi$ and
diphthongization are in a feeding relationship) and the linear order
in which the feeding rule precedes a <u>feeding</u> <u>order</u> (for example,
1. $\gamma > \varphi$, 2. diphthongization is a feeding order). Then one of the
principles that determine the direction of reordering is

I. Feeding order tends to be maximized.
Schematically:

$$\begin{array}{ll} \text{A.} \ [\varphi] > [\ \ ] \\ \text{B.} \ [\ \ ] > [\varphi] \end{array} > \begin{array}{ll} \text{B.} \ [\ \ ] > [\varphi] \\ \text{A.} \ [\varphi] > [\ \ ] \end{array}$$

A further example of I involves the several palatalizations in
Slavic. By the so-called first palatalization, *k* and *g* became *č*
and *ǯ*, respectively, before front vowels and *y*, for example,
*kĭto > čĭto 'what', **givŭ > *ǯivŭ* 'alive'.[1]

7. $\begin{bmatrix} + \text{ consonantal} \\ - \text{ diffuse} \end{bmatrix} \rightarrow \begin{bmatrix} - \text{ grave} \\ + \text{ strident} \end{bmatrix} / \underline{\quad} \begin{bmatrix} - \text{ consonantal} \\ - \text{ back} \end{bmatrix}$

But the resulting voiced affricate *ǯ* has become a continuant *ž* in
all Slavic languages by the rule

8. $\begin{bmatrix} + \text{ voiced} \\ - \text{ grave} \\ + \text{ strident} \end{bmatrix} \rightarrow [+ \text{ continuant}]$

For example, **ǯivŭ > živŭ*.

Subsequently new front vowels came to stand after velars by the
rule

9. ai → ě

By the so-called second palatalization k, and g,derived from k and g
by an earlier rule) became c and $ʒ$ before these new front vowels,
for example, $k,ěna > cěna$ 'price', $*g,ělo > ʒělo$ 'very':

10.
$$
\begin{bmatrix} + \text{ obstruent} \\ - \text{ grave} \\ - \text{ strident} \\ - \text{ diffuse} \end{bmatrix} \rightarrow \begin{bmatrix} + \text{ strident} \\ + \text{ diffuse} \end{bmatrix}
$$

The resulting affricate $ʒ$, unlike the earlier $ǯ$, is retained in Old
Church Slavic and in modern Polish. The grammars of these languages
have Rules 7-10 as phonological rules in an order that matches their
relative chronology. But elsewhere in Slavic, $ʒ$ also has been replaced by its corresponding continuant, namely z, for example,
$ʒělo > zělo$. These languages have the same four rules, but 8 must
here follow 10, in order to apply to the affricate produced by the
second palatalization as well. It is these two rules between which
the feeding relationship obtains. Rule 10 is the feeding rule and
the reordering establishes a feeding order between 10 and 8.

It should be noted that this relationship is a matter of the function and not of the form of the rules. In the Slavic example there
is, as is often the case elsewhere too, a formal similarity between
the related rules in that they mention some of the same features,
and so on. But it would not be possible to define the correct relationship on the basis of the form of the rules. The two Finnish
rules previously cited have very little in common, and the relationship is simply based on properties of the derivations the language
has.

Another possible functional relationship between two rules is that
A removes representations to which B would otherwise apply:

A.   [   ] > [$\sim\varphi$]
B.   [φ] > [   ]

Such a relationship holds for example between umlaut (A) and $o > ɔ$
(B) in the example of Section 2. Thus the application of umlaut
turns o into $ö$, a front vowel to which the lowering rule is no longer
applicable. If the lowering rule comes first in the ordering, it
applies, turning o to $ɔ$, and umlaut can then still apply. In the
terms of the Indian grammatical tradition, umlaut is here the *nitya*
or 'constant' rule. Call A a <u>bleeding</u> <u>rule</u> relative to B, the relationship between A and B a <u>bleeding relationship</u>, and the ordering
in which A precedes B a <u>bleeding order</u>. The principle which under-
lies the asymmetry of order in this case is the following:

II. Bleeding order tends to be minimized.

A. [ ] > [∿φ]		B. [φ] > [ ]		
B. [φ] > [ ]	>	A. [ ] > [∿φ]		

In this way the original order, in which umlaut preceded lowering,
became switched around into the new order, in which the bleeding did
not take place.

As another illustration of the effect of II, consider the relation
of two rules pertaining to voiced obstruents in German. One of them,
which is historically the older, is the devoicing of obstruents in
word-final position (for example, *bund > bunt*, *tāg > tāk*). This is
Rule 1, which has come up in the discussion several times already.
The other, found only in a certain group of dialects (Schirmunski
1962, p. 302), is the spirantization of postvocalic voiced stops,
for example, *tāgə > tāɣə*, *sāgt > sāɣt (>sāxt)*. Originally, devoicing
preceded postvocalic spirantization. Since, with this order, morphophonemic final voiced stops lost their voicing before spirantization
applied, they remained stops and the contrast of *tāk:tāɣə* resulted.
This bleeding order, in which word-final devoicing deprives spirantization of some of the voiced stops to which it would otherwise apply,
is still retained in some Alsatian, Bavarian, and Middle German
dialects. More frequently the reverse ordering is found, with final
voiced stops undergoing first spirantization (*tāg > tāɣ*) and then
devoicing *(tāɣ > tāx.)* This order is widespread and especially common in the Low German dialects. We know that this order is a secondary development because some words like *(a)wek* (Standard German *weg)*,
where the voicing of the stop had no morphophonemic support, failed
to spirantize even in the reordering dialects. This would be inexplicable unless we suppose that the devoicing was historically earlier even in these dialects in spite of the fact that it is synchronically later.

Another example can be cited from this same familiar area. A very
widespread sound change in German dialects (Schirmunski 1962, p. 212)
is the rounding of *ā* to *ɔ̄*. As *ǣ,* the umlaut of *ā,* is unaffected by
this change, it brings about alternations between *ɔ̄* and *ǣ* such as
šwɔ̄n 'swan', *šwǣn* 'Pl.', *špɔ̄t* 'late': *špǣtər* 'later'. Hence there
is a bleeding order between the rules:

a. umlaut
b. *ā > ɔ̄*

Many modern German dialects have just this system (see Rabeler 1911,
and Hotzenköcherle, 1934, for a Low German and Swiss German dialect,
respectively). In others (for example, Wanner, 1941) the system has

changed in that the umlauted form of $\bar{\partial}$ is $\bar{\bar{\partial}}$, for example, $\overset{\vee}{s}\overset{..}{w}\bar{\partial}n$, $\overset{\vee}{s}p\overset{..}{\bar{\partial}}ter$. The grammatical difference is that umlaut now applies after rather than before the rounding of $\bar{a}$. As phonemic $\overset{..}{\bar{\alpha}}$ in words like $ts\overset{..}{\bar{\alpha}}$ 'tough' and $l\overset{..}{\bar{\alpha}}r$ 'empty' stays unrounded (more proof of the correctness of the argument is in Section 5) it is clear that the possibility of a simplification of the rounding rule to all lone compact vowels is excluded and we are again faced with a case of re-ordering, which conforms perfectly to Principle II.

There is a more general principle underlying the two reordering tendencies (I and II) which combines them under a single wider concept of fuller utilization and makes their nature intuitively much clearer:

III. Rules tend to shift into the order which allows their
      fullest utilization in the grammar.

If I am right that such a principle determines the direction in which reordering proceeds, then it follows that the order toward which rules gravitate in this way is linguistically simpler than its opposite. It is hard to see what other explanation there could be for such a consistent tendency toward a specific kind of order in linguistic change. As a convenient designation for the order types which are shunned and preferred according to Principles I-III, I suggest marked and unmarked order, respectively. It may well be that marking conventions analogous to those which assign the un-marked feature values in segmental phonology are the appropriate device for reflecting the asymmetry of ordering relations as well.

Leveling and Extension

As further justification for my assertion that unidirectional re-ordering tendencies exist and that they obey Principles I-III, I want to adduce an unexpected parallelism which obtains between re-ordering, if so constrained, and rule simplification. We can begin with a distinction drawn in traditional and structural historical grammar between two types of analogy, one called leveling and the other called polarization or extension. By leveling was meant roughly that existing alternations are either curtailed or elimi-nated altogether, with the result that allomorphs of some morphemes become more similar to each other or merge completely. Thus the change of *bunt : bunde* to *bund : bunde* would have been regarded as a leveling of the alternation of voiced and voiceless stops in word-final position. The simplification of the umlaut rule (2) to its other version (3), which replaced *kraft : kreftig* by *kraft : kræftig* would have been regarded as a leveling of the height alter-nation in favor of the low vowel throughout the paradigm.

Polarization, or extension, on the other hand, refers to a type of
analogical change in which existing alternations spread to new instances. Here linguistic contrasts come to be more fully implemented
than before, whereas leveling has precisely the opposite effect. We
would presumably be dealing with extension if, for example, the alternation of medial voicing and final voicelessness in obstruents as
in *tāge : tāk, bunde : bunt*, instead of being eliminated altogether,
had become extended beyond its original domain to the sonorants, as
has in fact happened in Icelandic. The change of the limited Old
English vowel shortening rule (6) to its present more general form
(5) is another instance of extension.

This distinction, implicit in traditional historical studies,
though rarely drawn systematically (but see Hoenigswald 1960, pp. 63,
108), is a useful one, partly for reasons that have to do with linguistic reconstruction. Leveling will often be recoverable by historical reconstruction, because of the relic forms which reflect
older linguistic stages that leveling leaves behind. Extension,
however, will in general not be so recoverable because, with certain
very interesting exceptions, it cannot leave relic forms behind.
The difference between these two types of analogy can be defined in
terms of the formal differences of two kinds of rule simplification
in a very straightforward manner. Rules consist of two parts, a
structural analysis, which specifies to what forms the rule applies,
and a structural change, which says what happens to these forms. In
the customary notation for phonological rules, the structural change
is the part between the arrow and the slash and the structural analysis is everything else. Then any rule simplification which modifies
the structural change of a rule (whether or not it also modifies the
structural analysis) is a leveling, and any rule simplification which
does not modify the structural change of a rule is an extension.
Thus the loss of final devoicing (Rule 1) and the simplification of
Rule 2 to Rule 3 affect the structural change of the rule and are
hence levelings, but the change of the shortening rule in English did
not affect its structural change and is hence an extension.

It is a fairly surprising fact that the two kinds of reorderings
we have found, namely those governed by I and II, correspond pairwise
to these two kinds of rule simplifications and in turn to the traditional distinction between extension and leveling. Reordering by II
results in leveling and thus corresponds to simplification in the
structural change of a rule. For example, the effect of placing umlaut after *o > ɔ* is that the height alternation in *bɔdə : bödə* and
innumerable similar cases is leveled and the resulting forms, *bɔdə :
bödə*, retain the low vowel throughout the paradigm. So, too, the
reordering of spirantization and word-final devoicing results in the

dropping of a two-feature alternation, *tak : taɣə* (with change of
both voicing and continuance), in favor of a simpler one-feature alternation, *tax : taɣə* (with a continuant throughout the paradigm),
that is, again in leveling. In their effect on surface forms and on
the relation of surface forms, leveling by simplification in the
structural change of rules and leveling by reordering in accordance
with Principle II have similar effects in that they make more alike
the different shapes in which morphemes appear. But they bring this
effect about in different ways because leveling by rule simplification brings the forms closer to the base forms, whereas leveling by
reordering takes forms farther away from their base forms. But both
types share the property that they can leave behind relic forms
which make the recovery of these processes by linguistic reconstruction a possibility. What guarantees us the earlier grammar in each
of these cases are the forms like *weg* (in the case where the devoicing rule is lost and in the case in which it is reordered with
spirantization), *plötsli* (in reordering of umlaut and *o > ɔ*), and
so on.

On the other hand, reordering by I results in extension (polarization) and so corresponds to simplification which affects only the
structural analysis of rules. In the case of the Slavic palatalizations (see Section 8), for example, the voiced stop: voiced affricate
alternation is polarized into a voiced stop: voiced continuant alternation. It is clear that in this case any forms which undergo the
old form of the rules are also going to undergo them after the reordering, so that relic forms which would allow reconstruction of
the change could not be created.

These relationships are summarized in the following table.

Reordering	Corresponds to simplification of	Reconstructible by relic forms?	Surface effect
by I	Structural analysis only	No	Extension (polarization)
by II	Structural change	Yes	Leveling

Rule Opacity and Reordering

The reordering conditions proposed in Kiparsky (1968), that feeding
order tends to be maximized, and bleeding order tends to be minimized,
in most cases correctly predict the direction of reordering. The unmarked status of feeding order is not subject to any serious doubt.
Still, a number of examples have turned up where these conditions
are inadequate. There are three sorts of cases like this: (1) reordering contrary to the conditions; (2) reordering where the con-

cepts of feeding and bleeding are inapplicable; (3) reordering in
cases of "mutual bleeding." Some examples have been collected in
Kenstowicz and Kisseberth (1971).

In this section I will review the examples known to me where the
previously proposed conditions do not work. We shall see that they
reveal an inadequacy in the concept of bleeding order. I will tentatively suggest a reformulation of the conditions which accounts for
the problematic cases as well as for those which the old conditions
handle. This reformulation will make use of the concept of <u>rule
opacity</u>, which I will argue has an important role to play elsewhere
in lingustic theory as well.

I will begin with the syntactic example analyzed in Klima (1964).
Klima wrote this paper before it had been shown that reordering of
rules is a primary form of linguistic change. His analysis is
therefore formulated solely in terms of rule addition and subsequent
restructuring. However, it is now easy to recognize that the historical process Klima describes is essentially a series of downward
shifts in the order of case marking, which makes case in English
dependent on increasingly superficial configurations. For example,
the shift from *whom did you see?* to *who did you see?* is a shift from
a grammar in which case marking applies before Wh-movement (i.e. to
a representation of the form *you past see Wh+PRO*) to a grammar in
which case marking applies after Wh-movement (i.e. to something like
Wh+PRO you past see). From the drift-like progression of this reordering of case marking we can conclude that it constitutes a
natural development in the grammar of English. This raises the
question, what general principle lies behind the directionality of
the drift. The ordering asymmetries of feeding and bleeding order
(Kiparsky 1968) do not help us here. If anything, Klima's analysis
shows a drift towards *less* application of the case marking rule.

We can make an initial approximation to the required principle in
the following way. Let us make a distinction between <u>reordering
transformations</u>, which move constituents around, and <u>feature changing
transformations</u>, which add some morphologically realized mark onto
a constituent. Consider tentatively a principle which says:

(E') Feature changing transformations preferably follow reordering transformations.

This implies that the evaluation measure assigns a higher value to
a grammar in which a feature changing rule follows a reordering
rule than to the otherwise identical grammar in which the two
rules apply in the reverse order. This should, if correct, have
the usual consequences in terms of directionality of change, language acquisition (children should make mistakes in the direction
of the preferred order but not in the other direction), and frequency in the world's languages.

The study by Hale (1970) of the ergative and passive in Australian languages gives some support of principle (E'). On the basis of a comparative diachronic analysis of several languages Hale tentatively concludes that the ordering:

> Pronominalization
> Passive

is unstable. He shows that languages having this order tend either to reorder the rules or to make the passive structure obligatory and basic. It is possible, as Hale suggests, to attribute the reordering to the anti-feeding nature of the unstable order. However, perhaps a more natural way of looking at the change is that the drift is toward making pronominalization, a feature-changing rule, follow the passive transformation.

There is a phonological analog to this type of asymmetry in the order of transformations. In recent papers, Kisseberth and Kenstowicz (1971) and Kaye (1971) have discussed cases in which the unmarked order of phonological rules is not characterized by the bleeding or feeding relations. The examples of Kenstowicz and Kisseberth are of the following sort. In Yokuts, vowels are shortened in closed syllables:

$$V \rightarrow [- \text{long}] / \underline{\hspace{1cm}} C \begin{Bmatrix} \# \\ C \end{Bmatrix}$$

e.g. *do:s-ol* 'might report' but *dos-hin* 'reports'. This rule is critically ordered with respect to an epenthesis rule:

$$\emptyset \rightarrow i / C \underline{\hspace{1cm}} C \begin{Bmatrix} \# \\ C \end{Bmatrix}$$

which breaks up clusters and thereby turns closed syllables into open ones. Epenthesis bleeds shortening, but as Kenstowicz and Kisseberth note, the bleeding order:

> 1. Epenthesis
> 2. Shortening

in which the rules actually apply is quite natural, and the one which one would expect them to apply. In at least some cases, then, bleeding order seems to be unmarked.

Kenstowicz and Kisseberth do not actually give evidence that bleeding order really is unmarked in such cases. However, there are cases of historical change which support their conjecture. Wayne O'Neil (personal communication) has noted that Faroese has two rules:

> 1. Intervocalic spirantization
> 2. Vowel Syncope

which originally apply in the given order, e.g. *heidinir* → *heiđinir* → *heiđnir* 'heathen (pl.)', and have been reordered into a bleeding order:

1. Vowel syncope
2. Intervocalic spirantization

giving *heidnir*, where spirantization no longer applies.

Another possible example where diachronic evidence may point to the unmarked status of a bleeding order is discussed briefly in Hurford (to appear). Cockney English drops initial *h*. According to Hurford, there is an older dialect which says *a 'ouse*, whereas younger speakers say *an 'ouse*. We might say, then, that the non-bleeding order:

1. an → a / _____ C
2. h → ∅ / #_____

has changed into the bleeding order:

1. h → ∅ / #_____
2. an → a / _____ C

There are a couple of ways out. In the first place, we might say that the second dialect actually has no underlying *h*, but that words formerly ending in *h* have been restructured with an initial vowel. Secondly, we might argue that the rule for the indefinite article reads:

a → an / _____ V

in which case we no longer have a bleeding relationship. But it seems to me that these objections are really beside the point. Suppose that it is possible to motivate the underlying representations which Hurford assumes for the second dialect. Clearly this is a <u>possible</u> analysis. The change from *a 'ouse* to *an 'ouse* should be predicted under this analysis as well as under the other possible analysis. That this is the case is a flaw in the theory.

Kenstowicz and Kisseberth discuss two distinct ways in which the theory of phonology might be amended to characterize the markedness of ordering relations in the correct way. The first is that:

(E") Where one rule A stands in a bleeding relation with another rule B by virtue of A's altering a structure so that it no longer satisfies the environmental conditions of B, bleeding order is unmarked.

That is, a rule of the form:

K → L / M _____ N

is preferably bled (i.e. preceded) by a rule which destroys M or N

(the environment), although it is preferably <u>not</u> bled (i.e. followed)
by a rule which destroys K (the input proper).

However, they note that (E") does not take care of the following
sort of case. In some Slavic languages there is a vowel copy rule
of the form:

$$(C) \quad V \; R \; C \rightarrow 1 \; 2 \; 3 \; 2 \; 4$$

$$1 \quad 2 \; 3 \; 4$$

This rule, known to be a dialectal innovation of East Slavic, has to
apply before an old rule which accents the initial vowel of certain
words, as shown by the following derivations:

	/vórn + u/	/golv + u/
vowel copy	vórón + u	golov + u
accent insertion	"	gólov + u
later rules	vorónu	gólovu

It seems evident that this is indeed the expected ordering of vowel
copy and accent insertion. But here bleeding order is completely
irrelevant. Both rules will apply to underlying /golv-u/ in either
order, but with different results.

In view of this example, Kenstowicz and Kisseberth suggest an alternative principle (E'''), in terms of the <u>substantive</u> effect of the
rules. I formulate it here as follows:

(E''') Rules which affect syllabic structure (e.g., metathesis,
epenthesis, deletion) preferably apply before rules that
refer to syllabic structure (e.g., assimilation).

It is clear that Kenstowicz and Kisseberth are generally on the
right track. However, neither (E") nor (E''') can be correct. This
is shown by Kaye's Ojibwa example.

Kaye discusses the following two rules in Ojibwa:

<u>vowel coalescence</u>	$aw+i \rightarrow \begin{cases} \bar{a}/ \\ \bar{o}/ \end{cases} \underline{\quad\quad} \begin{matrix} k \\ n \end{matrix}$
<u>n-assimilation</u>	$n \rightarrow k/ \underline{\quad\quad} k$

He presents evidence that certain Ojibwa dialects have gone from the
above order to the reverse order. Underlying /nōntaw+in+k/ has
thereby changed from nōntōkk to nōntākk. Again, the bleeding (and
feeding) relations are inapplicable, so that principle (E") cannot
be invoked. However, principle (E''') also gives the wrong result,
since this reordering puts an assimilation rule <u>before</u> a rule that
changes syllable structure, whereas (E''') says that assimilation
rules preferably go <u>after</u> rules that change syllable structure.

In place of these principles, which are still somewhat unsatis-
factory, I would like to put forward tentatively a principle which
accounts for all the examples, including the syntactic ones.

Define the concept <u>opacity</u> <u>of</u> <u>a</u> <u>rule</u> as follows:

> <u>Definition.</u> A rule A → B / C _____ D is opaque to the extent
> that there are surface representations of the form
>   (i) A in environment C _____ D
> or (ii) B in environments other than C _____ D.

(The first of these two conditions has been referred to by structuralists as an alternation being "non-automatic" and by Stampe (1969)
as a rule being "contradicted on the surface.") Note that both
cases can arise in several ways. For example, CAD might arise
through a rule E → C / ___ AD, or a rule E → A / C ___ D. B might
appear in environments other than C ___ D either through some process that changes CBD to EBD, or through a process that introduces
B in other environments, etc. Of course, exceptions add opacity to
a rule according to the above definition. The definition can be
extended to syntax in the obvious way. Opacity as here defined is
a matter of degree, although I have no suggestions as to how to
quantify it formally. I suspect that the concept will ultimately
turn out to be more complicated than the above definition indicates.

Let us refer to the converse of opacity as <u>transparency</u>.

The hypothesis which I want to propose is that opacity of rules
adds to the cost of a grammar; more concretely, that opacity is a
property of rules that makes them, and the underlying forms to which
they apply, harder to learn. In particular, I conjecture that
transparent rules are learned first, and that the acquisition of
phonological rules proceeds roughly in the order of increasing
opacity.

As regards unmarked ordering, we can now derive, as a special case,
the following principle:

(E) <u>Rules</u> <u>tend</u> <u>to</u> <u>be</u> <u>ordered</u> <u>so</u> <u>as</u> <u>to</u> <u>become</u> <u>maximally</u> <u>transparent</u>.

This principle seems to cover the hitherto recalcitrant examples of
ordering asymmetry, capturing what is correct about the three principles (E'), (E"), and (E"').

For example, in Yokuts the preferred, unmarked order is that in
which shortening applies to the superficial, more phonetic representations reached after epenthesis, rather than the deeper, more
abstract representations that the derivation shows before epenthesis.
If shortening came before epenthesis, it would be a more opaque rule
by DEF., Case (ii). In Slavic, the rule "accent the first vowel in
words of the *golv* class" would be opaque if it preceded copying,
since copying would introduce a stressed vowel on the second syllable
of these words as well (DEF., Case [ii]). In Ojibwa, the awi → ō /
___ n rule is more opaque in the ordering that gives *nōntōkk* than in
the innovating ordering that gives *nōntãkk* (DEF., Case [ii]).

Similarly, in Klima's syntactic example the drift is towards making case marking an increasingly transparent process.

The reader will have noticed that these examples all involve Case (ii) of the definition of opacity. The same is true of the syntactic examples of Klima and Hale, and of the other examples discussed in the paper by Kenstowicz and Kisseberth. What about Case (i), then? This is simply a characterization of non-feeding order; the consequence that feeding order tends to be maximized is given by including Case (i) in the definition of opacity.

For example, suppose we have the two rules:

1. $\gamma \rightarrow \emptyset$ / V ___ V

2. $\begin{bmatrix} V \\ -lo \end{bmatrix} \rightarrow$ [+hi] / ___ V

Now the order given is the unmarked feeding order, in which we get derivations like *eγe → ee → ie*. This is also the order in which both rules are maximally transparent. Reversing the order would result in an output *ee* for the input *eγe*, making the vowel raising rule opaque by Case (i).

Our revised characterization of the ordering asymmetries now takes care of feeding order, one type of bleeding order, and certain cases where the concepts of feeding and bleeding are not applicable. Then what about cases of marked bleeding order of the type discussed in Kiparsky (1968), namely those in which two rules potentially apply in the same segment? For example, in Swiss German there is a re-ordering from

	/bode + Sg./	/bode + Pl./
1. Umlaut (e.g. in env.__Pl.)	----	böde + Pl.
2. o → ɔ /__[+ coronal]	bɔde + Sg.	----

to

	/bode + Sg./	/bode + Pl./
1. o → ɔ /__[+ coronal]	bɔde + Sg.	bɔde + Pl.
2. Umlaut (e.g. in env.__Pl.)	----	böde + Pl.

But these are exactly the cases in which the paradigm condition that allomorphy tends to be minimized, which we have seen to be needed on independent grounds, will give the correct result! In the Swiss German example, the innovating order preserves the stem shape between singular and plural. A review of the examples given in Kiparsky (1968), King (1969), and elsewhere, shows that the cases which have been cited as reordering from bleeding into non-bleeding order are all of this type.

The proposed reformulation seems necessary in order to account for
the examples brought up by Kaye and by Kenstowicz and Kisseberth,
and the syntactic cases discussed by Klima and Hale. It has at
least as clear a functional basis in language acquisition as the
notion of maximal applicability which it replaces. In addition, it
has some important further advantages which I will now mention
briefly.

The notion of rule transparency enables us to establish a profound
relationship between the two historical phenomena of rule reordering
and rule loss.

It has been pointed out by Stampe (1969) and Andersen (1969) (cf.
also Darden 1970) that rules tend to be lost from grammars through
historical change only under certain specific conditions. Basically,
we can say that rules are susceptible to loss _if they are hard to
learn_. And one of the major factors that makes rules hard to learn
(though not the only one) is precisely _opacity_ as defined above.

Consider the first condition that leads to opacity (Case (i) in
the Definition). A rule is opaque if representations of the sort
which it eliminates exist on the surface. Loss under this condition
is common (cf. the Algonquian example cited from Piggott (1971) in
§ 1 of this paper). To give just one more case, a similar situation
arose in early Iranian. The Iranian languages once had Bartholomae's Law, by which voiceless stops were subject to progressive
assimilation of aspiration and voicing after voiced aspirates, e.g.
/drugh+ta/ → *_drugdha_. Voiced unaspirated stops did not cause progressive assimilation, and were themselves subject to regressive
assimilation of voicing (with velars in addition being spirantized),
e.g. /bhag+ta/ → *_bhaxta_. Subsequently the voiced aspirates were
deaspirated. The resulting situation is one in which some voiced
stops (the old aspirates) cause progressive voicing assimilation,
but others (the original unaspirated stops) do not, e.g. (assuming
rephonemicization) /drug+ta/ → _drugda_ but /bag+ta/ → _baxta_. This
stage essentially survives in older Avestan. In later Avestan, however, the now opaque progressive assimilation rule is simply lost,
giving /drug+ta/ → _druxta_ like /bag+ta/ → _baxta_. Bartholomae's Law
is lost as a rule and survives only in isolated words in lexicalized
form, e.g. in _azda_ 'thus'. Other examples are given in Andersen
(1969).

We would also expect the second type of opacity (Case (ii)) to
lead to rule loss. There is not a great deal of evidence for this
being so. But a tentative analysis by Erteschik (1971) is, if
correct, exactly such a case. The Hebrew spirantization rule,
apparently applicable originally to all stops, has been limited to
_p_, _b_, and _k_. Erteschik suggests that _p_, _b_, and _k_ were, at the time

when the rule became restricted in this way, exactly the stops whose
spirantized cognates were not phonemic, the system being:

p	t	k	?
b	d	g	
	s		X
	z	r	

In support of this conjecture she notes what happens when children
learn spirantization in modern Hebrew. Here X has lost its pharyngealization, thereby merging with x, the spirantized form of k. This
means that spirantization of k has become opaque with respect to
Case (ii), since the output of spirantization of k now has another
source in the grammar. Spirantization of p, b, on the other hand,
remains transparent. According to Erteschik, children make mistakes
with spirantizing velars (but not, apparently, with labials). For
lexabes ⌒ *kvisa* she has observed children saying both *lexabes* ⌒ *xvisa*
and *lekabes* ⌒ *kvisa*. That is, children find it harder to learn the
opaque part of the modern Hebrew spirantization rule (and the underlying forms insofar as they are subject to this rule) than the
transparent part of the same rule.

Stampe has suggested other factors which make a rule susceptible
to loss, in particular the <u>unnatural</u> status of a rule. For example,
certain natural processes of vowel lengthening or shortening may be
unnatural as the corresponding tensing or laxing processes when the
length opposition changes into a tenseness opposition in the course
of historical change. Such rules might also be susceptible to loss.
Therefore not all cases of loss will necessarily involve rules which
are opaque in the sense defined here. Opacity will, however, be <u>one</u>
of the factors that bring about the loss of rules from a grammar by
historical change.

Rule opacity also plays a role in paradigm changes like those discussed above. Strictly speaking, Principle (B) is inadequate by
itself to deal with an example like the change of *honōs* to *honor*.
The *r* which is reintroduced in the nominative causes shortening of
the preceding vowel by a general rule of Latin. As a result we have
actually just traded in the s/r alternation of *honōs/honoris* for the
o/ō alternation of *honor/honōris*. Still, everyone would grant that
there is a real leveling here. It is obvious that the new paradigm
in some sense shows "less allomorphy" than the old one. But what
exactly does this mean formally? I would like to suggest as the
crucial difference that the shortening rule, which produces the ō/o
alternation, is transparent with respect to Case (i), whereas the
rhotacism rule, which produces the s/r alternation, is opaque with

respect to Case (i). That is, there are no words ending in -ōr in
Latin, but there are many words with intervocalic *s* (partly because
of exceptions to the rule, e.g. *miser* 'miserable', *positus* 'put
(pp.)', including loans like *basis, asinus* 'donkey', and partly because of *s* from other underlying sources, e.g. /cād+tus/ → *cāsus*
'fallen').

Finally, I should like to suggest that the concept of rule opacity
may prove to be useful in the theory of exceptions. It is hard to
find a clearcut division of phonological rule into those that may
and those that cannot allow exceptions. However, it is possible to
say that certain kinds of rules are much less likely to have exceptions than others. As a first approximation to the needed criterion
I propose opacity. The more opaque a rule, the more likely it is to
develop exceptions. More specifically, opacity by Case (i) leads
to input exceptions, whereas opacity by Case (ii) leads to environment exceptions (see Kisseberth (1970) and Coats (1970) for these
concepts). As an example of the first case, consider Finnish consonant gradation. This is a weakening affecting consonants in the
environment

$$\underline{\hspace{2cm}} VC \begin{bmatrix} \# \\ C \end{bmatrix}$$

The rule applies to single stops and geminate stops in the following
way:

1. Weakening of simple stops	t → d	(e.g. /maton/ → *madon* 'worm's')
	p → v	
	k → ∅,v	
2. Degemination	tt → t	(e.g. /matton/ → *maton* 'carpet's')
	pp → p	
	kk → k	

Degemination has virtually no exceptions (only certain very foreign
names might not be subjected to the rule, e.g. gen. *Giuseppen*, provided they are not assimilated in any way, including stress). On
the other hand, the weakening of simple stops normally fails to
apply in loans (*auton* 'car's'), as well as in many native personal
names (*Lempin* 'Lempi's'), brand names (*Upon* 'of Upo'), slang and
affective words *räkän* 'of snot'), etc. It seems reasonable to correlate this with the fact that degemination is nearly completely
transparent with respect to Case (i), whereas the weakening of
simple stops is rather opaque with respect to that case. That is,
the sorts of input representations that are destroyed by degemination
exist on the surface only in the rare exceptions, and in a few cases
where strong boundaries block the application of gradation, e.g.
Kekkosta 'Kekkonen (partitive)' (Karttunen 1970). But the sorts of

input representations destroyed by the weakening of single stops are quite frequent on the surface; indeed, they arise with every application of degemination. Thus, we might suppose that the weakening of simple stops, and the underlying forms subject to it, are harder to learn than the degemination rule, and the underlying forms subject to it. (This should be readily testable in child language.) The greater proneness of the weakening of simple stops to develop exceptions would, then, be a consequence of its greater opacity.

Examples of the second type (opacity by Case (ii) leading to environment exceptions) are commonplace. This case is simply the initial stage of the process of morphologization, by which rules lose their phonological conditioning and begin to be dependent on abstract features in the lexicon. The paradigm case is Germanic umlaut. The elimination of the conditioning i and j turned the umlaut rule opaque by Case (ii). At some point after this took place, umlaut started to be reanalyzed as a morphologically conditioned process.

Notes

[1]Other aspects of the Slavic palatalizations are dealt with by Halle and Lightner in a forthcoming study. My knowledge of the rules is based entirely on their work. I state the rule here with the Jakobsonian features rather than any of the recent alternative proposals which have greatly improved the system.

References

Andersen, H. 1969 "A study in diachronic morphophonemics: the Ukrainian prefixes," *Lg*. 45, 807-30.

Coats, H. S. 1970 "Rule environment features in phonology," *Papers in Linguistics* 2, 110-40.

Darden, Bill. 1970 "The fronting of vowels after palatals in Slavic," *Papers from the Sixth Regional Meeting, Chicago Linguistic Society*, 459-70 (Chicago: Chicago Linguistic Society).

Erteschik, Nomi. 1971 "The BeGeD-KeFeT or BeKeF mystery," Unpublished MS. (Cambridge, Mass.: M.I.T.)

Hale, Kenneth. 1970 "The passive and ergative in language change: The Australian case," in *Pacific linguistic studies in honour of Arthur Capell*, ed. by S. A. Wurm and D. C. Laycock (Canberra: Australian National University).

Hoenigswald, Henry M. 1960 *Language Change and Linguistic Reconstruction* (Chicago: University of Chicago Press).

Hotzenköcherle, Rudolf. 1934 "Die Mundart von Mutten," in *Beiträge zur schweizerdeutschen Grammatik* 19, ed. by Albert Bachmann (Frauenfeld).

Karttunen, F. 1970 "Problems in Finnish phonology," Unpublished Ph.D. dissertation (Bloomington: University of Indiana).

Kaye, J. D. 1971 "A case for local ordering in Ojibwa," Odawa Language Project, First Report (University of Toronto Department of Anthropology: Anthropological Series No. 9).

Kenstowicz, Michael and C. Kisseberth. 1971 "Unmarked bleeding orders," Unpublished MS. (Urbana: University of Illinois).

King, R. 1969 *Historical linguistics and generative grammar* (Englewood Cliffs: Prentice-Hall).

Kiparsky, P. 1968 "Linguistic universals and linguistic change," in *Universals in linguistic theory*, ed. by E. Bach and R. Harms, 171-202 (New York: Holt, Rinehart and Winston).

Kisseberth, C. 1970 "The treatment of exceptions," *Papers in Linguistics* 2, 44-58.

Klima, E. 1964 "Relatedness between grammatical systems," *Lg.* 40, 1-20. Reprinted in *Modern Studies in English*, ed. by D. A. Reibel and S. A. Schane, 227-46 (Englewood Cliffs: Prentice-Hall).

Rabeler, T.H.F. 1911 "Niederdeutscher Lautstand im Kreise Bleckede," *Zeitschrift für deutsche Philologie* 43, 141-202, 320-377.

Schirmunski, V. 1962 *Deutsche Mundartkunde*, Deutsche Akademie der Wissenschaften zu Berlin, *Veröffentlichungen des Instituts für deutsche Sprache und Literatur* 25 (Berlin).

Stampe, D. 1969 "The acquisition of phonetic representation," *Papers from the Fifth Regional Meeting, Chicago Linguistic Society*, ed. by R. Binnick, et al., 443-54 (Chicago: Department of Linguistics, University of Chicago).

Wanner, George. 1941 "Die Mundarten des Kantons Schaffhausen," in *Beiträge zur schweizerdeutschen Grammatik* 20, ed. by Albert Bachmann (Frauenfeld).

12   Competing Changes as a Cause of Residue

WILLIAM S-Y. WANG

Phonological change may be implemented in a manner that is phonetically
abrupt but lexically gradual. As the change diffuses across the lexicon,
it may not reach all the morphemes to which it is applicable. If there
is another change competing for part of the lexicon, residue may result.
Several fundamental issues in the theory of phonological change are
raised and discussed.

In the literature on sound change, much has been made of the neogrammarian doctrine that sound changes operate without exceptions.
Without some such hypothesis any description would be a long list
of unsystematic correspondences, with no assurance that the same
sound under comparable conditions would not change into a variety
of different sounds, with no governing principle whatsoever. This
point of view, which Hockett has termed the "regularity hypothesis,"
has been richly rewarding in historical research; as a celebrated
part of the heritage of modern linguistics, the point needs no
elaboration here.

When irregularities appear to leak through the net of postulated
phonetic laws, there should be an explanation for them. In the
words of Karl Verner, "There must be a rule for irregularity; the
problem is to find it." In searching for a rule that would explain
certain residues of Grimm's Law, Verner found it necessary to go
beyond the segmental environment into the accentual systems of Indo-
European and Germanic, though the condition in the rule he discovered
is still phonetic. In recent years, an impressive body of evidence
has accumulated that there are diachronic rules which depend on conditions that are altogether non-phonetic, e.g. factors which are
morphological and syntactic.[1] That this is so should not be surprising: in phonology, diachronic rules frequently leave counterparts in
the form of synchronic rules, and there are numerous instances where
synchronic rules are obviously dependent on 'grammatical prerequisites'.

From *Language* 45 (1969), 9-25. Reprinted by permission of William
S-Y. Wang and the Linguistic Society of America.

Furthermore, the stock of morphemes in a language is often partitioned into several layers according to non-phonetic criteria, where these layers exhibit different phonological behavior. To a large extent, such partitions correlate with the historical sources of the various layers, e.g. Romance versus native morphemes in English, or Chinese versus native morphemes in Japanese.

But what about the residual forms which remain, after we have taken into account the phonetic and morphological factors and the multilayered structure of the vocabulary?[2] What explanation can we give for sounds changing differently under completely comparable conditions? Here the usual points about borrowing, dialect mixture, analogy, homonym prevention, the effects of tabu and phonetic symbolism, and functional load suggest themselves.[3] Contrasted with the sweeping scope of phonetic laws, which have direct or indirect physiological motivation when internally induced, these suggestions appear unsatisfyingly ancillary and particularistic. In some cases, such suggestions are completely ad hoc and unconvincing, but they remain in the literature mainly for lack of alternative explanations.

In this study we will examine the various dimensions along which phonological change is implemented: chronological, lexical, and phonetic. Many types of change are phonologically abrupt and require long spans of time to diffuse across the lexicon, as will be discussed in detail below. Since living languages are constantly undergoing change, we should expect to find many seeming exceptions to changes which have not completed their course. These forms are not true residues, in one sense, even though we cannot specify them in general terms either phonetically or morphologically, since in time the appropriate phonological changes will reach them and make them regular. True residue may result, however, as a consequence of the chronological intersection of competing changes. To this extent the neogrammarian doctrine must be modified. A sound change is regular <u>if</u> <u>no</u> <u>other</u> <u>changes</u> <u>compete</u> <u>against</u> <u>it</u>. But there are situations in which two (or more?) changes are applicable to the same subset of morphemes at the same time. Such situations leave residues which are the direct consequences of sound changes that were prevented from running their full course.

1. *Relative Chronology.*
To develop this point we need to make two assumptions. First, we must assume that sound changes take varying periods of time for their operation. For lack of precise information, let us say that a sound change may take anywhere from several years to many centuries for its operation. The longer a sound change takes, the more likely it is to encounter a competing sound change.

Two sound changes may be complementary in their periods of operation. Indeed, many authorities on sound change seem to consider
only this type of time relation; at least, they do not mention other
types. Thus, in speaking of "relative chronology," Bloomfield (368)
refers to "the succession of changes," and Hoenigswald (1960:112) to
"the question of possible formal relationships between successive
sound changes" (emphasis added). In addition to successive (i.e.
complementary) time relations, we must also consider sound changes
in coincident, incorporating, and overlapping relations with each
other.[4] For convenience we will refer to these three non-complemen-
tary types of time relations as intersecting. Two sound changes are
intersecting if and only if the period of operation of one is partly
or wholly concurrent with the period of operation of the other.

Although it is extremely difficult to determine the exact chronological relations between two changes, it is possible to make some
elementary inferences. Let us think of phonological changes as diachronic rules, parallel in formal structure to the synchronic rules
in a grammar. Thus, consider two diachronic rules, R1 and R2, which
are related in a sense to be discussed in §4. Suppose that R1
changes some element X to Y, and R2 changes Y to Z; suppose, further,
that the two rules operate under the same condition C. If all X's
in condition C have changed to Z, then we can infer that R1 preceded
R2. Or, if all Y's have changed to Z and all X's to Y, then R2 must
have preceded R1. Since there is no residue, we conclude that R1
and R2 were virtually complementary.

The situation is more complex if, under some constant condition C,
R1 changes X to Y and R2 changes Y to X, yielding a case of flip-
flop.[5] Here, if all X's and Y's have indeed exchanged identities,
we may infer that R1 and R2 are virtually coincident—for had R1
extended beyond R2, some of the X's produced by R2 would have been
changed back to Y's; and similarly for R2.

2. *Flip-Flops*.

Flip-flops pose an interesting problem for rule formalism in phonological theory. It is easy to see that when the elements involved
contain the same number of segments, R1 and R2 may be collapsed by
using a binary variable.[6] This possibility of collapsing them
captures nicely the coincident nature of the two rules. In fact,
these cases strengthen the argument for binary specifications for
those features which participate in flip-flops, since a specification that ranges over three or more values will introduce obvious
difficulties when we try to collapse rules like R1 and R2.[7]

A problem arises, however, when X and Y do not contain the same
number of segments. We may consider an example from some Min

dialects of Chinese.[8]   In Amoy, the morphemes for 'fire', 'age', and
'skin' are pronounced with /(C)e/; in Lóngxī these same morphemes
are pronounced with /(C)we/. On the other hand, the morphemes for
'chicken', 'shoe', and 'plough' are pronounced with /(C)we/ in Amoy
but /(C)e/ in Lóngxī. If we assume for the sake of the present discussion that these morphemes retain in one dialect (say, Amoy) the
earlier forms from which the forms in the other dialect (say, Lóngxī)
are derived, then Lóngxī is separated from Amoy by two rules. One
rule changes /e/ to /we/, the other /we/ to /e/. These rules are
disjunctive in their application, for to apply them conjunctively
in one order would produce only /e/ and in the other order would
produce only /we/. This suggests the use of a variable. Yet the
variable cannot be attached to any distinctive feature, since it is
the entire segment /w/ that is involved. We need to extend the use
of the variable in a basic way to apply to whole segments in order
to be able to describe this particular type of flip-flop, as illustrated in the rule below. In such rules the specification '+' when
attached to the feature 'segment' denotes the presence of the segment with all its features, while the specification '—' denotes its
absence.

$$
\begin{bmatrix} \alpha\text{segment} \\ -\text{syllabic} \\ -\text{consonantal} \\ +\text{velar} \end{bmatrix} \rightarrow \begin{bmatrix} -\alpha\text{segment} \\ -\text{syllabic} \\ -\text{consonantal} \\ +\text{velar} \end{bmatrix} / \underline{\hspace{1cm}} \begin{bmatrix} +\text{syllabic} \\ -\text{consonantal} \\ +\text{palatal} \\ +\text{mid} \end{bmatrix}
$$

The phonetic history of these morphemes needs to be worked out in
detail to see if the assumption we made is true. It may be the case
that the two dialects developed along altogether different lines.
Or /we/ may have been /ø/ (i.e. a mid palatal labial vowel) at the
time of the flip-flop, which would permit the more usual type of
rule collapsing. In any case, it is at least possible that we have
here two coincident rules which require us to extend the way in
which variables are used in phonology. This extension is of great
interest for our understanding of phonological theory.[9]

3. *Lexical Diffusion.*

The second of the two assumptions referred to in §1 has to do with
the way in which a change operates within a given period of time.
Suppose that the change is from sound X to sound Y. Without concerning ourselves with the intriguing question of how the change came
into the language in the first place,[10] let us consider how it might
actually implement itself. Ideally, before the change, all speakers
will use sound X in all relevant morphemes; after the change, all

speakers will use sound Y in the same set of morphemes. The dimension of time may be studied in each of three relatively independent parameters: (1) phonetic, i.e. from sound X to sound Y; (2) lexical, i.e. from morpheme to morpheme in the relevant part of an individual's vocabulary; and (3) social, i.e. from speaker to speaker in the same dialect.[11]

With respect to the first of these parameters, we have in mind the familiar controversy of whether the change from X to Y is gradual or abrupt—i.e., whether sound changes occur always by successive slides, or always by abrupt leaps, or by both mechanisms, depending on the phonetic character of the sounds involved. By the term 'gradual' we refer to the 'imperceptible increments' type of shift as suggested, for instance, by Jespersen's metaphor of sawing logs, in which, in the absence of a standard measure, the errors may have a cumulative effect. Jespersen's metaphor has recently been quoted with approval by Hockett, who thinks that changes occur "mostly on a much finer-grained scale" still, and that they are "totally out of awareness" of the speaker.[12]

It is obvious that the gradual view of phonological change cannot be correct for many types of sound change, such as (1) when X and Y involve different articulators between which there is no physiological continuum (and it is implausible to imagine that there is any meaningful acoustical continuum; in the $t > k$ in Hawaiian, for example, there is no evidence whatever for a phonetically intermediate stage); (2) flip-flop and metathesis, which are paradigmatic and syntagmatic variants of each other, and where the gradualist would be forced to shunt one of the elements off the collision course onto an artificial detour; (3) voicing, nasalization, and related processes, where our control of the relevant articulators is quite gross; (4) segment addition or deletion, since many sound types are either present or absent, but never present in gradient quantitites. Furthermore, there is good reason to believe that many types of sound change must be regarded as operating at a phonological level that is much more abstract than the phonetic level, and therefore phonetically non-gradual. So, for a word like 'acclimate' in which the pronunciation changes from [əklájmɪt], the only pronunciation found in some older dictionaries, to [ǽklɪmejt], where all three vowels are different (in addition to the difference in accent pattern), it is surely unrealistic to suppose that there was a gradual and proportionate shift along all four phonetic dimensions. Clearly, the way to explain such a change is to posit a diachronic rule of accent fronting which is followed by the same body of stress adjustment and vowel-reduction rules which apply to a large sector of other English words.

Even more obvious than the points made above is the fact that non-phonetic changes (e.g. lexical, morphological, and syntactic) cannot be accommodated at all within the gradual view. In fact, it remains to be shown that the gradual view is applicable to any sound change at all, even to those cases where there is some degree of surface plausibility, i.e. where X and Y differ along continuous articulatory dimensions, as with vowels and tones, over which significant scattering is observed. As Hoenigswald (73) remarked, "The doctrine of gradual phonetic change may turn out to be a remnant from pre-phonemic days,"[13] when the multi-dimensional continua of speech had not yet been successfully quantized.

Without pursuing this topic further, it is sufficient for the argument here to grant that at least a large class of sound changes must be implemented abruptly, i.e. must go directly from X to Y without passing through minute intermediate stages. This is to say that the phonetic difference between X and Y is sufficiently gross to be potentially phonemic, and a normal speaker of the language can distinguish between X and Y easily and consistently without any special training.

The process of diffusion within a speaker's vocabulary may likewise be thought of as being either abrupt (i.e. all relevant morphemes change 'simultaneously') or gradual (i.e. the change affects the relevant morphemes severally in succession). There are then four logical possibilities in viewing how a sound change operates on an individual's vocabulary:

(1) phonetically abrupt   and lexically abrupt
(2) phonetically abrupt   and lexically gradual
(3) phonetically gradual   and lexically abrupt
(4) phonetically gradual   and lexically gradual

Of the two possibilities which involve a phonetically abrupt implementation, (1) is refuted by elementary observations: it implies that all morphemes with only X-pronunciations for a given speaker would suddenly have only Y-pronunciations, which is obviously unacceptable. A sound change takes time, not only for the collective vocabulary of a speech community, but for the vocabulary of individuals as well. (3) is the view taken by the neogrammarians and continues to be widely accepted today. The hypothesis of lexical diffusion stipulates (2) and (4). Of these two, (2) is the more compelling: for given that the phonetic implementation is abrupt, and that an individual's vocabulary does not change all that suddenly, the obvious conclusion is that what actually takes place is a kind of diffusion from morpheme to morpheme in his vocabulary. This diffusion within a lexicon is basically the same mechanism as the more observed forms of diffusion across dialects or languages, and diffuses only in its scope of operation; lexical diffusion is more local, the other forms are more global.

We do not need to insist that lexical diffusion is the only means by which the pronunciation of morphemes changes. It is sufficient for the argument here that this is one of the primary means through which a sound change implements itself. According to this view, during the early phase of the change only a small sector of the relevant morphemes is affected. Some of the affected morphemes may change to the X-pronunciation directly. Other morphemes, however, will at first have both the X-pronunciation and the Y-pronunciation, fluctuating either randomly or according to some such factor as tempo style. (For the most part, morphemes do not have more than two pronunciations. In the phonetic literature, these dual forms have sometimes been referred to as 'doublets'.) But the X-pronunciation will gradually be suppressed in favor of the Y-pronunciation.[14] These doublets, then, serve as a kind of psychological bridge between the two end-points of a sound change, carrying along with them even those morphemes which do not go through a doublet stage.

This hypothesis of lexical diffusion suggests that, at any given time in any living language, we should expect to find several sets of morphemes with dual pronunciations. Such examples are not difficult to obtain, although they are not abundantly reported in the literature, presumably because perception is a function of expectation; and their existence is not suggested by the dominant theory of sound change illustrated earlier in the works of Jespersen and Hockett. Thus, in Chinese dialects there are large sectors of morphemes which have two pronunciations, one 'literary', the other 'colloquial' (cf. Peking University 1962). For English, the pages of any good pronouncing dictionary (e.g. Kenyon & Knott 1944) show that many morphemes have two pronunciations, such as those involving accent pattern [ǽbdəmən / əbdówmən], postvocalic r [sərprájz/ səprájz], vowel labialization [kǽtəlɔg / kǽtəlag], vowel length [ruf /rʊf], syllabicity [táwl / táwəl], j-glides [nu / nju], voicing of intervocalic obstruent clusters [ɛ́ksɪt / ɛ́gzɪt], and so on. Dialect geography can tell us which areas favor which clusters of pronunciation. In actual fact, of course, many of the dual pronunciations are used by the same speaker.

As Vogt remarked (1954:367): "At any moment, between the initiation and the conclusion of these changes, we have a state characterized by the presence of more or less free variants, so that the speakers have the choice between alternative expressions. In each case the choice will be determined by an interplay of factors, some linguistic, some esthetic and social, an interplay so complex that most often the choice will appear as being due to pure chance. . . . What therefore in a history of linguistic system appears as a change will in a synchronic description appear as a more or less free variation between forms of expression, equally admissible within the system."[15] Recent advances in sociolinguistics hold the promise that perhaps some of the social factors determining linguistic choices of this kind can be investigated in a roughly quantitative way.

It is not always easy to determine if a given situation is the result of dialect borrowing, or if it is due to the process of lexical diffusion as described here. To say that dialect D_1 borrowed a particular set of Y-pronunciations from dialect D_2 can only be a partial answer at best. It merely tells us that the phonological explanation for the X-to-Y change does not lie in D_1. We must trace back to the dialect in which the change originated, if the question 'Why did X change into Y?' is to be fully answered. In those cases where we are fortunate enough to catch the inception of a change at one or two isolated sites, influence from neighboring dialects can be ruled out and we can have a clearer view of how the change implements itself. Thus when a dialect dictionary (Peking University 1962) shows that there is an ongoing change from the retroflex series to the labiodental series in Xian which is not reported in any of the neighboring dialects, we can hope that a detailed historical study of the Xian dialect will reveal the workings of lexical diffusion.

As the change continues to operate, an increasing portion of the relevant morphemes will become affected. Cases have been reported where, for extralinguistic reasons, a sound change ceased (or even reversed itself) after it had operated over only a part of the relevant vocabulary.[16] It is important to note that such cases (if they are real) are in direct conflict with the almost universally accepted view of how phonemic split can come about, as summarized by Moulton (1967:1394 f.). As Harms has recently put it (1967): "any claim for a split . . . must be supported by the environmental conditioning which gave rise to the putative split" (166) and "no other basis for split consistent with the synchronic structure of language is known" (169). If cases of incomplete changes can be established with certainty, then our understanding of the basis of phonemic split and, more broadly, of the regularity hypothesis itself must be revised.

If, however, the change runs its full course (which seems to be frequently the case), then all the X-pronunciations will be replaced by Y-pronunciations—unless another sound change comes into the picture to compete for some of the same morphemes relevant to the X-to-Y change. Notice that the view of sound change as competition between co-existing rivals is less constraining on the degree of

phonetic similarity between the two pronunciations than one which
construes one pronunciation as some sort of direct and gradual phonetic mutation of the other. There is thus no a-priori reason to
believe, for instance, that sound changes necessarily affect only one
distinctive feature at a time. A fortiori, I see no basis at all for
Sweet's assertion (1888:15) that "Such a change as the frequent one
of [ii] into [ai] presupposes a number of intermediate stages: [i:],
(Ii) [ei], [ɛi], [ɛ̈i], [ai], etc. Hence also there are no simultaneous changes of a sound, only successive ones. Thus we cannot suppose
a simultaneous opening and unvoicing of [m], but only such series as
[m], [b̃], [β], [φ]."[17] Nevertheless, the view of sound change exemplified by Sweet here may be actually the dominant view of this area
of linguistic scholarship. The notion of doublets as an intermediate
stage in sound change was specifically rejected by Wheeler (1887:5),
who wrote: "It is to be noticed that the operation of the laws of
sound is unconscious and gradual, so that the old form cannot, except
through mixing of dialects, survive alongside the new" (emphasis
added).

Given the picture roughly sketched out in this section, sound
changes can be seen to proceed very much along the same principles
as other, non-phonetic linguistic changes. A sound change may involve, simultaneously, several phonetic dimensions which are related
to each other by phonological rules, as illustrated by the word
'acclimate' above, though it is typically simple and physiologically
motivated. Over a half-century ago, Sturtevant described the situation quite well, though he did not use the term 'lexical diffusion',
when he wrote the following passage: "We have seen that many sound-
changes are irregular when they first appear and gradually become
more and more regular. The reason is that each person who substi-
tues the new sound for the old in his own pronunciation tends to
carry it into new words. The two processes of spread from word to
word and spread from speaker to speaker progress side by side until
the new sound has extended to all the words of the language which
contained the old sound in the same surroundings" (82). In addition,
he noted that "Such a spread of a sound-change from word to word
closely resembles analogical change; the chief difference is that in
analogical change the association groups are based upon meaning,
while in this case the groups are based upon form" (80).

Lexical diffusion may be schematized as in Table 1, which illustrates the basic paradigm of phonological change. At the beginning
of the time span, t_1, segment A occurs in four distinct contexts,
C_1, C_2, C_3, and C_4. These contexts may be specified in either phonological or morphological terms. At t_2, A has become B in the context
C_1, creating an alternation in the sound system. We may think of C_1

as the _primary_ context, as it is most likely the case that A is changed to B through an assimilatory process motivated by C_1.

All the morphemes which have A in the context C_1 will not change at the same time, of course. Some of them may even lag and change only after t_3, or maybe even later. It would be of interest to determine if such lags typically do or do not occur; and if they do, then to what extent. The table shows that by t_5 all of the A's have changed into B's. That is, the conditions for the change have re-laxed until finally the change has become unconditioned. Formally stated, this can be seen as a process of successive simplification in the diachronic rules that will ultimately have the effect of elim-inating whatever alternation was caused by the primary contest. In languages like Chinese, which have little morphophonemic alternation, since they have little morphological inflection, the effect of change upon the morphophonemic representations is correspondingly more direct. Unless we can reconstruct the history of this diffusion and determine what was the primary context, the change of A to B in the non-primary contexts will seem to lack phonetic motivation, or even to be counter-phonetic.

	t_1	t_2	t_3	t_4	t_5
C_1	A	B	B	B	B
C_2	A	A	B	B	B
C_3	A	A	A	B	B
C_4	A	A	A	A	B

Table 1. Basic Paradigm of Phonological Change

4. _Rule Relations._

The two assumptions we have made above allow us to conceive the fol-lowing situation. Suppose we have two diachronic rules which inter-sect in time. In the schema below, I, O, and C denote _input_, _output_ and _condition_; the subscripts denote the number of the rule.

$$R1 \qquad I_1 \rightarrow O_1 \ / \ C_1$$
$$R2 \qquad I_2 \rightarrow O_2 \ / \ C_2$$

Suppose, also, that R1 and R2 operate across the vocabulary in the manner of lexical diffusion suggested above. One further condition must be satisfied before these two rules can cause residue: they must be in competition with each other.

The competing relation in diachronic rules is approximately the counterpart of the ordering relation in synchronic rules. Two syn-chronic rules are ordered with respect to each other, if, for an _arbitrary_ input set, the output set differs according to the sequence in which the two rules are applied. Diachronically speaking, two

245

rules are in a competing relation if there are morphemes whose phonetic histories would differ according to the sequence in which the
two rules are applied. Since ordering is transitive, two rules may
be indirectly ordered via intermediate rules. From recent studies
we have learned that relations among phonological rules may be quite
complex: thus, rules which assign specifications to prosodic features for large syntactic constructions may need to be ordered cycli-
cally. There are rules which 'persist' in that they apply whenever
applicable;[18] such rules usually have strong phonetic motivations.
Rules may be conjunctive or disjunctive. Furthermore, there may be
cases where a rule may either precede or follow a block of rules but
must not apply within the block.[19] In the present discussion, however, we will consider only the simplest case: the relation between
two rules.

The relation between a pair of rules may be studied by reference
to the schema given above for R1 and R2. Recall that, in its formal
representation, each of the six parts in the two rules is a matrix
of feature specifications. Thus, given two matrices, M1 and M2,
neither of which is an empty matrix, M1 may contain M2 (M1 c M2),
M1 may be contained in M2 (M1 i M2), or M1 may equal M2 (M1 = M2).
The assertion M1 c M2 is of course equivalent to the assertion M2 i
M1. We use the formula M1 $\underline{c}$ M2 to denote that either M1 c M2 or
M1 = M2; and similarly for M1 $\underline{i}$ M2. The formula M1 $\neq$ M2 denies
both M1 $\underline{c}$ M2 and M1 $\underline{i}$ M2. On the other hand, M1 r M2 means either
M1 $\underline{c}$ M2 or M1 $\underline{i}$ M2.

The reader will note that if M1 c M2, then M2 actually refers to a
larger class of phonological situations. A matrix that represents
high front vowels will contain a matrix that represents high vowels,
though the latter of course refers to a more general class of segments. The formalism does not cover cases where M1 and M2 overlap
but neither contains the other. Such a situation would arise if M1
represented high front vowels and M2 represented a sequence of two
high vowels.

In terms of the formalism introduced above, it is easy to enumerate all the possible relations R1 may have to R2. Thus, we see that
the matrix O_1, for instance, may participate in any of the following
relationships. If $O_1 = \emptyset$, clearly R1 is a deletion rule.

If $O_1 \underline{c} I_2$, then we have a number of subcases. If $C_1 = \emptyset$, $C_2 = \emptyset$,
or $C_1 \underline{i} C_2$, then R2 will apply to O_1, as example 1 shows:

> (1) R1   mid vowels → high vowels /__C
> R2   V   →   Ṽ   /___nasals

246

If we impose the further condition that $I_1 \neq I_2$, we have what has been called a _feeding_ relation between the two rules (example 2):

(2) R1 $s \rightarrow z$ / ___V

       R2 $z \rightarrow r$ / V___V

In example 3, where $I_1 = I_2$ and $C_1 \subseteq C_2$, we have a _bleeding_ relation.[20]

(3) R1 $t \rightarrow \check{c}$ / ___i

       R2 $t \rightarrow d$ / ___V

In example 4, where $I_1 = O_2$ and $C_1 = C_2$, we have an instance of what might be called a _replenishing_ relation.

(4) R1 $n \rightarrow ñ$ / ___V

       R2 $l \rightarrow n$ / ___V

Example 5 illustrates a _voiding_ relation, where $C_1 = I_2$.

(5) R1 $a \rightarrow \mathrm{\mathcal{o}}$ / ___l

       R2 $l \rightarrow n$

It should go without saying that there are rules which are not in a competing relation, as in example 6.

(6) R1 $t \rightarrow s$ / ___V

       R2 $n \rightarrow m$ / ___labial stops

The four relations illustrated by examples 2-5 have interesting relations within themselves. _Replenishing_ and _feeding_, for example, are partial inverses of each other. If a pair of ordered rules includes a flip-flop rule, then the relation between the two rules is both _feeding_ and _bleeding_. (In fact, it is possible to obtain a simultaneous feeding and bleeding relation even when neither in the pair is a flip-flop rule.) In addition, there must be dozens of other possible relations that can be uncovered in an exhaustive study that exploits more fully the formalism introduced here. Two sound changes must have a competing relation to cause a residue; we must be satisfied here with merely illustrating some of the more obvious competing relations.

5. _Discussion_.

The conjecture offered here is that residue may be caused by two competing sound changes that intersect in time. A definitive proof of this conjecture must await case studies with careful and detailed documentation. My purpose here is merely to give it an airing, in the hope that scholars may be interested in investigating its validity in their respective areas of expertise.

If the picture of sound changes sketched above is valid, then the effects that they have on the phonological structure of the lexicon are certainly much more complicated than the neat universe suggested by the 'regularity hypothesis'. Given that R1, R2, and R3 operated in complementary periods, then the class of relevant morphemes can at most be partitioned into 2^3 subsets, where '+' indicates that the rule has been applied and '−' indicates that it has not, as shown in Table 2. Only subset I above is the perfectly regular class; subset VIII has somehow escaped all three sound changes.

If the three sound changes overlap, then the number of logical possibilities is significantly increased. The morphemes of subset I may be further divided according to the six possible orders in which the three rules may apply. Subsets II, III, and IV each further divides according to two possible orders. In fact, the very notion of 'residue' becomes quite subtle as it becomes increasingly difficult to determine which one of these numerous subsets of morphemes followed a 'regular' development.

	I	II	III	IV	V	VI	VII	VIII
R1	+	+	+	−	+	−	−	−
R2	+	+	−	+	−	+	−	−
R3	+	−	+	+	−	−	+	−

Table 2

This view of diachronic phonology has obvious implications for synchronic analysis. Current theories more or less assume that all morphemes uniformly go through the same full body of phonological rules, those which exhibit alternation as well as those which do not. It is clear from the diagram above, however, that there may be a considerable amount of cross-classification as to which rules are applicable to which morphemes, so that the neat picture of all-rules-apply-to-all-morphemes becomes highly suspect. We need to make much more use of rule features in synchronic phonology in order to capture the diversity in the lexicon that is due to the various cross-currents of sound change.

Some of the standard concepts of diachronic phonology will need re-examination. It is generally believed, for example, that splits can result only from a conditioned change, and that contrasts are possible only after something happens to the condition of the change. But if we accept the fact that a sound change (conditioned or unconditioned) may not complete its course due to other competing changes, then clearly we may also need to recognize incomplete sound changes as a cause of splits.

The conjecture presented here can only be invalidated by demonstrating that all (or at least competing) sound changes are complementary in their periods of operation, or that lexical diffusion is an untenable view of how sound changes spread. Both the assumption of relative chronology and the assumption of lexical diffusion, as they are sketched above, seem to me, however, to be eminently reasonable in the light of our present state of knowledge. Therefore, I would think it extremely unlikely that the conjecture will be invalidated on these grounds. Also, it should go without saying that the conjecture cannot be falsified by demonstrating that certain phonetic laws do not have residues or that certain residues are caused by other factors. (We cannot prove that the platypus does not lay eggs with photographs showing a platypus not laying eggs.)

Probably it is not much easier to validate the conjecture with an incontrovertible proof, primarily because such subtle factors are involved. But there are several considerations which give it indirect support. Although much more attention is usually given to the regular aspects of sound changes than to their residue, a closer scrutiny reveals that even the best phonetic laws are frequently ridden with irregularities.[21] When all currently available explanations fail, we must examine our premises and be prepared to accept a concept of sound change that is more detailed and more complex.

One of the most striking achievements of modern linguistics is the wealth of reliable information gathered about the phonetics of a great diversity of languages, on the basis of which we can make some preliminary historical guesses. The evidence is overwhelming that almost all sound changes come from an extremely small common inventory.[22] Many of these changes are now beginning to find explanations in laboratory phonetics. To the extent that they are phonetically motivated, they are unidirectional or asymmetrical. The degree of parallelism in phonological histories is such that every argument for a common history of dialects on the basis of a common sound change is suspect unless it is buttressed by additional independent considerations.[23] In fact, this small inventory of changes (e.g. umlaut, vowel nasalization before nasals, tone lowering with voiced consonants, palatalization and sibilation before grooved vowels,[24] etc.) constitutes the empirical foundation for much recent research on marking conventions in phonological theory, especially the use of these conventions as linking rules.

The observation that sound changes are few in kind suggests that, given any two sound changes, there is a significant possibility that they are formally in competition with each other. This line

of reasoning gives indirect support to the conjecture that residue
may be caused by two competing sound changes that intersect in time.

Another consideration has to do with time. The longer sound
changes take, the more likely it is that they will intersect, compete,
and leave a residue. To measure exactly how long a sound change took,
we would need to be able to determine the end points of its period
of operation, which is nearly impossible in our present state of
knowledge. Part of the difficulty stems from the fact that a sound
change may begin sporadically in the vocabulary (i.e. the class of
morphemes it affects can only be defined by enumeration); it then
consolidates itself and becomes regular but conditioned; and the
conditions may eventually be simplified until, finally, it becomes
an unconditioned change. The phonetic condition that originally
stimulated the change may create a 'snowball' effect across the lexicon, so that the condition itself eventually becomes irrelevant.
This means that, in a perfectly justifiable sense, one could argue
that most conditioned changes, even though they have no residue, are
really subchanges of larger changes which have not completed their
course. If we accept such arguments, then we must be prepared to
recognize sound changes as typically endowed with a much greater
longevity than is commonly thought.

As an interesting example, let us consider some English rules of
vowel shortening which have been recently discussed by Kiparsky. In
Old English, vowels were shortened either before three consonants
or before two consonants and two more syllables within the same word.
Beginning in Early Middle English, the condition of this rule was
simplified to either before two consonants or before one consonant
and two more syllables within the same word. The latter rule is
still with us, as evidenced by such morphophemic alternations as in
sleep / slept and *feline / felinity*. If we take these rules to be
synchronic manifestations of an underlying sound change,[25] then we
see that the deletion of a single consonant in the condition of the
change has operated over roughly a thousand years! Such examples,
of course, are not hard to find. Another sound change from the history of English is the loss of /h/ in presonorant position, which
still has residual forms in many dialects despite many centuries of
operation.

Surely, if we give more consideration to the dimension of time,
much of the 'unstructuredness' observed by dialect geographers and
in sociolinguistic studies of language usage can be better reconciled
with the necessary faith that our linguistic behavior is lawful.
Commenting on the general principles of biological evolution, Huxley
(1953:28) noted that in synchronic descriptions "we freeze the process into a set of unreal static pictures. . . . Only in the longest

perspective . . . do the overall processes of evolution become visible."[26] Within the narrow time perpectives available to us, numerous competing cross-currents appear to be vying for the phonological future of every word in the lexicon. Without adequate time-depth, it is often difficult for us to know which changes are sporadic, which will persist, which come from past millennia, which are receding, and which are just coming into the language. To understand such a complex dynamic situation, we must attempt to isolate for careful analysis each of the various interwoven factors—the physiological, the structural, the societal, and yet others. From the factors examined here, it seems that the 'regularity hypothesis' must be modified to allow for residue caused by competing sound changes which intersect in time.[27]

Notes

[1]That there should be non-phonetic conditions for sound change was expressed in this way by Sapir (1921:183 f.): "Every linguist knows that phonetic change is frequently followed by morphological re-arrangements, but he is apt to assume that morphology exercises little or no influence on the course of phonetic history. I am inclined to believe that our present tendency to isolate phonetics and grammar as mutually irrelevant linguistic provinces is unfortunate. There are likely to be fundamental relations between them and their respective histories that we do not yet fully grasp." It should be noted that Sapir's view is not compatible with that of the neo-grammarians, who "define sound-change as a purely phonetic process . . . (that) affects a phoneme or a type of phoneme either universally or under strictly phonetic conditions" (Bloomfield 1933;364). Non-phonetically conditioned sound changes are discussed at length in Postal 1968. In several recent works by Malkiel (e.g. 1968) we also find carefully documented histories of how morphological structures influence sound change.

[2]Cf. the following passage from Bloomfield (364): "We must suppose that, no matter how minute and accurate our observation, we should always find deviant forms, because, from the very outset of a sound-change, and during its entire course, and after it is over, the forms of the language are subject to the incessant working of other factors of change, such as, especially, borrowing and analogic combinations of new complex forms" (emphasis added). Bloomfield did not consider competing sound changes among the factors responsible for residue; and, as far as I know, neither has anyone else.

[3]I have attempted to provide a statistical basis for the notion of functional load in Wang (1967a). Results so far based on the measure developed in that article, or on various modifications of it, have led me to be quite pessimistic as to the value of this notion for our understanding of the causes of sound change. There is some surface plausibility to the suggestion that contrasts which distinguish larger numbers of higher frequency words are more resistant to loss. When we recall, however, the tremendous amount of various types of redundancy that is typically present in the speech situation, it appears that individual contrasts are not really all that crucial for effective communication. It is not difficult to find cases where contrasts have been lost on a grand scale: for example, the number of distinct syllables has been reduced by a factor of 3:1 from Middle Chinese to Modern Pekinese (cf. also the results of King 1968).

[4]These four terms are adopted from Wells (1949). They were used for still another purpose in Block (1953).

[5]I have elsewhere discussed a case of tonal flip-flop in a Min dialect of Chinese (Wang 1967b:102-3).

[6]Variable notation was introduced by Halle (1962).

[7]Binarily specified features can be used to describe alternations among three or four elements (as with vowels or tones) by attaching paired variables to different features; cf. Wang (1968).

[8]These examples are taken from Tung (1960:997-1010). Robert L-W. Cheng has called my attention to a similar situation with /e/ and /we/ in Northern and Southern Taiwanese.

[9]Note that in this formalism the deletion of w has a much more conventional interpretation than the addition of it. For the latter we have to assume that there is an implicit w in the underlying form which surfaces when the specification of the feature segment is changed.

Another use for the variable notation has been recently proposed by W. Labov to investigate statistical regularities in the application of rules. Later sections of this paper should make it clear that Labov's hypothesis on rule application and the hypothesis of lexical diffusion are related but distinct notions. Only in the latter hypothesis is it claimed that rule applicability in many cases must be specified vis-à-vis individual items in the lexicon.

[10]This question, as well as many related issues, is discussed with admirable balance and clarity in Weinreich, Labov, & Herzog (1968). Postal has recently expressed the rather extreme view of phonological change (p. 283 and elsewhere) in which all changes are stylistic and non-functional, and phonetics plays no role in considerations of sound change. It is difficult to see how such a view can be justified in the light of the abundance of different types of sound change which can easily be shown to have phonetic motivation, as against the paucity of attested 'counter-phonetic' changes. In fact, many changes are only apparently counter-phonetic since it can be shown that they are triggered by other changes in the system which are phonetically motivated. It may very well turn out upon deeper examination that all internal phonological changes are directly or indirectly actuated by phonetic factors, as envisioned in Whitney (1877).

[11]We preserve the convenient illusion of 'dialect' here for ease of discussion, realizing that isoglosses intersect in diverse fashions and that the concept is often no more than an idealization. Much of what we say here about lexical diffusion is true across dialects as well as within dialects.

[12]See Hockett (1965:202). For the cases where errors (or imprecision of pronunciation) build into a sound change, neither Jespersen nor Hockett explain why these errors should be cumulative in effect rather than mutually cancelling, or why the overwhelming majority of sound changes are unidirectional—i.e. why the relation between X and Y is anti-symmetric. The claim of sound changes occurring 'totally out of awareness' is based on the neogrammarians' belief that if the variation were noticeable, it would be corrected and sound change would not take place. Recent studies in sociolinguistics show, however, that speakers are very much aware of many types of subphonemic fluctuation which are socially marked; see especially Labov (1966).

[13]For a relatively early statement in favor of the 'abrupt leap' view, see Sommerfelt (1923). Still earlier, Sturtevant (1917:79) noted that "Even some changes which might take place by imperceptible stages are nevertheless observed to involve at certain times an easily perceptible variation between words or between speakers."

Contrast these opinions with that of Sweet (1888): "The most serious of my defects of method was my rejection of the principles of gradual sound-change in favour of change *per saltum* . . ." (vii); and " . . . all sound-change is <u>gradual</u>: there are no sudden leaps in the phonetic history of a language" (15). For his theoretical position, Sweet claims to "owe most to Paul and Sievers" (xii).

[14]We refrain at this point from speculating on certain fascinating questions: why some morphemes change earlier than others, whether morphemes follow the same change schedule from speaker to speaker, and how speakers influence each other's change schedules. These questions are probably in large part insoluble on the basis of purely linguistic considerations, since they appear to depend on many social factors. At any rate, the answer can not be as facile as Sturtevant pictured it when he wrote (83): ". . . it seems safe to say that the likelihood that a sound-change will become regular varies directly as the number and the frequency of the words which induce it." Opinions similar to Sturtevant's have been expressed more recently by Greenberg et al. (1954:148) (see also fn. 3 in the present paper for further discussion). Current work on sound change at a more microcosmic level (e.g. Labov) may eventually lead us to a better understanding of these questions, where consideration is given to the social aspects of language use, as well as to the structural aspects internal to the language.

[15]I am indebted to George Grace for drawing my attention to this clearly worded statement.

[16]Sturtevant (76) gives an example of an unsuccessful sound change: "In Latin there was at one time a tendency to lengthen short vowels before *gn* . . . . But . . . the pronunciation with a short vowel finally prevailed. In this case the net result of the incipient change was to leave things as they were at first." When the morphemes affected by an unsuccessful sound change do not get changed back, we have two classes of forms. Whether the new or the old forms should be considered regular is an interesting terminological question that depends in part on how unsuccessful the second change was. Examples of unsuccessful sound changes, which are noted as such, are scarce in the literature; of closely related interest here are cases that have been reported where *Y* changes back to *X*, which has been termed 'retrograde' (Weinreich 1958).

[17]I have replaced Sweet's Visible-Speech symbols with a more familiar phonetic notation. The theory that sound changes occur by single features is especially unacceptable with respect to epenthesis and deletion. For example, in Hankow Chinese an /ŋ/ has developed after /mu/. A theory that requires us to assign relative chronology to the various features of the epenthetic /ŋ/ is clearly misguided; and similarly for cases when segments are lost.

[18]For further discussion on ordering relations among phonological rules, especially regarding persisting rules, see Chafe (1967). For general theory, see also Postal (1968), and Chomsky & Halle (1968).

[19]The possibility of such cases was first suggested by C. Douglas Johnson in discussion (see Johnson 1967).

[20]The terms 'feeding' and 'bleeding' were proposed by Kiparsky (1968).

[21]Thus in Romance linguistics, a field that serves as a precious laboratory for historical methods, Bonfante writes (1947:345): "It would in fact be easy to show that for many of the so-called phonetic laws . . . the "exceptions" are more numerous than the 'normal' forms." It is unfortunate that most students of diachronic phonology, when they posit a sound change, do not take the trouble to enumerate the residual as well as the regular forms. Granted that the plausibility of a sound change does not rest exclusively on the number of attestations, it is surely important for an accurate

understanding of the linguistic processes involved to be able to explain both types of forms. If the evidence is too meager, the positing of the sound change may very well be in error; cf. Bennett (1966).

[22] Without a detailed specification of how broad a range of phenomena each sound change should encompass, it would be meaningless to offer an exact number at this time.

[23] Given dialects D_1 and D_2 and a sound change R which began at time T, we can argue with force that D_1 and D_2 must have split from each other at least since T, because they do not share R. But the other side of the argument is considerably weaker: that D_1 and D_2 must not yet have split at T because they share R. Languages, as well as dialects, can independently undergo the same sound change, with a probability that is directly correlated with the degree of similarity between the phonetic structures, but not necessarily related to the genetic affiliations involved.

[24] Palatalization and sibilation are two very different phonetic processes, though they frequently go together, and both are predominantly regressive, as are most assimilations. The former is an assimilation to the tongue position of a vowel such as [i], which is articulated with the vocal tract narrowest at the palatal region, as in *key* and *tea*. The latter is an assimilation to the tongue shape of the vowel. High front vowels are typically articulated with a groove in the center of the tongue, i.e. with the center down and the edges turned up against the lateral teeth. The presence of such a groove is the distinguishing property of sibilants, whereby the air stream is channeled against the upper edge of the lower incisors. So the English changes of [k] and [t] to [s] as in the letter 'c' and in *lunacy* need not have gone through a palatal stage at all.

[25] The statement by Greenberg et al. (148) that "in general, conditioned change is the diachronic aspect of the synchronic problem of conditioned allophonic variation" is, of course, quite incomplete. Morphophonemic variation also may reflect sound changes. Due to a variety of factors, synchronic rules may not faithfully reflect the phonological history. Thus, a sequence of diachronic rules may be telescoped into a single synchronic rule; i.e. $A \rightarrow B$, $B \rightarrow C$, and $C \rightarrow D$ go into just $A \rightarrow D$ if there is no synchronic motivation for positing B and C as intermediate stages. The English vowel shift may be such a case; cf. Wang (1968). Or the effects of a diachronic rule of the form $A \rightarrow B/C$ may be more simply accounted for synchronically by a reversed rule $B \rightarrow A/D$. For further discussion on the relation between synchronic and diachronic phonology, see Greenberg (1966) and Zeps (1966).

[26] The idea is expressed so well that the full paragraph should be quoted here: "When we take an instantaneous snapshot, we freeze the process into a set of unreal static pictures. What we need is the equivalent of a film. We all know how a film record can be speeded up to reveal processes that are hidden from ordinary view—the dancing movements of a growing twig, the adventurous transformations of a developing egg. The same applies to our moving picture of evolution. If this is run at what seems natural speed, we see only individual lives and deaths. But when, with the aid of our scientific knowledge and our imagination, we alter the time scale of our vision, new processes become apparent. With a hundredfold speeding up, individual lives become merged in the formation and transformation of species. With our film speeded up perhaps ten thousand times single species disappear, and group radiations are revealed; we see an original type, seized by a ferment of activity, splitting up and transforming itself in many strange ways, but all the transformations eventually slowing down and stabilizing in specialized immobility. Only in the longest perspective, with a hundred-thousand-fold speed-up, do the over-all processes of evolution become visible—the replace-

ment of old types by new, the emergence and gradual liberation of mind, the narrow and winding stairway of progress, and the steady advance of life up its steps of novelty."

[27] This study was supported in part by National Science Foundation Grant GS1430, and grew out of group discussions conducted at the Phonology Laboratory in Berkeley during the summer of 1967. Detailed comments from M. Beeler, W. Chafe, C. D. Johnson, K. Zimmer, and C.J. Bailey have helped me improve the presentation of several points. I am also grateful for a summer of research at the Pacific and Asian Linguistics Institute of the University of Hawaii, where I had the benefit of extended discussions with George Grace.

References

Bennett, William H. 1966 "The Germanic evidence for Bartholomae's law," *Lg*. 42, 733-37.

Bloch, Bernard. 1953 "Contrast," *Lg*. 29, 59-61.

Bloomfield, Leonard. 1933 *Language* (New York: Holt).

Bonfante, Giuliano. 1947 "The neolinguistic position," *Lg*. 23, 344-75.

Chafe, Wallace L. 1967 "The ordering of phonological rules," *IJAL* 34, 115-36.

Chomsky, Noam, and Morris Halle. 1968 *The sound pattern of English* (New York: Harper & Row).

Greenberg, Joseph H. 1966 "Synchronic and diachronic universals in phonology," *Lg*. 42, 508-17.

Greenberg, Joseph H., Charles E. Osgood, and Sol Saporta. 1954 "Language change," in *Psycholinguistics*, ed. by C. E. Osgood and T. A. Sebeok, 146-63 (Baltimore).

Halle, Morris. 1962 "A descriptive convention for treating assimilation and dissimilation," *MIT Research Laboratory of Electronics, Quarterly Progress Report*, 66, 295-96.

Harms, Robert T. 1967 "Split, shift and merger in the Permic vowels," *Ural-Altaische Jahrbücher* 39, 163-98.

Hockett, Charles F. 1965 "Sound change," *Lg*. 41, 185-204.

Hoenigswald, Henry M. 1960 *Language change and linguistic reconstruction* (Chicago: University of Chicago Press).

Huxley, Julian. 1953 *Evolution in action* (New York: Mentor Books).

Johnson, C. Douglas. 1967 "A note on the precedence relations in phonology," *Project on Linguistic Analysis*, report 2.2 (Berkeley).

Kenyon, John S., and T. A. Knott. 1944 *A pronouncing dictionary of American English* (Springfield, Mass.: Merriam).

King, Robert. 1967 "Functional load and sound change," *Lg*. 43, 831-53.

Kiparsky, Paul. 1968 "Linguistic universals and linguistic change," *Universals in linguistic theory*, ed. by E. Bach and R. Harms, 171-202 (New York: Holt).

Labov, William. 1966 *The social stratification of English in New York City* (Washington: Center for Applied Linguistics).

Lehmann, W. P., and Y. Malkiel (eds.) 1968 *Directions for historical linguistics: a symposium.* (Austin: University of Texas Press).

Malkiel, Yakov. 1968 "The inflectional paradigm as an occasional determinant of sound change," in Lehmann & Malkiel (1968): 21-64.

Moulton, William G. 1967 "Types of phonemic change," *To honor Roman Jakobson*, 1393-407 (The Hague: Mouton).

Peking University. 1962 *Hànyǔ fāngyīn zìhuì* [Phonetic dictionary of Chinese dialects] (Peking).

Postal, Paul. 1968 *Aspects of phonological theory* (New York: Harper & Row).

Sapir, Edward. 1921 *Language* (New York: Harcourt Brace).

Sommerfelt, Alf. 1923 "Note sur les changements phonétiques," *Bulletin de la Société de Linguistique de Paris* 24, 138-41.

Sturtevant, Edward H. 1917 *Linguistic change* (Chicago: University of Chicago Press).

Sweet, Henry. 1888 *History of English sounds* (Oxford).

Tung, Tung-he. 1960 "Four South Min dialects," *Bulletin of the Institute of History and Philology, Academia Sinica*, 30, 729-1042 (Taipei).

Vogt, Hans. 1954 "Contact of languages," *Word* 10, 365-74.

Wang, William S-Y. 1967a "The measurement of functional load," *Phonetica* 16, 36-54.

_____. 1967b "Phonological features of tone," *IJAL* 33, 93-105.

_____. 1968 "Vowel features, paired variables, and the English vowel shift," *Lg.* 44, 695-708.

Weinreich, Uriel. 1958 "A retrograde sound shift in the guise of a survival," *Estructuralismo e historia, miscelánea homenaje a André Martinet*, 2, 221-67 (La Laguna).

Weinreich, Uriel, William Labov, and Marvin Herzog. 1968 "Empirical foundations for a theory of language change: stimuli and constraints from structure and society," in Lehmann & Malkiel (1968): 95-195.

Wells, Rulon S. 1949 "Automatic alternation," *Lg.* 29, 99-116.

Wheeler, Benjamin I. 1887 *Analogy and the scope of its application in language* (Ithaca: Cornell University Press).

Whitney, W. D. 1877 "The principle of economy as a phonetic force," *Transactions of the American Philological Association* 8, 123-34.

Zeps, Valdis J. 1966 "A synchronic and diachronic order of rules: mutations of velars in Old Church Slavonic," *Approaches to linguistic methodology*, ed. by Irmengard Rauch and C. T. Scott, 145-51 (Madison: University of Wisconsin Press).

Postscript 1977

Since the above discussion, a good amount of empirical work has been done within the framework of lexical diffusion. Instances of diffusion have been investigated in many languages, including Chinese, English, German, Swedish. Much of this research is summarized in an article by Chen and Wang in *Language* 51, 255-81, 1975. In addition to language phylogeny, the concept of lexical diffusion has been applied in language ontogeny as well, in the work of Hsieh (*Glossa* 6, 89-104, 1972) and of Ferguson and Farwell (*Language* 51, 419-39, 1975).

It is clear by now that phonemes frequently are not the minimal units in historical change. Neither are they in the acquisition of phonological patterns. These observations highlight an intriguing issue which we may call *The Regrouping Problem*. If a phoneme is pronounced as several different sounds in a class of words, (and there are no phonetic conditions to relate the variants one to another), what are the mechanisms that guide the variants to regroup into the same sound again? In the case of acquisiton, the regrouping is more understandable since adult models are readily available. But for historical change, especially for languages with no writing or with nonphonetic orthographies, the degree of regularity that is believed to exist is quite puzzling. Weinreich, Labov and Herzog, in their important synthesis of 1968, attribute the regrouping to "a rise in the level of social awareness of the change and the establishment of a social stereotype" (p. 187). But what prompts all the affected words to establish the same stereotype? Surely phonetic factors must play an important role as well in some of the cases; but which ones?

The regrouping problem has not been given sufficient attention because lexical abruptness is usually assumed. Even with variable rules of the sort introduced by Labov, the problem does not emerge with clarity because these rules do not distinguish individual lexical items, but average out their usage by statistical methods. Yet it seems to me that the solution of this problem is crucial to a proper understanding of the sound patterns of language.

13   Phonetic Analogy and Conceptual Analogy

THEO VENNEMANN

1. *Background.*

Pre-transformational linguistics tried to account for analogic change
within the output of grammar, language, primarily by setting up pro-
portions of the type a : b = a': x,   x = b' (e.g. Lehmann 1962,
chapter 11). Transformational grammar tries to account for analogic
change within a grammar, without regard for its output, language, by
equating analogy with formal grammar simplification (Kiparsky 1968,
King 1969, chapter 5.3). That pre-transformational linguistics has
failed to create a coherent theory of analogic change is common
knowledge. I show in this paper that the existing transformational
model of analogic change has likewise failed. It failed because an
important distinction was not made, that between phonetic analogy
and conceptual analogy (Schuchardt 1885). I present a theory of
analogic change in which this distinction is made. This theory
agrees with the existing transformational model in describing analogic change as grammar change, but differs from it in recognizing
that only phonetic analogy is motivated by the internal structure of
the grammar, while conceptual analogy is motivated by irregularities
in the output of grammar, language. Regarding conceptual analogy,
it agrees thus with pre-transformational linguistics.

2. *The Function of Language.*

The function of language—more precisely, the function of a grammar—
is the symbolization of meaning in sound. In a conceptually ideal
human language, the linguistic sign (de Saussure 1966:65-7) is uniform: a single concept is symbolized by a constant sound image, and
the derivation of complex concepts is reflected in a corresponding

From Theo Vennemann and T. H. Wilbur: *Schuchardt, the Neogrammar-*
ians, and the Transformational Theory of Phonological Change (Frankfurt a.M., 1972, pp. 181-204). Reprinted by permission of Theo
Vennemann and the publisher, Akademische Verlagsgesellschaft
Athenaion, Wiesbaden. In memory of Hugo Schuchardt on his 130th
birthday, February 4, 1972.

derivation in sound (Humboldt 1971, Chapter 7, esp. p. 50). However, a conceptually ideal language need not be phonologically ideal. Natural phonological changes lead to preferred phonetic structures (Schane 1969, Vennemann 1969a) but may destroy the uniformity of the linguistic sign by introducing paradigmatic variation (Sturtevant's paradox, first half: Sound change is regular but causes irregularity). Paradigmatic variation, even though it may be regular phonologically, is suppletion conceptually. Suppletion is the antithesis of uniform linguistic symbolization. Suppletion is undesirable, uniformity of linguistic symbolization is desirable: Both roots and grammatical markers should be unique and constant. (I have called this innate principle of linguistic change Humboldt's Universal in Vennemann 1969b: §2.23.) Without this principle, paradigms of complex concepts such as A + S, A + P (root A, singular marker S, plural marker P) would be impossible. A succession of sound changes would convert A + S into B, A + P into C. The paradigm would be B,C. All paradigms would be totally suppletive, i.e. mere lists of phonetically dissimilar sound images. Human language would not exist.

The innate character of Humboldt's Universal is most clearly manifested in child language acquisition. All children show attempts to eliminate lexical suppletion, not only conspicuous cases such as *go : went* (which becomes *go : goed*), but also relatively minor deviations from perfect symbolization such as *mouse : mice* (which becomes *mouses*) and *house : houses* (which becomes [hausəs]). Likewise all children show attempts to eliminate grammatical suppletion, again both in its strong form such as the English umlaut plurals and ablauting past tense forms, and in mild cases such as *keep : kept* (which becomes *keeped*). This innate tendency toward uniform symbolization is strikingly demonstrated in the following steps in the acquisition of Russian (Dan I. Slobin, lecture at the Linguistic Institute 1971, August 3). Russian has overt marking of three genders and six cases, the case/suffixes depending upon gender (in addition, upon number and noun classes). The cases we are interested in here are the accusative and the instrumental in the singular of the most basic paradigms.

	Masculine	Neuter	Feminine
Nominative	∅	-o	-a
Accusative	∅	-o	-u
Instrumental	-om	-om	-oy

All children generalize the nominative:accusative distinction made in the feminine by carrying *-u* into all other genders and noun

classes. That this is not merely a matter of frequency (feminine
nouns account for about 70% of the children's vocabulary at this
stage because they include most diminutives) is shown by the children's initial generalization of *-om* for <u>all</u> instrumentals, later replaced by a generalization of *-oy* for <u>all</u> instrumentals, until
finally the gender and noun class distinctions are sifted out.

3. *Phonetic Analogy*.
The origin of phonological change is sporadic change (Schuchardt
1885). A sporadic change is a highly restricted phonological rule.
The primary basis for the development of sporadic rules into general
phonological rules is phonetic analogy. One individual acquired the
sporadic change formulated here as rule (1), owing to correction of
his original pronunciation of the name [nowm] by members of the
'in-group'.

(1) $\emptyset \rightarrow \ni$ / [now___m] Name

He was soon heard to say [nowəm] and [rowəm], then [nowən] (*Noam,
home, roam, known*). With his innate knowledge of what constitutes
a phonetic generalization, he had generalized his sporadic rule on
purely phonetic grounds. (The raised dollar sign marks a syllable
boundary, as in Vennemann 1972b.)

(2) $\emptyset \rightarrow \ni$ / $\begin{bmatrix} 0 \\ + \end{bmatrix}$ stress $\bigg]$ w $\underline{\quad}$ $\begin{bmatrix} C \\ +nasal \\ +labial \end{bmatrix}^{\$}$

(3) $\emptyset \rightarrow \ni$ / $\begin{bmatrix} 0 \\ + \end{bmatrix}$ stress $\bigg]$ w $\underline{\quad}$ $\begin{bmatrix} C \\ +nasal \end{bmatrix}^{\$}$

At this point, the individual consciously suppressed the rule (presumably relexicalizing /nowm/ as /nowVm/), and the rule did not
spread (Robert P. Stockwell, personal communication).

3.1 Rule generalization by phonetic analogy.
Norwegian (Oslo), Northern German, and Standard German have the
following rules, respectively:

(4) (a) s $\rightarrow$ š / $ ___1 (*$^{\$}$sr does not occur)
     (b) s $\rightarrow$ š / $ ___ {l r m n w} (*$^{\$}$sj does not occur)
     (c) s $\rightarrow$ š / $ ___ {l r m n w p t} (*$^{\$}$sk does not occur)

These three rules reflect three degrees of generality of the same
phonological process. The basis for this generalization is phonetic
analogy: Original phonetic constraints are given up.

(5) (a) s → š̆ / $ ___ $\begin{bmatrix} C \\ +\text{sonorant} \\ +\text{liquid} \end{bmatrix}$

   (b) s → š̆ / $ ___ $\begin{bmatrix} C \\ +\text{sonorant} \end{bmatrix}$

   (c) s → s / $ ___ C

One of Suchardt's (1885:8, 22-23) own examples of rule generalization due to phonetic analogy is the following.

(6) (a) s → h / V ___ V
    (b) s → h / V(#)___ V

In this case the generalization is not reflected as formal simplification, although this may be a shortcoming of my notation. (Schuchardt 1885 is the discoverer of rule generalization as a mechanism
of phonological change, cf. Vennemann 1972a.)

3.2. Rule reordering by phonetic analogy.
Kiparsky (1968:177-78) discusses the following case of rule reordering
in Finnish.

(7) (a) Standard: vee   teγe
                      vie   ---- Diphthongization
                      ---   tee   Loss of γ
                      [vie]   [tee]
     (b) Dialects: vee   teγe
                      ---   tee   Loss of γ
                      vie   tie   Diphthongization
                      [vie]   [tie]

In (7a), Diphthongization is restricted to deep long mid vowels. It
is not applied to long mid vowels deriving from Loss. This constraint is formally expressed by ordering Loss after Diphthongization.
In (7b), the constraint is given up. Diphthongization applies to
all long mid vowels, regardless of their origin. This is formally
expressed by ordering Loss before Diphthongization. The basis for
this reordering is phonetic analogy. No conceptual factors are involved. The difference between rule generalization by phonetic
analogy and rule reordering by phonetic analogy is that in the former
a process is extended to new domains of pre-existent deep environments derived by a later rule. No formal grammar simplification
seems to be involved. But this is merely a shortcoming of the phonological theory used by Kiparsky, cf. §6 below.

4. *Conceptual Analogy.*

Conceptual analogy is Humboldt's Universal in action. Seen from the conceptual side of a grammar, the addition of a phonological rule is a deplorable event. But Humboldt's Universal has to bide its time: Seen from the phonetic end of grammar, the added rule is a gain in naturalness. There is no way of driving it out of the phonological component. (I am not aware of a single case where a phonetically motivated rule is lost by analogy.) However, time is on the side of Humboldt's Universal: Vocabulary will be borrowed and further rules will be added to the grammar. Both obscure the phonetic motivation of the original rule (Chafe 1968).

4.1. Rule loss.

Rule loss is always caused by conceptual analogy (i.e. by Humboldt's Universal). It requires some further change such as the addition of another rule obscuring the phonetic motivation of the original rule (a factor which is not recognized in the existing transformational model of analogic change). Yiddish lost its Final Devoicing rule (Kiparsky 1968:177; King 1969:46-8).

(8)   [+obstruent]   →   [-voice] / ___ #

but only after the addition of an Apocopation rule (for which cf. King 1969:123) had placed new voiced obstruents in final position (*tok : tegə → tok : teg*), so that (8) was morphologized:

$$(9) \quad [+obstruent] \quad \rightarrow \quad [-voice] \ / \left[\underline{\quad\quad} \atop \text{(morpho-syntactic information)} \right] \ \#$$

Two factors must be noted. 1. Rule (9) has no value for the phonetic structure of Yiddish because unlike (8) it does not neutralize the voice distinction in word-final obstruents but merely changes the voice specification in some of them. 2. Rule (9) has no intrinsic value for the conceptual structure of the grammar of Yiddish: The morpho-syntactic information on which (9) is based is expressed more efficiently by other devices (e.g. the plural of /tog/ by umlaut). All that (9) does is introduce a redundant alternation into the root. By not learning (9) a new generation restored the uniformity of the paradigm: /tog/ unmodified symbolizes 'day' minus plural, [teg] (i.e. /tog/ plus umlaut) symbolizes 'day' plus plural. Note that no contrasts are lost in the process, as an extension of (9) to all final obstruents would have implied: *k/k : g/g* is a better resolution of *k/k : k/g* than *k/k : k/k* would have been. This seems to be true in general: Sound change neutralizes contrasts, analogy emphasizes contrasts by generalizing them. (That the lexical contrast had remained *k/k* : *g/g* all along follows not only from the outcome of this change but independently from the predictability principle: [k/k : k/g] cannot be predicted without a morphological classification from *k/k* : *k/k* but only from *k/k* : *g/g*.)

King's second example of rule loss (1969:48-51) shows once again that rule loss is not "another kind of primary change" (46) but is an aftermath of morphologization, the change of a phonetically motivated rule into a morpho-syntactically conditioned rule. Verner's Law was the addition of a phonetically motivated rule, (10).

(10) $\begin{bmatrix} +\text{obstruent} \\ +\text{continuant} \end{bmatrix} \rightarrow [+\text{voice}] \ / \ \begin{bmatrix} +\text{syllabic} \\ -\text{accent} \end{bmatrix} ([+\text{voice}]) \ \underline{\quad} [+\text{voice}]$

The fixing of the accent on word-initial syllables eliminated the phonetic motivation of the rule. Where alternations persisted, they had to be accounted for by reference to the morpho-syntactic categories which once bore the accent in a position which made them subject to rule (10):

(11) $\begin{bmatrix} +\text{obstruent} \\ +\text{continuant} \end{bmatrix} \rightarrow [+\text{voice}] \ / \ [+\text{voice}] \begin{bmatrix} \underline{\quad} \\ +\text{Verb} \\ +\text{past} \\ +\text{Ablaut} \\ +\text{Plural} \\ +\text{Subjunctive} \\ +\text{Participle} \end{bmatrix} [+\text{voice}]$

While the original rule (10) introduced phonetically plausible alternations, e.g.

(12) Infinitive   Past Sg. Ind.   Past Participle

      wérθana   wárθa   wr̥ðaná   'become'

its morphologized version (11) produced phonetically unaccountable alternations which were, furthermore, morphosyntactically redundant because the affected categories were more effectively marked by ablaut (and endings):

(13) Infinitive   Past Sg. Ind.   Past Participle

      wérθana   wárθa   wŕ̥ðana

All Germanic languages have given up this rule so as to restore the uniformity of the paradigm, e.g. Gothic:

(14) Infinitive   Past Sg. Ind.   Past Participle

      wairþan   warþ   waurþans

Again no contrasts were lost: Where ð/ð paradigms once contrasted with θ/ð paradigms, they contrasted with θ/θ after the loss of (11). (Note that in the case of Verner's Law, but not in the case of Final Devoicing in Yiddish, the phonetic root consonantism of the syntactically unmarked category, present-indicative, was generalized. These two examples of rule loss show that the predictability principle may override the unmarked category principle in determining lexical representations.)

In both examples, the loss of a morphologized rule leads to a more uniform phonetic representation of roots. I conclude that rule loss is one way of implementing Humboldt's Universal. Rule loss due to phonetic analogy does not occur. (This does not imply that a rule cannot be lost through purely phonetic developments. For example, Early Old Norse, which had (11), added a rule voicing all spirants in voiced environments. Since there is no connection between (11) and the new rule—the phonetic weakness of (11) is demonstrated by the loss of this rule in the other Germanic languages—one cannot speak of rule generalization. I call this situation rule absorption, cf. Vennemann 1972a. While Kiparsky (1968) considers rule loss as the extreme case of rule simplification, I argue in Vennemann 1972a that these two processes have nothing in common as far as their underlying motivation is concerned: Rule simplification—the formal correlate of rule generalization—is phonetically motivated and occurs only if a rule is felt to be a live process in the language; rule loss is conceptually motivated and occurs only if a rule is dead, both as a phonetic process and as a symbolic process. Cf. also the following section.)

4.2. Rule generalization by conceptual analogy.
It is uncertain whether such a mechanism of change exists. The following is a possible example. Late Middle High German added a rule of open syllable lengthening:

$$(15) \quad \begin{bmatrix} V \\ +\text{stress} \end{bmatrix} \rightarrow [+\text{long}] \quad / \quad \underline{\qquad} \quad [+\text{consonantal}]^{1} \quad V$$

This rule created paradigmatic alternations such as [tak] : [ta:gəs], [tal] : [ta:ləs] ('day', 'valley', nom. vs. gen. sg.). Length was then extended to vowels in a closed syllable, but only where a paradigmatic relationship to forms with long vowels existed, e.g. [ta:l] 'valley' vs. [val] 'wall' (cf. gen. [valəs]). This analogic extension occurred first before resonants, as contemporary dialects show, then also before obstruents, but again only where a paradigmatic relationship to forms with long vowels existed, e.g. [ta:k] 'day' vs. [špek] 'bacon' (cf. gen. [špekkəs]). Under one interpretation,

the resulting system had a generalized rule (16), ordered before a
rule shortening geminate consonants (Vennemann 1968a:14, 42, 45).

(16) $\begin{bmatrix} V \\ +stress \end{bmatrix}$ → [+long] / ___ [+consonantal][1]

(The interpretation of the change from (15) to (16) as rule simplification is only available in the notational framework of Chomsky
and Halle 1968. In a syllabic phonology, where (15) would be represented as in (15'), it would not be available.

(15') $\begin{bmatrix} V \\ +stress \end{bmatrix}$ → [+long] / ___ $

A more plausible interpretation is offered in §6.)

4.3. Rule reordering by conceptual analogy.
Kiparsky (1968:178-9) presents the following example of rule reordering from Swiss German dialects.

(17) Umlaut (simplified).

V → [-back] in certain morpho-syntactic environments,
              including plural.

(18) Lowering (abbreviated notation).

o → ɔ   before dentals, palatals, and *r*.

Some dialects (say A) preserve this historical order of the rules:

(19) bogə (sg.)	bogə (pl.)	bodə (sg.)	bodə (pl.)	
———	ö	———	ö	Umlaut
———	———	ɔ	———	Lowering
bogə	bögə	bɔdə	bödə	

The output is contrary to Humboldt's Universal: While the difference
in vowel backness in *bogə : bögə* is an optimal symbolization of the
singular : plural distinction, the additional height difference in
bodə : bödə disturbs this most direct symbolization by introducing
an irrelevant height difference. The obvious way to eliminate this
senseless deviation is to base the plural symbolization on the conditioned phonetic form of the singular, i.e. to order Umlaut after
Lowering. This has been done in other dialects (say B).

(20) bogə (st.)	bogə (pl.)	bodə (sg.)	bodə (pl.)	
----	----	ɔ	ɔ	Lowering
----	ö	----	ö̈	Umlaut
bogə	bögə	bɔdə	bödə	

The resulting singular:plural symbolization is again as perfect as
before the addition of Lowering. Kiparsky argues convincingly that
dialects B must once have had the two rules in the same order as
dialects A. His evidence consists of relic forms with an unlowered
ö before dentals and palatals: *plötsli, frösš*. These forms show
that the motivation for the lowering of ö was not phonetic but conceptual: Only ö's in a paradigmatic relationship to ə's were lowered
(e.g. *bödə ∿ bödə* because of *bədə*), but non-alternating ö's remained
unchanged. (The absence of phonetic motivation for this extension
of lowering from o to ö is discussed in Vennemann 1971b.) This case
of rule reordering is motivated by conceptual analogy.

4.4. Counter-phonological exemption from rules.

According to the phonological history of Spanish, the contemporary
language should have the following abbreviated paradigms (the forms
given are 1st ps. pl. pres.).

(21)

	'mark'	'pay'
Indicative	mar[k]amos	pa[g]amos
Subjunctive	*mar[s]emos	*pa[x]emos

One would expect these paradigms because Spanish underwent a series
of changes which would be reflected in the contemporary language as
in (22).

(22) 'Velar softening'.

$$\begin{bmatrix} k \\ g \end{bmatrix} \rightarrow \begin{bmatrix} s \\ x \end{bmatrix} / \underline{\quad} \begin{Bmatrix} i \\ e \end{Bmatrix}$$

(The examples of this and the following section are given in Harris
1970, 1971, though with a different interpretation.) The actual
forms of contemporary Spanish are not, however, as in (21) but as
in (23).

(23)

	'mark'	'pay'
Indicative	mar[k]amos	pa[g]amos
Subjunctive	mar[k]emos	pa[g]emos

The reason is obvious. The paradigm (21) predicted by rule (22) is
at variance with Humboldt's Universal. The 'irregular' paradigm
(23) is in accordance with it. The subjunctive subparadigm (a
'marked' category) was at one point in the history of the language
exempted from the ancestral form of rule (22) in order to reconsti-
tute a single phonetic form of the verbal root for the entire paradigm. Exemption of a marked morpho-syntactic category from a phonological rule not applying in the unmarked category of the same

paradigm is, therefore, a further way of implementing Humboldt's Universal, i.e. a further mechanism of conceptual analogic change.

4.5. Counter-phonological rule application.
Rule (22) predicts that contemporary Spanish should have the paradigms in (24).

(24)	'cook'	'protect'
Indicative	co[s]emos	prote[x]emos
Subjunctive	*co[k]amos	*prote[g]amos

The actual forms of the language are, however, as in (25).

(25)	'cook'	'protect'
Indicative	co[s]emos	prote[x]emos
Subjunctive	co[s]amos	prote[x]amos

Again the 'marked' category was remodeled so as to generalize the
phonetic shape of the root occurring in the unmarked category, this
time by applying a rule, (22), which according to its structural
description should not apply. The application of a phonological
rule contrary to its structural description in a marked category of
a paradigm in which the rule does apply in the unmarked category is,
therefore, a further way of implementing Humboldt's Universal, i.e.
a further mechanism of conceptual analogic change.

5. *Analogy and Relic Forms*.
Since rule generalization by phonetic analogy and rule reordering
by phonetic analogy are generalizations of an existing change proceeding by purely phonetic criteria, they do not normally leave
relic forms. (A relic form could only result either from the resistance of a functional element to the proceeding change, or else from
a reintroduction of the unchanged form due to conceptual analogy or
borrowing.) In particular, such a change will not distinguish between isolated forms and forms in paradigms. By contrast, rule
loss, rule reordering by conceptual analogy, counter-phonological
exemption from rules, and counter-phonological rule application
typically leave relic forms. They affect only those forms which
stand in a paradigmatic relationship to a form or forms on which the
analogical extension is modeled. (If there are no such isolated
forms in the language, as in the example of rule reordering by conceptual analogy in Vennemann 1970:79, then there naturally cannot
exist relic forms.) Kiparsky (1968:202) correctly relates the occurrence vs. non-occurrence of relic forms to the various forms of
change in rule systems. But they appear in his account as inexplicable correlates of changes because the changes are not differenti-

267

ated according to underlying motivations. In a theory of analogy distinguishing phonetic from conceptual motivation, the correlations are seen to be a trivial consequence.

6. *Analogy as Simplification.*

In the theory of analogy presented in Kiparsky (1968) and King (1969), rule generalization, rule reordering, and rule loss are indiscriminately labeled "grammar simplification," while rule addition is considered as the primary mechanism of grammar complication ('innovation'). A critique of this simplistic view of phonological change is inherent in Stampe's (1969) "natural phonology." Stampe recognizes three mechanisms of phonological simplification: rule addition, rule generalization, and rule unordering. All three changes are simplificatory because they eliminate constraints. The addition of a rule allows the speaker to neutralize certain less natural phonological structures into more natural ones. Generalization of a rule similarly leads to further neutralization by elimination of restrictions imposed on the earlier form of the rule. Unordering of rules leads to neutralization of contrast by eliminating an ordering constraint previously imposed on two rules. "Unordering" in Stampe's sense is the same as "reordering by phonetic analogy" (§3.2 above) and as reordering by Kiparsky's principle "I. Feeding order tends to be maximized" (1968:197). Since Stampe is concerned exclusively with phonetic simplification, he has no way of accounting for the mechanisms of change discussed here in §4 under the heading "conceptual analogy" (cf. Stampe 1969:453, n. 14). This very inability of his model points to a fundamental difference between the changes here assigned to 'conceptual analogy' and those here assigned to 'phonetic analogy', and thereby to a deficiency of Kiparsky's model.

The contention that rule generalization, rule reordering, and rule loss are simplificatory grammar change permits two different interpretations. If we understand 'grammar' as the representation of the native speakers' linguistic competence in their minds, and if we accept the assumption made by Kiparsky and King that those three mechanisms of change originate in the children's language acquisition process which is generally recognized as leading only to simplification, never to complication of grammars (cf. Halle 1962), then the contention becomes tautological. If we understand 'grammar' as a theory describing the native speakers' linguistic competence (i.e. 'grammar' in the previous sense) in an explanatory way, then the representation of those mechanisms of change as formal simplification can never be a research result but only a goal: An explanatorily adequate linguistic theory must require us to write grammars in such a way that rule generalization, rule reordering, and rule loss are in fact reflected as formal simplifications of the grammar.

This goal has been achieved in the cases of rule generalization and rule loss. The first difficulty arises with reordering. Kiparsky (1968:196-200) distinguishes two types of reordering: one in which a later rule is ordered before another so as to increase the input of the other rule (reordering into feeding order), and one in which an earlier rule which takes away input from a later rule is ordered after the later rule so that this rule can now apply to part of the input of the reordered rule (reordering out of bleeding order). He proposes two universals: "I. Feeding order tends to be maximized." "II. Bleeding order tends to be minimized," and goes on to reformulate them into one general principle, "III. Rules tend to shift into the order which allows their fullest utilization in grammar." While rule reordering is not formally reflected as simplification, it is declared simplificatory by labeling the reordered state the "unmarked" order. This monistic treatment of the two kinds of reordering is inadequate, as can be seen from the fact that it does not explain why feeding order reordering does not normally leave relic forms while bleeding order reordering does. We can add a further difference inexplicable by Kiparsky's theory: Feeding order reordering never creates new marked segments, but only more segments of the same kind (in the example of §3.2. more *ie*'s from new *ee*'s); by contrast, bleeding order reordering can create new marked segments and frequently does so (in the example of §4.3. a new *ö*). But all this follows as a matter of course if we study reordering types as to their motivation rather than simply as to their relational properties within the grammar. Feeding order reordering is reordering by phonetic analogy, i.e. unordering in Stampe's terminology; we could add: a change from extrinsic order to intrinsic order. It is the extension of an existing powerful phonetically-motivated rule to a newly arising set of inputs of the same sort. By contrast, bleeding order reordering is reordering by conceptual analogy. It is <u>not</u> unordering in Stampe's sense but a change from one extrinsic order into another with the sole motivation of regularizing linguistic symbolization. Characteristically, this kind of reordering invariably orders a symbolic (i.e., morphosyntactic) process, such as Umlaut, after a merely phonological process, such as Lowering. It can be contrary to phonological naturalness (the creation of a low front round vowel *ö* before dentals in an unnatural phonological process if viewed in purely phonetic terms). The absence of phonological naturalness from the process explains why forms not under paradigmatic pressure do not undergo it and survive as relic forms. Clearly, if bleeding order reordering is to be reflected as grammar simplification this simplification cannot be expressed in the phonological component but only in the grammar as a whole.

The dilemma of the monistic view of phonological change becomes even more obvious in the case of irregular exemption from rules and irregular rule application. As Harris (1970) argues convincingly, these processes are actually formal complications in a transformational-generative grammar of Spanish built on the present linguistic theory (Chomsky and Halle 1968), because they require the introduction of costly exception feature apparatus into the grammar. Yet these processes are analogic in precisely the same sense as rule loss and bleeding order reordering. Here a theory which equates analogy with formal simplification in existing transformational grammars fails completely.

I too consider all the changes discussed here as simplificatory. The difference between my theory and Kiparsky's (1968) is that I consider the motivations for change and the functions of change in grammars as symbolization devices with two 'ends', a conceptual and a phonetic one, while Kiparsky (1968) studies only the formal and relational aspects of change within the phonological component. I agree with Halle, Kiparsky, and King that linguistic change has to be studied as grammar change. However, I agree with a great number of pre- and non-transformational grammarians that the explanation of change cannot come from an inspection of the formal properties of models of grammar (such as Chomsky and Halle 1968) but only from the study of the dual aspect of change in language as a symbolic system. Such a study shows that there are two different simplificatory tendencies in language: one leading to simplifications in the phonological structure of language, formally reflected as addition of natural rules, rule generalization, and rule unordering, the other leading to simplifications in the phonological representation of the conceptual structure of language, i.e. to optimization of linguistic symbolization, formally reflected as rule loss, rule reordering, counter-phonological exemption from rules and counter-phonological rule application, and perhaps a special kind of rule generalization. (The relevance of paradigms to phonological change has been pointed out repeatedly; within transformational grammar, in Vennemann 1968b, Harris 1970). Thus, while the existing transformational-generative model of phonological change distinguishes innovation from simplification as in (26),

(26) The transformational-generative classification of phonological change.

I. Innovation	II. Simplification
1. Rule addition	1. Rule generalization 2. Rule loss 3. Rule reordering

I consider all phonological changes of the kinds considered here as simplificatory, but as simplificatory from two opposite and often conflicting points of view, cf. (27).

(27) A new classification of phonological change.

I. Phonetically motivated simplification	II. Conceptually motivated simplification
1. Addition of natural rules 2. Rule generalization 3. Rule unordering (into "intrinsic order" or "feeding order")	1. Rule loss 2. Rule generalization (?) 3. Rule reordering (from one "extrinsic order" into another, or from "bleeding order") 4. Exemption from rules 5. Counter-phonological application of rules

These two simplificatory tendencies are in conflict because a phonetic simplification quite commonly leads to conceptual complication by splitting paradigms, and conceptual simplification commonly leads to phonetic complication by introducing phonetic elements into structures from which they had previously been banned by rules. Thus, a hypothetical singular:plural change $as+a : as+i$ to $as+a : a\check{s}+i$ is 'good' phonetically but 'bad' conceptually, while the analogic reconstitution of $as+a : as+i$ is 'good' conceptually but 'bad' phonetically. The interplay of these conflicting tendencies is part of the history of each language. This, in addition to lexical borrowing and other types of change not considered here, answers the question, "If everything gets simpler, why don't languages get simpler?"

Transformational-generative theory has succeeded in formally representing rule generalization and rule loss as simplifications. Tentative proposals for the formal characterization of rule addition as simplifications have been made (Vennemann 1968a:183-4; 1969a), but a more direct result can probably be obtained by incorporating

a form of Stampe's "natural phonology" into generative grammar. Rule
unordering can be reflected as formal simplification by deleting a
notation characterizing extrinsic rule order. However, the existing
theory has failed to represent all conceptually motivated changes,
except rule loss, as formal simplification. If we take seriously
the goal of representing all acquisitional simplifications as formal
simplifications of grammars, then we have to reconsider both the
structure of the phonological component and the nature of lexical
representation. In particular, phonological components seem to be
much shallower than has been assumed by generative phonologists,
with relexicalization and rule morphologization occurring readily
as a by-product of new rule additions and borrowing. For example,
the case of rule generalization by conceptual analogy tentatively
offered in §4.2. is probably more adequately interpreted as a case
of graded relexicalization with the lengthened vowel: /tal/[tal]:
[ta:ləs] ∿ /ta:l/ [ta:l] : [ta:ləs] : /tag/ [tak] : [ta:gəs] ∿
/ta:g/ [ta:k] : [ta:gəs]. Similarly, the case of rule reordering
by conceptual analogy discussed in §4.3 invites an interpretation
as relexicalization with the lowered ɔ (perhaps with a lexical morpheme structure rule expressing the redundancies in the distribution
of /o/ and /ɔ/). The example of exemption of marked forms from a
rule could be simply interpreted as the morphologization of this
rule: Velar Softening ceased operating as a phonetically motivated
phonological rule when exemption became possible. Finally, the
example of counter-phonological application of a rule given in §4.5
is not this at all but rather a case of relexicalization with the
conditioned variant introduced by Velar Softening: /kok/ [kos-e-] :
[kok-a-] ∿ /kos/ [kos-e-] : [kos-a-]. Nominalizations such as
co[k]tion on which Harris bases a synchronic representation of such
verbs with /k/ are quite irrelevant to the problem: the verb is
basic and shows the lexical representation of the root; nominalizations, if they are to be represented with the verbal root at all
rather than simply with their own phonetic shape, have to be derived
by morphophonemic rules which are the inverse of the original rules
(Hooper 1971), e.g.

(28) $\begin{Bmatrix} s \\ x \end{Bmatrix}$ → k / ___ C in forms specified as undergoing
this change.

Once a rule is morphologized anyway, considerations of phonological
naturalness cease to play a role, and inverse rules such as (28) are
no worse than morphologized versions of the original rules. (cf.
Vennemann 1972c for a discussion of inverse rules and rule inversion.)
A detailed study of the process of relexicalization may well lead to

the result that the types of change labeled II. 2-5 in table (27) are mere artifacts of a linguistic theory lacking proper constraint by universal conditions on the depth of grammars, and that a more appropriate classification of phonological changes is that in (29).

(29) A future classification of phonological change.

I. Phonetically motivated simplification	II. Conceptually motivated simplification

1. Addition of natural rules
2. Rule generalization
3. Rule unordering (into "intrinsic order" or "feeding order")
	1. Rule loss
	2. Relexicalization, with
	  a. a resulting lexical redundancy rule
	  b. a morphologized rule
	  c. an inverse rule

While generative grammars provide an optimal basis for the study of both phonetically and conceptually motivated phonological changes, the formal equation of the two as 'simplifications' has in my opinion hindered progress in the study of both of them. Both a typology of phonetically motivated simplifications and a typology of conceptual-analogic changes as grammar changes are still desiderata of linguistic theory. Hopefully this paper will help prepare the ground for this work.

References

Chafe, Wallace L. 1968 "The ordering of phonological rules," *International Journal of American Linguistics* 34, 115-36.

Chomsky, Noam, and Morris Halle. 1968 *The sound pattern of English* (New York: Harper and Row).

Halle, Morris. 1962 "Phonology in generative grammar," *Word* 18, 54-72.

Harris, James W. 1970 "Paradigm regularity and naturalness of grammar," Paper read at the Annual Meeting of the Linguistic Society of America, Washington, D. C.

_____. 1971 "On the order of certain phonological rules in Spanish," MS.

Hooper, Joan. 1971 "The role of borrowing in the phonology of Spanish," MS, University of California, Los Angeles.

Humboldt, Wilhelm von. 1971 [1836]. *Linguistic variability and intellectual development*. Trans. from the German by George C. Buck and Frithjof A. Raven (Coral Gables, Florida: University of Miami Press).

King, Robert T. 1969 *Historical linguistics and generative grammar* (Englewood Cliffs, N.J.: Prentice-Hall).

Kiparsky, Paul. 1968 "Linguistic change and linguistic universals," in *Universals in linguistic theory*, ed. by Emmon Bach and Robert T. Harms (New York: Holt, Rinehart and Winston), 170-202.

Lehmann, Winfred P. 1962 *Historical linguistics: an introduction* (New York: Holt, Rinehart and Winston).

Saussure, Ferdinand de 1966 *Course in general linguistics* (New York: McGraw-Hill).

Schane, Sanford A. 1969 "Natural rules in phonology," in Stockwell and Macaulay (1972).

Schuchardt, Hugo. 1885 *Über die Lautgesetze: gegen die Junggrammatiker* (Berlin: Oppenheim). Translation in Schuchardt et. al. (forthcoming).

Stampe, David. 1969 "The acquisition of phonetic representation," *Papers from the Fifth Regional Meeting, Chicago Linguistic Society,* 443-454 (Chicago, Illinois: Department of Linguistics, University of Chicago).

Stockwell, Robert P., and Ronals K. S. Macaulay, eds. 1972 *Linguistic change and transformational theory. Essays from the Conference on Historical Linguistics in the Perspective of Transformational Theory, UCLA, February 1-2, 1969* (Bloomington: Indiana University Press).

Vennemann, Theo. 1968a "German phonology," Dissertation University of California, Los Angeles (Ann Arbor, Michigan: University Microfilms).

_____. 1968b "On the use of paradigmatic information in a competence rule of Modern German phonology." Paper read at the Summer Meeting of the Linguistic Society of America. Urbana, Illinois.

_____. 1969a "Sound change and markedness theory: on the history of the German consonant system," in Stockwell and Macaulay (1972).

_____. 1969b *Zur synchronischen und diachronischen Phonologie des Deutschen* (Munich: Max Hueber, forthcoming).

_____. 1970 "The German velar nasal: a case for abstract phonology," *Phonetica* 22, 65-81.

_____. 1971 "The interpretation of phonological features in assimilation rules," *Working Papers in Phonetics, University of California, Los Angeles* 19, 62-68. The complete version of this paper appeared in *Language* 48, 863-92 (1972) as "Phonetic detail in assimilation: problems in Germanic phonology."

_____. 1972a "Hugo Schuchardt's theory of phonological change," in Schuchardt et al.

_____. 1972b "On the theory of syllabic phonology," *Linguistische Berichte* 18, 1-18.

_____. 1972c "Rule inversion," *Lingua* 29, 209-242.

_____, and Terence H. Wilbur. 1972 *Schuchardt, the Neogrammarians, and the Transformational Theory of Phonological Change* (Frankfurt a.M.: Athenäum-Verlag).

14 On the Use of the Present to Explain the Past

WILLIAM LABOV

Just ten years ago, at the Ninth International Congress of Linguistics, Jerzy Kuryłowicz issued the following strong statement on the independence of linguistics from worldly considerations:

> Once we leave languages *sensu stricto* and appeal to extra-linguistic factors, a clear delimitation of the field of linguistic research is lost. Thus, e.g., the physiological (articulatory) aspect may be a consequence of social factors, the latter being themselves due to certain political or economic facts (conquest, migrations involving bilingualism). . . . It seems that the field of linguistic explanation in the literal sense must be circumscribed by the <u>linguistic</u> aspect of the change in question, i.e. by the actual state of the system before and after the change ("l'état momentanée des termes du système"—de Saussure) (1964:11).

Kuryłowicz urged that we purify linguistic argument by renouncing all support from dialect geography, phonetics, psychology and cultural anthropology. Our reconstructions of the history of language would then rise to a "higher conceptual basis" (1964:30).

This position departs from the older tradition of historical linguistics, which had established deep roots in all of these areas. Kuryłowicz projects into diachronic studies the synchronic tradition of Saussure and Baudouin de Courtenay: linguistics is to be restricted to abstract operations upon emic units defined by referential contrasts. This was of course a fruitful restriction, and we admire the good use made by extending it into historical matters by Martinet (1955) and Kuryłowicz. And one can fully appreciate the motivation behind their linguistic *apartheid* policy in reviewing the mass of sociological, physiological and genetic arguments that they were reacting against (Sommerfelt 1930).

But a retreat once started is not easily checked. If we study the various restrictions imposed upon linguistics since Saussure, we see

From *Proceedings of the Eleventh International Congress of Linguists* (Bologna, 1974, pp. 825-51; Vol. 2.) Reprinted by permission of William Labov and the publisher, Società Editrice Il Mulino. A shorter version of this paper was read at the 11th International Congress of Linguists, August 1972.

more and more data being excluded in a passionate concern for what linguistics is <u>not</u>. Every field of substance has come under attack at one time or another: semantics, phonetics, social factors, and finally speech itself. The culmination of this puristic program is the generative view of linguistics as the study of an ideal homogeneous structure, revealed in the intuitions of the most highly sophisticated members of the community who create through introspection both the theory and the data.

At the same International Congress of 1962, Chomsky delivered his important paper on "The logical basis of linguistic theory" which sharply criticized the taxonomic work of previous decades and opened a whole new perspective for many linguists. In his comments on "objectivity of linguistic data" he stated that the subject matter of linguistics was to be the speaker's introspective judgments:

> . . . One might ask how we can establish that. . . "John's eagerness to please. . . " is well-formed while "John's easiness to please. . ." is not, and so on. There is no very satisfying answer to this question; data of this sort are simply what constitute the subject matter for linguistic theory. . . . Operational tests, just as explanatory theories, must meet the condition of correspondence to introspective judgments (1964:939).

This development represents the most complete exploitation of what I have called "the Saussurian Paradox." If we carry to its logical extent Saussure's notion that *langue* represents the knowledge of the language in the possession of all members of the speech community, it follows that we can study *langue* through intuitions of any one member, even the linguist himself. He can then examine the <u>social</u> aspect of language in the privacy of his office; but *parole*, the individual aspect of language, can only be pursued through a sociological survey of the population.

One must look with admiration and astonishment at the boldness of linguists who have thus discarded the great body of data produced by ordinary citizens arguing, conversing, orating, corresponding, etc., proceeding with full confidence to recreate linguistics out of their own intuitions. And indeed, linguistic theory of the past decade has flourished in this otherworldly setting: it has produced a vast corpus of deep argumentation which makes the theory of previous decades seem shallow by comparison.

But this philosophical mode of investigation is quite unsuited to the study of change, where we have no intuitions at all. We have not inherited the intuitions of the eighteenth century, and it is unlikely that the twenty-first century will accept ours, intermingled as they are with our theoretical persuasions. It is clear that the study of history must rest on some point outside of the

linguist's mind, in the secular world. When generative linguists
turn to historical questions, they must deal with the same residual
data as anyone else, perhaps leaning more upon the reported intuitions of grammarians than others would. But they share with Kuryłowicz the firm determination to wrest this data from its social setting, analyzing the successive emic structures without regard to
the social factors which produced it. In recent years, generative
grammar has been applied to this program, beginning with Halle's
article on "Phonology in a generative grammar" (1962) and followed
by the work of Kiparsky (1968), King (1969) and many others. They
proceed in the conviction that operations with distinctive features,
markedness conventions, and rule re-orderings can solve the fundamental problems of linguistic change.

There is no doubt that recent linguistics has been dominated by
the drive for an autonomous discipline based on purely internal
argument, in both synchronic and diachronic studies. But it seems
that the most notorious mysteries of linguistic change remain untouched by such abstract operations and become even more obscure.
It is still unclear why the neogrammarian principle appears to be a
good working basis for comparative reconstruction when both studies
of change in progress (e.g. Gauchat 1905) and careful reviews of the
historical record (e.g. Chen 1972) show large-scale oscillation,
massive splitting and lexical diffusion. It is still unclear
whether simplicity arguments which seem to be essential tools for
grammatical description have any explanatory force in the explanation of sound change (cf. Bach and Harms 1972, Cohen 1970). The
long-term drift of particular languages in particular directions
which appeared so puzzling to Sapir (1921) is still as puzzling as
ever, despite King's broad assurance that drift is nothing but the
uniform result of rule simplification (1969:202).

In this paper I will ask for a sharp change of direction. I will
try to show that long-standing problems of historical linguistics
can be resolved only if we are willing to use general principles
drawn from phonetic and sociolinguistic research. I will consider
one notorious problem in the history of English: the reported mer-
ger of $\overline{ea}$ words with long $\overline{a}$ and their later separation to merge
with long $\overline{e}$. In Section 1, I will draw upon sociolinguistic studies
of present-day speech communities to show how such a merger could
have been reported in the first place, and why there is so much disagreement about it. In Section 2, I will draw upon spectrographic
analyses of sound change in progress to show how the $\overline{ea}$ class could
be re-separated from one class and joined to another. To do so, I
will present fresh data on a second well-known and parallel case:
the reported merger and later re-separation of *line* and *loin*. In

the course of this discussion we will see the fundamental weakness of
the minimal pair test and the inadequacy of uncontrolled intuitions
and self-report as a basis for describing phonological systems; and
the strength of a technique which uses the speech of everyday life
as the empirical base for linguistic theory.[1]

1. The merger of *mate* and *meat*: did it occur?
In the history of the English language, there is no issue which is
more puzzling than the behavior of the vowel spelt $\overline{ea}$ in Early
Modern English, derived from Middle English long open $\bar{\varepsilon}$. Since the
class containing this vowel is spelled fairly consistently with $\overline{ea}$,
I will refer to it as the $\overline{ea}$ words: *meat, mead, meal*, etc. The
great majority of these words now rhyme with the reflexes of ME
long close $\bar{e}$ in [i:]: *meet, seed, feel*, etc. There are five well-
known exceptions that still have mid vowels, along with reflexes of
ME long $\bar{a}$. Thus *great, break, yea, drain* and *steak* have the same
vowel as *made, mate*, and *male*. The sub-class of $\overline{ea}$ words before *r*
is split almost down the middle: *fear, tear, near, dear* vs. *bear,
tear, wear, pear*, etc. The issue is whether or not the whole class
of $\overline{ea}$ words was once merged with long $\bar{a}$ and if so, how did they
separate?

I have followed the debates and historical evidence on this case
with the help of Geoffrey Nunberg of the University of Pennsylvania,
who observes that the only thing on which philologists agree is that
sometime around the end of the sixteenth century all of these word
classes showed long mid-front vowels. For theories of language that
depend upon the model of a homogeneous speech community, this is a
particularly difficult and confused case. It involves many of the
features that we are now familiar with in the study of normal, heterogeneous speech communities: widespread systematic variation, asymmetrical word classes, regional dialects, class stratification, and
finally the reversal of a reported merger. It is a comfortable situation for those who study language in its social context, but awkward
for those who would prefer to ignore that context.

The evidence for and against the merger can be summed up as follows.
Quite a large body of evidence from rhymes and puns has been presented by Wyld (1936) and Kökeritz (1953) in arguing for the merger.
A number of misspellings are cited by Wyld to show the merger, such
as *to spake to her* (C. Stewkley in *Verney Mem.*, iv., 464, 1695,
cited in Wyld 1936:211); *maneing* 'meaning' (*Lady Brill Harley* 40,
1639); *St. Jeamsis Park* (*Later Verney Letters*, 1: 37, 1697); *to have
her bed mead* (*Later Verney Letters*, 1: 75, 1700, these cited by
Wyld 1936:401).

The reports of the English grammarians are divided on this question. They give evidence of three possible sub-systems:

I	II	III
meet	meet	$\begin{bmatrix} \text{meet} \\ \text{meat} \end{bmatrix}$
meat	$\begin{bmatrix} \text{meat} \\ \text{mate} \end{bmatrix}$	
mate		mate

John Hart clearly had sub-system I in 1569, with all three word classes distinct. Mulcaster (1582) and Whythorne (Palmer 1969) agree. But $\bar{ea}$ and $\bar{a}$ are said to be the same or rhyme or are placed in a list of homonyms by Laneham in 1575, Bullokar in 1580, Bellot in 1580 and Delamothe in 1592. They thus indicate the existence of sub-system II above. There was also a sub-system III in which $\bar{ea}$ words have already merged with long $\bar{e}$, as shown for example by rhymes in Shakespeare such as *teach thee—beseech thee* (*Venus and Adonis* 404,406); Spenser's *seas—these*, *streeme—seeme*, etc.; and spellings such as *spyking* (*Henry Machyn* 1550), *birive* (*Harvey Letters* 1573, cited by Wyld 1936:209).

In the seventeenth century, we find that grammarians no longer reported sub-systems I or II. The great bulk of $\bar{ea}$ words were distinct from $\bar{a}$ for Florio in 1611, Gill in 1621, Wallis in 1688, Price in 1665, Miège in 1680 and Cooper in 1687. By the end of the century, the $\bar{ea}$ words not before $\bar{r}$ had almost all been assigned to the $\bar{e}$ class.

Faced with this evidence, the historians of English give radically different chronology for the raising of these vowels. The traditional view is that the first merger could not have happened, and therefore it did not. Jespersen (1909), Luick (1921) and Dobson (1968) thus concluded that $\bar{a}$ and $\bar{ea}$ had never merged, on the principle that if they had merged, they could not afterwards have separated, and arranged their chronologies accordingly. Zachrisson was at first of the same opinion (1913) but in later writings he saw that there were some dialects in which the merger had taken place. Wyld (1936) and Kökeritz (1953) also accepted the reports of the grammarians that at least for some dialects, long $\bar{a}$ and $\bar{ea}$ merged. They argued that the first merger was never actually reversed; they see the situation as a replacement of one dialect for another. The sub-system III was a Southeastern importation, arriving with speakers from Kent and Essex, which gradually won out over the older London dialect. The south-east was well advanced in the general upward movement of the long tense vowels; both O. E. $\overline{ae}^1$ and $\overline{ae}^2$

for example, were raised to a tense mid $\bar{e}$ in Kentish, often spelled *ie* as in *gier* and *cliene* (Wyld 1936:41). Newcomers entering London in the sixteenth century from Kent and Essex brought this dialect with them.

Wyld is a leading exponent of the view that social factors play an important role in linguistic change, and he has documented many such cases of regional features becoming sociolinguistic variables in London. His views fit in closely with the scheme put forward by Sturtevant (1947) and with the patterns found in our studies of sound change in Martha's Vineyard and New York City (Labov 1963, 1965).

A linguistic change begins as a local pattern characteristic of a particular social group, often the result of immigration from another region. It becomes generalized throughout the group, and becomes associated with the social values attributed to that group. It spreads to those neighboring populations which take the first group as a reference group in one way or another. The opposition of the two linguistic forms continues and often comes to symbolize an opposition of social values. These values may rise to the level of social consciousness and become <u>stereotypes</u>, subject to irregular social correction, or they may remain below that level as unconscious <u>markers</u>. Finally, one or the other of the two forms wins out. There follows a long period when the disappearing form is heard as archaic, a symbol of a vanished prestige or stigma, and is used as a source of stereotyped humor until it is extinguished entirely. If the older pronunciation is preserved in place names or fixed forms it is then heard as a meaningless irregularity.

The case of $\bar{ea}$ fits this model quite well. The change must be seen as a relative acceleration of processes that had already been operating, off and on, for more than a thousand years. These are in fact the continued raising of tense vowels in English which follow the general principle that <u>in chain shifts</u>, <u>long or tense vowels rise</u> (Labov, Yaeger and Steiner 1972, Ch. 4). This process was accelerated by the arrival of a large southeastern population in London operating at a more advanced level of the shift. There is strong evidence for the existence of socially marked dialects, in which the two forms are associated with opposing populations. Thus in a well known quotation of 1621, Gill stigmatized the affected or effeminate pronunciation of the Mopsae, who used an "Eastern Dialect," saying *kēpn* for 'capon' instead of *kāpn* for 'capon'. Later in the seventeenth century, we follow evidence for the progression of the shift by lexical diffusion in favor of the higher value for $\bar{ea}$ in orthoepists like Cooper (1687). The opposition was still a live one in the eighteenth century: Thomas Tuite reported in 1721 that the English differed in using high or low vowels for many $\overline{ea}$ words, with Londoners leading in the use of high vowels. Today the issue is a dead one; it survives in the well-known irregularities noted above, and in occasional place names like Preakness, New Jersey [pre^{I}knIs] and Leakey, Texas [le^{I}ki]. We cannot doubt the existence of competing $\overline{ea}$ dialects in London.

But Wyld's explanation for the current status of $\overline{ea}$ words is not entirely persuasive; on one obvious point, it cannot stand as it is. Neither the older London system I or the Southeastern system III had the merger. How then did London speakers acquire it?

At this point we can begin to apply principles derived from our sociolinguistic studies of change in progress. In so doing, we necessarily rely upon the uniformitarian principle—that is, the forces which operated to produce the historical record are the same as those which can be seen operating today. Of course, we cannot solve historical problems as we can synchronic ones: the phonetic and social data are too fragmentary. But we can provide some plausible interpretations with principles which have full empirical support and so illuminate the past by the present as we do the present by the past.

In these descriptions of change, it should be clear that we do not distinguish on principle between the origin and the propagation of a change. For if we take seriously the view of language as a form of social communication, the language can only be said to change when a new form is transmitted from one speaker to another, and accepted as an arbitrary social convention for conveying meaning. The analogy with biological evolution is clear: for a species can only be said to have changed when a new trait is propagated to future generations.

In studying sound change in progress, we continue the tradition of Louis Gauchat, who showed in 1899 that the assumption of a basic homogeneous speech community had no empirical support, even in the remote village of Charmey in the Suisse Romande (1905). Like Charmey in the nineteenth century, sixteenth century London was a normally heterogeneous community with regular class stratification and style shifting. Within such a community we can locate change in progress by a specific configuration. This is the sociolinguistic pattern shown in Figure 1: the raising of (oh) in New York City. This is the long open *o* vowel in *caught, off, lost, all*, which rose in three generations from low [ɔ] to high [U^ə]. In Figure 1, the vertical axis is the height of the vowel. The horizontal axis is the range of socio-economic class groups. The values for each speech style are connected by solid lines: the highest value of the variable are found in casual speech. The most advanced forms do not appear in the highest or lowest social groups, but in the

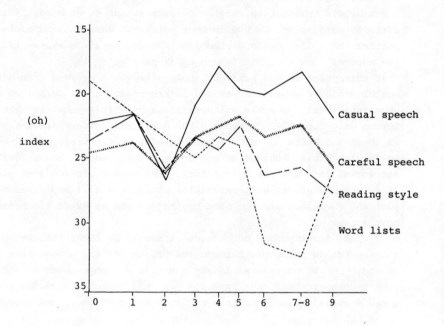

Socio-economic class	"Lower class"	"Working class"	"Lower middle class"	"Upper middle class"
Stylistic stratification	None	Slight	Extreme	Moderate
(oh) in casual speech	low	High	High	Low

Figure 1. Development of style stratification of (oh) in socio-economic sub-classes of New York City.

intermediate Lower Middle Class. This group also shows the strongest correction in more formal styles. In this curvilinear pattern, the sociolinguistic variable is not aligned with the socio-economic hierarchy in any one-to-one fashion. The general principle is that stable sociolinguistic variables will show a linear correlation with social class, so that the highest status group uses the highest degree of a prestige form or the lowest degree of a stigmatized form. But when change begins in an interior group, as it usually does, we see the curvilinear pattern which is associated with change in progress.

Of course, it is possible for a change to begin in the highest or lowest social group, but this is not the usual case. A curvilinear social stratification seems to be regularly associated with stratification in apparent time: that is, a regular increase of the variable through the various age levels of the population. When this is correlated with reports from earlier points in real time, it may then appear clear that we are indeed dealing with linguistic change in progress. This correlation was found for (oh) in New York City and the parallel variable (æh). It appears again in the study of Panamanian Spanish by Cedergren (1970). Table 1 shows the distribution of five sociolinguistic variables in Panamanian Spanish, which may be defined briefly as follows:

(R): the devoicing, fricativization, pharyngealization, and deletion of syllable-final /r/, with values ranging from 1 to 6 in the direction of these processes.

(PARA): the alternation of the full form of the preposition *para* with *pa*, with values of 1 and 2 respectively.

(ESTA): alternation of the full form *esta* with *ta*, assigned values of 1 and 2 respectively.

(S): the syllable-final alternation of [s], [h], and [∅], with values of 1, 2 and 3 respectively.

(CH): palatal vs. retroflex and reduced stop onset of /c/, with values of 1 and 2 respectively.

One of these variables, (CH), shows a curvilinear distribution, with a peak in social group II (second highest). The sound change therefore consists of a movement towards the retroflex sound centered in the second highest socio-economic group. Table 2 shows the age distribution for each socio-economic group. No particular trend appears except for (CH), where it is immediately evident that the younger the speaker, the higher the value of the variable.

A fourth example of this correlation appears in the recent study of Norwich, England, by Trudgill (1971). Figure 2 shows the pattern

Table 1. Social Stratification of Five Spanish Variables in Panama
[from Cedergren 1970]

Social Groups:	I	II	III	IV
(R)	1.62	1.88	2.29	2.29
(PARA)	1.11	1.37	1.39	1.69
(ESTA)	1.26	1.56	1.62	1.71
(S)	2.03	2.24	2.31	2.36
(CH)	1.88	2.24	2.13	2.00

Table 2. Development of Five Spanish Variables by Age Groups
[from Cedergren 1970]

Age:	11-20	21-30	31-40	41-50	61-70 years
(R)	2.28	1.90	1.95	2.23	1.46
(PARA)	1.31	1.34	1.48	1.33	1.39
(ESTA)	1.64	1.50	1.67	1.57	1.41
(S)	2.34	2.22	2.15	2.18	2.19
(CH)	2.15	2.29	2.05	1.81	1.31

of stylistic stratification for the (el) variable in Norwich; the
progressive backing of short /e/ before /l/ in *help, belt*, etc.,
which moves from [e] to [3] to [ʌ]. The index is constructed as the
numerical average (x100) of values: [e] = 1, [3] = 2, [ʌ] = 3.
Whereas all other variables in Norwich showed a linear pattern of
social stratification, this is curvilinear, with a peak in the upper
working class. Note that the groups immediately neighboring to the
originating group show a marked pattern of stylistic differentiation,
though not as steep as the upper working class. The upper middle
class is the most remote from the point of origin, and shows no significant trace of this backing. The pattern of Figure 2 would lead
us to predict a wave model of distribution in apparent time, and

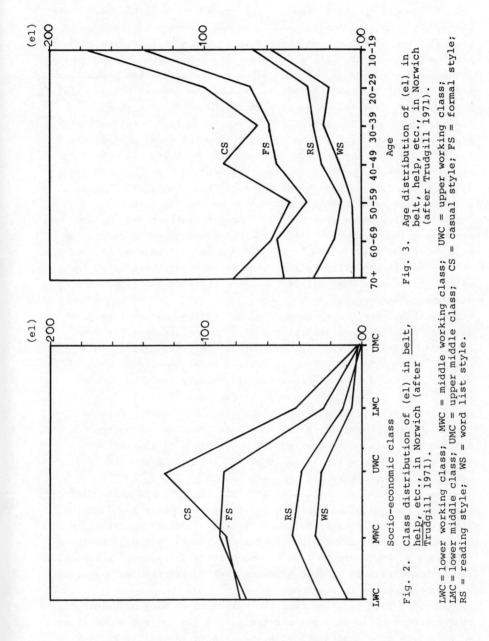

Fig. 2. Class distribution of (el) in belt, help, etc., in Norwich (after Trudgill 1971).

Fig. 3. Age distribution of (el) in belt, help, etc., in Norwich (after Trudgill 1971).

LWC = lower working class; MWC = middle working class; UWC = upper working class;
LMC = lower middle class; UMC = upper middle class; CS = casual style; FS = formal style;
RS = reading style; WS = word list style.

285

Figure 3 shows that this is indeed the case. Trudgill demonstrates
that (el) is in an early stage of change in progress. In all styles
there is a regular progression upward of (el) values, reaching a
maximum in the 10-19 age group. There is some sign of correction in
the middle-aged speakers, since their values are a little lower than
the oldest speakers, but the sudden upward movement in the younger
groups is unmistakable. We carried out instrumental studies in Norwich to follow up Trudgill's findings, and found clear spectrographic
evidence of the move to [3] and [ʌ] in the working-class population.

Following up Trudgill's findings on (el), we carried out parallel
exploratory interviews in Norwich for our instrumental studies
(Labov, Yaeger and Steiner 1972). The spectrographic evidence
appears in Figures 4a, 4b and 4c which show the vowel systems of
James Wickes, 74; Les Branson, 42; and Jean Suffling, 15. The vertical axis shows the position of the first formant and the horizontal
axis the position of the second formant. This two-formant space is
a close analogue of what linguists hear as the "front-back" and
"high-low" dimensions when they do impressionistic transcription.
Throughout this and other discussions of spectrographic records we
will refer to "high," "low," "front," and "back," bearing in mind
that we are in actuality referring to formant positions which may
match our acoustic impressions but are correlated much less closely
with articulatory gestures.

Using this instrumental record, we can follow the progression of
(el) in Norwich across generations (i.e. change in apparent time).
For James Wickes, in Fig. 4a, half of the (el) tokens are front
vowels, while others overlap central /ʌ/. For the middle-aged
speaker in Fig. 4b, we see that (el) is totally included in a mid-
back /ʌ/; for the youngest speaker in Figure 4c, (el) is in a low-
back position, further back and lower than /ʌ/, overlapping and extending beyond the broad /a/ class. This provides strong spectrographic confirmation of the regular progression of the variable
through age levels which is reflected in Trudgill's precise articulation scores of Figure 2.

These convergent patterns indicate that the basic sociolinguistic
principle can be relied on to locate change in progress. It is not
likely that it will apply to every case we encounter in future research, but it now seems clear that a curvilinear social distribution is a strong indication of a wave pattern in apparent time, and
the combined pattern is good evidence that we are viewing the early
stages of a change in progress.

There is reason to think that the sixteenth century movements of
long a̅ and e̅a followed a pattern similar to the current sound changes
we have been studying. In London, the long a̅ and e̅a variables were

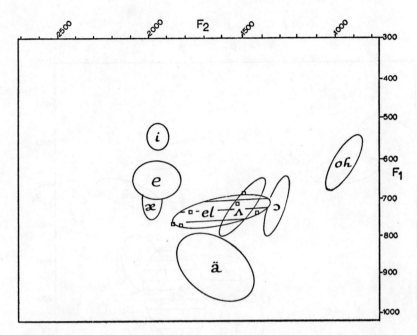

Figure 4a. Backing of (el) in Norwich: James Wicks, 74.

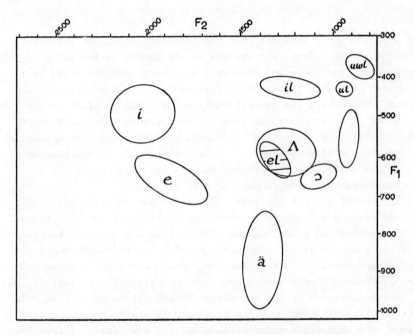

Figure 4b. Backing of (el) in Norwich: Les Branson, 42.

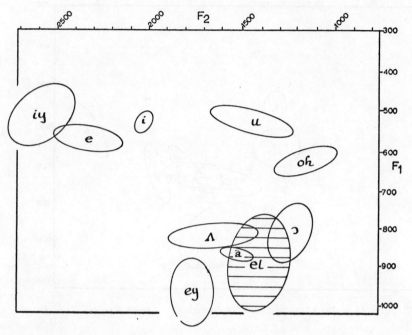

Figure 4c. Backing of (el) in Norwich: Jean Suffling, 15.

most advanced among speakers from the merchant class, not the highest social class. Hart, who was one of the landed gentry and a
court herald, had low ā and lower-mid ēa. Those who testified to
the merger of ēa and long ā were tradesmen's sons, like Bullokar and
Laneham. We can see the general outlines of a middle-class pattern
opposed to an upper-class pattern. If our present understanding of
sociolinguistic patterns is at all applicable, we would not expect
to find sharp divisions between the two which would establish them
as separate dialects. The predominance of the merchant class in
the raising was a matter of more or less.

Within this framework of class differentiation, we must introduce
a second principle which is involved in the reported merger. When
a set of associated sound changes spreads from one group to another,
different elements are advanced more rapidly by different groups.
That is, structural relations are not preserved and may even be reversed. Thus in Martha's Vineyard, the centralization of (ay) to
[əI] was accompanied by the secondary centralization of (aw) to [əu]
among the Yankees. When the change spread to the Portuguese and
Indians, the emphasis was reversed, with (aw) now leading (Labov
1963). In sixteenth-century London, it is clear that the raising of

long $\bar{a}$ was seen as the primary sociolinguistic variable. We have seen that Gill in 1621 heavily stigmatized the custom of pronouncing $\bar{a}$ as a higher-mid vowel. But $\bar{ea}$ was never mentioned.

The merger of long $\bar{a}$ and $\bar{ea}$ was then characteristic of Londoners who were influenced by the Southeastern model to accelerate their raising of $\bar{a}$ without raising $\bar{ea}$. Eventually $\bar{ea}$ was raised, but not until a century later was the raising completed.

Those who would try to write a uniform chronology for sixteenth-century London as a homogeneous speech community are bound to encounter contradictions. These are as baffling as those found by linguists trying to write a uniform description of New York City, who ended by describing it as a case of massive "free variation" (Labov 1966, Chapter II). Thus Dobson writes of sixteenth-century London: "The direction of the changes were mostly convergent, and therefore destructive of the distinctions which an educated language must seek to preserve." (1955). But our sociolinguistic studies suggest that this convergence is not confusion; it is rather the indirect evidence of the regular style, class and age stratification that must have prevailed in that area of the vowel system. This is the pattern which Weinreich calls "orderly heterogeneity," a normal characteristic of all communities that have been carefully studied (Weinreich, Herzog and Labov 1968).

2. The Reversal of Irreversible Mergers

We must now turn to a deeper problem: if the reported merger of long $\bar{a}$ and $\bar{ea}$ did occur, how was it reversed?

Wyld and Kökeritz suggest that contact with the Southeastern dialect was sufficient. But there is a general principle in dialectology that mergers expand at the expense of distinctions. Large groups of speakers do not re-learn word classes, which are essentially massive sets of historical accidents.

In Halle's 1962 paper on "Phonology in Generative Grammar" he discussed this merger and reversal on the basis of data supplied by Keyser. He simply explained the reversal as the re-organization of the rules for realizing the same set of underlying forms; $\bar{e}$, $\bar{ea}$ and $\bar{a}$. But how could these three underlying vowels be preserved? There are a limited set of alternations which might identify the $\bar{ea}$ class as opposed to the long $\bar{a}$ class: *break-breakfast, clean-cleanliness, mean-meant*. If the shortened $\bar{ea}$ forms were distinct from the short $\bar{a}$ forms in *sanity, tan*, etc., then it would be possible for sixteenth century speakers to distinguish the underlying form of *break* as distinct from *brake* and *breek*. But this strategy would only serve for those few words which showed alternations. It would be of no value in distinguishing *beat* from *bate, meat* from *mate, feat* from *fate*.

Chomsky and Halle (1968) assign underlying forms to entire classes of long vowels on the basis of alternations shown by some members though there is considerable disagreement as to whether this should be done (Krohn 1969, Hoard and Sloat to appear). But no mergers are involved: it is simply a case of rotating the sets of long vowels by a phonetic rule to match the underlying forms of sets of short vowels. Limited sets of grammatical alternations have no value in explaining the re-separation of a reported merger. On the contrary, the very existence of *break-breakfast* and *clean-cleanliness* would motivate the splitting of the original ēā class, with *break, clean,* and *mean* joining long ē and the others remaining with long ā. Halle does not discuss any of these issues in his 1962 article, which remains as an unmotivated claim for the retention of underlying forms. In *The Sound Pattern of English* (1968), Chomsky and Halle take John Hart as representative of sixteenth-century English.[2] Since Hart shows no merger at all, the problem of ēā is no longer of any concern to them.

The regularity of irregular sound changes. The well-known irregularities of the ēā class may be taken as evidence that the reversal of the merger was not in fact achieved: *great, break, yea, steak* and *drain,* along with *wear, swear, tear, pear* and *bear* might show that speakers were not in fact able to identify the ēā class accurately because of the merger with long ā. These ten forms are then seen as a random residue, testifying to the impossibility of re-separating a merged class. But a re-examination of the historical evidence, along with data from our spectrographic studies of parallel changes now in progress, shows that this impression of irregularity is largely illusory. Let us consider first the five words not before *-r,* which Samuels refers to as "those *enfants terribles* of traditional *Lautlehre*" (1965). With or without a merger with ā, the very existence of these exceptions has posed a difficult challenge for the traditional neogrammarian view of the regularity of sound change.

The form *yea* can first be set aside as an entirely different phenomenon. It seems to have risen to [yi:] as part of the regular process in the seventeenth century, but afterwards reformed to [ye:] along with *nay.*[3]

We can understand how a great many place names were left behind, and rare and learned words, since their assignment to a particular word class may be problematical, but these five are common ordinary words, and their irregularity is puzzling. If the shift of ēā words to high position was the product of irregular dialect mixture, why did it work so regularly for all but these five? On the other hand, if sound change is basically regular, why do so many sound changes show residue like these which give comfort to the opponents of the

neogrammarian doctrine? The five residual words are too many to fit
the model of regular change, and too few to be explained by random
mixture.

We cannot hope to resolve the major question posed here by one investigation, but I believe that we can throw some light on the issues
by drawing again on our instrumental studies of sound change in progress and some new sociolinguistic principles as well.

First of all, we observe that the irregularity is not so great as
it seems. Three of the five words begin with consonants plus *r*. Of
course historical linguists have noted this fact, but they have been
quick to discount it because it immediately becomes obvious that a
great many words were raised after initial /r/. "In *great* and *break*
it is often explained as due to *r*, which is not probable, seeing that
r is followed by [i:] in *read, treason, breach, grease, cream, preach*,
etc." (Jespersen 1909 [1949 edition:338]).

To this list we can add *ream, real, reap, rear, dream, bream,
scream, treat*, etc. Jespersen did not let the matter rest there,
since the primary task of the historical phonologist is to reduce
such irregularities to rules or account for them somehow. He develops intricate arguments by analogy for *great, break*, and *yea*. ·But
historical linguists under-estimated the subtlety of phonetic conditioning in sound changes such as the raising of ēa. Our own work on
sound change in progress has steadily increased our respect for the
power of phonetic factors to differentiate word classes in the middle
stages of a change.

At the beginning of our work on sound change, we found naturally
enough that the major influence on English vowels was the following
consonant, especially /l/ and /r/, but more recently we have discovered that there are dialects in which initial /r/ has just as
strong an influence as final /r/. For example, in Glasgow, we find
that the vowel of short /e/ in *rest* winds up in exactly the same
position as short /e/ in *person*, somewhat lower than the main body
of short /e/ words. And in every dialect, a preceding post-consonantal /r/ has a strong effect on the vowel nucleus. In our studies
of the tensing and raising of short *a* in various American cities, we
find that words like *grab* are lower and more central than *stab*. This
on-going sound change is quite parallel to the original raising of
long ā, [mat] having been lengthened in open syllables to [ma:tə]
and reduced to [ma:t]. It was then gradually raised to [mæ:t] and
[mɛ:t] and [me:t]. In the present situation, short *a* as [æ] is
being tensed and lengthened by a separate rule to [æ:] and then
raised to a mid and even high ingliding vowel: [ɛ:ə], [e:ə] and
[I:ə]. We will refer to this variable class as (æh).

This raising of (æh) follows the first of three unidirectional principles of chain shifting that we have located: in chain shifts, tense or long vowels rise. Somewhat to our surprise, examination of this change in progress throughout the Northern tier of cities in the United States—Rochester, Buffalo, Detroit, Chicago—has not yet shown us lexical irregularities. Instead, we see an extraordinarily regular phonetic process, illustrated in Figures 5 and 6 for a father and son from Detroit. Figure 5 shows the vowel system of James Adamo, 55, interviewed in the sociolinguistic survey carried out by Roger Shuy, Walt Wolfram and William K. Riley (1967). Adamo shows short *a* in a low front position, ranging from lower low to upper low. But the sound change is already in progress: we see the characteristic fine-grained phonetic differentiation which arises when (æh) begins to move upward. The highest and most peripheral vowels are those before front nasal consonants, as we now expect, with the velar nasal in a lower position. (From this point on I will use the expression "velar stop" to indicate "vowels before velar stop"). Voiced stops are lower; voiceless fricatives are lower yet and more central, with /f/ lower than the others; and the voiceless stops are lowest of all. Among the voiceless stops, the palatal /č/ is relatively highest and /k/ is the lowest and well back to a central position.

The effect of preceding and following /l/ can be seen in a subtly graded series of restraints of (æh): initial /l/ has some effect in *land* and *last*; next, post-vocalic /l/ in *Italian* and *challenge*. Returning to the voiced stops, we see that *flag* is more central than *bad* with a velar final and preceding post-consonantal /l/. In a word, the relative position of almost every item can be accounted for by phonetic conditioning. This spacing out of phonetic sub-classes is characteristic of the intermediate stages of change in progress, like the spacing out of runners in a race; at the beginning they are all bunched together; in the midst of the race, they are strung out according to their individual abilities and speeds; at the finish, they are brought together again.

Figure 6 is a view of (æh) in the system of the thirteen-year-old son, Chris Adamo, where we see even greater phonetic dispersion. The sound change has advanced until the words ending in front nasals are in lower-high position; the rest are in upper and lower-mid position. Voiced stops are just behind the nasals; below them the voiceless fricatives, then the voiceless stops, and one word ending in /kt/ in the lowest position of them all. And most importantly for our analogy with the case of *great*, *break* and *drain*, there is one item ending in a voiced stop well below all the others, in lower

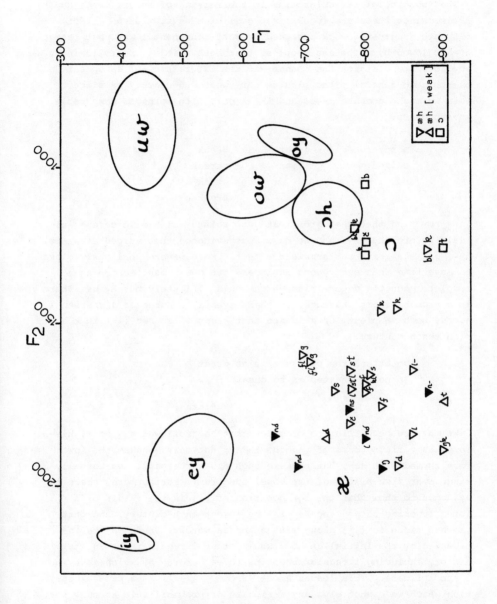

Figure 5. Phonetic conditioning in the raising of
(æh) and fronting of (ɔ) in the vowel
system of James Adamo, 55, Detroit.

mid instead of lower high position: *grabbed*, showing the effect of the postconsonantal /r/.

The two crucial irregularities in the raising of $\overline{ea}$ are *great* and *break*, since these are regular reflexes of ME $\overline{\epsilon}$ from OE $\overline{æ}^2$. Not only are *great* and *break* preceded by post-consonantal /r/, but they are followed by voiceless stops so that both initial and following environments disfavor the change—if the EME raising of $\overline{ea}$ operated on the same general principles as our twentieth-century raisings.[4] Thus we might compare *great* and *break* only with words in comparable environments:

not raised:	great	break
raised:	treat	streak
		creak
		freak

We now find that the words that were raised all had voiceless initials before the *-r-*, and we have some evidence that voiced clusters, *dr-*, *gr-*, *br-* have the heaviest effect. Here we are perilously close to asserting that every word is indeed its own class, absorbing a complete phonetic determinism which would ultimately betray us. There is a probabilistic character to these events, because as Jespersen notes, we have plenty of evidence that *great* often had [i:] in the eighteenth century.

> Doubtless the pleasure is as great
> In being cheated as to cheat

> (Hudibras)

We may now be willing to consider that *yea* followed a special history, as various forms of *yeah* do today; not only because the lower form rhymed with *nay*, but because such discourse particles normally range over five-sixths of the vowel spectrum. Furthermore, there is evidence to show that the low position of *yea* is the result of a later lowering of *yea* and *nay* in the seventeenth century, and that *yea* had risen to [ji] along with other $\overline{ea}$ words. *Drain* may be influenced by the initial *dr-* but shows other irregularities in its history including irregular breaking to $\overline{ea}$ before *-h*, which make it a special case. This leaves *steak* (from ON *steik*) as a true exception which we cannot give any rationale or probabilistic account for. Since this was [e:] in the sixteenth century, it should now have a high vowel.

One might wonder why we should be concerned over the small irregularities in *ea* words when there is apparently massive irregularity

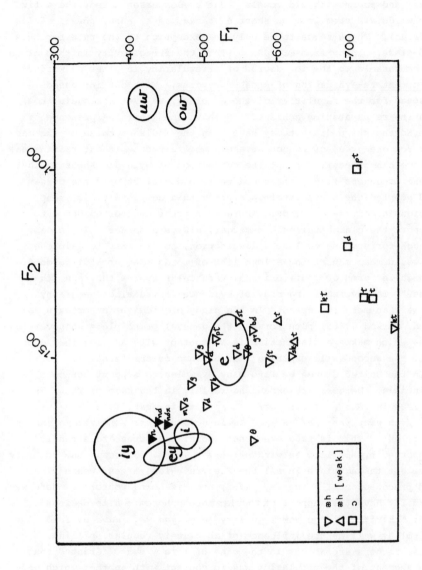

Figure 6.   Phonetic conditioning in the raising of
(æh) and fronting of (ɔ) in the vowel
system of Chris Adamo, 13, Detroit.

in *ea* words ending in *r*: *fear, beard, dear, hear, clear, near, tear, year*, with high vowels as against *bear* (vb), *bear* (n), *pear, tear, wear*, and *swear* with mid vowels. But as Jespersen noted, these five low words all stem from OE short ĕ (*bĕran, bĕre, pĕru, tĕran, wĕrian, swĕrian*). There seems to be only one exception to the rule for this sub-class: *spear* from OE *spĕru*. Thus the irregularity in this class is comparable to the low degree of irregularity in other $\overline{ea}$ words.[5]

Current re-evaluation of speaker reports. With our increased respect for the regularity of the $\overline{ea}$ class, we must ask again, how was the re-separation achieved? We have seen that the presence of the Southeastern dialect may have been the indirect cause of the merger for one group of London speakers who raised $\overline{a}$ without raising $\overline{ea}$. But we cannot easily accept the suggestion of Wyld and Kökeritz that these Londoners simply abandoned their old dialect with the merger and adopted the Southeastern pattern with a completely different assignment of the $\overline{ea}$ words. There is a great deal of evidence to support the claim that once a merger, always a merger. It is easy enough for someone to lose a distinction, not so easy to gain one. It would mean memorizing a long list of words that are "different" though in terms of their original vernacular system they are "the same." The overwhelming body of evidence from dialect geography shows that mergers expand. In his study of Yiddish in northern Poland, Herzog (1965) puts forward the general principle: whenever an area which makes a distinction is in contact with an area that does not, the second will expand at the expense of the first.

In the United States we find many examples to support Herzog's principle. Mergers are expanding rapidly in the case of /hw-/ vs. /w-/ as in *which, witch*; /or/ vs. /ɔr/ as in *four, for*; /-in/ vs. /-en/ in *pin, pen*; /a/ vs. /ɔ/ as in *cot, caught*; /æ/ vs. /a/ as in *aunt, ant*. This is true even when social pressures are strongly supported by spelling as with *which* vs. *witch*. There is one contrary movement taking place in all the Eastern *r*-less areas, where final and preconsonantal *r* in *car, guard*, etc. is being restored. Here we normally have the support of regular morphophonemic alternations [ka: ∿ kar##ænd] and vowel quality (e.g. *god* vs. *guard* as [gad ∿ gɑ:d] as well as the influence of absolutely regular spelling. These factors are absent in the case of *mate* ∿ *meat*. Granted that one segment of the population was in contact with another which made the distinction, we would normally expect the merger to expand. We still have no plausible explanation as to how this re-separation was accomplished, especially when we note that the re-assignment of $\overline{ea}$ to $\overline{e}$ is not reported until the middle of the next century.

We can now throw some light on this question by turning to some of the most unexpected and striking results of our current spectrographic studies of change in progress, supported by the National Science Foundation. These concern the relation of reported mergers to spectrographic records of connected speech. The reports of mergers are usually made through minimal pair and commutation tests, which show the ability of the speaker to label two sounds as the same or different. Minimal pair tests are still fundamental tools of phonological analysis, though their importance has declined from the peak period in the 1940s and '50s when many structural linguists argued that no phonetic data was required besides these reports of "same" and "different." Recent sociolinguistic work has underlined the dangers of relying upon pronunciations of isolated words that are produced with full deliberation and upon the conscious elicitation of intuitions about these words. It has been known for some time that speakers can make distinctions in these formal tests which they do not make in everyday speech. But it has not been reported before, to our knowledge, that these tests are doubly defective: speakers can report two sounds as "the same" even though they regularly make the distinction in their own natural language (Labov, Yaeger and Steiner 1972: Ch. 6).

The first case we encountered was in New York City, where native speakers reported *sauce* and *source*, *law* and *lore* as "the same" whenever they did not pronounce the final *-r*. But the spectrographic records of twenty-six speakers drawn from the larger sample of the Lower East Side (Labov 1966) shows that these vowels have distinct distributions in every case. The nucleus of *source* is higher and/or further back than the nucleus of *sauce* (F1 and/or F2 lower). Since then we have found seven other cases in our studies of the general principles of chain shifting in English and American dialects. We found the same relation between *fool* and *full* in Albuquerque, New Mexico. The two vowels were approximated in minimal pair tests, but in connected speech the nucleus of *fool* had distinctly lower second formants (was further "back") than the nucleus of *full*. In Boston, we found that many younger working-class speakers heard *beer* and *bare*, *cheer* and *chair* as "the same," but these word classes showed up with distinct distribution in their speech.[6]

These findings have general implications for our understandings of the relation between production and (conscious) perception of speech. In my own linguistic training, I absorbed the principle that if two word classes differ systematically by any particular sound feature, no matter how small, then native speakers used this distinction to distinguish words. This is the principle behind Bloomfield's declaration "Such a thing as a 'small difference of sound' does not exist in language." (1927). We now see that such small differences do exist. To the native speaker, they may not be worth noticing and may

in fact be impossible for him to label; nevertheless, he regularly
produces these differences.

The most dramatic example of asymmetry between production and perception occurred in Norwich, England. There the class ME of long
open $\bar{\text{ɔ}}$ words has risen to high position and the nucleus fronted to
mid position; for some speakers, coinciding with the nucleus of ME
long close $\bar{\text{o}}$ words. Thus *too* is pronounced [tʰᵾ⁺] and *toe* is pronounced [tʰᵾᵘ]. Impressionistically, the distinction is a subtle
one, though the outside phonetician can hear it consistently after a
few minutes practice. Spectrographically, it appears as a distinct
difference in the direction of the glides. The *t-o-o* class glides
up, and the *t-o-e* class glides up and to the back. Figures 7a and
7b show the differentiation of the vowels used in a commutation test,
a random alternation list of *too* and *toe* as spoken by two fourteen-
year-old Norwich boys. The second boy, Keith, was totally unable to
hear the distinctions being made by David in Figure 7a though David
was trying as hard as possible, face to face, to get it across to him.
But when Keith read the list off himself, he produced the clear pattern shown in Figure 7b, which David deciphered without any trouble.
Thus Keith could produce the distinction but could not use it to
distinguish words. We should not then be surprised to find vacilla-
tion in the reports of sixteenth century observers, since there are
apparently great personal differences in the ability to label such
marginal pairs even when the productive rules are the same.

We can apply this evidence most directly to our present problem of
ea by examining first the modern reflexes of a parallel case: the
reported merger and re-separation of long $\bar{\text{i}}$ and *oi* in *line* and *loin*,
vice and *voice*, *file* and *foil*. These two vowels are said to have
merged in the seventeenth and eighteenth centuries, but re-separated
in the nineteenth to yield our modern /ay/ and /oy/.

The case of *line* and *loin*. Present day /oy/ includes the reflexes
of at least two ME diphthongs, *oi* and *ui*, and perhaps more. The *oi*
type is found in words ultimately derived from Latin *au + i* (*joy*,
choice, *noise*); *ui* from Lat. ŏ + *i* (*annoy*, *oil*) or from Lat. *ō/u + i*
(*point*, *join*, *toil*). (The commonest /oy/ word, *boy*, is of obscure
origin and seems to have had a close labialized onset in Early Modern
English [*bwoi*]). The first signs of merger with ME long $\bar{\text{i}}$ words
appear in fifteenth century misspellings; the general tendency
appears in the late seventeenth century when Coles (1674) identifies
line and *loin*, *bile* and *boil*, *isle* and *oil*, including both *ui* and *oi*
types, and a wide variety of words are shown as merged by other
phoneticians of the period. Free variation appears in the rhymes of
Dryden, Butler and Pope. The traditional theory of Sweet connects
this merger with the unrounding and lowering of short ŭ which became

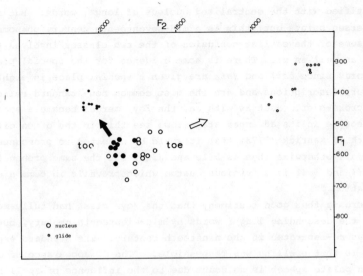

Figure 7a.   Nucleus and glide positions
for <u>too</u> and <u>toe</u> commutation
test as pronounced by David,
14, Norwich, England.

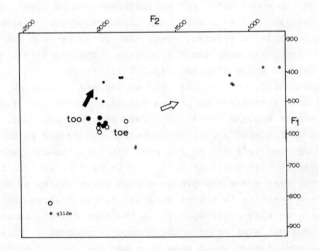

Figure 7b.   Nucleus and glide positions
for <u>too</u> and <u>toe</u> commutation
test as pronounced by Keith,
14, Norwich, England

identified with the centralized nucleus of long ī words. But as
Jespersen points out, this is a mid-seventeenth century phenomenon,
and some of the earlier confusion of the two classes involves the *oi*
type as well as *ui*. There is some evidence for the special place of
ui words since *boil* and *join* are given a special place in eighteenth
century descriptions and are the most common non-standard relics of
the cross-over. Just as with ēa, the /oy/ merger became a social
stereotype in its advanced stages; we see this in the often cited
remark of Kenrick (1773) that it would be affected to pronounce *boil*
and *join* otherwise than as *bile* and *jine*, but the same pronunciation
in *oil* and *toil* is a "vicious custom which prevails in common conversation."

There is thus good testimony that the /oy/ class had fully merged
with the descending long *i* words by mid-eighteenth century, but that
it was re-separated in the nineteenth century. The standard explanation is that spelling was responsible. "The disappearance of *ai* for
oi in polite speech is no doubt due to the influence of spelling."
(Jespersen 1949: 330).

This argument is put forward because it is the only conceivable
one, but it is not convincing. The general problems raised for ēa
hold here as well. If spelling could reverse the merger of /ay/ and
/oy/ in the nineteenth century, it could reverse the merger of /α/
and /ɔ/ in the twentieth. But our observations of speakers who
learned English with this merger in their vernacular system find it
almost impossible to reverse, even under pressure from teachers and
peers who regularly make the distinction. The irreversibility of
mergers has not ended with the rise of literacy.

But beyond this, we find that the merger and separation of /ay/
and /oy/ is not confined to polite society: throughout the local
vernaculars of England and America /ay/ and /oy/ are distinct. In
the south of England /ay/ is often backed and raised to the original
position of /oy/ [ɔ^I] but at the same time /oy/ moves upward in a
chain shift to high-position [u^I]. It is hard to explain this clear
separation, even under the pressure of a chain shift, by the effect
of standard spelling in London speech. Figure 8 shows the vowel
system of a working class speaker in the East End of London, taken
from our current studies of sound change in progress. This diagram
is merely one of many which show that the /ay/ ∿ /oy/ distinction is
normally preserved without any difficulty. Though /ay/ is raised to
a lower mid position, /oy/ is quite distinct with a high back
nucleus.

This dialect is the direct inheritor of the "common speech" stigmatized by Kenrick for its merger of /ay/ and /oy/. The same pattern appears in many other dialects that seem to have once shown a

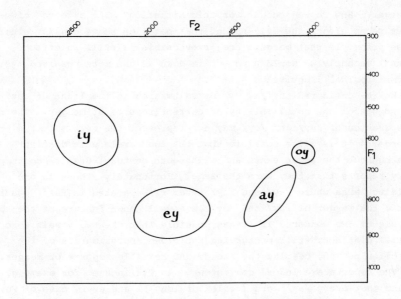

Figure 8.   Vowel system of Marie Colville,
39, Hackney (London), England

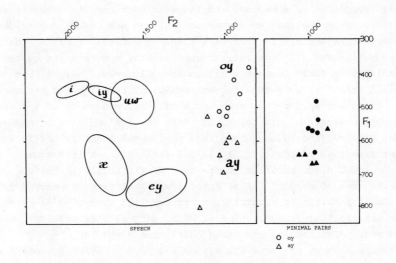

Figure 9.   Distribution of /ay/ and
/oy/ in the vowel system
of Jack Cant, 85, Tillingham (Essex), England

merger. How do we account for this situation? The evidence of merger seems clear; the evidence of re-separation seems equally clear;
the principle that mergers are irreversible is still in effect.
Until recently we would have put it down as one more unsolved mystery
of historical linguistics.

We re-considered the /ay/ ∿ /oy/ situation in the light of our
findings on the unreliability of current reports of merger. The re-
separation of /ay/ and /oy/ may not represent the reversal of a true
merger: it is quite possible that the two vowels were distinct
throughout the seventeenth and eighteenth century, despite contemporary reports that they were the same. Fortunately, there is one
dialect area where /ay/ and /oy/ never re-separated in Essex County;
here the merger of /ay/ and /oy/ is a well known feature of the rural
dialect. We wondered if it was possible that the two vowels were
still distinct, still preserving the close approximation of the
earlier period, despite the steady and reliable reports of merger.

The reports are indeed consistent. In Tillingham, for example, we
find that every /ay/ word (reflex of long ī) and every case of /oy/
shows exactly the same representation in Volume III of Orton and
Dieth's *Survey of English Dialects* (1970): a simple /ɔ^{I}/. Neighboring towns show some fronting in various words, but no differentiation
of the two classes. The field worker heard this as a merger, it is
well recognized as a merger, and there is no reason to doubt it as a
merger. Nevertheless, we suspected that the nucleus of /oy/ might
indeed be higher and further back than the nucleus of /ay/: that is,
more peripheral. In general, it appears that speakers are quite
sensitive to first formant position (roughly, vowel height) but not
at all sensitive to second formant position (fronting and backing).
The field worker for that area had kindly allowed us to do a spectrographic analysis of his tapes, and from the limited data it appeared
that /ay/ may indeed have been less peripheral than /oy/.[7] To investigate this possibility, I visited eastern Essex last summer, and
interviewed older speakers in the town of Tillingham in the center
of the area of merger. In my interviews, I elicited as many /oy/
words as possible in natural conversation, and succeeded in getting
the unreflecting pronunciation of such pairs as *line* and *loin*, *voice*
and *vice*. The results are shown in Figures 9 and 10.

Figure 9 shows the over-all system and /ay/ ∿ /oy/ relations for
Jack Cant, 85, a retired farm laborer and reportedly the brother of
one of the original informants for the Orton survey. In response to
direct questions about the minimal pair *loin—line*, he reported them
"the same." But the actual distribution of the two sets of words in
his speech is quite different: /oy/ is clearly higher than /ay/;
the only overlap is found with the word *point* in the minimal pair

question. (Note that *point* is a lexical item that has crossed over to the /ay/ class for many speakers in this area.)

As Jack Cant began to think about the minimal pair, his *line* moved up, closer to *loin*, as shown by the solid triangle, and his *loin* down, as shown by the solid circles. We find the same phenomenon in New Mexico, where *fool* and *full* were more different in natural speech than in minimal pairs and in New York City for *source* and *sauce*. This means that the act of labelling the two forms as "the same" is not due to an inability to hear the difference; rather the speaker appears to have an intuitive norm that they are the same sound, and approximates that norm in minimal pairs, eliminating most of the difference found in natural speech.

Several of the /ay/ forms are found along the less peripheral path, and the only /ay/ form which is as high as /oy/ is differentiated by its less peripheral position. This fits in with our previous view of /ay/ with a lax nucleus and a less extreme second formant position than /oy/. Figure 10a shows the vowel system of Mrs. Leonard Raven, of the same age group, a retired domestic worker. Again we find that /ay/ and /oy/ are quite distinct; even the minimal pairs show /oy/ higher and further back than /ay/. Though the over-all distribution of /ay/ is lower than /oy/, they would not be clearly separated if it were not for the second formant difference.

Mrs. Raven also found *loin* and *line* "the same," though in her case they became even more distinct in pronunciation: the solid circles show *loin* shifting back and the solid triangles *line* shifting down, still heard as "the same." On the other hand, she clearly heard a difference between *voice* and *vice*. In natural speech, the difference between *voice* and *vice* is of the same order as *loin* and *line*, but the second were "the same" while the first were different, and became more different as she repeated the pair. (If /ay/ and /oy/ are now re-separating in Essex, it would be expected that the "merger" would last longer before nasals. We find in the Southwestern U.S. that the on-going merger of /a/ and /ɔ/ occurs first before nasals.)

Figure 10b shows the vowel system of Mr. Leonard Raven, a retired farm superintendent, seventy-two years old. His speech is generally less "Essex" than his wife's, and closer to the standard in grammar; he heard *line* and *loin* as different, but the general pattern of /ay/ and /oy/ is the same. The highest vowels on the chart for each class are the words *buy* and *boy*; they are in close approximation but *buy* is still slightly less peripheral than *boy*. Again, the two sets of vowels would be merged if it were not for the second formant position. The one exception is the word *joined* which appears among the less peripheral /ay/ vowels. This is one of the two common

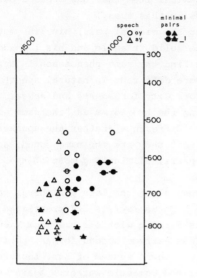

Figure 10a.

Distribution of /ay/ and
/oy/ in the vowel system
of Mrs. Leonard Raven, 69
Tillingham (Essex) England.

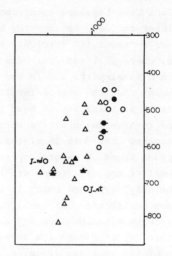

Figure 10b.

Distribution of /ay/ and
/oy/ in the vowel system
of Leonard Raven, 70,
Tillingham (Essex) England.

items, *boil* and *join*, that crossed over to the /ay/ class and were
perfectly natural in the /ay/ class according to Kenrick in 1773.

This data clearly shows the disjunction between normative, intuitive reactions to phonological pairs and the reality of language as
it is used. We find that words pronounced as minimal pairs are more
closely approximated than in natural speech, and the speakers' judgments indicate that they cannot <u>label</u> the word classes as different.
If they were to write reports of their language for some future
generation, they would have to state that *line* and *loin* are the same.
But they are not; these classes are plainly maintaining their separate paths even after several centuries of near merger. This data
has to be given more weight than most, because it is not an accident
that it came to our attention. I went to Essex to investigate this
phenomenon, led by previous findings to the conclusion that the reported merger of *line* and *loin* may not have been a merger. In fact,
it seems to be a conclusive demonstration that the intuitions of the
native speaker about contrast do not necessarily give us reliable
information about the sound system of the language and cannot be
used alone as a secure base for a theory of linguistic change.

In the summer of 1972, we added a new chapter to the study of *line*
and *loin*. We returned to Tillingham and met again with the three
older speakers whose vowel systems we had analyzed, bringing with us

a commutation test prepared from the connected speech of Jack Cant.
The first ten items were a random alternation of his pronunciations
of *line* and *loin* extracted from his unreflecting, connected speech.
Two tokens of *loin* had nuclei at F1-510, F2-990 and F1-575, F2-975;
two tokens of *line* had nuclei at F1-645, F2-990, and F1-605, F2-1015.
The second formant positions were thus quite close, with *loin* showing slightly lower F2 as usual. The first formants were also close,
but with *loin* showing distinctly lower F1 (that is, occupying a
higher position). The second ten items alternated utterances of
loin and *line* made when Jack Cant was reflecting directly on whether
or not they were "same" or "different"; *loin* was at F1-575, F2-1015
and *line* at F1-685, F2-1005. These positions were typical of the
vowel nuclei displayed in Jack Cant's chart given above in Figure 9.

None of the three informants were able to pass the commutation
test. Jack Cant, who originally rated *loin* and *line* as "the same,"
gradually began to feel that there was a small difference between
them. In fact, his comment demonstrates clearly that native speakers naturally contradict Bloomfield's dictum that small differences
do not exist: "There's a little difference but sometimes they seem
to be both the same." At the same time, Jack Cant was totally unable to identify his own productions of *loin* and *line*. His actual
score was below chance: that is, he mis-identified *line* as *loin*
and *loin* as *line* sixty percent of the time. Correct and incorrect
identifications ran in blocks, indicating that Jack Cant may have
been hearing "same" and "different" with some degree of accuracy
without being able to utilize the direction of the difference. In
further discussion, he reacted to *voice* and *vice* as "the same," and
insisted that there was no possible difference between *file* and *foil*.

Mrs. Raven had the greatest degree of success in identifying Jack
Cant's *line* and *loin*, though she had originally reacted to her own
pronunciations as "the same." Nevertheless, she mis-identified
seven of the twenty cases. The first ten judgments were all correct,
though some hesitations and reversals occurred; the mistakes were
concentrated in the minimal pair test. Mr. Raven, who originally
thought they were different, had much less success in hearing the
difference.[8]

Both Mr. and Mrs. Raven came to the opinion that there was a strong
difference between *line* and *loin*, and their own pronunciations of the
two became increasingly differentiated. Mr. Raven, in particular,
was able to exaggerate his natural pronunciation in this maximally
reflective situation:

> When you try to sound that L-O-I-N [loˇːɪn] I think
> people try to put that *o* in, more than they would do
> if they just said [lʌɪn].

Mrs. Raven did not produce such a strong contrast in her own speech, maintaining the slight differentiation shown in Figure 10a, but she insisted that the sound difference was useful in differentiating the two words:

> Loin of lamb, you do go like that, [lɔˆIn], loin o'
> lamb, 'n if you want the [lɔ‹In], the linen line or
> anything like that, you go like, "Put the linen line,
> [lɔ‹In, lɔ‹In]," see?

Nevertheless, she was not able to use the differences made by Jack Cant to identify words accurately, contrary to her expectation. As noted above, the contrast from unreflecting speech was easier to hear than the series from the minimal pair test: reactions to the former were much faster, as well as more accurate. This corresponds to the process we have observed in other cases, such as *fool—full* in Albuquerque: on first reflection in minimal pair tests, the difference made in natural speech tends to disappear or be narrowed as the subject judges the two words to be "the same." This is what Jack Cant does. On further conscious discussion, the difference may be re-established or exaggerated if the subject can consciously imitate other dialects, as Mr. Raven does.

These commutation tests confirm our finding of the asymmetry between production and perception. In these cases, speakers consistently make small differences in natural speech which maintain the identity of word classes, but they cannot accurately label these differences on conscious reflection, either in their own speech or in the speech of their close associates who speak the same dialect. Both minimal pair tests and commutation tests are helpful in identifying this marginal situation, a fact of considerable importance for an understanding of linguistic change. But these tests will give a very faulty view of the underlying forms and phonological rules of the language, if they are not coupled with accurate studies of the actual use of segments in the course of connected, unreflecting speech.

From these results we infer the strong possibility that /ay/ and /oy/ have remained in close approximation in Tillingham for several hundred years, heard as the same, yet not the same in fact. They are now re-separating in the speech of younger Tillingham speakers, as /ay/ becomes progressively more central. We may further infer that /ay/ and /oy/ never merged at all in the history of English. The rhymes and reports of "the same" may only be the results of the fact that the differences between the two sounds at a certain stage were too small to be relied on to distinguish words; but the phonological system continued to produce a peripheral nucleus for /oy/ and a less peripheral and lower nucleus for /ay/ (basically tense $\bar{o}y$ and lax ay).

The resolution of the $\overline{ea}$ problem. We can now apply these findings to the problem of the merger and re-separation of the $\overline{ea}$ words. From all that has been said, it follows that we cannot use the reports of orthoepists on "same" or "different" as direct evidence for the existence of a merger. It seems clear that the ability to label a difference is not a determining factor in the evolution of the language. Without instrumental records of the use of language in the past, we must base our conclusions on the actual course of linguistic history.

There is no question that a merger of $\overline{ea}$ and long $\bar{a}$ was reported in the sixteenth century, and that many speakers heard *meat* and *mate* as the same. That does not mean that they were the same. It does mean that they were in close approximation, and could not be relied on—for a time—to distinguish words. The later history of English in the seventeenth century showed that $\overline{ea}$ and $\bar{a}$ had not merged in the sixteenth. This conclusion seems to resolve effectively the contradictions in which this problem has been embroiled, and we submit our findings to historians of English with the hope that they will find them illuminating.

We can never claim to have resolved an historical issue decisively, as we might do for a synchronic problem; the best that we can do is to develop the most plausible reconstruction of past events, in the light of other past and present data. We suggest that historical linguistics can continue to benefit by drawing upon the rich and inexhaustible store of data to be found in the study of change in progress. The case of $\overline{ea}$ is but one of a great many where subjective reports of past observers need further interpretation; and the problem of merger and re-separation is but one of many unresolved contradictions in the past which can be illuminated by the present.

3. *Turning Outward*

In this analysis of the $\overline{ea}$ problem, we have introduced a number of findings that have general implications for linguistic theory. We must reject the principle of Bloomfield that there is no such thing as a small difference in sound, since this is precisely what we have in the oppositions of *meat—mate, loin—line, too—toe*. Native speakers hear these as small differences—if they hear them at all— and react to them as small differences, quite distinct from the major phonemic distinctions such as *meet* and *mate, line* and *loin*.[9] In other words, the set of phonemic categories does not exhaust the set of distinctions in the phonological system.

This finding is also a dramatic demonstration of the inadequacy of intuitive reports as a basis for describing a phonological system. In some sense, speakers who regularly produce a distinction must perceive it, but that perception is not available for introspection on command.

By comparing such formal tests with the unreflecting behavior of everyday speech, we are better able to interpret them. We now see them as direct evidence for the degree of structural organization imposed by the speaker on the continuous phonetic sub-stratum. The fact that there are marginal phonemes does not destroy our interest in the phonemic system of contrasts; the fact that intuitions can be deceptive does not diminish our interest in using intuitions in a controlled way.

The most important conclusion to be drawn from this work is that linguistics must turn outward if it is to pass beyond the contradictions set up by our manipulation of abstract models. I would like to submit this example of the interpretation of the past by the present as evidence that we cannot continue to exclude phonetic and social data from linguistic explanation. Nothing I have said here should suggest that I would reject or neglect the many insights gained through structural analysis of the type advocated by Kuryłowicz and Martinet. We have built heavily on the views of Martinet (1955) and profited from the analyses of Haudricourt and Juilland (1949) in our studies of sound change in progress (Labov, Yaeger and Steiner 1972). It should also be clear that our results strongly support the views of Chomsky and Halle on the role of contrast in phonological rule systems (Chomsky 1964, Halle 1962).

But as fruitful as the period of internal linguistic argument may have been, I am afraid that we have paid a fearful price for this withdrawal. One cannot miss the sense of isolation and alienation in many areas of linguistics today. We see linguistics alienated from phonetics, dialectology removed from linguistic theory, historical linguistics divorced from dialectology, and the study of language alienated from speech itself. We see linguists so alienated from other sciences that they have lost the lesson learned by those sciences from bitter experience: that the theorist cannot produce the theory and the data at the same time.

At a number of recent meetings I have been much encouraged by signs of a different direction. I think that linguistics is turning back to the secular world and to the real speakers in it, a world in which the systematic and rational character of language is fully revealed. We are now offered many tools for the exploration of that world which were not available to nineteenth century linguists: the instruments of acoustic analysis and acoustic recording, survey methodology,

participant-observation, as well as our own techniques of structural
analysis. We can use these tools to re-enter the world, with full
confidence that its rational character will reward our efforts to
understand it. We should have no hesitation in projecting this
understanding to past events that are no longer accessible to direct
observation. Granted that the world of everyday speech is rational,
there is no reason to think that it was any less so in the past. If
there are contradictions in the historical record, we have no doubt
that they can be resolved: the most likely route to such a resolution is through a deeper understanding of the use of language in the
ordinary world of the present. Only when we are thoroughly at home
in that everyday world, can we expect to be at home in the past.

Notes

[1]The studies reported here were carried out in connection with "A
Quantitative Study of Sound Changes in Progress," a research project
sponsored by the National Science Foundation under contract NSF GS-
3287 at the University of Pennsylvania. The instrumental spectrographic analyses were carried out with the help of Malcah Yaeger and
David Depue, at the University of Pennsylvania and Benji Wald and
Virginia Hashii at Columbia University. I am greatly indebted to
these researchers for the many insights they have contributed to the
analysis. The historical investigations have been carried out as
part of a larger project, investigating the possibilities for the
mutual interpretation of data on past and present sound changes. As
noted at several points in the text, I am greatly indebted to Geoffrey Nunberg, who has reviewed the original texts of the English
orthoepists as well as the secondary sources. The present version
has benefited from a number of critical and insightful comments of
C.-J. Bailey.

[2]The Chomsky-Halle approach to the history of English appears to be
the realization of Chomsky's approach to synchronic linguistics: that
we are concerned only with the study of the ideal speaker-listener
and that all social variation ("data-flux") is to be disregarded.
Thus Hart, Cooper, Wallis, etc. are taken as exemplars of the language in this sense, and history is written as a series of successive
models. The Saussurian Paradox can then be exploited in historical
as well as in synchronic linguistics.

[3]*Nay* is itself irregular. It is derived from OF *ei*, and should
have risen to long ē as well as *yea*. The fact that these vowels are
both lowered indicates sociolinguistic processes affecting words of
affirmation and disaffirmation, in which the vernacular favors more
open forms. Compare the variant forms of *yes* as [jeə, jɛə, jɪə] and
French *oui* as [wɛ, wæ].

[4]We must be particularly cautious about interpretations involving
/r/, since it is possible that Early Middle English speakers used a
tongue-tip /r/, flapped or trilled, especially in post-consonantal
position, and this may have less influence on neighboring vowels.
We are exploring this question with English speakers who use such an
/r/; but as noted above, the Scots patterns seem to show essentially
the same relative influence.

[5]The position of these lengthened short ĕ words poses an astonish-
ing problem for historical linguistics, and it is remarkable that
Jespersen accepted so easily the idea that their origin in short ĕ
explained their continued separation. The lengthening in open
syllables of *bĕre, pĕru*, etc. took place at least three centuries

before long ǣ rose to the ε position. Therefore at the time of the lengthening, *fear, beard,* etc. were *lower* than *bear, pear,* etc. How did it then happen that the ær words moved from this lower position to a higher position than the lengthened short *e* words without merging with them, giving us [fɪːər, bɪːərd] as against [bɛːər, pɛːər]? It is clear that the other ǣ words moved gradually up to the [ɛː] position, and were then raised to [i]. This problem is parallel to several other examples from past changes, such as the fact that Germanic long ī fell to [ai] without merging with *ei* in Yiddish and several other dialects. Even more striking is the central puzzle of the Great Vowel Shift of English: that long ī fell to [ai] without merging with M.E. *ai* as it rose to [ei]. The solution is indicated in the view of phonological space provided by our current studies of sound change in progress, in which both front and back vowels are clearly divided into peripheral and non-peripheral areas. The continued raising of long vowels takes place along the peripheral track, and vowels with less peripheral nuclei can remain quite distinct without being involved in this raising. It is reasonable to assume that lengthened short ĕ remained in a less peripheral position throughout Middle English, similar to the treatment of *where, bear,* etc. by some New York City speakers today. This view is supported by recent observations of Nunberg of the rhyme patterns in Chaucer; it appears that ĕr words are not rhymed with words from OE ǣr.

[6]The near merger of *fear* ∿ *fair,* etc., appears even more clearly in Norwich. Trudgill has independently located there the same phenomenon: many speakers report the two sounds as "the same" even though their distributions are close but distinct.

[7]I am greatly indebted to Howard Berntsen for the use of his Essex materials, and for drawing my attention to the problems involved in this merger.

[8]This difference between the Ravens may be entirely due to hearing problems. Mr. Raven is acknowledged to be hard of hearing, while his wife has no difficulty at all. Of course, hearing problems are not likely to be responsible for the general phenomenon we have been studying here, since most of the eight cases of inability to hear small differences have been with young adolescent subjects.

[9]Such small or marginal phonemic distinctions have many properties which distinguish them from normal, full distinctions: asymmetry, grammatical conditioning, idiosyncratic distribution, onomatopoetic support, as well as close phonetic approximation.

References

Bach, Emmon and Robert T. Harms. 1972 "How do languages get crazy rules?", in R. P. Stockwell and R. K. D. Macaulay (eds), *Linguistic Change and Generative Theory* (Bloomington, Ind.: Indiana University Press), 1-21.

Bellot, J. 1580 *Le Maistre D'Escole Anglois,* Theo. Spira (ed.) (Halle, 1912).

Bullokar, W. 1580 *Booke At Large for the Amendment of Orthographie for English Speech,* M. Plessow (ed.), *Fabeldichtung in England* (Berlin: Palaestra, 1906).

Cedergren, Henrietta. 1970 "Patterns of free variation: the language variable." Paper presented to Canadian Sociology and Anthropology Meeting.

Chen, Matthew. 1971 "The time dimension: contribution toward a theory of sound change," *Project on Linguistic Analysis Reports,* Second Series, No. 14 (June).

Chomsky, Noam. 1964 "The logical basis of linguistic theory," in H. Lunt (ed.), *Proceedings of the Ninth International Congress of Linguists* (The Hague: Mouton), 914-1008.

_____, and Morris Halle. 1968 *The Sound Pattern of English* (New York: Harper and Row).

Coles, C. 1674 *The Compleat English Schoolmaster* (Scolar Press facsimile, Menston, England, 1967).

Cooper, C. 1687 *The English Teacher*, B. Sundby (ed.) (Lund, 1953)

Delamothe, G. 1592 *The French Alphabet*.

Dobson, E. J. 1968 *English Pronunciation 1500-1700* (Oxford).

Florio. 1611 *Dictionary*.

Gauchat, Louis. 1905 "L'unité phonetique dans le patois d'une commune," in *Aus Romanischen Sprachen und Literaturen: Festschrift Heinreich Morf* (Halle: Max Niemeyer), 175-232.

Halle, Morris. 1962 "Phonology in a generative grammar," *Word* 18, 54-72.

Hart, John. 1569 *An Orthographie*, B. Danielsson (ed.), *John Hart's Works . . .*, Part I (Stockholm, 1955).

Haudricourt, A. G., and A. G. Juilland. 1949 *Essai pour une Histoire Structurale du Phonêtisme Français* (Paris: C. Klincksieck).

Herzog, Marvin I. 1965 *The Yiddish Language in Northern Poland: Its Geography and History (Publication 37 of the Research Center in Anthropology, Folklore, and Linguistics)* (Bloomington, Ind.)

Hoard, James E., and Clarence Sloat. To appear. "English irregular verbs," *Language*.

Jerspersen, O. 1909 *A Modern English Grammar*, Vol. 1 (Heidelberg).

_____. 1949 *A Modern English Grammar on Historical Principles*, Part 1 (London: Allen and Unwin).

Kenrick, James. 1773 Cited in A. J. Ellis, 1874, *Early English Pronunciation*, Vol. 4 (New York: Greenwood Press reprint, 1968).

King, Robert D. 1969 *Historical Linguistics and Generative Grammar* (New York: Holt, Rinehart and Winston).

Kiparsky, Paul. 1968 "Language universals and linguistic change," in E. Bach and R. Harms (eds.), *Universals in Linguistic Theory* (New York: Holt, Rinehart and Winston), 171-204.

Kökeritz, Helge. 1953 *Shakespeare's Pronunciation* (New Haven: Yale University Press).

Krohn, Robert K. 1969 "English Vowels." Unpublished dissertation (University of Michigan).

Kuryłowicz, Jerzy. 1964 "On the methods of internal reconstruction," in H. G. Lunt (ed.), *Proceedings of the Ninth International Congress of Linguists* (The Hague: Mouton), 9-31.

Labov, William. 1963 "The social motivation of a sound change," *Word* 19, 273-309.

_____. 1965 "On the mechanism of linguistic change," in J. Alatis (ed.), *Georgetown Monograph* No. 18, *Languages and Linguistics* (Washington, D.C.: Georgetown University), 91-114.

_____. 1966 *The Social Stratification of English in New York City* (Washington, D.C.: Center for Applied Linguistics).

_____, Malcah Yaeger, and Richard Steiner. 1972 *A Quantitative Study of Sound Change in Progress*. Report on National Science Foundation Contract GS-3287 (Philadelphia: U.S. Regional Survey).

311

Laneham, Robert. 1871 "Letter," in Furnwall (ed.), *Captain Cox, His Ballads and Books* (Ballad Society).

Luick, K. 1921 *Historische Grammatik der Englischen Sprache*.

Martinet, André. 1955 *Économie des Changements Phonétiques* (Berne: Francke).

Miège, G. 1688 *The English Grammar* (Menston, England: Scolar Press Facsimile, 1970).

Mulcaster, R. 1582 *The First Part of the Elementarie* (Menston, England: Scolar Press Facsimile, 1970).

Orton, Harold, and Eugen Dieth. 1970 *Survey of English Dialects*, Vol. III: *The East Midland Counties and East Anglia* (Leeds: D.J. Arnold).

Palmer, R. 1969 *Thomas Whythorne's Speech* (Copenhagen).

Price, O. 1665 *The Vocal Organ* (Menston, England: Scolar Press Facsimile, 1970).

Sapir, Edward. 1921 *Language: An Introduction to the Study of Speech* (New York: Harcourt Brace).

Shuy, Roger, Walt Wolfram and William K. Riley. 1967 *A Study of Social Dialects in Detroit*, Final Report, Project 6-1347 (Washington, D. C.: Office of Education).

Sommerfelt, Alf. 1930 "Sur la propagation de changements phonétiques," *Norsk Tidsskrift for Sprogvidenskap* 4, 76-128.

Sturtevant, Edgar. 1947 *An Introduction to Linguistic Science* (New Haven: Yale University Press).

Trudgill, P. J. 1971 *The Social Differentiation of English in Norwich*. Unpublished Edinburgh University dissertation.

Tuite, T. 1726 *The Oxford Spelling Book* (Menston, England: Scolar Press Facsimile, 1967).

Wallis, J. 1936 Excerpted and discussed in M. Lehnert, *Die Grammatik des Englischen Sprachmeisters John Wallis (1616-1703)*.

Weinreich, Uriel, William Labov and Marvin Herzog. 1968 "Empirical foundations for a theory of language change," in W. Lehmann and Y. Malkiel (eds.), *Directions for Historical Linguistics* (Austin, Texas: University of Texas Press), 97-195.

Wyld, H. C. 1936 *A History of Modern Colloquial English*, 3rd Ed. (Oxford: Basil Blackwell).

Zachrisson, R. 1913 *Pronunciation of English Vowels, 1400-1700*. (Goteborg).

15   Abductive and Deductive Change

HENNING ANDERSEN

This article takes as its point of departure an unusual phonological change
in a Czech dialect. It then proposes a model of phonological change which
would make possible the understanding of structural innovations in the
phonology of a homogeneous speech community. The model, which distinquishes
two logically different modes of change (abductive and deductive), helps
clarify the essential difference between 'internally motivated' change and
change 'induced from without'. The model uses our experience of observed
phonetic changes, and may consequently have some bearing on our understanding of the structure of phonology.

1.1. In some localities in the Litomyšl area in northeastern Bohemia,
traditional dialects as still spoken toward the end of the 19th century differed from the surrounding Czech dialects by a striking
peculiarity: the occurrence of apico-alveolar consonants /t d n/
corresponding to Proto-Slavic bilabial consonants *p *b *m in a
small and diminishing number of very common lexemes, e.g. /koutit/
(Standard Czech *koupiti*) 'buy', /tekňe/ (*pěkně*) 'nicely', /di:lej/
(*bílý*) 'white', /dežet/ (*běžeti*) 'run', /dřemeno/ (*břemeno*) 'burden',
/ni:t/ (*míti*) 'have', /nesto/ (*město*) 'town'.[1]

The Litomyšl dentals are mentioned in several 19th century works on
Czech dialectology; they were even used in literary works as late as
the 1890's to characterize folk speech in that area. But even at
that time, the dentals occurred only in the speech of the oldest
generation of speakers and were an object of ridicule, celebrated in
alliterating jeers like /ti:te ti:vo šak je s tenou/ (*Píte pivo však
je s pěnou!*) 'Drink your beer, never mind the head!' or /holoude f
troude na di:li: ni:se/ (*Holoubě v troubě na bílí míse*) 'The young
pigeon in the oven is on a white platter.' Now only a couple of
etymologically isolated lexemes preserve this peculiarity of the old
Teták dialects—as I will call them—e.g. /prati:sko/ (*prapísek*)
'door post', /didla/ (*bidla*) 'flail', if they are indeed still used.[2]
But it is clear from the evidence that at one time in the past—as
recently as the 1840's, according to Hodura (cited in Bělič 1966:40)

From *Language* 49 (1973), 765-93. Reprinted by permission of
Henning Andersen and the Linguistic Society of America.

—the dialects in question regularly had dentals as reflexes of
Proto-Slavic labials in certain environments.

1.2. The phonological change by which this peculiarity arose is in
some respects—at least superficially—of an unusual type. Nevertheless, it has not attracted much attention. Jakobson [1938] 1962:
275) cites it as an example of the change of grave to acute consonants before acute vowels, i.e. as a parallel to the palatalization
of velar consonants before front vowels. But this is an error; the
Teták change is not a case of regressive assimilation, as will be
shown below. Incidentally, Jakobson makes no attempt to elucidate
the process of change involved.

The Teták dialects have been discussed by Utěšený (1960:175ff.),
who also fails to deal with the interesting question of how the
change of labials to dentals actually came about. But he does
classify it correctly among the changes that led to the complete
loss of phonemic sharping in almost all dialects of Czech.

Most recently the Teták change has been discussed by Bělič in an
article devoted specifically to the problem of the process of change.
As Bělič sees it, this problem is one of articulatory phonetics, to
be solved by constructing a series of hypothetical intermediate
steps which would make it possible to conceive of the change from
the original sharped labials to the later dentals as a gradual progression, rather than as the abrupt shift which the lack of articulatory contiguity between labials and dentals seems to indicate.
Accordingly he posits a sequence of complicated articulatory innovations—in part with uncertain auditory effects—all of which are
unmotivated by any force other than their originator's determination
to convert labials into dentals by gradual articulatory steps.

Bělič's account of the Teták change has a number of factual and
methodological shortcomings which will not be detailed here. But it
would fail as an explanation even without these, for the concept of
phonological change on which it is based is unrealistic. Bělič
apparently assumes that a phoneme is definable as a complex of articulatory gestures, and that each stage in a phonological development
is derived from the preceding one by the language learners' more or
less successfully imitating the articulation of their elders. He
ignores the fact that language is a system of auditory signs, and
that language learners acquire the phonology of their language by
ear, not by visual inspection of articulatory movements. Further,
his concept of change makes no allowance for the fact that the
speech of each individual speaker is directly related to only one
thing, namely to that speaker's internalized grammar.

If we wish to understand how changes such as that of sharped labials to dentals in the Teták dialects come about, we need a model of
linguistic change which takes this essential fact into consideration.
We cannot use Bělič's physiological model. Nor can we use the more
recent model espoused by proponents of 'systematic phonemics' (e.g.
Halle 1962, King 1969), which views linguistic change simply as
grammar change. Viewed in the light of that concept, the Teták
phenomenon could be described very succinctly as a 'rule additon'.
To paraphrase King (108), a rule changing certain labials to dentals
was added to the speakers' grammar; this changed certain labials to
dentals. But this concept would provide no answer to the question
of where the speakers of these dialects got the rule which they
supposedly added to their grammar. Judging from King's exposition
(e.g., p. 85), one would have to surmise that they conceived it
spontaneously.[3] Nor would this model of change suggest an answer
to the question of why the speakers would add such a rule. Indeed,
this theory can do nothing with the Teták change—or any other
phonological change—except restate the diachronic correspondences
to which it gave rise (cf. Andersen 1972:12-13).

What is needed is a model of phonological change which recognizes,
on the one hand, that the verbal output of any speaker is determined
by the grammar he has internalized, and on the other, that any
speaker's internalized grammar is determined by the verbal output
from which it has been inferred (cf. Figure 1). The model that is
needed must show how phonological innovations can arise in a homogeneous speech community (in the sense of Labov 1970:70), given
these limitations.

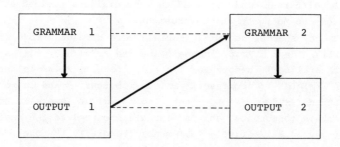

Figure 1. The essential links in the transmission of language
from generation to generation (heavylines) and the pseudo-connections
discussed by Bělič and King (dotted lines).

I will propose such a model in the following pages. To illustrate
the considerations motivating different aspects of this model, I will
try to give an account of the development of the original sharped
labials in the Teták dialects, explaining how the Teták peculiarity
arose and how it was eventually eliminated. But in order to do this,
I must first, however briefly, sketch the historical and geographical
context of the Teták innovation.

2.1. The historical background of the Teták change is the phonological system of Old Czech in the 1200's, which contained an opposition
sharped vs. plain, phonemic in dental consonants (/t, d, n, s, z,
t d n s z/) and labial consonants (/p, b, m, p b m/—as well as in
liquids and glides, which for simplicity I will disregard in the
following. This stage in the development of Czech can be established
with a high degree of confidence on the basis of historical and comparative evidence, and is amply reflected in the spelling conventions
of Old Czech.

During the period from around 1300 to the end of the 1400's, to
judge by the textual evidence, the majority of Czech dialects lost
the phonemic opposition sharped vs. plain. There is some textual
evidence that the opposition was lost earlier in dentals than in
labials. This evidence can be correlated with the fact that Czech
dialects show great uniformity in their reflexes of sharped dentals,
but considerable diversity in their reflexes of the sharped labials.
Sharped dentals simply lost their sharping; cf. OCz. /t,eb,e/ 'thee',
/ten/ 'that', /d,en,/ 'day', /dence/ 'bottom', /vz,al/ 'took',
/rzal/ 'neighed' and Modern Cz. /tebe/, /ten/, /den/, /dence/,
/vzal/, /rzal/. Sharped labials, on the other hand, developed differently in different dialects, and in many dialects yielded different reflexes depending on the environment.

In Old Czech, sharped and plain labials were opposed before /i/
(e.g. /m,ili:/ 'dear', /miš/ 'mouse'), before /u/ (/b,u/ '(I) strike',
/budu/ '(I) will be'), before /e/ (/b,eře/ 'takes', /bez/ 'alder'),
before /a/ (/m,a:stv i/ 'confuse', /ma:slo/ 'butter'), and in word-
final position (/xudi:m,/ 'bad, instr. sg.', /di:m/ 'smoke'). Before
/ě/ and certain consonants, sharped labials occurred to the exclusion
of plain (e.g. /p,ět,/ 'five', /b,řemeno/ 'burden'). Before /o/ and
certain other consonants, only plain labials were found.

Leaving the Teták dialects aside for a moment, we can sum up the
development of sharped labials as follows. In all dialects of Czech,
the opposition of sharped vs. plain labials was lost before /e/,
before consonant, and in word-final position, sharped labials becoming plain. Subsequently, phonemic sharping was lost in labial consonants in still other environments, but it was lost in different

ways in different dialects. Either sharped labials lost their sharping and merged with the corresponding plain consonants, or the
sharped labials changed into sequences of (plain) labial + /j/. In
the former case, the phonemic distinction of sharped and plain labials was simply lost; in the latter, it was replaced by another distinction. In various dialects of Czech, these two possibilities
were realized to different extents depending on the following vowel.
The dialects apparently fell into six types according to their reflexes of OCz. /p,i p,ě p,a/ (types A-F in Table 1), to which we may
add the Teták dialects (type G), in which sharped labials changed to
dentals before /i ě ř/. This fairly clear picture has been partly
obscured by a subsequent change of /ě/, which in Old Czech probably
was an [ie] diphthong, into /je/ in most dialects.[4]

We will not be concerned with all this diversity, however. The
Teták dialects which interest us, were spoken in an area of type A,
in which /ě/ was monophthongized and merged with /e/. (These are
the dialects mentioned in fn. 2 as the Peták dialects.) In our
further discussion of the Teták dialects, it will be useful to contrast their development with that of the Peták dialects that surrounded them.

A	B	C	D	E	F	G
pi	pji	pji	pji	pi	pi	ti
pě	pě	pje	pje	pje	pě	te
pa	pa	pa	pja	pja	pja	pa

Table 1. The reflexes of Old Czech sharped labials before OCz.
/i ě a/ in different dialects, before the change of /ě/ to /je/.

2.2. In discussing a phonemic change such as the one before us, it
is important to understand, first of all, that phonemes are not the
smallest units of phonological structure. The phoneme is a syntagm
(or construction) whose ultimate constituents are phonemic 'feature
values'—or, speaking traditionally, terms of phonological oppositions. The phoneme differs radically from other syntagmatic structures of language, such as the complex work or the phrase, by being
a simultaneous rather than a sequential combination of signs; but it
still shares the essential organizing principles with its isomorphic
counterparts on other linguistic levels. In the [—voiced, —continuous, +grave, —compact, +consonantal, —vocalic] segment /p/ of
Czech, each of the constituent phonological terms is a member of a
minimal (binary) paradigm and—like each of the adjectives present
in a noun phrase like a *small, heavy object*—implies the absence
of its opposite. And just as the adjectives are subordinated

to the substantive in this noun phrase, so the phonological terms
which constitute a phoneme present a hypotactic rather than a para-
tactic structure, in which any higher-ranking immediate constituent
is of more central importance in the syntagm than the corresponding
lower-ranking immediate constituent.

An essential fact about the terms of phonological oppositions, by
which they differ from other linguistic signs, is their identity of
meaning. The meaning of any phonological term is that it denotes
'otherness' (cf. Jakobson [1939] 1962:304). This has the important
consequence that phonological terms cannot be synthetic signs. In
the lexicon, each morpheme is a single signans having as its signatum a complex of semantic feature values. In inflectional morphology,
grammatical feature values may be expressed either asynthetically or
synthetically: the -s of Eng. *sheep's*, which merely means 'poss-
essive', and the -s of *thinks*, which means 'third person, singular,
present, indicative', illustrate these two possible signans—signatum
relations. In phonology, on the other hand, only one of these exists:
each phonological term has one and only one diacritic function.[5]
Still, the very fact that phonological terms, although asynthetic
and relational, must be manifested by simultaneous, concrete acoustic
attributes may give rise to ambiguities which typologically—by the
kinds of resolutions they allow—are very similar to the ambiguities
presented by synthetic morphemes.

Let us consider the situation in a language with phonemic sharping
in dental and labial consonants, like Old Czech. In most languages,
each diffuse consonant is a syntagm of phonological terms one of
whose constituents defines the tonality of the segment. In a language like Old Czech, this constituent, in turn, is a hypotactic
syntagm constituted by terms of two tonality oppositions, one of them
defining the basic tonality of the consonant as high [—grave] or low
[+grave], the other qualifying its tonality as heightened [+sharped]
or not heightened [—sharped]. Such a simultaneous two-constituent
syntagm demands that the language learner, who has to interpret its
acoustic manifestations, make a number of decisions. He has to
decide how many constituents the syntagm has, i.e. how many phonological oppositions are involved—one, two, or more. If he identifies it as a two-constituent syntagm, he must still decide which of
the constituents is superordinate and which subordinate. Furthermore
he must decide whether the syntagm is simultaneous or sequential. A
wrong decision on any of these points, it should be clear, is tantamount to a structural innovation.[6]

The loss of phonemic sharping in the dialects of Old Czech which
we are concerned with was the outcome of several structural innova-

tions in which two-constituent tonality syntagms were reinterpreted as having only one constituent.

	I	II	III	
Heightened high tonality	t,	t	t	High tonality
Non-heightened high tonality	t			
Heightened low tonality	p,	p,	p	Low tonality
Non-heightened low tonality	p	p		

Table 2. Tonality distinctions in diffuse consonants at three different stages in the development of the Peták dialects.

	I	II	III	
Heightened high tonality	t,	t	t	High tonality
Non-heightened high tonality	t			
Heightened low tonality	p,	p,		
Non-heightened low tonality	p	p	p	Low tonality

Table 3. Tonality distinctions in diffuse consonants at three different stages in the development of the Teták dialects.

2.3. In the Peták dialects (type A in Table 1), tonality syntagms in diffuse consonants were reduced twice, first in the [—grave] consonants, later in the [+grave] consonants (cf. Table 2).

In the Teták dialects, too, there were two reductions of tonality syntagms in diffuse consonants, the first identical to that of the Peták dialects, the second having a different outcome (cf. Table 3).

The reason it was possible for the Peták and Teták dialects to reduce their tonality syntagms in different ways is to be found in the ambiguous character of the acoustic manifestations of these syntagms. The acoustic dimension of frequency is a continuum which the language learner has to bisect—in different ways in different environments—in order to discriminate correctly between the [+grave] and the [—grave] phonemes of his language. Within this continuum, the manifestations of heightened low tonality fall in an intermediate range—again varying according to environment. If these manifestations are not analysed correctly in their relation to non-heightened low tonality, they must be interpreted either as manifestations of simply low tonality (i.e. as realizations of undifferentiated labials), as happened in the Peták dialects, or as manifestations of simply high tonality (i.e. as realizations of dentals), as in the Teták dialects.[7]

319

The Teták change has a parallel in the early Latin change of initial *$d\underset{\sim}{u}$ (and perhaps of initial *$t\underset{\sim}{u}$) to b (and p). This is not an exact parallel, for it involves a different phonological opposition; but this only makes it more instructive. We may assume for early Latin (4th century B.C.) a three-way distinction in initial diffuse stops—simple dentals, e.g. *tegō* 'cover', *doceō* 'teach'; labialized dentals, e.g. */t°ariēs/ 'wall' (if *pariēs* is indeed cognate with Lith. *tvorà* 'fence'), */d°ellum/ (archaic *duellum*, classical *bellum*) 'war', */d°is/ (archaic *duis*, classical *bis*) 'twice', */d°onus/ (archaic *duonoro*, gen. pl., classical *bonus*) 'good'; and labials, e.g. *pater* 'father', *bibō* 'drink'—a set of distinctions based on the phonemic oppositions of gravity and flatting forming simultaneous two-constituent syntagms as in Table 4.[8]

The change by which this three-way distinction was reduced to a two-way distinction is a clear typological parallel to the Teták change. Since the manifestations of lowered high tonality are intermediate between the extremes of high tonality and low tonality, they are potentially subject to misinterpretation as manifestations either of simple high tonality or—as in our Latin example—of simple low tonality.

Parallels to the Teták change can be found in the development of vowel systems as well. Consider the change by which the rounded

	I	II	
Non-lowered high tonality	t	t	High tonality
Lowered high tonality	t°	p	Low tonality
Low tonality	p		

Table 4. Tonality distinctions in diffuse consonants in archaic and classical Latin.

	I	II	
Non-lowered high tonality	ī	ī	High tonality
Lowered high tonality	ȳ		
Low tonality	ū	ū	Low tonality

Table 5. Tonality distinctions in diffuse non-compact vowels in Old English and Middle English.

front vowels of Old English merged with their unrounded counterparts (Table 5). As a matter of fact, such reductions of two-constituent tonality syntagms are far from uncommon in vowel systems. The

English change (cf. Brunner 1960:253) has exact counterparts in the development of Greek, Czech, High German dialects, Danish dialects, and elsewhere.

3.1. We have examined the phonological aspects of the Teták change and have established that it is typologically identical to the superficially different change in the Peták dialects, and that both these changes belong to a type of change which is common. Furthermore we have seen that this type of change can be understood as motivated by the nature of the acoustic manifestations of the phonemic feature relations which the learner of the language has to analyse.

However, it is one thing to understand how a learner might reinterpret a complex of phonemic distinctions at some stage in the process of acquiring his language; it is another thing to explain how the phonetic consequences of such a reinterpretation could be acceptable to the speech community. If the changes examined were mere changes in the distribution of non-phonemic features, one might suppose that they were simply not noted by the speakers. But each of the changes discussed involved the loss of a phonemic distinction, and hence entailed the distortion of the phonemic shape of words, and the creation of homonyms. One would expect that phonemic differences between a learner's forms and those of his elders would be noted—if not by the learner, then at least by the bearers of the received norms—and that an attempt would be made to eliminate such differences. After all, any member of a speech community who considers himself responsible for a child's linguistic acculturation will routinely correct the child's deviations from the norms, and young children appear genuinely anxious to imitate the speech of their models. Can one suppose that these innovations were not censured, or that the learners who introduced them did not heed the corrections?

Hardly. But it would seem that, when a learner becomes aware of differences between his speech and the speech of those he considers his models, there are two ways in which he can adjust his grammar. He can revise his analysis of the linguistic units in question so that his grammar will naturally produce the desired output. Or he can devise ad-hoc rules to cover up the inadequacy of his analysis. Let us consider a concrete example.

3.2. If we assume that a language learner whose phonology does not include the phonemic feature sharped vs. plain would naturally perceive sharped labial consonants as dentals, we may suppose that, at a certain point in the history of the Teták dialects, children's speech came to be characterized by dentals corresponding to the sharped labials of their elders. This deviation might be tolerated

in the speech of small children; but at some point in their development, children would presumably become aware (perhaps be made aware)
of their deviant pronunciation, and would try to adjust it. Some
might achieve this by re-analysing the tonality relations manifested
in the received pronunciation, revising their lexical representations
and morphophonemic rules accordingly. Others might not succeed in
re-analysing the phonemic feature relations, but would adapt their
pronunciation to the norm by formulating what will be called an
adaptive rule (A-rule; see further below), applicable to certain
lexical items and to the output of certain morphophonemic rules.
Thus, at an earlier time, all speakers of the dialect would have an
underlying sharped labial stop in /p,i:vo/ (St. Cz. *pivo*) 'beer',
realized as [p,i:vo]; but at a certain point some speakers would have
an underlying dental stop in /ti:vo/, which—thanks to the adaptive
rule (roughly of the form [t] → [p,] in morphemes marked [+A-rule])
—would be realized as [p,i:vo].

Superficially, speakers of both categories would adhere to the
traditional pronunciation, but they would evaluate children's speech
differently. While speakers with underlying sharped labials would
consider the childish dentals a distortion, speakers with underlying
dentals would consider them a natural simplification and would very
likely be more tolerant of them. An increased tolerance in the
speech community toward this deviation would naturally allow children
to acquire the received pronunciation later, and in time more and
more speakers would derive it from underlying dentals by means of an
adaptive rule rather than from underlying sharped labials. Furthermore, for the speakers who adjusted their pronunciation to the received norms late, the adaptive rule which they had to apply to
speak like their elders would naturally be associated with the difference in age. Instead of being an obligatory rule, motivated
solely by the need to produce acceptable surface forms, it would
become a stylistically motivated rule, used in some speech situations,
but suspendable in others. A rule of this kind would tend to be
eliminated. First, as a phonostylistic rule, it would be used only
in certain speech situations, and even in these would not be simply
obligatory, but applicable with greater or lesser consistency depending perhaps on the degree of formality of the speech situation, on
the character of the speech content etc. Second, since its domain
would be defined in terms of individual lexemes specifically marked
as subject to it, the number of lexemes to which it applied would
tend to be reduced with the passage of time (cf. Andersen 1969b:
826-7 and fn. 22)

We can picture the final stage in this process as a situation in
which all speakers would have underlying dentals for the original

sharped labials. All would normally pronounce these as dentals, but
members of the oldest age group might produce them as labials
(sharped?) in a very formal style, at least in some of the lexemes
that originally had sharped labials, perhaps hypercorrectly in some
that did not. The essential phases in the development which has been
outlined can be represented schematically as in Table 6.

I	II	III
/p,i:vo/	/ti:vo/	/ti:vo/
I-rule: /p,/ → [p,]	I-rule: /t/ → [t]	I-rule: /t/ → [t]
	(A-rule: [t] → [p,]/ $\begin{bmatrix} \underline{\quad\quad} \\ +\text{A-rule} \end{bmatrix}$)	
[p,i:vo]	Style 1: [p,i:vo]	[ti:vo]
	Style 2: [ti:vo]	

   Table 6. Three stages in the development sketched in §3.2, showing the derivation of surface forms from underlying representations
by implementation rules (I-rules, cf. §6.3) and adaptive rules
(A-rules).

3.3. In the last few pages I have outlined a model of phonological
change, which, it would appear, overcomes the deficiencies of some
of the traditional models by taking into account the essential
elements of reality disregarded, in different ways, in the conceptions of change mentioned in §1.2.
   The assumptions on which this model is based are (1) that innovation in the phonological structure of a language (symbolized by the
different underlying representations /p,i:vo/ and /ti:vo/ in Table 6)
can only be explained on the basis of ambiguities in the corpus of
utterances from which the new grammar is inferred; and (2) that
observed phonetic innovations in a language (symbolized by the forms
[p,i:vo] and [ti:vo] in Table 6) can be explained only as manifestations of the phonological structure of the language.[9] These assumptions, which I will try to justify below, are tantamount to recognizing two different modes of change, for which I propose the terms
abductive innovation and deductive innovation.[10] Let us briefly
examine the logical basis of this model of linguistic change.

4.1. It is usual to distinguish two modes of inference, induction
and deduction. Both modes operate with the three propositions that
constitute a syllogism: the rule or law(e.g. 'All men are mortal'),
the case (e.g. 'Socrates is a man'), and the result (e.g. 'Socrates
is mortal'). While inductive inference proceeds from observed cases
and results to establish a law, deduction applies a law to a case

and predicts a result. These two modes of inference share two important characteristics: first, the conclusion asserts nothing which is not given in the two premises; second—and this is a natural corollary—if the premises are true, the conclusion is certain to be true.[11]

There is a third mode of inference, termed abduction by Charles S. Peirce, which is often confused with induction. Abduction proceeds from an observed result, invokes a law, and infers that something may be the case. E.g., given the fact that Socrates is dead, we may relate this fact to the general law that all men are mortal and guess that Socrates was a man. This inference differs essentially from the conclusion reached by inductive and deductive reasoning. Although it, too, is based strictly on its premises, it is not necessarily true, even though its premises are: if we have matched the given result with the wrong law, our conclusion may be false.

The law to which an abductive inference appeals may be an already established truth; or it may be a new, tentative generalization. In either event, it will serve as an explanation of the observed fact only provided it can be validated—i.e. only if the inferred case is found to be true, and if similar cases are consistently linked to similar results. The process of probing the validity of a hypothesis is the business of deduction and induction. Deduction tests the hypothesis by predicting what results the law entails in particular cases. Induction tests it by matching it to new observed cases and results.[12]

The conclusions reached by abductive inference afford none of the security offered by induction and deduction. Since abduction inference goes beyond what is given to suggest that something may be the case, it is always a weak argument, sometimes a reasonable guess, but often a mere surmise. Still, abduction justly holds the prominent place in a theory of scientific method which Peirce accorded it, for it alone of the three modes of inference can originate new ideas; it alone gives us an understanding of things. The experience of facts prompts the inquirer to suggest an explanatory hypothesis, and predicted experience strengthens the hypothesis; but it is the hypothesis, not experience, that makes the real contribution to the progress of science (Reilly, 38). 'Every item of science came originally from conjecture, which has only been pruned down by experience. . . . The entire matter of our works of solid science consists of conjectures checked by experience' (Peirce 1966:320).

It is interesting that Peirce emphasizes the essential identity of the processes involved in the abductive inference and the perceptual judgment, noting that one shades into the other without any sharp line of demarcation. Here is how he describes the perceptual abduction (1940:305): 'A well-recognized kind of object, M, has for its ordinary predicates P_1, P_2, P_3, etc., indistinctly recognized. The suggesting object, S, has these same predicates, P_1, P_2, P_3, etc. Hence, S is of the kind M.' The similarity between this process and the process by which a law and an observed result serve as basis for the inference of a case is obvious, and it is not a merely superficial similarity (cf. Reilly, 46ff.) It is clear that our first premises, the perceptual judgments, may be regarded as nothing but the most extreme type of abductive inferences.

4.2. It was natural for Peirce, the scientist and philosopher, to concentrate his attention on the formation of explanatory hypotheses in science and the nature of the perceptual judgment, the most sophisticated and the most elementary activities of the human mind. But between these two extremes, as Peirce was well aware, lies the whole range of abductive reasoning based on 'common sense', the practical application of previous experience in the evaluation of everyday experiences, which is the substance of our day-to-day lives. Between them, too, lies what is the most important abductive activity in the life of the individual, the acquisition of a cultural pattern —including, in particular, the formation of a grammar—based on the observed behavior of the other members of the community in which he is brought up.

In acquiring his language, a learner observes the verbal activity of his elders, construes it as a 'result'—as the output of a grammar —and guesses at what that grammar might be. He has little positive knowledge or experience, comparable to what we use in our everyday abductive reasoning, to provide his major premise in this process. What he has, however, is a more reliable set of 'laws', which he shares with all members of his species, viz. the properties of his constitution that completely determine the nature of linguistic structure, and hence the relation between a grammar and its output. It is one such property, e.g., which makes the learner who is faced with sound perceptions ranging over a frequency continuum analyse these perceptions in terms of binary oppositions—as shown in §2.3— rather than learning them as a continuum and reproducing them un-analysed, as a parrot would.

As he builds up his grammar, in his attempt to explain the utterances he has observed, the learner constantly tests its validity by use of both induction and deduction. He checks new utterances produced by his models against the relevant parts of his grammar, to see whether these new data ('results') can be reconciled with the linguistic structure he has formulated (the posited 'case') in conformity with the 'laws' of language; this is induction. If they cannot, there can be only one reason: his grammar is inadequate. He will then be prompted to make new abductions to make the grammar conform to all the observed facts. E.g., hearing diffuse consonants in three discernible ranges within the frequency continuum, the learner who has bisected this continuum into high tonality and low tonality will determine by induction that his analysis is deficient. As he attempts a new analysis, he may view the three frequency ranges as manifestations of two binary oppositions, or he may view the intermediate frequency range as derived from one of the extreme ranges by an A-rule (cf. §3.2).

This cyclical application of induction and abduction, by which a grammar is built up, is a goal-directed process, analogous in all essentials to the teleological models described by Miller, Galanter & Pribram (1960:29ff.), and termed TOTE units (for Test-Operate-Test-Exit). Induction corresponds to the Test phase, abduction to the Operate phase; the process is repeated until induction provides no further cause for abduction, and the Exit phase is reached. It is worth noting that the language learner's goal is the formation not of a specific ('true' or 'optimal') grammar, but only of a grammar which in some way conforms to the observed data (cf. fn. 15). Inductive inference naturally tends to eliminate errors that may arise through abduction. But it may serve merely to minimize the effects of such errors (as was seen in §3.2), and is actually no safeguard against abductive innovation.

As he builds up his grammar, the learner listens to the speech of his models; and he also speaks, testing his grammar by using it to produce utterances in conformity with the laws of language. This is deduction, the process by which an abductive inference is evaluated on the basis of the consequences it entails. If his analysis is deficient, the learner's utterances may cause misunderstandings or elicit corrections, which may prompt him to revise his analysis. This part of grammar formation, too, is a goal-directed process describable in terms of the TOTE model. Deduction corresponds to the Test phase. But the Operate phase, which follows when deduction produces negative feedback, is itself a TOTE unit, consisting of induction-abduction-induction, like the one described in the preceding paragraph. In other words, the process of deductive testing includes induction, and can be described as a TOTE unit with an embedded TOTE unit (cf. Miller, Galanter & Pribram, 32-7).[13]

For instance, having abductively interpreted the frequency continuum (over which the diffuse consonants of his language range) in terms of the single binary opposition of high vs. low tonality, the learner produces forms implementing this opposition—according to the universal laws of phonetics—as a distinction between dental and labial consonants. If some of his models have not two, but three distinct frequency ranges in their diffuse consonants, the learner may be corrected; and the correct forms, which induction tells him are irreconcilable with his grammar, will trigger new abductions. Suppose he hypothesizes that the intermediate frequency range is derived from one of the terms of his single tonality opposition by an A-rule applicable to the lexemes he has pronounced wrong. Renewed deductive testing will permit him to produce these lexemes in accordance with the norms, and he will have no reason to suspect that his analysis is 'wrong'. For his purpose—and everybody else's—it will be adequate; cf. Fig. 2.

5.1. We have seen above that the conception of language acquisition assumed for our model of phonological change involves processes that are basic to all activities of the human mind. We could now return to the discussion of phonological change which we interrupted in §3.3, and comment on some aspects of abductive and deductive change not illustrated by the Teták change, but which should at least be mentioned. However, we are not quite finished with the development of the original sharped labials in the Teták dialects.

We have examined in some detail the change by which the Old Czech sharped labials changed to dentals in the 1300's. Five hundred years later, in a change that perhaps occurred over three or four generations, almost all traces of the Teták peculiarity were eliminated from the dialects. This was a very different change from the earlier one. The change in the 1300's was an <u>evolutive change</u>, i.e. a change entirely explainable in terms of the linguistic system that gave rise to it. The more recent change was an <u>adaptive change</u>, i.e. a change not explainable without reference to factors outside the linguistic system in question. The extraneous factor in this change was the Peták dialects, with whom the Teták speakers came into closer contact as communication improved during the 19th century.

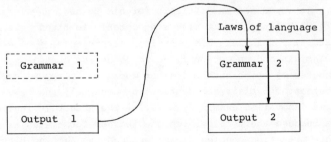

Figure 2. Abduction and deduction in the acquisition of language.

Evolutive and adaptive change both involve abductive and deductive innovations, but they do so in essentially different ways, and it is therefore instructive to contrast the two changes through which the Teták dialects have gone.

5.2. Let us first note that, with respect to the diffuse consonants, there were no structural differences between the Teták and the Peták dialects, but only a difference in the lexical and morphophonemic distribution of dentals and labials. Both types of dialects had dentals for original dentals and labials for original plain labials. But the Teták dialects had dentals for original sharped labials, where the Peták dialects had labials.

The Teták speaker who came in contact with the world outside his native village would soon discover that outsiders had a different distribution of labials and dentals, and that he could adapt his speech to theirs by replacing dentals with labials in certain morphemes.[14] Note that the mere realization that the outsiders' speech was different is an inductive inference; but the A-rule, by which the speaker would replace certain dentals with labials, amounts to an abductive guess as to how this difference might be produced.[15]

During the 19th century, as far as we can judge, the Teták peculiarity had come to be regarded by Teták speakers as a symbol of social inferiority. We know that they were exposed to ridicule from outsiders, and apparently they accepted the outsiders' evaluation of their peculiarity as something best suppressed. In growing numbers, they acquired the A-rule and the necessary lexical markings to produce the more widely acceptable pronunciation; they would then use these adaptive means not only when speaking to outsiders, but also increasingly among themselves in speech situations requiring a style comparable to the one used with outsiders.

A learner whose models pronounced certain lexemes with both dentals and labials would have to decide which to take as the underlying consonants. It would not be difficult for him to see, however, that the doublets with labials were always acceptable to his models; so he would naturally formulate his phonology accordingly, i.e. with underlying labials and an optional A-rule to derive dentals. Note that the process by which such a learner would reinterpret the lexical distribution of labials and dentals is completely analogous to the abductive innovation examined in §3.2. The abductive innovation is possible because the A-rule which the learner formulates as part of his reinterpretation enables him to produce the same doublet forms that he has heard from his models. As a consequence, his abduction will not be invalidated by deductive testing.

Once native Teták speakers were producing the socially preferred
labials directly from underlying labials, the regular use of the
local peculiarity would quickly decline, becoming limited to the
speech of old people. This is the situation attested from the 1890's.

5.3. The foregoing brief account of the decline and fall of the
Teták peculiarity makes it possible to define several differences
between evolutive change and adaptive change. We will note first two
differences in degree of complexity.

As we have seen, an evolutive change can be described as a single
abductive innovation followed by deductive ones, where the abductive
innovation consists in a reinterpretation of the phonological structure, compensated for by an A-rule; the deductive innovations that
follow gradually permit the new interpretation of the structure to
be manifested, as the domain of the A-rule is curtailed. An adaptive
change, by contrast, necessarily involves two abductive innovations.
The first introduces the A-rule(s) needed to adjust the speaker's
output to new norms; this has immediate overt consequences, in that
the speaker's pronunciation changes. The second abductive innovation
occurs when learners of the language take this observable output at
face value; this too has immediate overt consequences (though it does
not result in any change), since it produces the more highly valued
pronunciation. If it involves the formulation of an A-rule, as in
our example (cf. §5.2), that rule is stylistically restricted from
the very beginning: it is not needed to make the output conform to
the received norms, but only to produce what the learner evaluates
as deviations from these norms.

Adaptive change is more complex than evolutive change in one other
respect. An abductive innovation in the evolution of a single phonological system can be entirely explained as motivated by ambiguities
in the corpus of utterances from which the system has been inferred.
As was seen in §4.2, the premises from which a grammar is inferred
in the normal course of events are an observed corpus of utterances
and the laws of language. In adaptive change, by contrast, the
speaker who adjusts his pronunciation to new norms necessarily interprets these norms in terms of the phonological structure of his own
grammar. In this way the premises from which he infers his A-rule(s)
are (1) the corpus of utterances embodying the new norms; (2) his
internalized phonological structure; and (3), one step removed, the
laws of language, to which his own phonological structure already
conforms, and to which his A-rule(s) must conform.

The fact that adaptive change is a more complex phenomenon than
evolutive change must be considered in forming hypotheses about
attested changes in phonology. It means that, of two alternative

explanations of a change—one of which interprets the change as
evolutive, the other as adaptive—the former should be valued more
highly for its greater simplicity.

Let us note finally the very different relations between phonetic
and structural innovations in evolutive and adaptive change. In
evolutive change as described here, it is a reinterpretation of the
phonological structure that motivates a phonetic innovation. In
adaptive change, the reinterpretation of the phonological structure
is the result of a phonetic innovation.

The case discussed here exemplifies one particular type of adaptive
change—change resulting from language contact—and I should perhaps
conclude this section by pointing out that the definition of adaptive
change suggested above (§5.1) is wide enough to comprise other kinds
of change where an innovation in a linguistic system might be said
to be induced by factors outside that system. Such extraneous factors may be linguistic, as in cases of language contact. But they
may also be extralinguistic. A change in the material or spiritual
culture of a speech community may motivate innovations in the semantic structure of its language. Similarly, though seldom, the adop-
tion of a new custom, like the use of labrets, may motivate innovations in the phonological structure. When a linguistic code changes
in response to any circumstance which is extraneous to the code, one
may speak of that circumstance as the cause of the linguistic
change. But the causality involved is not efficient causality, but
final causality. It is this goal-directedness which our term
'adaptive change' is intended to reflect.

6.1. Now that we have seen examples of both evolutive and adaptive
change, we can continue our discussion of the abductive-deductive
model of change which has been proposed.

The model implies the assumption that a language learner makes
abductions of two sorts in formulating a phonology. He abduces a
phonological structure, which one may conceive of as a structured
system comprising all the synchronically motivated rules for the
combination and concatenation of phonemic and non-phonemic feature
values. (I will make some further remarks on the character of this
phonological structure below, §6.3). And he abduces a set of
adaptive rules which adjust his pronunciation to the received norms
in all respects where these norms cannot be derived from the phonological structure he has set up. These A-rules are formulated in
terms of the phonological structure, and hence are subordinate to
it; but they form an additive system which can be elaborated and
revised throughout the speaker's life.[16]

There can be no doubt that our notion of the A-rule reflects reality. Many speakers of English are capable of producing anything
from a pseudo-Gallic flavor to a real French pronunciation of lexemes
which are marked 'French' in their lexical representation.[17] Most
educated speakers of English are able to derive a [x], probably from
an underlying /k/, in lexemes or names of Scottish, German, or Slavic
provenience. Some native speakers of General American English—among
them some radio announcers—are able to simulate a more prestigious
dialect by inserting a [i̯] in words like *duty* [di̯uti] and *new* [ni̯u],
and sometimes in words like *noon* [ni̯un] and *noodle* [ni̯udl̩] as well.
These are rather crude and obvious examples suggesting the reality of
A-rules. Much more important, though somewhat more subtle, are the
means with which speakers of any language are able to adjust their
pronunciation to different speech situations, to match (to whatever
extent they consider appropriate) the stylistic level of their interlocutors. It is A-rules, apparently, that account for the complex
linguistic behavior, so well discussed by Labov 1966; Weinreich,
Labov & Herzog 1968; and Labov 1970.

From the examples just given, and from the discussion in §3.2, it
is clear that A-rules can apply in domains defined in terms of individual lexemes. In this respect they resemble morphophonemic rules.
Like them, A-rules also lack the intrinsic, structural motivation
which characterizes the pronunciation rules that are part of the
phonological structure; hence A-rules are unproductive (cf. Andersen
1969b:826-7). But unlike morphophonemic rules, which describe
alternations between phonemes of a language, A-rules may derive
simultaneous and sequential combinations of phonetic feature values
which are not provided for in the phonological structure. Our
example of this was the [p,b,m,] derived from underlying /t d n/ when
the Teták peculiarity originated. Another example, closer at hand,
is provided by the New Yorkers whose 'ingliding system of vowels
shows a seven-membered series. . . in their most formal speech. . .
but produced in a most irregular and unreliable manner', but whose
most spontaneous speech will yield a very regular system of four
members (Weinreich, Labov & Herzog, 134-5). Like the Teták change,
the change by which the vowel system of the New York dialect has been
simplified is 'a regular and rational process of linguistic evolution' (Labov 1966:559ff.) Although the abductive innovation has taken
place, and lexemes like *beard, bared, bad* are strictly homonymous in
their underlying phonological representation, the speakers are still
able to render the traditional norms their due by pronouncing such
lexemes differently (though not consistently so) in their most formal
style.

6.2. We have seen that an abductive innovation may involve both the phonological structure and the system of A-rules. As we now proceed to consider deductive innovations, we may begin by noting that it is necessary to distinguish two basic categories of innovations by which the relations defining the phonological structure of a language may be manifested in its phonetic output. One of these categories of innovations concerns the phonological structure; the other concerns A-rules. Let us consider first the latter type, which is the one exemplified in this article.

Since A-rules enable the individual speaker to adhere to the received norms of his speech community even if his phonological structure does not correspond to these norms, they serve the essential end of ensuring relative uniformity of usage, regardless of differences in phonological structure among the grammars of the speakers. In diachronic terms, this means that even though 'grammar change is abrupt'—or, more accurately, structurally different consecutive grammars are discrete—A-rules ensure continuity in usage by permitting structural innovations to be reflected only gradually in the speech of the community.

An A-rule provides in three ways for a gradual manifestation of the structural innovation that has made its formulation necessary. First, the domain of the rule may be gradually curtailed, so that the rule is applied to fewer and fewer lexemes or in progressively circumscribed phonological environments. Second, the effect of the rule, i.e. the phonetic modification it produces, may be gradually diminished as successive learners produce phonetic compromises between the received pronunciation and what is motivated by their own underlying structure. Third, the stylistic value of the rule may gradually become more and more circumscribed; i.e., the rule may become increasingly 'marked' and hence be applied in fewer and fewer speech situations. We will consider these three possibilities in turn.

A gradual curtailment of the domain of an A-rule is exemplified by the loss in Standard Russian of the phoneme /ɣ/. At an earlier time, Standard Russian had voiceless and voiced velar stops and fricatives /k g x ɣ/; but by the end of the 19th century, [ɣ] had ceased to be interpreted as part of the phonological structure—i.e. as the voiced counterpart of /x/—and was instead a stylistic variant of /g/, produced from underlying /g/ by an adaptive rule applying to a dwindling number of lexemes. As the number of lexemes marked as subject to this special rule diminished, underlying /g/ came to be realized as [g] in such lexemes as *lëgok* 'light', *mjagok* 'soft', *nogot'* 'nail', *kogot'* 'talon', *bogatyr'* 'hero', *bogatyj* 'rich', *blago* 'good', etc. [18]

It is a deductive innovation of precisely this character which I
posited for the Teták change, where sharped labials at some point
were reinterpreted as stylistic variants of dentals, produced by an A-
rule applying to certain lexemes and to the output of certain morphophonemic rules; they were then eventually lost as this rule was permitted to lapse (cf. §3.2).

As an example of the gradual weakening of the phonetic effect of
an A-rule, one can mention the change of [x] > [f] in dialects of
Macedonian and Bulgarian, which may still be in progress. Here,
apparently, onset and coda variants of original /x/ have been dissociated. While the original onset variants have been weakened and
reinterpreted as glides (/v/ or /j/) or zero, the original coda
variants have been reinterpreted as realizations of /f/. This latter
abductive innovation entails the formulation of an A-rule which produces the [x] of the traditional norms from underlying /f/ by re-
specifying some of the acoustic properties associated with /f/. As
the effect of this rule is gradually permitted to be weakened, more
and more of the acoustic properties of /f/ come to be realized, and
the pronunciation of original syllable-final /x/ changes from a
weakly fricative [x] to an increasingly fricative bilabial [$^{u}_{\wedge}$f] or
[^{w}f], and eventually to a labiodental [f].[19]

Finally, as was mentioned, the stylistic value of an A-rule may
gradually change so that the rule is applied with decreasing consistency. In my account of the Teták change, I supposed simply that
the speakers who produced [p, b, m,] from underlying /ƫ d n/ by an
A-rule applied this rule primarily when addressing speakers older
than their own peer group, i.e. that the stylistic value of the rule
was defined with reference to the interlocutors' relative age. An
A-rule characterized in this way will gradually go out of use, as
the speakers who have it grow old. But any speech community of some
size presents parameters other than age in terms of which the stylistic value of A-rules may be defined. If a rule comes to be characterized with reference to some parameter of greater permanence
than age—say, social class—the normal process by which an A-rule
is eliminated may be retarded or even reversed. An example of this
kind is the development of /h/ in England. Here /h/ was lost in
most of the folk dialects, but preserved in the standard language.
Thus the development in some places, e.g. London, stopped at the
transitional stage where /h/ was already lost in the phonological
structure; but initial [h] could still be produced in some styles
of speech by means of an A-rule. The increasing influence of R.P.
may eventually effectively reverse the loss of /h/ (cf. Brunner,
414ff.)

For simplicity, each of the examples given here illustrates primarily one of the three ways in which A-rules gradually are eliminated.
In reality, the loss of an A-rule involves two or three of these processes of gradual restriction simultaneously.[20]

Changes such as these are radically different from abductive innovations as defined above (cf. §§3.3, 4.2, 5.3). An abductive innovation is motivated by ambiguities in the corpus of utterances from
which it is inferred, and may be compensated for by adaptive means
in such a way that it has no overt manifestations; but a change in
an A-rule—of any of the three types just described—has immediate
observable consequences in the form of deviations from the received
norms. It cannot possibly be motivated by these norms, with which
it is at variance.

The term 'deductive innovation' for changes of this type is
prompted by considerations of two kinds. First, it is clear that,
when viewed in the context of the model of language acquisition
sketched in §4.2, these deviations from the norms are the result of
incomplete learning, and arise in the deductive process of testing
the validity of the phonology the learner has inferred. That these
deductive innovations can be described as changes in the formulation
of A-rules is surely a secondary fact. They are deviations from the
norms which the learner's models fail to (effectively) correct, and
which consequently become codified in the phonological rules the
learner formulates.

The question of what motivates innovations of these types leads us
to the second justification for the term 'deductive innovation'. The
term is consistent with the assumption that, given a certain phonological structure and the laws of language, one can predict that a
certain phonological rule will be unproductive and hence subject to
elimination, and also the way in which its effects will be curtailed.
It may be assumed that speakers of a language evaluate deviations
from the received norms in the speech of other members of the community in terms of such deductive inferences, and will accept only such
deviations as are consistent with the phonological structure. This
is the assumption which forms the basis of the account given in §3.2.

6.3. We may now turn to the second of the two categories of deductive innovation, the category with which we have not been concerned
in this article, but which must be the focus of attention in a theory
of diachronic phonology, since no understanding of evolutive change
is possible without an understanding of this category of innovations.
It contrasts with the loss of A-rules just considered by consisting
not in the elimination of rules which are unmotivated by the phono-

logical structure, but rather in the inclusion in the phonological
structure of rules which are consistent with its defining relations.

There are two kinds of such implementation rules (I-rules), as I
will call them, and correspondingly two types of deductive innovations by which I-rules are introduced into a phonology: neutraliza-
tion changes and variation changes. Neutralization changes concern
the phonemic oppositions: in such a change, the two terms of an
opposition come to be realized identically in a certain context or
contexts. Variation changes may affect the terms of phonemic oppositions, as in diphthongization, or non-phonemic features: in such a
change, different values for a certain phonetic feature (associated
or not with a phonemic opposition in the language) come to be distributed in such a way that the more marked value appears in marked
contexts, and the less marked value in unmarked contexts (cf. Andersen 1972:44-5).

Like A-rules, I-rules serve the essential function of transforming
a phonological representation, expressed in purely relational terms,
into a phonetic representation sufficiently explicit to be realized.
But otherwise they differ in function. Since a phonology is a semiotic system (cf. §2.2), one may expect phonological rules to have a
semiotic function, and it is important to define the differences in
semiotic function between different kinds of phonological rules. The
function of A-rules is defined exclusively in terms of the output of
the phonology, which has to conform to the norms of the speech community regardless of the underlying representations. It seems that
if a phonological rule has a stylistic or social value, and thus
refers to extralinguistic reality, the output of that rule will be
conventional signs—i.e. symbols, in Peirce's terminology. For example, centralized diphthongs stand for island allegiance on Martha's
Vineyard (Labov 1963). This is the only semiotic function that A-
rules can have. I-rules, on the other hand, transform underlying
phonological relations into relations between phonetic feature values,
and can thus be said to connect phonological signata with signantia.
The semiotic character of I-rules is determined by the fact that both
their signata, and the signantia they assign to them, are relations:
they are diagrammatic (cf. Peirce 1940:105ff.) and constitute the
phonological counterpart of the ' "system of diagrammatization,"
patent and compulsory in the entire syntactic and morphological pattern of language' (Jakobson [1965] 1967:357).

The way in which new I-rules are introduced into a phonological
structure can be described here only in outline, but is largely comparable to the elimination of A-rules. I-rules can be characterized
as codified deviations from the received norms—deviations which are
deducible from the laws of language and the phonemic relations of the

phonological structure, and which are acceptable to the bearers of the received norms precisely because they are deducible. For, as mentioned above, one may assume that, to the extent that any deviations from the received norms are tolerated, only those will be accepted by a homogeneous speech community—and hence reflected in new I-rules in the learners' grammars—which can be predicted from the relations that define the phonological structure. It may be noted that when a deduction produces a deviation from the received norms which is acceptable, that deviation serves to validate the learner's analysis of the phonemic relation(s) it implements. (Andersen 1969a, 1969c discuss the introduction of different kinds of I-rules from this point of view.)

Even though a new I-rule is thus motivated by the phonological structure, its full effect may be permitted to be manifested only by degrees. (For a fairly detailed example, see Andersen 1972:16.) This is perhaps because when an I-rule is introduced, its effect from the beginning is attenuated by an A-rule which is permitted to lapse only gradually, at a rate determined by the speech community's demands for continuity of usage.

By the gradual accumulation of pronunciation rules that are motivated by the phonological structure, the phonological structure of a language becomes more and more explicitly implemented. However, there are no safeguards against the introduction of I-rules which produce an ambiguous phonetic output, i.e. an output which would warrant the abduction of a phonological structure different from the one from which it is derived. Thus deductive innovation is the mainspring of evolutive change. Although individual neutralization and variation changes merely serve to elaborate the implementation of a given phonological structure, their cumulative effect may be to obscure it, and hence indirectly to motivate abductive change.[21]

7.1. The purpose of a theory of diachronic phonology is to explain fully and explicitly how sound change takes place and why. In this paper I have been concerned primarily with the problem of understanding the differences between abductive and deductive change, which is only one of several basic questions that must be clarified before a coherent theory of phonological change can be formulated. But it has been necessary, for the purposes of the discussion here, to allude to tentative solutions to a number of other questions, particularly concerning the structure of phonology. For this reason it seems appropriate, before concluding this article, to consider how the theory of phonological change adumbrated here is relevant to some traditional issues in diachronic phonology.

Traditionally a number of questions have been debated concerning the way in which sound change takes place. I will discuss very briefly the questions of whether sound changes are gradual or abrupt; whether they are regular; and whether they are internally motivated or motivated from without. Finally I will consider the causes of sound change.

7.2. Are sound changes gradual or abrupt? This question has been discussed primarily by linguists who have conceived of phonological change exclusively as change in output or as change in grammars— i.e. linguists who have defined change in terms of the pseudo-connections indicated in Fig. 1. If a distinction is made between abductive and deductive innovations, this issue loses much of its meaning. Abductive innovations cannot be said to be either abrupt or gradual, since they arise in the process of grammar formation. As for deductive innovations, all the different types examined here have been observed as gradual processes. Even where phonemic distinctions are involved—as when a neutralization rule is introduced, and the distinction in question must in principle be made or not made, tertium non datur—stylistic variables provide for graduality of change.

One type of abductive innovation may immediately result in deductive innovation; that is the primary abductive innovation in adaptive change, by which a speaker adopts new norms of pronunciation. Whether changes of this kind are in fact gradual or abrupt must depend on the capacity of individual speakers to change their habits of pronunciation.

7.3. Are sound changes necessarily regular? The well-known neogrammarian claim that sound changes know no exceptions, and that all apparent exceptions are of secondary origin, does not appear to be borne out by sound changes that have been observed in progress. As a change progresses, the phonetic innovation is usually manifested to different extents in different age groups or social classes, or even in the speech of the individual speaker in different styles, or within a single style in different phonological environments or lexical categories. If the neogrammarian claim were to be judged solely on the basis of empirical data of this kind, it would have to be rejected.

But the fact remains that however irregular a sound change in progress may appear, when it has run its course—if it is permitted to do so—it yields regular correspondences. It is obviously regularities of this kind that first motivated the neogrammarian doctrine, and in a way justify it. But the problem of reconciling the observed

irregularity of sound changes with the attested regularity of their
outcomes has hitherto been unsolvable. This problem can be approached
only if the traditional, vague notion of 'sound change' is replaced
by a consistent differentiation of abductive and deductive innovations, and if a distinction is made between the two parts of a
phonological system that have here been called the phonological
structure and the system of A-rules.

In the first place, the observed irregularity concerns only deductive innovations. It would be a mistake to take at face value the
apparent irregularity with which deductive innovations are made—
i.e., to assume that observed variation in usage is not rule-governed.
On the contrary, one must assume that however complex the observed
manifestations of a deductive innovation may be, they are the product of phonological rules; and one must assume that it is possible
to establish the linguistic and/or extralinguistic parameters to
which these rules refer. Even if it is found, in the case of some
change, that the variant which is basic for one member of a speech
community is stylistically marked for another (cf. Fónagy, 269),
this does not mean that the variations is not rule-governed, but
merely that the variants are evaluated differently by different individuals. Indeed, this is precisely what one would expect, e.g.,
when a change like the Teták one is in progress. Speakers with
underlying sharped labials, as well as speakers with none, would
presumably both be able to produce innovating forms containing dentals—the former by applying an adaptive rule replacing underlying
sharped labials with dentals in deference to the new norms, the
latter by not applying the A-rule that enabled them to adhere to the
old norms. Speakers of these two categories could not but differ in
their evaluation of new and old forms (cf. §3.2).

The fact that the apparently disorderly progression of a change
eventually yields a set of regular correspondences can be understood
as a diachronic consequence of the synchronic relation between the
phonological structure, in terms of which all underlying representations are written, and the system of A-rules. Since a speaker cannot
produce a deviation from the norms except by applying the rules he
has formulated to the underlying representations he has set up,
every observed deductive innovation is necessarily preceded by a
corresponding abductive innovation (cf. Andersen 1969b:829). This
means that, before a change begins to be manifested little by little,
its end result is already given in the underlying representations.[22]
In short, the regularity of the outcome of a phonological change is
present throughout the progression of the change in the underlying
representations; it is merely obscured by the A-rules that permit
the speakers to produce compromises between the traditional norms

and the pronunciation that would naturally be derived from their phonological structure.

7.4. Are sound changes motivated from within or from without? It is customary, in discussions of linguistic change, to dintinguish two phases in each change: the innovation proper, and its subsequent spread within the speech community. While the second of these phases has been thought to pose no particular problems, the first phase, the actual source of the change, has created difficulties. The lack of a theory which could explain linguistic innovation has made some linguists conclude that the distinction between 'innovation' and 'spread' is illusory, while it has led others to define linguistic change narrowly as 'spread' ('borrowing').

It is clear that an actual change in which an innovation has been made in one place and has subsequently spread to other areas involves both the mechanisms of change that have been considered in this article. The 'innovation' is an evolutive change, and its 'spread' is an adaptive change. It is obvious that an actual 'innovation' (e.g. the Teták one) cannot be an adaptive change—there can be no 'borrowing' without a source of borrowing. It is less obvious, and therefore worth mentioning, that an innovation may very well occur in one place at one time, and subsequently in contiguous areas, without any 'borrowing' being involved. In other words, an evolutive change may very well appear to have spread even though in fact it has not. This is often the case where structurally similar contiguous dialects evolve at different rates. It is obviously inappropriate to apply the 'innovation'—'spread' dichotomy to such instances.[23]

To return to the question posed at the beginning of this section, whether sound changes are motivated from within or from without, it may be said that some changes are of one kind, some of the other. Both adaptive and evolutive change may result in convergent developments. Linguistic divergence, on the other hand, can be the result only of evolutive change.

7.5. We may finally consider the question of the causes of phonological change. It has long been recognized that this question must be put in teleological terms (cf. Jakobson 1928); but hitherto it has been impossible to advance beyond a purely programmatic stage, in part because it has not been sufficiently clear what change is, in part because the concept of teleology itself has been poorly understood. The notion of teleology has traditionally been erroneously identified with purpose in the sense of '(conscious) intent'; and most students of linguistic change have been wary, and rightly so, of either ascribing (conscious) intent to linguistic systems or claiming that all change is the result of willful distortions of inherited patterns. However, there is no reason to think of purpose narrowly as 'intent.' It is perfectly proper to speak of some constituent element of a structured system as serving a certain purpose in the sense of 'function.' Defining the function of an element within the system of which it is part thus amounts to a teleological explanation (cf. Emmet 1958:45ff.) In speaking of phonological change, it is necessary to distinguish this teleology of function from the teleology of purpose.

I have defined three types of innovation: abductive innovation in evolutive change, the primary abductive innovation in adaptive change and deductive innovation. The first of these cannot be said to have either purpose or function. The learner who formulates a grammar on the basis of the verbal output of his models has as his goal a grammar that will produce that output. Whether his grammar actually is identical to or different from that (those) of his models has no practical relevance in the speech community, which can only be concerned with observable usage. The source of abductive innovations is to be found in distributional ambiguities in the verbal output from which the new grammar is inferred. These ambiguities are causes of change, however, only to the extent that they do not prevent the abductive innovations any more than they occasion them. They are necessary but not sufficient conditions for the innovations to which they give rise.

The primary abduction by which a speaker adapts his pronunciation to new norms is an innovation which is not only goal-directed, as was mentioned in §5.3, but purposeful. Whether or not a speaker is conscious of his attempt to adjust his pronunciation to that of others, he can be said to modify his phonology with a definite intent. Here, then, one may speak of teleology of purpose, and define the final cause of the innovation as the intended new pronunciation.

Deductive innovation, the process by which learners of a language produce acceptable deviations from the received norms, involves teleology of function in two distinct ways. Since it is produced deductively, any acceptable deviation fulfills the important function in the process of grammar formation of validating the learner's analysis of the stylistic values (in the case of A-rules) or phonemic relations (in the case of I-rules) with which the deviation is consistent. Besides this validating function, a deductive innovation consisting in the introduction of a new I-rule serves a function definable in terms of the phonological structure into which the rule is introduced. Since I-rules manifest phonological relations, the addition of a new one serves to make more explicit the relations that constitute the phonological structure.

8. It may be useful, in conclusion, to return once more to the diagram presented in Fig. 1.

While the task of descriptive phonology has long been correctly understood as the investigation of the relation between phonemic patterns and their phonetic realizations, the object of study of historical phonology has not been so clear. For the most part, attention has been concentrated on the study of diachronic correspondences either between phonetic units or between phonemic units or rules (the pseudo-connections in Fig. 1). Much extremely valuable work has been done on this basis, establishing the phonetic or phonemic character, respectively, of attested sound changes. But the study of diachronic correspondences does not by itself lead to an understanding of sound change.

Phonetic correspondences have been investigated since the second half of the 19th century, primarily as results of articulatory modifications. But this study has not yielded a theory explaining phonological change; nor can it, for the study of phonetic correspondences divorced from phonemic relations is tantamount to the study of effects isolated from their causes. The introduction of phonemic considerations into the study of diachronic phonology made it possible, as Jakobson demonstrated long ago (1931), to classify phonemic correspondences between consecutive linguistic states into a number of logically possible types. More recently it has also been shown that diachronic correspondences in terms of phonological rules can be classified into a small number of logically possible types (cf. Kiparsky 1968). But a typology of diachronic correspondences is not a theory of phonological change. It explains nothing, nor does it suggest what questions the investigator should ask of his data in order to explain them. It merely provides him with a set of classificatory labels, and leaves him to wonder vaguely about 'transitional probabilities' between linguistic states. What seems to have been insufficiently appreciated is that the internalized grammars of individual speakers are discontinuous. Since there can be no direct causal relation between discontinuous entities, the mere study of correspondences between consecutive states of a language cannot yield any explanations of change.

Since diachronic phonology is concerned with language in its historical aspect, it must focus attention on the abductive connection that links a phonology to the phonetic output from which it has been inferred, and on the deductive connection that links it to its own output. These two essential links in the ongoing process of using and transmitting language can and must be investigated empirically. Weinreich, Labov & Herzog must be given credit for having insisted on the importance of studying synchronic variation in all its complexity with the explicit aim of gathering evidence for the process of deductive change. But the abductive process must also be investigated. Language acquisition can be studied directly, and the study of phonology acquisition in different languages can provide important insights into the interplay of universal and language-particular determining factors in this process. Again, experiments with the perception of speech sounds can contribute much to our understanding of the learner's task in analysing a phonetic corpus into its underlying phonological relations.[24]

But of course the main data of diachronic phonology will continue to be diachronic correspondences. It is the linguist's task to construct detailed and mutually consistent hypotheses as to how these correspondences have come to be, and as to what motivated the innovations that gave rise to them. To do this, he must understand the place of correspondences in the total context of language transmission (cf. Fig. 1), and must consistently attempt to break diachronic correspondences down into the individual deductive and abductive innovations that produced them. Given a diachronic correspondence between two consecutive stages of a phonological system, the analyst must posit the phonetic ambiguities in the output of the antecedent stage which made possible the abductive innovation involved. And he must show how the pronunciation rules that produced these phonetic ambiguities were motivated by the phonological structure of the antecedent stage—or, in other words, served to implement its phonemic relations.

If this approach is followed, it becomes possible to reformulate radically the goals of diachronic phonology. Early structuralism viewed phonological systems as being more or less at the mercy of phonetic alterations, and consequently could insist only that every phonetic innovation be interpreted in terms of the system that under-goes it (cf. Jakobson [1928] 1962:2, and 1962:651 et passim); but the theory sketched here shows how it is possible to interpret every phonological innovation—abductive or deductive—in terms of the system that gives rise to it. This must be the goal of diachronic phonology.

Notes

[1] Sources of information on these dialects are mentioned in §1.2.— Since I am not concerned with details of articulatory phonetics in this article, I will refer to the apico-alveolar and bilabial consonants simply as 'dentals' and 'labials' respectively.

[2] There is apparently no established name for these dialects. However speakers of neighboring dialects who say /pet/ for Standard Czech pět /pjet/ 'five' are called petáci (sg. peták); and in the Teták dialects the word for 'five' was /tet/. I have named them accordingly.

[3]Seen in the larger perspective of the history of linguistics, this theory should perhaps be understood as merely a vulgarized version of a conception of linguistic change proposed by some structuralists, e.g. Jakobson (cf. [1931]1962:219). According to this conception, phonological change is a recoding. Members of an innovating generation possess the code of their elders, but of their own accord modify it to suit their expressive purposes. The theory of Halle and of King differs from this conception primarily by not posing the question of why speakers of a language would intentionally change its phonological system. I have commented on this conception of linguistic change elsewhere (1969b:928ff., 1974).

[4]The preceding account is based on Komárek 1958, especially pp. 86-94.
The different dialect types defined in Table 1 have a very interesting geographical distribution; cf. Utěšený, map VIII A. It may be noted that the change of OCz. /ě/ > /je/ differentiated the type A dialects into a larger group in which the change occurred (from which the standard language has developed), and a smaller group, the Peták dialects. The change also obliterated the original isoglosses between types B and C and between types E and F. In his discussion of this diversity (p. 175), Utěšený does not mention types B and C at all, but they can be inferred from the map (see, e.g., the localities Svojanov and Svratka); nor does he mention a distinction between types E and F, which seem to be contrasted in the Litovel area on the map.

[5]Jakobson ([1939] 1962:304-5) has an interesting discussion of the signans-signatum relations in phonology and grammar, in which the 'cumul de signifiés' of the synthetic morpheme is likened to the phoneme with its complex of phonemic feature values. It would seem, however, that there is no basis for speaking of the latter as a 'cumul de signifiants' parallel to the 'cumul de signifiés', as Jakobson does. In the phoneme, each of the constituent signantia has its separate signatum, its own diacritic function.

[6]It may be noted here that such classifications of phonemic changes as Jakobson 1931 or Hoenigswald (1960:75ff.) are implicitly based on (partial) enumerations of the logically possible wrong decisions of language learners regarding the constituency, constituent rank, or dimension of syntagms of phonological terms. I discuss this matter in some detail in Andersen 1974.

[7]It would be desirable at this point to cite acoustic data showing that, in languages with phonemic sharping in labial but not in dental consonants (stage II in both Tables 2 and 3), the tonality of sharped labials is indeed intermediate between that of plain labials and undifferentiated dentals. Unfortunately, no such data are available. It is of some interest to consider the acoustic properties of sharped and plain consonants in a language like Russian, but it must be remembered that the plain dentals of Russian are of perceptibly lower tonality than those of languages like English or French (and presumably stage II in the development of the Peták and Teták dialects), where dentals are undifferentiated with respect to sharping. According to Fant (1960:331), average F2 and F3 positions for Russian diffuse consonants are as follows: /f p m/—920 and 2025 cps; /f,p,m,/—1820 and 2400 cps; /s t n/—1440 and 2640 cps; /s,t,n,/—1700 and 3050 cps. (Cf. also Halle 1959:149ff.) For some further remarks, see fn. 22, below.

[8]Cf. Safarewicz (1969:113) and Brandenstein (1951:490). The etymology of *pariēs* is disputed, and the change of *tu > p hence doubtful (cf. Sommer 1913:114, and Walde & Hoffman 1938, s.v.). On the development of *su, see Horecký (1949:40) and Brandenstein.

[9]Phonological structure' is used here and elsewhere in this article in the quite specific sense described in §6.1.

[10] Andersen 1969b:828-9 presents a short outline of this model as it applies to morphophonemic change. What is there called 'inductive change' is more accurately termed 'abductive', as will become clear just below.

[11] The account given in this section is based on the excellent monograph of Reilly 1970.

[12] Note that the mere process of joining one particular with another as result and case—the procedure which is usually called 'induction' —implies the previous existence of a hypothesis, viz. that the two particulars may belong together as case and result. In this way abduction necessarily precedes induction.

[13] The structure of this complex strategy, T(TOTE)TE, underscores the unique role of abduction (O) vis-à-vis the other modes of inference, which merely test what has been arrived at by abduction.

This may be a convenient place at which to note that, in the process of communication, the speaker and the hearer use quite different strategies. Without attempting to define these in detail, one can evidently describe the process of encoding as essentially deductive, and that of decoding as abductive. The signal the hearer receives (a 'result') 'conveys' no meaning as such; he has to guess at the meaning (the 'case') that prompted it. A knowledge of a grammar effectively identical to the speaker's (the 'law') is useful, but strictly speaking is neither necessary for correct decoding (distinct languages may be mutually intelligible to some extent), nor sufficient for correct decoding (in cases of ambiguity). The facts that actual linguistic ambiguity plays such an insignificant role in normal communication, and that people can decode messages in languages they cannot speak, suggest that the hearer as a matter of course brings all his knowledge, linguistic and extralinguistic, to bear in the abductive process of decoding. If this is so, one may well question the wisdom of defining the object of the study of grammar as 'the competence of the ideal speaker-hearer' (thus Chomsky 1965:4).

[14] In addition to his replacement of underlying dentals with labials, he would have to suspend those morphophonemic rules which in the Teták dialects replaced underlying labials with dentals before certain derivational and inflectional suffixes. Bělič suggests that the morphophonemic alternations of labials and dentals in the Teták dialects had been curtailed through an internally motivated development. This could be true, but we do have evidence that these alternations persisted until the 1890's; cf. such pairs of lexemes as /kupova-t/ 'buy, impf.', /kout-i-t/ 'perf.'; /holub/ 'pigeon', /holoud-e/ 'young pigeon'; /troub-a/ 'oven, nom. sg.', /troud-e/ 'loc. sg.' Our knowledge of the morphophonemics of the dialects is too slight for firm conclusions, however, so we will omit this matter from the present account.

[15] Here, as in §4.1, I assume that the speaker's abductive activity is determined by his desire to imitate the phonetic output of his models. So he guesses at how he himself might produce that output— not at how his models actually go about producing it, or at how an ideal speaker-hearer of his dialect would do it.

[16] This division of phonology into a structured core system and an additive ad-system is grosso modo comparable to Coseriu's distinction between 'sistema' and 'norma', but differs from the latter in essential respects. Note in particular that Coseriu considers implementation rules part of 'norma' (1962:71ff.), whereas I consider them integrated into the core structure (see §6.3, below).

[17] See, e.g., the different degrees of Frenchness recognized by the *Concise Oxford dictionary* (Appendix II, 'Pronunciation of non-English words', pp. 1534-9).

[18] The state of this change at the beginning of this century is described in some detail by Ušakov 1928. Lundell 1890 cites the evidence of 18th- and 19th-century grammarians (pp. 20,40, et passim). For a more recent evaluation, see Panov (1967:332-3).

[19] The account given here, and the phonetic symbols used, are from Seliščev 1918:114ff. (see also Koneski 1967:89ff., Mirčev 1963:142, and Stojkov (1962:129).

Ralkov 1933 reports from the Trojan area that in some villages, speakers over 30 years of age have [x] for the original syllable-final /x/, whereas speakers under 30 have [f], but with an interesting further difference (216): 'while older children perceive this *f* as a *v*, and sometimes write instead of *xodixme* ['we walked'] *xodivme*, the young children, from pre-schoolers through the first two grades, already perceive it as a pure *f* and therefore often say . . . *Svetago Dufa* ['the Holy Ghost', for *Duxa*] when we insist that they speak "properly"'.

On the background of this example one may wonder if there were any intermediate acoustic stages between the original [p,b,m] and the new [t d n] when the Teták peculiarity arose—and, if so, how they were articulated. The dorso-labial compound stops and nasal constructed on paper by Bělič 1966 do not seem to correspond to any known types of co-articulation. But alveolar-labial compound articulations ([p͡t b͡d]) are known from various languages. In some they have resulted from vowel syncope, e.g. in Margi and Balanta (I am grateful to Professor Joseph H. Greenberg for this information.) In Gur languages such as Dagbani these sounds are allophones of /k͡p/ and /g͡b/ which occur before front vowels (Ladefoged 1968:11). But there is no reason to think that acoustic values intermediate between those of sharped labials and those of dentals could be produced only by compound articulations. Simple dental (alveolar) stops with appropriately adjusted tonality would seem just as possible.

[20] Fónagy 1956 offers an ample collection of examples and further literature.

[21] I plan to return to this subject in a future publication.

[22] In Coseriu's terse formulation, 'el cambio fónico no termina, sino que empieza con la "ley fonética"' (1958:57).

[23] For a particularly striking example of a sound change which appears to have spread radially from a center of innovation, but did not take place there, see Andersen (1969a:565, §13, and 570-71).

[24] Specifically, a cross-linguistic experiment like that of Cooper et al. 1952 might serve to establish the acoustic cues associated with sharped labials and—in languages which do not have sharped labials in their phonemic system—with dentals. Such data would obviously be of value for a full understanding of changes such as the Teták innovation.

References

Andersen, Henning. 1969a "Lenition in Common Slavic." *Lg.* 45, 553-74.

_____. 1969b "A study in diachronic morphophonemics: the Ukrainian prefixes." *Lg.* 45, 807-30.

_____. 1969c "Indo-European voicing sandhi in Ukrainian." *Scando-Slavica* 15, 157-69.

_____. 1972 "Diphthongization." *Lg.* 48, 11-50.

_____. 1974 *Bifurcating changes and binary relations*. Proceedings of the First International Conference on Historical Linguistics, to appear.

Bělič, Jaromír. 1966 "K otázce zaniklého litomyšlského *t*, *d*, *n* za někdejší *p'*, *b'*, *m'*," (Slavica Pragensia 8; Acta Univ. Carolinae, Philologica, 1-3.) Prague: NČAV.

Brandenstein, W. 1951 "Kurze Phonologie des Lateinischen." *Geschichte der lateinischen Sprache*, by Franz Altheim (Frankfurt: Klostermann) pp. 481-98.

Brunner, Karl. 1960 *Die englische Sprache, ihre geschichtliche Entwicklung*, I. 2nd ed. (Tübingen: Niemeyer)

Chomsky, Noam. 1965 *Aspects of the Theory of Syntax*. (Cambridge, Mass: MIT Press).

Cooper, Franklin S., Pierre C. Delattre, Alvin M. Liberman, John M. Borst, and Louis J. Gerstman. 1952 "Some experiments on the perception of synthetic speech sounds." *JASA* 24, 597-606.

Coseriu, Eugenio. 1958 *Sincronía, diacronía e historia: el problema del cambio lingüístico*. (Montevideo: Universidad de la República).

_____. 1962 "Sistema, norma y habla." In his *Teoría del lenguaje y lingüística general* (Madrid: Editorial Gredos), pp. 11-113.

Emmet, Dorothy. 1958 *Function, purpose, and powers*. (London: Macmillan).

Fant, C. Gunnar M. 1960 *Acoustic theory of speech production*. Description and analysis of Contemporary Standard Russian, 2. (The Hague: Mouton).

Fónagy, I. 1956 "Über den Verlauf des Lautwandels." *Acta Linguistica Academiae Scientiarum Hungaricae* 6, 173-278.

Halle, Morris. 1959 *The sound pattern of Russian*. Description and analysis of Contemporary Standard Russian, 1. (The Hague: Mouton).

_____. 1962 "Phonology in generative grammar." *Word* 18, 54-72.

Hoenigswald, Henry M. 1960 *Language change and linguistic reconstruction*. (Chicago: University of Chicago Press).

Horecký, Ján. 1949 *Fonologia latinčiny* (Bratislava: SAVU).

Jakobson, Roman. 1928 "O hláskoslovném zákonu a teleologickém hláskosloví." *Časopis pro Moderní Filologii* 14, 183-4. [Translated in Jakobson 1962:1-2.]

_____. 1931 "Prinzipien der historischen Phonologie." *TLCP* 4, 247-67. (Revised version, "Principes de phonologie historique," published as appendix, pp. xv-xxix, to *Principes de phonologie*, by N. S. Troubetzkoy, Paris 1949; reprinted in Jakobson 1962:202-20.)

_____. 1938 "Observations sur le classement phonologique des consonnes." Proc. 3rd Intl. Congr. Phonetic Sciences, 33-41. Ghent. [Reprinted in Jakobson 1962:272-9.]

_____. 1939 "Zur Struktur des Phonems." Lecture, University of Copenhagen. [First published in Jakobson 1962:280-310.]

_____. 1962 *Selected writings I: phonological studies* The Hague: Mouton).

_____. 1965 "Quest for the essence of language." *Diogenes* 51, 21-37. [Reprinted in his *Selected writings II: word and language* (The Hague: Mouton, 1967), pp. 345-59.

King, Robert D. 1969 *Historical linguistics and generative grammar* (Englewood Cliffs, N.J.: Prentice-Hall).

Kiparsky, Paul. 1968 "Linguistic universals and linguistic change." *Universals in linguistic theory*, ed. by R. T. Harms. (New York: Holt, Rinehart & Winston) pp. 171-204.

Komárek, Miroslav. 1958 *Historická mluvnice česká I: hláskosloví* (Prague: Státni Pedagogické Nakladatelství).

Koneski, Blaže. 1967 *Istorija na makedonskiot jazik* (Skopje: Kultura).

Labov, William. 1963 "The social motivation of a sound change." *Word* 19, 273-309.

_____. 1966 *The social stratification of English in New York City.* (Washington, D.C.: Center for Applied Linguistics).

_____. 1970 "The study of language in its social context." *Studium Generale* 23, 30-87.

Ladefoged, Peter. 1968 *A phonetic study of West African languages,* 2nd ed., (Cambridge: University Press).

Lundell, J. A. 1890 *Étude sur la prononciation russe: compte-rendu de littérature,* 1. Stockholm.

Miller, George A., Eugene Galanter, and Karl H. Pribram. 1960 *Plans and the structure of behavior* (New York: Holt, Rinehart & Winston).

Mirčev, Kiril. 1963 *Istoričeska gramatika na bălgarskija ezik,* 2nd ed., (Sofia: Nauka i Izkustvo).

Panov, M. V. 1967 *Russkaja fonetika* (Moscow: Prosveščenie).

Peirce, Charles S. 1940 *The philosophy of Peirce: selected writings.* Ed. by Justus Buchler (New York: Harcourt Brace).

_____. 1966 *Selected writings.* Ed. by Philip P. Wiener (New York: Dover).

Ralkov, Lal'o. 1933 "Govorni različija meždu mladi i stari." *(Kăm dialekti na văzrastnite v Trojansko: prexod x-f.) Rodna Reč* 6, 215-17.

Reilly, Francis E. 1970 *Charles Peirce's theory of scientific method.* Orestes Brownson series, 7 (New York: Fordham University Press).

Safarewicz, Jan. 1969 *Historische lateinische Grammatik* (Halle: Niemeyer).

Selišcev, A. M. 1918 *Očerki po makedonskoj dialektologii,* 1. Kazan´.

Sommer, Ferdinand S. 1913 *Handbuch der lateinischen Laut- und Formenlehre* (Heidelberg: Winter).

Stojkov, Stojko. 1962 *Bălgarska dialektologija.* (Sofia: Nauka i Izkustvo).

Ušakov, D. N. 1928 "Zvuk *g* frikativnyj v russkom literaturnom jazyke v nastojaščee vremja." *Sbornik Otdelenija Russkogo Jazyka i Slovestnosti* 101:3, 238-40.

Utěšeny, Slavomír. 1960 *Nářeči přechodného pásu česko-moravského: hláskosloví* (Prague: Nakladatelství ČAV).

Walde, A., and J. B. Hofmann. 1938 *Lateinisches etymologisches Worterbuch,* vol. I, 3rd ed. (Heidelberg: Winter).

Weinreich, Uriel, William Labov, and Marvin I. Herzog. 1968 "Empirical foundations for a theory of language change." *Directions for historical linguistics,* ed. by W. P. Lehmann and Yakov Malkiel (Austin: University of Texas Press), pp. 95-188.

16 Formalization as Degeneration in Historical Linguistics

RAIMO ANTTILA

One of the central themes in recent historical linguistics has been
the so-called revolution brought about by generative theory. It has
become clear, however, that the revolution is *social*, rather than a
new scientific breakthrough, and the movement is thus extremely interesting from the point of view of the sociology of scientific inquiry. I have recently surveyed the situation (Anttila, 1973a), and
out of it I repeat a summary in diagrammatic form(Figure 1). The diagram delineates two main camps of "generative" historical linguistics.
The orthodox one launched by Paul Kiparsky and summed up by Robert
King can be called "taxonomic-generative," because it concentrated
on various strict rule taxonomies without paying attention to history. In contrast, the more open-minded group could be called sys-
tematic-generative, but a more accurate designation seems to be
"*traditional*-generative," although by now the constituent "generative" turns out to have rather doubtful value. In fact, it has only
obfuscated the discussion of historical linguistics. Curiously, the
taxonomic-generativists remained in the same structuralist island as
American structuralism, Hjelmslev, or Kuryłowicz, whereas the functional structuralists on the mainland are much more generative. The
state of the art (since about 1970) has been active emigration from
the island onto the continent, although the terminology used obscures
the movement. In fact, many do not realize at all that they are
entering traditional territory. The latest significant move that
proved this analysis was King's retreat from the taxonomist camp
(Umeå, June 1973), although he retained the earlier vocabulary. There
are now at least four productive lines in the traditional camp as
indicated in the diagram. The most notable cluster of campshifters
represents various "natural" linguists.

From *Historical Linguistics*, edited by John M. Anderson and Charles
Jones, (Amsterdam, 1974), Vol. 1, pp. 1-32. Reprinted by permission
of Raimo Anttila and North-Holland Publishing Company.

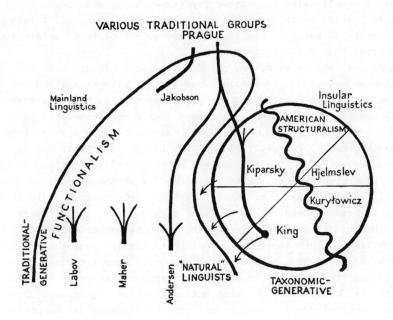

Figure 1

State of the art map of "generative" historical linguistics
delineating two main camps, traditional and taxonomic, and
showing movement from the latter into the former. (Simplified from the Proceedings of the second international conference of Nordic and general linguistics [Karl-Hampus
Dahlstedt, ed.] Umea, Skytteanska samfundet.)

I am not going to repeat all the arguments for the configurations in the diagram, nor all the evidence for the camp-shifting (it is indeed very impressive); rather, I will discuss one more aspect against this background. Incidentally, judging even by the abstracts of this conference, at least the pre-conference sentiment runs more along the lines I have delineated than against them, and I expect to get further substantial argumentation for my position, however implicit it be. In discussing the influence of formalization as one of the factors in taxonomic-generative historical linguistics I will no doubt overlap with many other reports at this conference, but I hope to justify my appearance from a complementary angle. I take the liberty of being on the general side so as not to interfere too much with other contributions.

As I said, and as is by now rather well known or accepted, the taxonomic-generative group eliminated history altogether, and replaced it with mere formalisms on paper, decreeing that rule taxonomy alone was sufficient to explain change (for a criticism of this approach see also Newton, 1971:52-53, Weinreich-Labov-Herzog, 1968, Bever-Langendoen, 1971:442,443,448,452; Labov, 1972:1111; and many of the reviewers of King's book; see Anttila, 1973a; and further Chen, Jeffers, Vincent, Ohala, Vachek, and Koefoed at the present conference). *Descriptions* under names like "rule reordering," "rule loss," "rule insertion," etc., were taken as *explanations*. Generative-transformational grammar rose together with the appeal of Marxism (which likewise practices history without history), and there also Marx's *questions* have been taken as *answers*. Formalizations per se are neither bad or good, in fact, they represent an essential part of the goal of science, but what matters is what use is made of them. In the taxonomic-generative group one *described* what had happened, since the formalism represents a recursive device for producing the correct outcomes. Now, this is a long way from history, where something happens, or even psychology, which could have been used for explanation. "Psychological reality" is referred to, it is true, but it refers rather to the "reality" that the linguist has created a notation which is real in the sense that it can be, say, photographed from paper. It refers to a kind of Cartesian private mind, which is totally unworkable in society, as the Wittgensteinian tradition has shown beyond doubt. Whenever inadequacies in applying this theory to history were encountered one pleaded for sharpening the synchronic theory (e.g. Kiparsky, 1971:578). Of course, synchronic theory is where the trouble began (cf. Newton, 1971). This synchronic theory was excessively influenced by formal languages (Itkonen, 1973a), which come to existence with their rules. In a way such a language and its use is one and the same phenomenon.

Natural languages are radically different; they exist in a society
which is subject to history. A formalized grammar cannot *explain* or
predict in the positivistic sense assumed by the transformationalists.
Thus it is totally unfit for historical explanation. "Taxonomic
grammar" in the Chomskyan sense and transformational grammars have
the same metascientific status (Itkonen, 1973a; another reason for
the term "taxonomic-generative"). Note also that this formalism gave
devices to simplify descriptions, in itself a very legitimate undertaking. "Generative" came to mean description of "sentences in terms
of their formal, explicit derivation from the axiomatic S-symbol"
(Itkonen, 1973b). When this apparatus of simplification was transferred into historical linguistics, it forced the interpretation that
change must be a formal operation within such a notation. For almost
ten years this attitude was taken as a scientific breakthrough, because the notation at least *looked* new or different. Ultimately,
however, the facts became by necessity more impelling and overrode
the notation, leading to the camp-shifting, whereby traditional content was put under the ("old") "generative" terms, and the second
breakthrough was announced. This is the general course of events,
without consideration of any contributions here and there. My topic
is *degeneration*, and in gross outline both "breakthroughs" exemplify
it: the first one in that an incompatible formalization was forced
on historical linguistics and decreed explanation, and the second in
that the history of historical linguistics came to be badly distorted.

Now, I seem to be denying an essential factor in science, to quote
two Nobel prize winners in physics: the essence of science "lies
not in discovering facts, but in discovering new ways of thinking
about them" (Sir Lawrence Bragg; Koestler, 1967:234) and "it is more
important to have beauty in one's equations than to have them fit
experiment" (Paul Dirac; Koestler, 1967:245). Or further:

> 'One central aspect of any revolution is, then, that
> some of the similarity relations change. Objects that
> were grouped in the same set before are grouped in
> different ones afterward and vice versa' (Kuhn, 1970:
> 262).

Very well, this is indeed what happens, but there should be some kind
of goodness of fit with the objects also. Note how the taxonomic-
generativists combined the notions of sound change and analogy into
rule change, because they could be unified under one notation on
paper. This new "similarity relation," however, just impeded understanding linguistic change, since it was a mere archiving device to
store facts, a change of locks only, not a regrouping in the cabinets
or shelves. As historical linguistics is returning to traditional
notions, the field is now running into the problem of translation,
because

> 'many additional research results can be translated
> from one community's language into the other's. As
> translation proceeds, furthermore, some members of
> each community may also begin vicariously to under-
> stand how a statement previously opaque could seem
> an explanation to members of the opposing group.
> The availability of techniques like these does not,
> of course, guarantee persuasion. For most people
> translation is a threatening process, and it is en-
> tirely foreign to normal science. Counter-arguments
> are in any case always available, and no rules pre-
> scribe how the balance must be struck. Nevertheless
> as argument piles on argument and as challenge after
> challenge is successfully met, only blind stubborn-
> ness can at the end account for continued resistance'
> (Kuhn, 1970:265-266).

What has become apparent in recent historical linguistics is indeed the threatening character of translation. By 1971, when
Kiparsky gave his Maryland state of the art paper, the situation
had cleared up (and the camp-shifting was halfway accomplished).
Let us recall the tripartition of that paper for the question of the
structure of terminology that is in use today. First Kiparsky tack-
les *abstractness conditions* (an issue initiated by him earlier) and
shows that Chomsky and Halle's evaluation measure is wrong, because
it is formal only (579), and so is absolute neutralization, and
simplicity is not the only measure (583). Reanalyses proceed from
a nonabstract synchronic analysis of merged segments (588), and in
fact clever underlying analyses can be faulty (591f.). In other
words, terms like "conditions," "constraints," and the like represent the requirement that actual language data in real speech situations must also be taken into account in studying grammar change.
This is a healthy traditional requirement (with modern notational
rigor, which is not at issue here). His second point is acceptance
of *paradigm conditions*, a very clear and old traditional notion,
earlier known under the name of *Systemzwang* or *leveling*, and extensively treated in the literature, although the school does not acknowledge it, witness a recent statement like

> 'Although my impression is that I have heard, and
> participated in, a fair amount of loose discussion
> of phonological rules becoming morphologized, it is
> nevertheless surprisingly difficult to find in print
> explicit discussion of specific examples. The case
> just cited, umlaut in German, is, as far as I know,
> the only one that has provoked extended and explicit
> discussions in the generative literature' (James
> Harris, 1973).

Kiparsky feels that we should be able to *predict* which alternant
will win in a given tug-of-war, and we are not even close to this
(599), and in fact paradigm leveling is not reducible to formal
properties of the generative system of a language (600). We have
here the actuation problem of Coseriu and Weinreich-Labov-Herzog.

The third point is *rule opacity* which corresponds to the structuralists' "non-automatic." It is in fact *surface ambiguity*, which is the
traditional name for a situation characteristic of an invitation to
reanalysis. Kiparsky has to conclude that he has no suggestions as
how to quantify it formally (622). It is of course not rule opacity,
but surface opacity, which is quite well treated by abduction, as has
become explicit in Andersen's work (1972, 1973). In other words,
Kiparsky is not quite willing to accept the mental factors of change.
His change of position out of the taxonomic camp is not total, however, since reordering of rules (taxonomy) is still a primary form
of linguistic change (612), or Latin *honor/honestus* might need a
crazy *minor rule* $r \rightarrow s$ (598).

"Minor rule," "rule opacity," and the like, show that it is desirable to have the term *rule* in as many contexts as possible, because
it *sounds* more formalistic and theoretical. Note also Vennemann's
(1972) term *via-rule* for relations like the *honor/honestus* (or *cool/
chill*, *sit/seat*, etc.) case. It seems to have precise formal con-
notation as compared to e.g. Saussure's *rapports associatifs* or
Bloomfield's *morpholexical alternations*. I think Bloomfield's term
is much superior, because it states exactly what is at issue (and so
does Saussure's). Bloomfield scores here over our generation exactly
like Harris over Chomsky in that Harris did not elevate his taxonomy
into illegitimate explanation (cf. Itkonen, 1973b). (Note that
taxonomy is always very important, and thus also the taxonomic-generative rule apparatus for diachronic correspondences has a place.)

What we have seen from the above sketchy discussion is that 1) a
strict formalism was created for the formalism's sake (more or less).
2) When it was not adequate for treating linguistic change, the
terms had to be supplied with traditional content. 3) But now the
notions were no longer formalizable or quantifiable, although the
vocabulary remained theoretical-sounding (after the example of the
"exact sciences"). This last point will be very important in what
follows, and it is advisable to return to it now. The parties that
settle on the mainland from the island have found the following
stumbling blocks: explanation is difficult, prediction is impossible,
the degree of opacity does not yield to formal quantification.
Robin Lakoff regrets that she cannot characterize formally the notion
of drift; no mechanism within the present theory of transformational
grammar allows an explanation (1972). Characteristically she re-
names drift *metacondition* supplying thus further evidence for what
was said above about terminology. Bever and Langendoen (1971) find
out that linguistic structure and evolution are a joint function of
the various systems for the *use* (my emphasis—RA) of language, not
just grammatical structure or formal rules. We need also perceptual

and productive systems for speech behavior (451). The authors find
out that grammars change by *minimal* steps through structures that
are close to the already learned structures. But the definition of
structural "closeness" must be left open (450-451). One could add
that Kiparsky would like to characterize *optimality* independently of
any particular language in terms of paradigmatic and phonotactic
properties of the output (1971:604-605).

One fully appreciates these problems of recalcitrant scales and
the challenges they offer. The current concensus seems to be that
even loose perception models are still useful, rather than no models
at all. Aspects of perception strategies and complexity have totally
evaded measurement and formalization. These have been impossible
to express coherently, rather all solutions are arbitrary, as the
current cry proclaims. A historical linguist at least of the old
training is very sympathetic toward such fluid entities, since he
has to live with historical complexity. But what one cannot condone
is the taxonomic-generative attack against the "vagueness" of the
traditional notion of analogy (cf. Jeffers, Vincent, Kiparsky, Ohala
here). It seems that this very vagueness was the one they bumped
into on the traditional mainland. "Loose perception or vagueness"
might have been approached from the wrong end with wrong tools, perhaps? Note that the mainland was not uninhabited when the colon(ial)-
ists entered. Should not one expect that the natives might have
developed certain tools to cope with the terrain they lived in? Of
course one need not assume that they would be able to eliminate all
obstacles, but would they have a system of understanding that would
make life easier to live? Or a system that would point out desirable
goals? After such a long cultural tradition we can indeed guess that
this is the case.

A workable philosophical frame for linguistic change (or any change)
is provided by the work of Charles Sanders Peirce (all information
taken from the selection in Buchler, 1955; and Feibleman, 1970;
Knight, 1965; Reilly, 1970). Note that linguistics is above all
part of semiotics (which has been ignored by transformational grammar) and Peirce's achievements in semiotics surpass Saussure's.
Figure 2 delineates in very crude form some of his basic categories,
but his sign types and logical categories have been omitted, because
Andersen has already shown their relevance for language learning and
linguistic change (e.g. 1972, 1973, and here), and I have myself
used them elsewhere (Anttila, 1972a, 1972b, 1973b). The basic phenomenological scheme is that, first, qualities (feelings) impinge
on the cognizer. This leads secondly, to a reaction (main lesson of
life), and thirdly, ultimately to a representation, mediation between
the two. It is thirdness that is the domain of science, the highest

Phenomenological categories modes of phenomena	Metaphysical categories modes of being	modes of existence	Meaning for epistemology	Cosmological categories
FIRSTNESS quality	possibility	chance (freedom) (spontaneity)	simples (qualities)	chance TYCHISM (quality) (feeling)
SECONDNESS reaction	actuality (fact) (existence)	Law	recurrences (facts)	habit AGAPISM (growth) (evolution)
THIRDNESS represent- ation mentality	destiny law (freedom) (necessity)	habit order legislation	comprehensions (laws)	continuity SYNECHISM (generality) (regularity)

Figure 2

Table of Peirce's phenomenological and other categories and their interrelations in approximate arrangement. (After Buchler, 1955; Feibleman, 1970; Knight, 1965; and Reilly, 1970.)

cognitive area. It is here that generalities and regularities manifest themselves, and this is where a grammar belongs, too. Naturally
I cannot really justify this in the present context; instead I will
concentrate on the modes of existence and the cosmological categories.
At first blush this sounds of course like utter confusion for those
who have thought that all we need is a Cartesian clear and distinct
mind. But such simplification we do not need. It is in the first
flash of chance that all novelties start. If repeated they start to
become habitual. Chance feeds into diversity, habit into uniformity,
which eventually leads to law. Evolution is the product of habit,
and it is the only category that shows no exceptions. According to
Peirce we exaggerate the part that law plays in the universe (cf.
Chen here). The culmination of everything is synechism, the doctrine
that all that exists is continuous. I have pointed out earlier what
synechism might do for phonology and how the terms *syn-echism* and
où tout se tient are parallel (Anttila, 1972c). Generality is the
heart of science (Reilly, 1970:111), and it is generality as continuity that leads to explanation: ". . . . Once you have embraced the
principle of continuity no kind of explanation of things will satisfy
you except that they *grew*" (1.175) (Knight, 1965:143). Certainly
historical linguistics has always tended to use genetic explanation,
which the transformationalists claim is worse than formal description.
Fallibilism and exception keep the system functioning by allowing for
change and thus preventing an end to progress. Absolute laws cannot
grow, and language has to change to stay the same (Anttila, 1972a:
380, 393, 1972c; cf. Baron here). It should be noted that Peirce
was able to make "chance" and "habit" metaphysical notions, not to
be confused with Bloomfield's psychological "habit," or behaviorism
in general. Looked at from the Peircean point of view even transformationalists are rather antimental behaviorists. This Peircean
frame gives one good reason for the inadequacy of synchronic transformational theory as pointed out by Itkonen: entrance to the area
of thirdness through formal languages is the wrong way. We have to
explicate language *use*, and thus we have to proceed from firstness.
And if possible, it is even more true of linguistic change, which is
language use in action, in a definite context. This will be discussed below. It should also be remembered that Peirce's cosmological categories are also formal, but they observe the objects they
represent.

The first leap out of the original indeterminate chaos into some
quality must have been through hypothetic inference, or abduction,
giving a generalizing tendency. Note how this supports a hermeneutic
frame of reference: mind is the measure of everything. Andersen has
shown the role of abduction for change, it is the crucial single

factor. A variant (an extreme form) of abduction is perceptual judgment, some aspects of which have to be briefly mentioned (see Anttila, 1972b). Perceptual judgments are not subject to criticism (Reilly, 1970:46-47), although science is ultimately built up from them. Both perceptual judgment and abductive inference share important similarities: both contain elements of generality, and both are in some aspect beyond the control of reason. Both have newness or originality, and both are interpretative (Reilly, 1970:47-50). Perceptual judgment is abstract in that the knowable aspects are never exhausted, and it cannot be corrected (Reilly, 1970:50-51). The scientific explanation suggested by abduction renders the observed facts necessary or highly probable, and this explanatory hypothesis is based on facts that are different from the facts to be explained, these being often not directly observable (Reilly, 1970:35). This is an important aspect of explanation. Note also that even vehement antirationalists like Hume had to acknowledge natural relations, empirical laws of association. Thus everything has to start in here, in the (biological) composition and working of the human mind.

Now we see the main reasons for the difficulties encountered by the taxonomic-generative approach or its aftermath: abduction is unpredictable (cf. Knight, 1965:118) and perceptual judgment is beyond control or criticism. They cannot be formalized, and no strict rules of procedure exist for them, even if there are certain requirements (Reilly, 1970:37). The same problem applies to analogy as well, and it is thus no wonder that the taxonomic-generativists were unhappy with both. Attempts to formalize it have not been successful. Descriptions of the results had to be elevated post facto into explanations (cf. Anttila, 1972a:202). An age-long philosophical problem is that resemblance cannot be formalized or justified. Peirce solved the problem better than others by making similarity a central concept in his philosophy. He (and also Hume) accepted it to avoid the Cartesian bogs, which the transformationalists do not seem to mind. Unformalizable similarity is the moving force of linguistic change, and not formalization derived from elsewhere (from above).

The Peircean categories form a circle, not a row, since knowledge or science has no beginning or end. In fact, the obligatory phenomenological link in any science necessitates it, as does also the hermeneutic circle (everything depends on the mind). Thus, e.g. "freedom" can occur both in firstness and thirdness, and "law" and "habit" change places between secondness and thirdness. Also in language one must acknowledge such relativity over against the one-track approach of taxonomic generativism. The notion of habit has been completely misunderstood by the transformational grammarians. Habit as the third category of existence characterizes existence and

gives it direction. It is the character of the symbol which is indispensable to the application of any intellectual habit (Feibleman,
1970:192). Habit derives from chance, and its product is evolution.
Only the principle of habit can span the chasm between chaos and
order (407). Final causes are primary (and generativists have also
ignored teleology completely), but the law of habit adds a law of
efficient causation (Buchler, 1955:359). Note how close Bever and
Langendoen come to this total set-up: "This ontogenetic independence
of the *perceptual* and *predictive* systems implies that the perceptual
system could influence the form of the predictive system as it is
learned" (438). Perceptual judgments are feeding here into the laws
of habit. It is generally recognized that "mortal minds, even those
of genius, are not governed by logic but by habit" (Koestler, 1967:
207). There is also a completely automatic strain (apart from unconscious intuitions):

> 'The formation and gradual automatization of habits
> of all kinds, of muscular, perceptual, thinking
> skills, follows the principle of economy. Once a new
> skill has been mastered, the controls begin to func-
> tion automatically and can be dispatched underground,
> out of sight; and under stable conditions strategy
> too will tend to become stereotyped. I call this the
> "downward" stream of mental traffic' (Koestler, 1967:
> 208).

It is interesting what economy, strategy, and depth can mean; and
these also exist, and belong to linguistic operations as well.

But habit in research activity has been quite apparent, since

> 'If a skill is practised in the same unvarying condi-
> tions, following the same unvarying course, it tends
> to degenerate into stereotyped routine, and its de-
> grees of freedom freeze up. Monotony accelerates
> enslavement to habit; it makes the *rigor mortis* of
> mechanization spread upward in the hierarchy'
> (Koestler, 1971:134).

and

> 'Habit is the enemy of freedom; the mechanization of
> habits tends towards the "rigor mortis" of the robot-
> like pedant. . . . Machines cannot become like men,
> but men can become like machines' (Koestler, 1971:
> 251).

Here the taxonomic-generativists have followed Saussure's formula
"Le linguiste n'a nul besoin d'être un phonologiste consommé, il
demande simplement qu'on lui fournisse un certain nombre de données
nécessaires" (*Cours:*77). Koestler's two books have also brought
out a kind of Peircean position in that there is no essential difference between the artist and the scientist (cf. Fig.3). Fig. 3
also indicates Peirce's answer to Descartes. His solution is objective idealism: matter is effete mind, inveterate habits becoming
physical laws (Feibleman 1970:412). Thus evolution is the agent
that mediates between mind and matter.

	Mind-matter controversy	Theory of inquiry	Its methodo- logical con- clusions	Human beings
1st	mind	belief	fallibilism	artists
2nd	matter	doubt	common- sensism	business men
3rd	evolution	habit	pragmatism	scien- tists

Figure 3

Peirce's categories applied to man and the sociology of science.

Here I must briefly (at least) mention a few consequences, implications, and clarifications provided by Peirce's system. Why would
evolution be so important? Because synchronic inquiry is helped by
diachrony: "Gonic" inquiry helps "nomic" inquiry. "Tell us how the
laws of nature came about, and we may distinguish in some measure
between laws that might and laws that could not have resulted from
such a process of development" (1.408) (Reilly, 1970:139). Hjelmslev
tackled similar problems in linguistics and in Finland Paavo Ravila
used such a maxim, and then also Kiparsky made it his own (1968).
But note the relevance of these categories for any structuralism.
Similarity and consistency (firstness and secondness) are the two
crucial factors in any semiotic system that "predicts" the future
(thirdness). Such properly understood structuralism is far superior
to taxonomic generativism with its binding formalism derived from
the wrong end. In fact, similarity and consistency are obvious
factors in sound change and the like, even if one cannot absolutely
predict what similarity will be seen. It is also quite well known
that likeness and repetition are the foundations of analogy (i.e.
iconicity and indexicality; cf. metaphor and metonymy, etc.). There
is always an analogy to be drawn and ultimately any analogy always
breaks down (cf. Buchler, 1955:225). Thus the notion understandably
met with such hostility within "generative" linguistics; we have a
gradient circle which cannot be formalized. Still analogy is the
very essence of language, its learning, and its use (Householder,
1971; Anttila, 1972a; Hsieh, 1972; and Jeffers, Vincent, and Ohala
here):

> 'It would seem that the strongest candidate for
> this hypothetical linguistic faculty is the
> "power of association," or "analogical power."
> It is quite plausible that by the help of this
> power, a subject responds to a new or unfamiliar
> word by associating it with one or more already-
> known words that are similar in some respects to
> the new or unfamiliar item. He then supplies
> responses that he would give to the already-known
> items being associated' (Hsieh, 1972).

Here we see similarity again, that ultimately leads also to a kind
of lexical synechism, since

> 'we infer that the dichotomy between actual and
> artificial words is more apparent than real.
> Further, that there is a "continuum of reality"
> which extends from words that may be called "most
> real" (such as words appearing in everyday con-
> versation) on one end to words that may be consi-
> dered "least real" (such as words used in a most
> bizzare test) on the other' (Hsieh, 1972).

Another imperative of evolution is that, as Peirce thought, biological evolution must be drawn into philosophy (Reilly, 1970:141).
Any kind of true mentalism requires it (see Koestler's works), and
recent historical linguistics is crying out for it, and many linguists have in fact done it (see e.g. Anttila, 1972a:§22). Not that
biology would have given answers to all the problems, but it would
at least have lessened e.g. the ignorant marveling displayed by
Robin Lakoff. Such drift (metacondition!?) is extensively treated
in literature. Note the evolution of the bird. It was not only the
development of the wings, but the whole bone structure had to be
synchronized with it, etc. Of course this cannot be characterized
formally. Or take the parallel developments of the placentals and
marsupials which both produce a jerboa (jumping rat), flying squirrel,
and a wolf (Koestler, 1971:169-172). Or consider the mammalian
whale, bat, and terrestial creatures, all matched by the sauruses of
the Reptilian Age (cf. Vennemann here). Why should everything be a
universal (cf. Lakoff, 1972:192). One has to consider function,
environment, etc., and not structure alone. The notion of optimality is rather well developed in evolutionary biology, and it would
seem that Kiparsky's language-independent optimality measure would
run into serious difficulty, since defining the total environment
would bring in the particulars. You cannot define change from above
like that. And if Sapir was "feeling his way toward an understanding" of drift (Lakoff, 1972:176), he had the right tools for it: he
was a hermeneutician, not a mechanist (Itkonen, 1973b). I have
elsewhere discussed grammatical, sociolinguistic, and biological
parallels of optimization (1973b), and their consequences for notions
like generalization. Be it just briefly remarked that the generative-transformational use of "generalization" corresponds to "psycho-

logical reality" (as description vs. universals). Since the latter
is inadequately treated "generalization" gets also derailed. Notable
for generalization is that analogy and metaphor represent it, and
these have been banned. On the other hand, "the chief end of man is
to form general propositions. And no generalization is worth a damn"
(Justice Holmes) (Homans, 1967:9-10).

But back to linguistics. There is a problem in comparative linguistics that is cleared up by the fact that similarity once perceived is correct and beyond criticism. This is the question of
known parallels. Often the linguist has to posit a change that does
not look quite commonplace in order to justify his reconstruction or
etymology. The change need not even be 'way out', and still our
colleagues are not happy unless they know, or are provided with,
parallels. Of course a change may have a parallel that nobody knows
(a mere accident), or be so well established that it is superflous
to ask for a parallel. Still, the requirement of parallels reigns
in the field, and of course it is a very useful one. For years David
Francis (of Yale University) has been saying that a good case needs
no parallels. Indeed, we have seen that the Peircean framework gives
a solid logical foundation for this position. Again we have support
for hermeneutics.

Comparative linguistics brings out another contradiction in taxonomic-generative historical linguistics. The model elevated internal
reconstruction into the main guideline of phonology thereby eliminating most of morphology. Still, such a past-oriented approach was
expected to predict future. Weaseling out monolithic underlying
forms is of course a perfect manifestation of the ahistorical narrow
approach, although every logical explanation must unify observed
variety (Feibleman, 1970:413). But this way one does not explain
evolution which shows tendency toward *both* law *and* variety, and for
linguistic history we need the latter (the law of habit works in
front of final causation and is efficient causation), cf.:

> 'In so far as evolution follows a law, the law of
> habit, instead of being a movement from homogeneity
> to heterogeneity, is growth from difformity to uni-
> formity. But the chance divergences from law are
> perpetually acting to increase the variety of the
> world, and are checked by a sort of natural selection
> and otherwise (for the writer does not think the
> selective principle sufficient), so that the general
> result may be described as "organized heterogeneity,"
> or, better, rationalized variety' (Buchler, 1955:359).

In fact, these two tendencies have always been obvious in linguistics
(cf. Vachek here); it was only in the "generative" movement that such
facts were ignored. Rationalized variety is very obvious in sociolinguistics (Anttila, 1973b), and there is the launching pad for
linguistic change, as is well known. We have to resolve the law side

(Saussure's *où tout se tient*) with Sapir's *all grammars leak*. Chomsky has himself condoned two kinds of creativity, one the capacity to create an infinite number of sentences, the other to use language in new situations. He has even complained that linguists have generally not acknowledged this. His first kind of creativity keeps language as it is, the second changes language. One should rather regret the fact that he concentrated only on the first kind, since it is not creativity at all, but mere recursion. There seems to be no reason to call mechanistic recursion creativity, but what happened was that the taxonomic-generative group applied formalized recursion to language change. The proper procedure would have been the reverse (Anttila, 1972c). Others are subscribing to this requirement now. Paillet (1972) recognizes that we sterilize our work in descriptive linguistics by paying too much attention to normal patterns, which are imperfect selections to begin with. In fact, we have to change from description of objects to one of processes, and to pay as much attention to the deviations as to the norm. The same is even more forcefully (and correctly) expressed by Dominguez (1972; and cf. Vachek here). He suggests that only the static mechanistic aspect be called "generation," and the dynamic unpredictable part "creation." Generation corresponds now to the formalizable algorithmic part of language, and creation is responsible for the evolution of language. Creation constantly renews the language, and refers to what exceeds mechanical possibilities. There is always a part of language which is not formalizable. And there is trading between the two parts (tendency toward both variety and law). The creative part is in no way less important than the mechanistic sector, because it tends to modify the formalizable core, and is thus a fundamental factor in linguistic change. This part resists formalization. Note now that if the creative counterbalance is omitted, "generative" means the kind of sterile automatization described in the Koestler quotes above. One feels that an explicit Peircean framework would have considerably enhanced these worthwhile modern tendencies. Even the rudimentary exposition above suggests it. In this context rule opacity as a criterion in the "theory of exceptions" (Kiparsky, 1971: 631-632) would seem to remain without new interpretation, not to speak of Halle's "original" idea of listing exceptions (1972:410). Poor Bloomfield!

Mechanical law can never produce diversification (Buchler, 1955: 357), and thus we need spontaneity. Note that in the early days when sound change was viewed from the outside it was supposed to be mechanical. Sound change is a good example of objective idealism (matter is effete mind), because viewed from the inside it is mental (Andersen). Rise of allomorphy represents rationalized variety.

Once a linguistic sign (symbol) is learned, it takes on iconic character within that language (inside view). Allomorphs add considerable indexical overlay to morphemes. In other words, they refer beyond their own boundaries towards larger syntagmatic stretches, and in that sense they exemplify contiguity within the structure of grammar. Thus in a case like *duch-ess* (to take Bloomfield's example) *duch-* refers beyond *duke* to the suffix *-ess* and the semantic feature [+fem]. Whatever remains common to allomorphs retains the iconic overlay of symbols, and whatever comes to be different indicates at least grammatical distribution iconically. In other words, similarity represents lexical meaning, difference, grammatical. This function is thus diagrammatic, a subtype of iconic (e.g. with English *sane/san-ity* we have something like *s-n-* vs. *ey* ∿ *æ*, perhaps cutting arbitrarily the nonhigh front vowel with the alternation). However, for naive speakers the grammarian goes too far, because both aspects can be indicated by the allomorphs *seyn-* and *s æn-*. The development can proceed all the way to complete suppletion, e.g. Latin *ocul-us/ ocul-ī* to French *œil/yeux* (Anttila, 1972a:101). This new arrangement is a switch back to symbols, the "similarity relations" within language structure have changed, due to abductive change. Thus it cannot be predicted when this happens. All this indicates that large stretches can be learned as lumps, and in this sense, the rise of allomorphy is also "generalization," although it sounds of course totally irrational within taxonomic-generative theory. Indeed, syntactic units can be learned as holistic lumps which subsequently fossilize (e.g. *willy-nilly, maybe, quamvis, peut-être*). Metaphors fade similarly. These phenomena are quite well known, but note that here also we have to do with effete mind. Fig. 4 crudely sketches this fact that both sound change and lexicalization feed into lexicon and morphology (here "lexicalization" covers also all sorts of re-cutting phenomena). Of course in these grammatical phenomena the mind never gets stone-dead, but enough to get juggled around. Here belongs also the fact that today's morphology tends to be yesterday's syntax. The obvious importance of morphology and lexicon comes out clearly.

After the recent rehabilitation of the classical phoneme it was to be expected that morphemic variants would come back with a new lease for existence. This has now happened, independently from the philosophical/semiotic reasoning presented above. In Anttila, 1972c and 1973b, I have pleaded for a linguistics of variants in which variants have direct semiotic function of their own. Communication does, although it need not always, bypass underlying forms. In our non-nudist culture clothing has direct social meaning in particular contexts, and anthropologists do not devise an abstract underlying

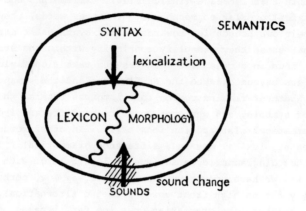

Figure 4

Morphology and lexicon as centers of attraction
of change.

garment from which all the variants can be derived. That would in
fact be ridiculous. Much of the time underlying forms (UFO's
according to J.P. Maher) in linguistics are likewise. I built my
plea on Mati Hint's work (see. e.g. 1972 in which he sums up his output over the years). Because of the great number of Estonian gradation types and their often small number of members, Hint concludes
that a single principle will not do, and thus there is a place for
a word-paradigm or item-and-arrangement model in the overall description of Estonian. In fact, even regular (even if not automatic)
alternations are really no different from suppletion (cf. Hudson at
this conference). There is a difference between inflection and
derivation, and this should be observed also in the generative interpretation: "it follows that morphology (paradigmatics) must be
taken as an independent component of generative grammar" (31). Surface forms are surfacing again, since requirements for their specification both in morphology and lexicon are increasing (Skousen,
1973; Takahasi, 1973):

> 'Already there is evidence that the child's lexicon
> is a "surface-forms-too" kind of lexicon. Accord-
> ingly, the adult's lexicon should also be a "surface-
> forms-too" type. In other words, contrary to current
> belief that only phonological underlying forms are
> needed in the lexicon, it is necessary for us to list
> phonological surface forms in the lexicon' (Hsieh,
> 1972; cf. Ohala here).

The Umeå conference (see under Anttila, 1973a) also tried to re-
surrect morphology for generative grammar. It became apparent,

however, that the requirement of "generative grammar" was irrelevant. There was a sentiment among the champions of generative grammar that all schools have neglected morphology. True, perhaps, but the generativists lead here by a wide margin indeed. In fact ignorance and exaggeration combine now in statements that we do not know anything about morphology and its change (see James Harris above and Kiparsky, 1972a:277). Morris Halle has culminated this outrage with an utter insult to the field of linguistics (1972, 1973), as is shown succinctly by Lipka (1973). Others have apparently been so stunned that they have been unable to write, and this indeed was the reaction in Bologna. Now he wants to attract others on the topic. Imagine the scores of linguists in the 1960s who were suffocated by syntactic trees or barred in with plus-and-minus matrices! Halle can see no difference between inflection and derivation, and he is totally unaware of the word-paradigm tradition. But enough, these articles do not deserve any attention; I have presented them as extreme warnings and as evidence for the taxonomic-generative colonialism.

Still, Kiparsky thinks that some progress in historical linguistic theory was made in the 1960s, particularly in that surface alternants are derived from underlying forms by means of ordered phonological rules (1972a:277). This progress is hard or impossible to see if you are not initiated. Naturally we need both the synchronic principles of morphological organization and the surface forms to characterize analogical change (280-281, 282). This has never been seriously doubted. It was actually clear already in Brugmann's 1878 manifesto, and this understanding runs through Saussure (see Skousen, 1973), Sturtevant, Kuryłowicz, and others. The program was available, even if *all* the linguistis have not followed it (cf. Anttila, 1973c: 111). This is true of all linguistic change, or any change whatever (e.g. biological evolution), witness:

> 'While early structuralism viewed phonological systems as being more or less at the mercy of phonetic alternations and consequently could insist only that every phonetic innovation be interpreted in terms of the system that <u>undergoes</u> it, the theory that has been sketched here shows how it is possible to interpret every phonological innovation—abductive or deductive —in terms of the system that <u>gives rise</u> to it. This must be the goal of diachronic <u>phonology</u>' (Andersen, 1973, end).

In other words, the end results are already given in the underlying representations, or in still other words, we must always use an explicitly teleological explanation or point of view. In this connection observe closely the following statement about synchronic morphological rules:

> 'Such rules represent the result of many historical processes of reanalysis and generalization. Their

original nucleus can be a sound change, a difference in morphemic composition, or simply a pattern
perceived at one point by speakers in a paradigm
composed of unrelated morphemes, much as an imperfect gestalt is seen in a random arrangement of
pebbles. Once these rules become established,
however, they serve as the tracks along which
"analogical change" proceeds. Forms not conforming
to them are now "exceptional" and over long periods
of time get reshaped so as to become regular. This
process of regularization, I would claim, is what
"analogical change" really refers to.'

Do we have here a rare occasion of Peirce himself talking about the
increase of iconicity in morphology, since this is totally in the
framework presented above? Or do we have here a summary of Michel
Bréal's conceptions about linguistic change? Bréal was rather clear
in understanding the role of abduction and teleology in this sense
(Anttila, 1972b, 1973b). No, this particular traditional statement
is by Kiparsky (1972a:280; for increase in iconicity as a central
factor in change see Anttila, 1972a and Skousen, 1973). Hereby (and
through his contribution here) the evidence for almost a total camp-
shifting is closed. The obscuring effect comes from propositions
like "I claim" or "I propose" (Halle), even when the issue has been
so obvious for so many for such a long time. In short, there is no
doubt that the above quote is accurate, except historically, of
course.

Finally, we can turn to Finnish morphology to see how the increase
in iconicity works, or might work (cf. Lightfoot here for modals).
We will also get evidence against Halle's claim that speakers "know"
morphological segmentation the way he wants them to know it. Still,
they create and use language. Over the years the colloquial suffix
-*ari* has increased its territory e.g.

(A) kunnari   kunniajuoksu
     pannari   pannukakku   'pancake'
     demari   demokraatti
     kommari   kommunisti
     tikkari   tikkukaramelli   'lollipop'

In general, longer compounds and derivatives are cut up after the
first consonant (cluster) and the suffix is appended to this trunk.
A single consonant can also be doubled.

(A´) folkkari   folksvaagen   'VW'
     rekkari   rekisterilaatta   'license plate'
     synttäri   syntymäpäivä   'birthday'
     nimmari   nimipäivä   'namesday'

and in fact doubling is normal as compared with rarer formations like *demari*. It would seem that the general rule is then <u>doubling</u> + - *ari*. But that is not so simple because the suffix can have a clear variant -*kkari* (-*ppari* after *m*):

(B) puukkari   puuro   'porridge'
     olkkari   olohuone   'living room'
     talkkari   talonmies   'janitor'
     telkkari   televisio   'TV'
     yökkäri   yöpuku   'pajamas'
     lumppari   lumipallo   'snowball'
     limppari   limunaati   'lemonade'

In a way this is an extra degree of the lengthening, and the -*kkari* might have been segmented out of the numerous -*kk*- words like *tikkari*. Note that in Finnish one single word, *tytär* 'daughter', has produced a feminine suffix -*tar*'-ess' that is productive (*laulaja-tar* 'singer-ess'). On the other hand, there is a device for double stop (-*kk*-/-*pp*-) hypocoristic proper names:

(C) Taukka   Tauno
     Eikka   Eino
     Aukku   Aulis
     Olkku   Olli
     Terkko   Terho
     Arkko   Armas
     Timppa   Timo
     Imppo   Ilmari
     Jorttu   Jorma

Here -*tt*- is completely exceptional. Note further that the final vowel cannot be predicted although the process is productive. The problem of consonant doubling recurs with another affective/descriptive suffix, -*u*. Austerlitz was the first to draw linguistic attention to it (1960). By 1960 it was by no means only nascent; its origin could perhaps go at least to the 1920s. But its use has steadily increased. There need be no doubling in the preceding consonant.

(D) kultu   kulta   'dear'
     nenu   nenä   'nose'
     poju   poika   'boy'
     kapu   kapteeni   'captain'
     laku   lakritsi   'licorice'

367

but it can occur also

(D1) jallu   jaloviina   'brandy'
      essu   esiliina   'apron'
      känny   käsi   'hand'
      Ellu   Elina
      Sellu   Selene

and both types are in a way combined in cases where a cluster is
assimilated to a geminate:

(D2) possu   porsas   'pig'
      kessu   kersantti   'sergeant'

  Again the suffix -u combines with -kk- to give -kku:

(E)   brenkku   brannvin   'licor'
      valkku   valkoviini   'white wine'
      punkku   punaviini   'red wine'
      pöykky   pöytäviina   'vodka'
      telkku   televisio   'T.V.'
      orkku   orava   'squirrel'
      farkku   farmari   'jeans'
      omppu   omena   'apple'
      kymppi   kymmenen   'ten'

In the "spirited" terms the usage owes its strength to the old
brenkku, which itself, however, cannot be explained in terms of such
analogy. The suffix -u can be further preceded by an affrication
of *t*:

(F)   Antsu   Antti
      Matsu   Matti
      pontsu   pontikka   'moonshine'
      rantsu   ranta   'shore'
      hintsu   hintelä   'shaky'
      kätsä   kätevä   'handy'
      Martsa   Martti

where the last two items end in -*a*, but show the same process. A
process of affrication is by no means the whole truth, however,
because in some cases there is no *t* to begin with:

(F1) poitsu   poika   'boy'
      kaltsu   kallio   'cliff'
      Kaitsu   Kai

The suffix is now clearly -tsu. A suffix -sa would seem to occur in
the following formations

(G) pulsa   pulpetti   'desk'
    palsa   palttoo   .'overcoat'
    mansa   maantieto   'geography'
    kilsa   kilometri   'kilometer'
    bilsa   biologia   'biology'

and these merge again with type (F) on one side (l as dental). But
then we have the most recent pattern where we have both assibilation
and a -k- element:

(H) notski   nuotio   'campfire'
    jätski   jäätelö   'ice cream'
    matsku   materiaali   'material'
    potsku   potilas   'patient'

A case like *pitsku* for *piha* 'courtyard' does not even have underlying *t*. But before these forms came to be, a suffix with -sk- was
in existence after nasals:

(H1) romsku   romaani   'novel'
     pansku   banaani   'banana'
     jänskä   jännittävä   'exciting'
     vänskä   vänrikki   'ensign'
     penska   penikka   'cub/kid'

   The presentation here is quite sketchy and ignores many facets of
the configuration (to be treated elsewhere). No attempt is made to
provide exact chronology for each particular word, but the increase
of these items is substantial, as a decade of absence from Finland
has shown to me. The -kk-ari and -kk-u suffixes intersect also in
that there seems to be shifting from the former into the latter:
farmarit to *farkut*, and *telkku* is now much more prevalent than
telkkari. From two loose pebbles we have gotten clear patterns,
discernible increase in regularity (law). The target is a limited
set of cononical forms (variety). But still one cannot predict what
particular formation will be used in any case (unpredictability).
In general the main line of development seems to be (vowel *u* only):
1. *-u*, 2. *-CC-u*, 3. *-kk-u (-kku?)*, 4. *-ts-u (-t-su?)*, 5. *-tsu*,
6. *-sku*, 7. *-ts-ku (-t-sku)*, and finally even deeper penetration
like *pitsku*. Similar development can be perceived in *-kkari* as
well, note *pul-tsari (puliukko* 'wino'). This situation is of course
in no way unique; undoubtedly such cases can be found freely in many
languages. The phenomenon is typical in two senses, however. The

colloquial area is outside the norm (cf. Paillet) and the pebbles are still too scattered for tight formalization. The linguist's safe selection bypasses such areas.

Postscript in response to discussion at the conference. It was pointed out at the conference that another interpretation of the generative position on historical linguistics is possible, in other words, that the generative terminology meant right from the beginning what I say above. The problem is typical in the unfolding of very recent history, since those involved are either conscious of posterity, or do not yet want to become historical persons. But I am definitely not alone in my criticism. Many of the papers at this conference say the same from at least one perspective each (Ohala, Chen, Koefoed, Campbell, Jeffers, Vincent, Vachek, Vennemann), although these did not draw the above criticism, apparently because they show the inadequacy of "generativism" through specific problems. My purpose was to sum up such studies under a more general frame showing a possibility of wider explanation. Further, there are those linguists who themselves have *felt* a distinct shift out of the generative paradigm that was too confining (Traugott, King, etc.; see Anttila, 1973a). Even the Lakoffs can accept no more the old homogeneous speech community. When scientists see things in a new way, they should make it known in exact terms, as the above ones have in fact done. Unfortunately it seems that I have to repeat some of the evidence for my thesis, although a detailed exposition cannot be undertaken here. But the following points can be noted.

1) The original generative position that linguistic change is *simplification* (Kiparsky, 1968; King, 1969) has been changed. Now Kiparsky reports that Maori children failed to learn the generalization linguists would have made about Maori grammar (1971:590-94; and cf. Ohala here). This makes it impossible to continue making the assumption that children are constrained to learn the maximally simple grammar (the Maoris did not learn it); so, the shortest grammar cannot be assumed a priori to be psychologically real any longer. The implication for historical linguistics is that if in some cases children might not learn the simplest grammar, we can no longer assume that all linguistic change (other than rule addition by adults) is simplification. Thus the former dogma on rule mechanisms has given way to an appeal to "substantive constraints" (Kiparsky, 1971:579), and simplification is now wrong.

2) But what are the substantive constraints? Analogy was not originally worthy of serious study in generative treatments (Postal, 1968:234 and 259 fn. 12, quoting Kiparsky's 1965 position, King, and

others), but it is precisely cases of analogy which show that over-reliance on simplification or simplicity was wrong. This brings Kiparsky to his paradigm conditions (1971:596). Thus his "leveling condition" (1972b:195) is nothing more than a restatement of analogy, while his "distinctness condition" (same page) is exactly the same as the old 'one meaning, one form', or analogical prevention (see Anttila, 1972a:100-1, 143-6, 170-1, 181-4, and passim). It is the classical examples of analogy he discusses (Latin *honor:* 1971:597; 1972b:206-7).

What he really shows is that his original reliance on formalism is proven wrong by cases of analogy and so he had to back off from the negative attitude about the role of analogy and fix up his theory to include it (see also his paper here, which increases precision in the Kuryłowiczian frame).

3) Similarly, he now says (1972b:189) that the theory has come far enough to return to traditional questions of functionalism. But, in fact, the examples he discusses (such as distinctness requirements using Labov's output [197], morphological conditioning [198f.], Latin *honor*, etc.) all show that the return to functionalism is forced upon him by examples handled traditionally but which his theory did not handle.

In each case Kiparsky makes it sound like the theory is constantly progressing to handle new things, but in fact each change in the theory seems to be backing down from the sterile formalism of earlier positions to accommodate pressing counter-examples. Each retreat, however, is caused by traditional causes and examples, and the resulting revised theory (which he views as progress) seems to be moving closer to traditional ways of doing things or looking at things. In his view this is progress (and it is progress any time one gets closer to truth), but outsiders (outside the in-group) will naturally see this as retreat or camp-shifting, as was succinctly summed up by Lyle Campbell here.

4) In the early days both Kiparsky and Postal lamented that with the new revolution historical linguistics would have to start from scratch (they should have read Hoenigswald, 1950: 364, fn. 8). Weinreich, Labov and Herzog (1968:126) listed things that happen any time there is a change in the theory of synchronic linguistics:

a) there will be a reinterpretation (reclassification) of existing changes in terms of the new theory (which is what King's book is); i.e. there will be a translation of the old theories and their results into the new one.

b) there will be a proposal of fresh constraints on change.

c) there will be new causes of change proposed.

Of the three, generative studies have done mostly *a*, but only *b* and especially *c* really help advance historical linguistics. Until recently all the work in generative historical linguistics was either translating (into rule mechanisms), or arguing that the constraints of the old school were not good enough. When they are forced to propose new constraints (such as Kiparsky's paradigm constraints), we see that they are forced back to much more traditional views than they originally set out for.

However, the important aspect here is that the tune about c, the causes of change, has changed. Postal said that there were only cultural reasons (like the length of skirts [1968:283]; i.e., he had no explanation for causes of change), and King did really no better, other than to talk a little about it, using traditional notions like drag and push chains, and saying mostly that traditional 'causes' were not too good. His book also banned statements of 'tendency' as worthless. Now we see an about-face, where Kiparsky talks little about actual causes, but proposes certain tendencies which are analogues of traditional explanations for why. But, as they now move toward Weinreich-Labov-Herzog's third point, they are forced to abandon much of the original dogmatism about b and c, softened exactly towards traditional notions (cf. also the first Gellner quote below).

One might still want to look at the scene from a Cartesian point of view: some of the earlier ideas might quite well be true, but they should be rediscovered and proved in an orderly way in a strict deductive system. This is indeed basically what Kiparsky now wants to do to many traditional notions (e.g. 1972b). But I have shown above that there is no such system, because the newly rediscovered ideas bring with them largely the old system as well.

Concurrently with this conference the IXth International Congress of Anthropological and Ethnological Sciences included substantial discussion also on generative theory in historical linguistics. Interventions by Haugen, Slama-Cazacu, Oksaar, Wurm, and particularly Maher support exactly my position here. To sum up the results (from Maher's comment on Cook):

> 'What does transformational grammar offer anthropology and ethnology?—The cult of personality, a priori dogma, esprit de corps, notation (but also notational flimflam), history without history, language without speakers, speakers without societies, societies without environments, in sum linguistics without language(s).'

Maher also points out a parallel for the current linguistic scene from the Linguistic Philosophy at Oxford, through Gellner, 1959 [1968]:

> 'In its earlier stages, it was claimed to be *revolutionary*; more recently the stress has been on *continuity* with the past. Novel ideas had to be claimed to justify the introduction of such novel practices: continuity is now claimed mainly in order to avoid

the drawing up of balance sheets of how much the
revolution has achieved. If it is merely a continuation, it is at least no worse than philosophies
which preceded it, it is claimed, and there is no
call for abrogating it if it has failed—as it has—
to deliver the promised goods' (191 [212]).

What I apparently run against in my paper is a sense of decorum, to
take another Gellner quotation from Maher's assessment of the linguistic scene:

'A particularly important consequence of success and
establishment is that Linguistic Philosophy [read
'generativism'--RA] has acquired a fine and powerful
sense of decorum. Any fundamental criticisms of it
are ruled out as indecorous. . . . This powerful
sense of decorum is curious in a movement descended
from the castigation of past thought as *nonsense*,
and which itself described past thought as *pathological*' (191 [212]).

(Cf. this with early Postal). It would be rather easy to go on
quoting Gellner for highly relevant observations also on the linguistic scene, but I leave it at this.

  Lest I be accused of relying on fellow indecorous linguists let me
also refer to a linguist who certainly enjoys independent status.
W. Haas' recent work on the status of generative rules is very compatible to my ideas above, although he does not speak of historical
linguistics. In e.g. a recent paper in *Language* (1973), he discusses the choice of semantic *tendencies* which defy the strongest
syntactic rules:

'It is in this freedom of ad-hoc choice, rather than
in any generative mechanism of rules, that we find
the truly creative aspect of language. There is a
discipline as well as an art in the use we make of
this freedom. Recent investigations by linguists
brought up in the generative mode have turned toward
exploring this discipline. It may seem puzzling at
first that, though their several efforts give the
impression of utter disarray, there can yet be no
doubt about their genuine <u>collective</u> achievement.
The puzzle has an interesting solution: we need only
discard that generative fiction, shared by them,
which substitutes a computational mechanism for our
freedom of semantic choice; then the genuine insights
of their rival fictions all become viable and compatible' (292).

or consider further:

'The computational framework of generative grammar
seems to have become a hindrance for the further
development of syntax as well as of semantics,
which it has greatly enhanced during the last
fifteen years. Syntactic analysis seems incapable
of attaining greater adequacy, unless it succeeds
in at least freeing itself from the dogmatic acceptance of traditional "surface structures"; and progress in semantic investigations seems impossible as
long as the creative interaction of meanings is
viewed as subject to a "government of generative
rules"' (293).

Mutatis mutandis the arguments are even more impelling for historical linguistics, as I said above.

And if classical generativists always meant exactly what current
criticism finds lacking in their approach (to return to the beginning of my comment), why did they not say so in the first place?
Surely if this was meant, camouflage has been used, and it would of
course be typical of a social revolution, since the kind of "typo-
graphical jargon" (to use Collingwood's term, Gellner, 1959 [1968]:
97 [108]) has no other justification. I think that this conference
showed extensive unity in our thinking about linguistic change. But
those who would say that the present position was indeed the generative program all along resort to a private language which is con-
veniently defined post facto. Such a defense gives no hold for any
criticism, because those who interpreted the school through the
normal community language are wrong by definition. This sense of
decorum is certainly degenerative.

References

Andersen, Henning. 1972 "Diphthongization." *Language* 48, 11-50.

_____. 1973 "Abductive and deductive change." *Language* 49,
765-93.

Anttila, Raimo. 1972a *And introduction to historical and comparative linguistics.* (New York: Macmillan).

_____. 1972b "Child language, abduction, and the acquisition
of linguistic theory by linguists." *Proceedings of the international symposium on first language acquisition,* Florence, Sept.
4-6, 1972 (Walburga v. Raffler-Engel, ed.). University of Ottawa
Press.

_____. 1972c "Exception as regularity in phonology." *Phono-
logica* 1. (Proceedings of the second international phonology
meeting, Vienna, Sept. 1972).

_____. 1973a "Was there a generative historical linguistics?"
*Preprints of the Second international conference of Nordic and
general linguistics,* Umeå, June 14-19, 1973 (Karl-Hampus Dahlstedt,
ed.) 8-14. Final version to be published by Skytteanska sumfundet,
Umeå, Sweden.

_____. 1973b "Generalization, abduction, evolution, and
language." *Concerning the generative-transformational paradigm:
against the MITniks* (E.F.K. Koerner and J.P. Maher, eds.).

_____. 1973c "Onko strukturalismin aika kielitieteessä jo
ohi?" Virittäjä 2/1973:109-122.

Austerlitz, Robert. 1960 "Two nascent affective suffixes in
Finnish." *American Studies in Uralic Linguistics, Indiana University Publications in Uralic and Altaic,* Vol. 1:1-5.

Bever, T. G. and D. T. Langendoen. 1971 "A dynamic model of the
evolution of language." *Linguistic Inquiry* 2, 433-463.

Buchler, Justus (ed.). 1955 *Philosophical writings of Peirce.*
T217 (New York: Dover).

Dominguez, Carlos Rafael. 1972 "Creation in syntax and generation in syntax." *Preprints of the 11th international congress of linguists,* 1019-1023. Bologna.

Feibleman, James K. 1970 *An introduction to the philosophy of Charles S. Peirce.* (Cambridge, Mass.: MIT Press)

Gellner, E. 1959 (1968) *Words and Things.* London.

Haas, William. 1973 "Rivalry among deep structures." *Language* 49, 282-93.

Halle, Morris. 1972 "Morphology in a generative grammar." *Preprints of the 11th international congress of linguists,* 408-416. Bologna.

_____. 1973 "Prolegomena to a theory of word formation." *Linguistic Inquiry* 4, 3-16.

Harris, James. 1973 "Morphologization of phonological rules: an example from Chicano Spanish." Paper read at the Romance historical conference, April 1973.

Hint, Mati. 1972 "Generatiivinen fonologia sekä viron astevaihtelu ja kvantiteettisysteemi." *Virittäjä* 1/1972: 27-33.

Homans, George C. 1967 *The nature of social science.* H 62. (New York: Harcourt).

Hoenigswald, Henry M. 1950 "The principal step in comparative grammar." *Language* 26, 357-64.

Householder, Fred W. 1971 *Linguistic speculations.* (London & New York: Cambridge University Press)

Hsieh, Hsin-I. 1972 "On listing phonological surface forms in the lexicon." MS.

Itkonen, Esa. 1973a "Transformational grammar and the philosophy of science." *Concerning the generative-transformational paradigm: against the MITniks* (E.F.K. Koerner and J.P. Maher, eds.).

_____. 1973b "Linguistics and metascience." MS of a book.

King, Robert D. 1969 *Historical Linguistics and Generative Grammar.* (Englewood Cliffs, N.J.: Prentice-Hall)

_____. 1973 "Integrating linguistic change." *Preprints of the Second international conference of Nordic and general linguistics,* Umeå.

Kiparsky, Paul. 1968 "Linguistic universals and linguistic change." *Universals in linguistic theory* (E. Bach and R. T. Harms, eds.), (New York: Holt), 170-202.

_____. 1971 "Historical linguistics." *A survey of linguistic science* (W. O. Dingwall, ed.), 576-649. Linguistics Program, University of Maryland.

_____. 1972a Review of Watkins, *Indogermanische Grammatik III: 1. Foundations of Language* 9, 277-286.

_____. 1972b "Explanation in phonology." *Goals of Linguistic Theory* (S. Peters, ed.), ch. 6. (Englewood Cliffs, N.J.: Prentice-Hall)

Knight, Thomas S. 1965 *Charles Peirce.* W.885. (New York: Washington Square Press.)

Koestler, Arthur. 1967 *The act of creation.* Laurel 0015. (New York: Dell)

_____. 1971 *The ghost in the machine.* (London: Pan Books.)

Kuhn, Thomas S. 1970. Postscript 1969. *Foundations of the Unity of Science* 2, 236-272. University of Chicago Press.

Labov, William. 1972 "On the use of the present to explain the past." *Preprints of the 11th international congress of linguists,* 1110-1135. Bologna.

Lakoff, Robin. 1972 "Another look at drift." *Linguistic change and generative theory* R.P. Stockwell and R.S.K. Macaulay, eds., (Bloomington, Indiana: Indiana University Press), 172-198.

Kipka, Leonhard. 1973 "Prolegomena to 'Prolegomena to a theory of word formation'." MS.

Newton, B.E. 1971 "Ordering paradoxes in phonology." *Journal of Linguistics* 7, 31-53.

Paillet, Jean Pierre. 1972 "Levels, processes, and realisation." *Preprints of the 11th international congress of linguists,* 196-199. Bologna.

Postal, Paul M. 1968 *Aspects of Phonological Theory.* (New York: Harper & Row)

Reilly, Francis E. 1970 *Charles Peirce's theory of scientific method.* (New York: Fordham University Press)

Skousen, Royal. 1973 "On the nature of morphophonemic alternation." MS.

Takahashi, Sakutaro. 1973 "On the assumption that every morpheme has a single phonological representation." MS.

Vennemann, Theo. 1972 "Rule inversion." *Lingua* 29, 209-242.

Weinreich, Uriel, William Labov, and Marvin I. Herzog. "Empirical foundations for a theory of language change." *Directions for historical linguistics.* W. P. Lehmann and Y. Malkiel, eds. (Austin, Texas: University of Texas Press), 95-195.